International Human Rights Law and the Framework Convention on Tobacco Control

This book reviews the challenges and opportunities in the implementation of the WHO Framework Convention on Tobacco Control (FCTC) at the regional and national levels in Africa. It contains an analysis of the relevant norms and monitoring mechanisms at the regional level, and case studies from selected African and other developing countries.

The WHO has noted that tobacco use or exposure to tobacco is a major health risk factor for non-communicable diseases (NCDs). This volume highlights the importance of taking measures to control tobacco use in Africa with a view to preventing these risks. With contributions from experts from the Global South, the book provides a critical analysis of the role that human rights can play in mitigating the impact of tobacco use and NCDs, and the implementation of the FCTC. The book contains a systematic and in-depth analysis of how efforts to realise the right to health under international and regional law can help to address the incidence of tobacco use in the developing world.

The collection will be an important resource for academics, researchers and policymakers working in the areas of public health law and international human rights.

Ebenezer Durojaye is Professor and Head of the Socio-Economic Rights Project at the Dullah Omar Institute, University of the Western Cape, South Africa.

Lucyline Nkatha Murungi is Senior Lecturer and Assistant Director at the Centre for Human Rights, University of Pretoria, South Africa.

Routledge Research in Health Law

Workplace Mental Health Law
Comparative Perspectives
Takenori Mishiba

Mental Health Law in China
A Socio-legal Analysis
Bo Chen

International Human Rights Law and the Framework Convention on Tobacco Control
Lessons from Africa and Beyond
Edited by Ebenezer Durojaye and Lucyline Nkatha Murungi

For more information about this series, please visit: www.routledge.com/Routledge-Research-in-Human-Rights-Law/book-series/RRHL

International Human Rights Law and the Framework Convention on Tobacco Control

Lessons from Africa and Beyond

Edited by Ebenezer Durojaye and Lucyline Nkatha Murungi

Routledge
Taylor & Francis Group
LONDON AND NEW YORK

First published 2023
by Routledge
4 Park Square, Milton Park, Abingdon, Oxon OX14 4RN

and by Routledge
605 Third Avenue, New York, NY 10158

Routledge is an imprint of the Taylor & Francis Group, an informa business

British Library Cataloguing-in-Publication Data
A catalogue record for this book is available from the British Library

Library of Congress Cataloging-in-Publication Data
A catalog record for this book has been requested

ISBN: 978-1-032-20576-2 (hbk)
ISBN: 978-1-032-20579-3 (pbk)
ISBN: 978-1-003-26424-8 (ebk)

DOI: 10.4324/9781003264248

Typeset in Galliard
by Apex CoVantage, LLC

Contents

Tables

Acronyms and abbreviations

ACHPR	African Charter on Human and Peoples' Rights
ACRWC	African Charter on the Rights and Welfare of the Child
African Commission	African Commission on Human and Peoples' Rights
CEDAW	Convention on the Elimination of Discrimination against Women
CRPD	Convention on the Rights of Persons with Disabilities
FCTC	Framework Convention on Tobacco Control
HRC	Human Rights Committee
ICCPR	International Covenant on Civil and Political Rights
ICESCR	International Covenant on Economic, Social and Cultural Rights
Maputo Protocol	Protocol to the African Charter on the Rights of Women
SDGs	Sustainable Development Goals
WHO	World Health Organization

Contributors

Adetoun T Adebanjo, LLD, Free State, is a law and human rights researcher in Queensland, Australia. Her areas of specialization include human rights, with a focus on women's rights and sexual and reproductive health and rights; constitutional law, and company and insolvency law. she is the author of several book chapters and articles in peer-reviewed international journals.

Adhip Amin, Researcher, Institute of Public Health Bengaluru, India

Isabel Barbosa, Adjunct Professor at Georgetown University Law Center and a Senior Associate at the O'Neill Institute for National and Global Health Law, working at the Global Center for Legal Innovation on Food Environments

Lucía Berro Pizzarossa, LLB, LLM (Oxon), PhD; Research Fellow, UdelaR

Upendra Bhojani, Director, Institute of Public Health, Bengaluru, India

Margherita M Cinà, Associate at the O'Neill Institute for National and Global Health Law, working at the Global Center for Legal Innovation on Food Environments.

Andrés Constantin, J.D., LL.M., Assistant Director of Health Law Programs at the O'Neill Institute for National and Global Health Law at Georgetown University

Riddhi Dsouza, Researcher, Institute of Public Health, Bengaluru, India

Ebenezer Durojaye, Professor and Head of the Socio-economic Rights Project, Dullah Omar Institute, University of the Western Cape, South Africa. Together with Gladys Mirugi-Mukundi and Charles Ngwena, he is the co-editor of the book *Advancing Sexual and Reproductive Health and Rights in Africa: Constraints and Opportunities* (Routledge 2021)

Christian Garuka, LLM, is a human rights lawyer with more than 10 years in legal practice where he has litigated cases related to the right to health and also has published in the area of human rights . He has extensively consulted for various institutions on human rights at the national and international level. He holds a Master's Degree in Human Rights from the University of Pretoria

Lucía Giudice, PHD candidate, Universidad Autónoma de Madrid; LLM in Global Rule of Law, Institute Tarello for Legal Philosophy, Università di Genova. Research fellow at the Law School, Universidad de la República, Uruguay

Pragati Hebbar, Researcher, Institute of Public Health Bengaluru, India

Rachel Kitonyo, McCabe Centre for Law and Cancer

Roopanand Mahadew, (LLD) is a senior lecturer in Law at the University of Mauritius. His research interests are international human rights and his teaching areas are public international law, human rights law and legal research methods. He is currently serving as an external expert in the Working Group on Children's Rights and Business to the African Committee of Experts on the Rights and Welfare of the Child. Dr Mahadew has also authored a number of journal articles and book chapters on various issues related to human rights law.

Michelle Rufaro Maziwisa, LLD UWC, Post-doctoral Researcher, Dullah Omar Institute, University of the Western Cape, South Africa

Lucyline Nkatha Murungi, Assistant Director, Centre for Human Rights, University of Pretoria, South Africa

Robert D Nanima, LLD, LLD, is a Senior lecturer in the Department of Criminal Justice and Procedure in the Faculty of Law, University of the Western Cape, and a research fellow at the Dullah Omar Institute. He is also a member of the African Committee of Experts on the Rights and Welfare of the Child and Special Rapporteur for Children affected by Armed Conflict. His areas of research include socio-economic rights of vulnerable persons, and human rights

Chipo Mushota Nkhata, Lecturer, University of Zambia; LLD Candidate, University of Cape Town, South Africa. She is a human rights, inclusion and gender specialist and legal practitioner who is passionate about the rights of vulnerable and marginalised groups. Currently, she is researching on women inmates' participation in health-related decision making and programming as a means of enhancing their health rights

Bright Nkrumah, PhD, scholar-activist at the Center for Human Rights, University of the Free State. He is the author of Seeking the right to food: food activism in South Africa (Cambridge University Press 2021)

Lucía Berro Pizzarossa, post-doctoral fellow at the O'Neill Institute for National and Global Health Law at the University of Georgetown. She holds a Ph.D. in International Law from the University of Groningen, an MJur from the University of Oxford, and an LLB from the Universidad de la Republica in Uruguay. She has consulted for Ipas, RSFU, inroads, and others on various topics related to reproductive justice and abortion

Belice Odamna, LLM, is a health rights advocate with experience in socioeconomic and political issues that affect the enjoyment of the right to health. She has experience working in the Civil Society sector implementing programs on governance. She has further experience in litigating on HIV and TB, challenging punitive laws and practices that lead to stigma, and discrimination while working with communities of PLHIV and key populations on related advocacy

Amiti Varma, Researcher, Institute of Public Health, Bengaluru, India

Emma Wanyonyi, International Institute for Legislative Affairs, has over 12 years' experience working in tobacco control. She has previously served as CEO of International Institute for Legislative Affairs in Kenya and on the Boards of the Kenya Tobacco Control Alliance (KETCA) and the Africa Tobacco Control Alliance (ATCA), through which she has led civil society advocacy for tobacco control policy development and implementation in Kenya and supported capacity strengthening for tobacco control civil society in various countries in Africa, including Kenya, Nigeria, Ghana, The Gambia, Botswana and Zimbabwe. Ms Wanyonyi's background is in public health

Preface

This book was conceived to address a very important and challenging issue confronting Africa. Tobacco-related non-communicable diseases (NCDs) are one of the major causes of deaths in developing countries, especially those in Africa. The book explores the link between human rights and tobacco control, using the WHO Framework Convention on Tobacco Control (FCTC) as the reference point. The burden of NCDs in Africa has grown considerably in the recent past. NCDs related to tobacco use have received particular attention in the wake of the adoption of the FCTC. In response to this development, some policy proposals have been put forward at the continental level. These policy proposals predominantly approach the subject of tobacco control and NCDs as more of a public health concern and much less as a human rights issue. The FCTC provides a global frame of reference on the regulation of tobacco use, as well as the response to NCDs related to tobacco use.

The approach to regulation of tobacco use and related NCDs varies significantly from country to country within Africa. In most countries, however, initiatives in this regard are shaped by competing interests in the tobacco industry and public health. In most cases, the link between tobacco control, NCDs, and human rights is not articulated in legislation or policy. At the regional level, the role of the African human rights system, particularly the African Commission on Human and Peoples' Rights, in responding to the incidence of NCDs in general and those related to tobacco use specifically, remains largely unexplored.

This book provides timely insight into the link between tobacco control as envisaged under the FCTC and NCDs associated with tobacco use, through a human rights prism. The existing academic discourse on the link between tobacco use and NCDs has mostly coalesced around the adoption of the FCTC. However, even within this literature, there is little about the implementation of the FCTC in Africa or the link between human rights, tobacco use and NCDs. The focus on Africa and the human rights approach adds to its value as a pioneering contribution on the past and potential impact of the FCTC on reducing the incidence of tobacco-related NCDs in Africa. The book will be useful to students, researchers, activists, civil society groups and policymakers.

Acknowledgements

The editors are grateful for the support received from colleagues at the Dullah Omar Institute, University of the Western Cape and the Centre for Human Rights, University of Pretoria during the preparation of this book. Thanks go especially to Temitayo Lawal and Keathélia Sapto for providing the needed support towards the finalisation of the manuscript.

Part I
Introduction

1 Introduction

Ebenezer Durojaye and Lucyline Nkatha Murungi

1.1 Background

This book provides a nuanced analysis of the link between human rights and tobacco control. It highlights the importance of taking measures to control tobacco use in Africa with a view to preventing the risk factors for non-communicable diseases (NCDs). The first of its kind in the African region, the book examines the implementation of the World Health Organization (WHO) Framework Convention on Tobacco Control (FCTC) in selected African and other developing countries from a rights-based perspective. With contributions from experts across Africa and other countries in the Global South, the book provides a critical analysis of the role that human rights can play in mitigating the impact of tobacco use and NCDs, an issue that affects the lives of millions of people across the world, particularly in Africa. The WHO has noted that tobacco use or exposure to tobacco is a major health risk factor for NCDs.[1] The book contains a systematic and in-depth analysis of how efforts to realise the right to health under international and regional law can help to address the incidence of tobacco use which can, in turn, lead to NCD-related deaths in selected countries in Africa and other developing regions. It will be an important read for anyone interested in addressing the negative impact of tobacco use as a risk factor for NCDs in society.

The book engages with the value and relevance of applying human rights to public health hazards such as tobacco use, noting that this can cause NCDs. It uses the FCTC as a case study in this regard. The book emphasises that both international and national laws play a significant role in regulating the affairs of people and can go a long way in addressing major social ills or public health challenges. Echoing Roscoe Pound, who asserts that law should be viewed as a tool for social engineering, the book discusses the importance of developing effective legal framework at the national level to address the incidence of tobacco use.[2] Nowhere is this better evidenced than in the adoption of the FCTC.

1 WHO 'Fact sheet on tobacco' (2019) https://www.who.int/news-room/fact-sheets/detail/tobacco (accessed 26 April 2021).

2 L McManaman 'Social engineering: The legal philosophy of Roscoe Pound' (1958) 33 *St John's Law Review* 1.

DOI: 10.4324/9781003264248-2

1.1.1 The normative framework on the right to health and NCDs

The right to health is guaranteed in numerous international and regional human rights instruments. At the global level, these include the Universal Declaration of Human Rights;[3] the International Covenant on Economic, Social and Cultural Rights;[4] the Convention on the Elimination of Discrimination against Women;[5] the Convention on the Rights of the Child;[6] and the Convention on the Rights of Persons with Disabilities.[7] In the African region, these include the African Charter on Human and Peoples' Rights (African Charter);[8] the Protocol to the African Charter on the Rights of Women (Maputo Protocol);[9] and the African Charter on the Rights and Welfare of the Child (the Children's Charter).[10]

The most authoritative provision on the right to health is contained in article 12 of the Committee on Economic, Social and Cultural Rights (CESCR). The CESCR in its General Comment 14 has expounded on the meaning and nature of states' obligations to realise the right to health.

The Committee notes in this regard that the enjoyment of the right to health has implications for other rights such as dignity, non-discrimination and equality, life, privacy, and freedom from torture, inhumane and degrading treatment. According to the Committee, the right to health must be available, accessible, acceptable and of good quality. It further identifies states have the obligation to respect, protect and fulfil the right to health. In this regard, the Committee emphasises the need for states to take proactive steps to prevent and treat epidemics and diseases within their jurisdiction. This clarification by the Committee is crucial to addressing tobacco use and its risk factors for NCDs at the national level. The obligation to protect requires states to take adequate measures to control the activities of tobacco companies so that they do not undermine the right

3 Universal Declaration of Human Rights, adopted 10 December 1948, art 1, GA Res 217A (III), UN Doc A/810 (1948).

4 UN General Assembly, International Covenant on Economic, Social and Cultural Rights, 16 December 1966, United Nations, Treaty Series, vol 993, p 3 (16 December 1966) UN Doc A/6316 (1966) (entered into force 2 September 1990).

5 UN General Assembly, Convention on the Elimination of All Forms of Discrimination Against Women, 18 December 1979, United Nations, Treaty Series, vol 1249, p 13 (entered into force 3 September 1981).

6 UN General Assembly, Convention on the Rights of the Child, 20 November 1989, United Nations, Treaty Series, vol. 1577, p 3 (1989) UN Doc A/44/49 (entered into force 2 September 1990).

7 UN General Assembly, Convention on the Rights of Persons with Disabilities, 24 January 2007, UN Doc A/RES/61/106 (2007) (entered into force 3 May 2008).

8 Organisation of African Unity, African Charter on Human and Peoples' Rights, adopted 27 June 1981, OAU Doc CAB/LEG/67/3 rev 5, 21 ILM 58 (1982) (entered into force 21 October 1986).

9 African Union, The Protocol to the African Charter on the Rights of Women in Africa, adopted by the African Union in 2003 (entered into force 27 November 2005).

10 Organisation of African Unity, African Charter on the Rights and Welfare of the Child, adopted 11 July 1990, art 5, OAU Doc CAB/LEG/24.9/49 (entered into force 29 November 1999).

to health of the people. Furthermore, the obligation to fulfil requires states to adopt legislative, budgetary and other measures to regulate tobacco use.

Under the regional human rights system, the various provisions of the African Charter, the Maputo Protocol and the Children's Charter are relevant in addressing NCDs. In this regard, the right to health, guaranteed in article 16 of the African Charter, article 14 of the Maputo Protocol, and article 14 of the African Children's Charter are relevant for this purpose. The African Commission on Human and Peoples' Rights (the Commission) has elaborated on the nature of this right by adopting a broad interpretation that links its violation to other rights such as life, non-discrimination, housing and food.[11] Also, the Commission has noted that the right to life guaranteed in the Charter requires states to take positive measures to prevent loss of life.[12] This broad approach by the Commission is significant in framing states' obligations to address tobacco use and its risk factors for NCDs in the region. It can be argued that states are expected to take positive measures with a view to preventing NCD-related deaths caused by tobacco use in the region. More importantly, it requires states to develop legislative framework in response to tobacco use.

In addition to binding human rights instruments on deaths resulting from NCDs attributable to tobacco use, the United Nations General Assembly in 2011 adopted a Declaration on the Prevention and Control of Non-communicable Diseases. The Declaration recognises the burden of NCDs in the world, especially among poor countries, and calls on states to take urgent steps to address this. It further reaffirms the right of everyone to the enjoyment of the right to health in the context of NCDs. The Declaration recognises the

> importance of reducing the level of exposure of individuals and populations to the common modifiable risk factors for non-communicable diseases, namely, tobacco use, unhealthy diet, physical inactivity, and the harmful use of alcohol, and their determinants.[13]

It is further noted that women tend to bear a disproportionate burden of NCDs in the world. More importantly, the Declaration calls on states to adopt a multisectoral, cost-effective intervention in order to reduce the impact of common NCDs such as tobacco use, unhealthy diets, physical inactivity and consumption of alcohol, and to adopt comprehensive National Action Plans to address NCDs.

11 See the *International Pen on behalf of Saro Wiwa v Nigeria* (1998) AHRLR 212 (ACHPR 1998); Communications 137/94, 139/94, 154/96 and 161/97; see also, *Social and Economic Rights Action Centre (SERAC) v Nigeria* (2001) AHRLR 60 (ACHPR 2001).

12 See for instance, General Comment 3 on the African Charter: The Right to Life (art 4), Adopted During the 57th Ordinary Session of the African Commission on Human and Peoples' Rights Held from 4–18 November 2015 in Banjul, The Gambia.

13 UN General Assembly 'Political Declaration of the High-Level Meeting of the General Assembly on the Prevention and Control of Non-Communicable Diseases' Doc A/66/L.1 (2011) para 35.

Furthermore, the Sustainable Development Goals (SDG), particularly SDG 3 on healthy lives and well-being, and even more specifically SDG 3.A on strengthening implementation of the FCTC, are anchored in human rights.

During the 66th World Health Assembly in May 2013, the WHO adopted the Global Action Plan for the Prevention and Control of Non-communicable Diseases. This Action Plan contains a number of very important commitments to addressing tobacco use and its risk factors for NCDs. There were six objectives and nine voluntary targets towards addressing NCDs. States are enjoined to take concrete and coordinated measures, including policy formulations, with a view to addressing four major NCD-related deaths. One of the important objectives of this Action Plan was that states should take adequate measures towards achieving a 25 per cent reduction in mortality from cardiovascular diseases, cancer, diabetes or chronic respiratory diseases by 2025 and reducing the risk factors for NCDs. The Action Plan also aims at addressing four shared behavioural risk factors: tobacco use, unhealthy diet, physical inactivity and harmful use of alcohol. It is hoped that this Plan of Action will galvanise states to implement measures to address tobacco use and NCD-related deaths.

1.2 Linking tobacco use and NCDs

According to the WHO, the tobacco epidemic is one of the major health challenges facing the world.[14] Tobacco use is associated with heart- and lung-related diseases across the world.[15] An estimated 7 million people worldwide die of the consequences of tobacco use each year.[16] Of these deaths, about 6 million are caused by direct tobacco use, while around 890,000 are the result of non-smokers being exposed to second-hand smoke.[17] About 80 per cent of the 1.1 billion smokers worldwide live in low- and middle-income countries, particularly Africa, where the burden of tobacco-related illnesses and deaths is heaviest.[18] It is a known fact that tobacco smokers are likely to die prematurely, thereby causing socio-economic hardships to their families. Through a range of instruments, the international community has committed to addressing the incidence of NCDs, including those caused by tobacco use.

On 23 May 2003, the WHO adopted one of the most important health rights treaties, the FCTC, during the 56th World Health Assembly held in Geneva, Switzerland. The Treaty came into force on 27 February 2005. So far, about 181 countries have ratified the Convention, including many African countries.[19] The FCTC is the first major health-specific Treaty grounded in human rights that addresses the various aspects of tobacco use. It reaffirms the right of people to

14 WHO (n 1).
15 As above.
16 As above.
17 As above.
18 As above.
19 See WHO 'WHO framework convention on tobacco control' (2003) (FCTC).

the highest standard of health, provides legal dimensions for international health cooperation and sets high standards for compliance. Some of the important provisions of the Treaty include rules that govern the production, sale, distribution, advertisement and taxation of tobacco. FCTC standards are minimum requirements, however, signatories are encouraged to be even more stringent in regulating tobacco use than the Treaty requires them to be. The FCTC is also the first internationally binding instrument to address the link between tobacco and NCDs.

Almost two decades after the adoption of the FCTC, is it imperative to take stock of how African countries have fared in implementing the commitments under the Treaty. More importantly, it is apposite to review what has worked well, what is not working and why this is so. In other words, this is an opportune time to document lessons learned among countries in the region and beyond and to share the good practices and challenges in the implementation of the FCTC.

This book is the first of its kind to embark on case studies of selected countries in Africa and other developing countries regarding the challenges and opportunities presented by the implementation of the FCTC at the national level. Given the benefits of cross-fertilisation of knowledge and ideas, this book also features chapters from other regions in a comparative context. The chapters from outside Africa were selected to represent other comparable regions, particularly Asia (India) and Latin America (Uruguay). The third chapter in that section provides a regional look at the experience of the Inter-American Human Rights System. In recent times, both India and Uruguay have experienced some interesting developments with regard to tackling of NCDs in general and those caused by tobacco use in particular. The combination of legal reforms and social mobilisation in this regard provides useful lessons for African countries. Moreover, the efforts of the Inter-American Commission and Court of Human Rights in developing norms and standards on NCDs in general and tobacco use in particular present a nuanced comparative study for the African human rights system. It is hoped that the lessons and good practices emerging from other countries from the Global South will impel African countries to take more concrete measures towards addressing NCDs, particularly those related to tobacco use.

1.3 Significance of the book

This book examines the link between human rights and tobacco control, using the FCTC as a case study. It further discusses the relevance of the right to health to addressing tobacco control at the national level. It also assesses the degree of domestication and implementation of the FCTC at the national level in selected African countries. This analysis also identifies challenges and good practices with regard to the implementation of the FCTC and provides suggestions on how to effectively incorporate and implement the provisions of the FCTC at the national level.

The book adopts a nuanced approach to evaluating the implementation of FCTC at the national level. It is a collection of rich chapters by scholars from

Africa and other developing countries who engage in prodigious discussion and analysis of serious threats to the health and well-being of millions of people. The country case studies provide critical analysis of the development in the selected countries and not merely general reports. In each chapter, the authors present an in-depth analysis of the legal framework to address tobacco use and the extent to which this is consistent with the country's obligations under international law. As such, it is a significant contribution to knowledge and scholarship on an important issue affecting not only Africa but also the international community.

The book responds to the needs of researchers, academics, students, policymakers and civil society groups working in the area of tobacco control and NCDs as a whole. In addition, the book seeks to stimulate debate about the relevance of the FCTC as a means of addressing tobacco use in Africa and beyond. The central message of the book is to reaffirm the relevance of a rights-based approach to tobacco control and related NCDs. It underscores the point that states are obligated under international law to respect, protect and fulfil the right to health in the context of tobacco control. The book further presents a unique and compelling message to policymakers and other stakeholders on the need to address the negative consequences of tobacco use in Africa and beyond. It advocates for proper implementation of the FCTC at the national level as a means for reducing NCD-related deaths associated with tobacco use.

1.4 Literature gap analysis

There are very few books on the same topic across Africa and internationally. Two major books on tobacco use in the region focus on different aspects of tobacco control. The first book is Jeffrey Drope's *Tobacco Control in Africa: People, Politics and Policies* (2011), which focuses on the work initiated and executed under the African Tobacco Situational Analyses, a recent major public health initiative sponsored by the Canadian International Development Research Centre. Drope's approach entails case studies of selected countries in Africa and examines topics such as the prevalence of smoking, the status of relevant smoking-related policies and the politics of public health policy reform, as well as the role played by the tobacco industry in each of these key areas. However, to the extent that Drope merely focuses on socio-political factors relating to tobacco use, it differs from the current book, which adopts a rights-based approach to tobacco use in Africa and draws on experiences from other jurisdictions.

The second book is Johann van Loggerenberg's *Tobacco Wars: Inside the Spy Games and Dirty Tricks of Southern Africa's Cigarette Trade* (2019). It deals marginally with corrupt practices relating to tobacco use in South Africa. Van Loggerenberg notes that tobacco not only kills but also corrupts, given the amount of money involved with the selling and marketing thereof. Thus, one could say that the focus of the book differs greatly from the current book, which examines the state of implementation of the FCTC in selected African countries.

In comparison to the two books mentioned, this book adopts a rights-based approach to tobacco use in Africa. Unlike these books, which deal with socio-political issues relating to tobacco use, the central focus of the proposed book is the application of a human rights-based approach as envisaged under the FCTC to address tobacco use at the national level, and particularly linking such measures to the control of tobacco-related NCDs. It contains an analysis of the provisions of the FCTC and adoption of national laws to ensure effective implementation. It offers useful insights in assessing efforts made so far by African governments to reduce tobacco use and the challenges associated with the implementation of the FCTC. This is very important, as it resonates with SDG 3 of the Sustainable Development Agenda 2030 and the African Union Agenda 2063.

A more recent book, *Human Rights and Tobacco Control* (2020) by Marie Elske Gispen and Brigit Toebes, addresses the human rights issues raised by tobacco control across the world. The book focuses on tobacco control from an international perspective and provides an insight into the role of law and human rights in addressing NCDs caused by tobacco use. However, the book contains only one chapter on the African human rights system. To this extent, the focus of that book differs from this book, insofar as the latter examines the relationship between the right to health and tobacco control in African countries, drawing on good practices from other jurisdictions in Asia and Latin America. Using the FCTC as a focal point, this book emphasises the link between the enjoyment of the right to health, poverty, and NCDs, including those associated with tobacco use, in developing countries. The focus on the link between these issues, and on Africa with some limited comparable countries from other developing regions, clearly distinguishes the present book from the one by Gispen and Toebes.

1.5 Summary of the chapters

This book is organised into three parts. Part I introduces the link between tobacco use and human rights, as well as the role of the African human rights system in addressing tobacco use and related NCDs in Africa. This link is important, because it provides a basis for the analysis of the implementation of the FCTC from a human rights point of view. In Part II, the book explores the implementation of the FCTC in eight African countries. Part III focuses on comparative case studies from other regions, specifically Uruguay, India and the Inter-American Human Rights System.

1.5.1 Part I: introduction

In this first chapter, the editors provide a general overview of the book, including a summary of the scope, rationale and significance of each of the chapters. The chapter also provides a brief summary of the legal frameworks relevant to the right to health, NCDs and the link between tobacco use and NCDs.

In Chapter 2, the editors discuss the role of the African human rights system in addressing tobacco use in Africa. The chapter examines the potential of the African human rights system, with a focus on the African Commission on Human and Peoples' Rights (African Commission) to address tobacco use from a human rights perspective. Given the increasing challenges posed to the health and lives of Africans, the editors argue that the institutions of the African human rights system, particularly the African Commission, play an important role in holding African governments accountable to address tobacco use in order to meet their human rights obligations under the relevant human rights instruments in the region. They emphasise that while tobacco use may undermine various rights under the African Charter and the Maputo Protocol, the rights to health and life are more directly affected by tobacco use. They particularly seek to establish the link between the implementation of the FCTC and the response to tobacco-related NCDs in Africa. Further, they assess whether the African Commission till now has truly lived up to its obligation to hold states accountable for the human rights violation caused by tobacco use. The editors identify the shortcomings of the African Commission in this regard and propose ways it could improve on realising its mandate to hold states accountable with regard to tobacco use. They propose that the African Commission can learn from other human rights bodies such as the Committee on Economic, Social and Cultural Rights and the Inter-American Commission on Human Rights in this regard.

1.5.2 Part II: country case studies

In Chapter 3, Nkrumah examines the incidence of NCDs and tobacco use in Ghana. He discusses the link with the realisation of the right to health in Ghana. While observing that the right to health is not explicitly recognised in Ghana, he notes that the government of Ghana is obligated to respect the various international and regional human rights instruments that have been ratified on this issue. Further, he discusses the various attempts by the Ghanaian government to regulate tobacco use in the country. In this regard, he analyses the provisions of the FCTC in comparison with the national law. The chapter highlights the provisions on the right to health in Ghana and their relevance to addressing tobacco use as a risk factor for NCDs. Nkrumah then evaluates efforts made by Ghana to ensure the effective implementation of the FCTC at the national level. He observes that tobacco consumption abounds in Ghana despite the requirement by the FCTC that States parties' should adopt policies and institutional frameworks towards limiting the use of tobacco among the people. He notes that while Ghanaian laws have complied with the provisions of the FCTC, proper implementation on the ground remains a serious challenge in the country. The chapter then offers some recommendations for the way forward.

In Chapter 4, Nanima explores the challenges and opportunities in the implementation of the FCTC in South Africa. At its core, the chapter takes a human rights approach that underscores the highest attainable standard of health underpinned by high standards for compliance. It points out the link between tobacco use and NCD-related mortality. Nanima discusses the obligations of the South African government to realise the right to health at the national and international levels and the implications for addressing tobacco use in the country. He further traces the historical attempt at regulating tobacco use in the country and then discusses the relevance of the FCTC in addressing tobacco use in the country and whether the South African government has lived up to its obligations to comply with this treaty. In this regard, the chapter analyses some of the provisions of the FCTC vis-à-vis the South African laws, discusses some case law relevant to the attempt to control tobacco use in the country and offers some recommendations for a way forward.

In Chapter 5, Adebanjo provides an overview of Nigeria's efforts in addressing NCDs within the framework of the FCTC. The author notes that the incidence of NCDs in general and tobacco use in particular is relatively high in Nigeria compared to other countries in the region, and discusses the obligations of the Nigerian government under international law to realise the right to health in general and in the context of tobacco use. The author notes that the right to health is not constitutionally guaranteed in Nigeria but nevertheless concludes that the country is obligated under international law to respect, protect and fulfil this right, including controlling tobacco use. The chapter then examines the provisions of the FCTC and how they have been incorporated into the Nigerian legal framework. From a right to health perspective, the author argues that the Nigerian government would need to exhibit more political will to effectively implement the FCTC in the country. Adebanjo notes that despite the enactment of the National Tobacco Control Act (NTCA) 2015, which aims at incorporating the provisions of the FCTC, tobacco use in the country has continued to increase, thereby posing a threat to the enjoyment of the rights to health and life in Nigeria. The chapter proffers some recommendations to the Nigerian government in this regard.

In Chapter 6, Wanyonyi, Kitonyo and Odamna explore tobacco control and the right to health in Kenya, focusing on the implementation of the FCTC. Their chapter covers the development of tobacco control laws in Kenya before and after the ratification of the FCTC and makes the link between tobacco use and NCD-related deaths in the country. Also, the chapter examines the evolution of the tobacco legal and policy framework vis-à-vis the promotion and protection of the right to health as provided for in article 43 of the Kenyan Constitution. The authors discuss Kenya's compliance with essential provisions of the FCTC, including packaging and labelling, protection from tobacco smoke exposure, tobacco promotion, advertising and sponsorship, public education and information, sale to minors, regulation of tobacco product disclosures, price and tax measures, regulation of contents of tobacco products, and support for other alternate activities that are economically viable. Good practices and challenges faced during implementation of tobacco control laws are also discussed in this chapter. The authors point out some good practices and discuss challenges in effective implementation of tobacco policies and laws in Kenya. They explore litigation in Kenya, brought by the tobacco industry since 2006, challenging the constitutionality of the Tobacco Control Act and the regulations created therein.

In Chapter 7, Nkhata examines tobacco-related health rights in Zambia in light of the FCTC. She examines the prevalence of tobacco use in Zambia, noting that it is responsible for numerous NCDs and deaths in Zambia. Using the FCTC and international human rights standards on the right to health as benchmarks, the author analyses Zambia's health rights obligations with regard to tobacco control. She examines specific provisions of the FCTC and how the Zambian government has incorporated these into its national laws. Nkhata notes that to some extent Zambia has complied with the provisions of the FCTC; however, much is required to ensure effective implementation in the country. She suggests that the Zambian government would need to take more concrete measures towards removing barriers to the effective implementation of the FCTC at the national level. Some judicial challenges to government efforts to regulate tobacco use in the country are also discussed.

In Chapter 8, Garuka explores the progress, challenges and perspectives on tobacco smoking and the law in Rwanda. The chapter examines the incidence of tobacco use and its risk factors for NCDs in the country. The author notes that countries around the globe have adopted laws to regulate tobacco use, and in some instances these laws have prohibited the sale of tobacco to specific persons and limited smoking to specific areas. The potential of the right to health in responding to challenges associated with tobacco use in Rwanda is discussed. Garuka notes the role of the FCTC in the regulation of tobacco use and observes that as a party to the FCTC, Rwanda has adopted some laws that directly and indirectly deal with tobacco use. The author then critically assesses whether the current Rwandan national legal framework complies with the FCTC and other international and regional human rights instruments from the right to health perspective. The chapter concludes with recommendations for the way forward.

In Chapter 9, Maziwisa and Durojaye analyse the efforts by Zimbabwe to implement the FCTC. The chapter discusses the incidence of tobacco use and its link to NCDs in Zimbabwe. The authors highlight the provisions on the right to health and their relevance to tobacco control in Zimbabwe. They consider the history of the attempts made by the Zimbabwean government to address tobacco use through laws and policies, and further discuss the obligations of the Zimbabwean government to realise the right to health in the context of tobacco use. They then critically evaluate the legal framework on tobacco use in Zimbabwe and whether this is consistent with the FCTC. While some of the laws and policies would seem to be in line with the FCTC, there are challenges with regard to effective implementation of these laws and policies at the national level. The chapter concludes by making recommendations on how the government of Zimbabwe can better address tobacco use in the country.

In Chapter 10, Mahadew assesses the level of compliance of the domestic normative framework on tobacco products of Mauritius with the FCTC. The author notes that Mauritius reacted to the growing concern about the number of deaths caused by tobacco products by ratifying the FCTC in May 2004. The chapter makes the link between tobacco use and NCD-related deaths in the country and explores the obligations of the government to realise the right to health, which includes addressing tobacco use. Mahadew notes that while some positive steps have been adopted by the government to address tobacco use, there is still considerable legal reform that needs to be implemented at the national level to ensure compliance with the FCTC. He notes that in 2008, the Public Health (Restriction on Tobacco Products) Regulations were enacted, which encapsulated the spirit of the FCTC. However, the author questions the effectiveness of this law in capturing the main substance of the FCTC. He then assesses the level of compliance of domestic laws on tobacco with the FCTC, concluding that while the domestic legal framework addresses concerns regarding tobacco use in Mauritius, certain gaps exist that require further actions from the government to address tobacco use.

1.5.3 Part III: lessons from other jurisdictions

In Chapter 11, Pizzarossa, Constantin and Giudice explain that Uruguay was the first Latin American country to adopt a comprehensive smoke-free national law as part of its nationwide tobacco control campaign. They note that this step was crucial to addressing NCD-related deaths in the country. The chapter describes Uruguay's strategy to address smoking and the different measures adopted by the country to tackle this global health challenge. The authors then discuss the tobacco industry's resistance to these measures and the arbitration procedure initiated by Philip Morris against the country before the International Centre for Settlement of Investment Disputes. They explore the relevance of a rights-based approach to addressing tobacco use in the country and reflect on the corporate practices and the challenges they pose to countries adopting tobacco control policies. The impact of Uruguay's policies on tobacco use is explained. The chapter concludes by reflecting on the case of Uruguay and the next steps to be taken to address the challenges posed by tobacco use and exposure in the region.

In Chapter 12, Bhojani and colleagues examine the extent to which the Indian government has implemented the FCTC at the national level. They evaluate the activities of the tobacco industry and its implication for the right to health of the people. They discuss the burden of NCDs in India, emphasising that marginalised groups are more likely than other members of the population to bear that burden. The chapter also explores the incidence of tobacco use and the health-related challenges for millions of people in India and examines the history of tobacco regulations in India pre- and post-ratification of the FCTC. The authors analyse the tobacco laws in India and their consistency with FCTC, noting that while the tobacco laws in India have incorporated the provisions of the FCTC to a great extent, there are gaps with regard to effective implementation at the national level. The authors recommend a rights-based approach relying on India's obligations under human rights instruments to realise the people's right to health.

In Chapter 13, Barbosa and Cinà discuss lessons on NCDs from the Inter-American Human Rights System. They consider the role regional human rights bodies in the Inter-American Human Rights System can play in addressing tobacco use as a means of reducing NCDs. The authors note that NCDs that are attributed to modifiable risk factors such as tobacco use, alcohol consumption, unhealthy diets, and physical inactivity are on the rise all over the world, especially affecting low- and middle-income countries. They note in particular the great risk that NCDs pose to the realisation of a wide range of health and health-related human rights. The authors argue that while tobacco control has been at the forefront of the NCD fight, particularly since the adoption of the FCTC, human rights frameworks at the international and regional levels have also proven to be useful tools to address NCD risk factors. Thus the chapter explores the Inter-American Human Rights System's development around NCDs, shining a light on how regional human rights systems, including the African Human Rights System, can create opportunities to examine NCD risk factors outside of their topic-specific silos, particularly in the absence of internationally binding treaties for all the major NCD risk factors.

1.6 Conclusion

This book makes a valuable contribution to the burgeoning literature on NCDs and human rights, and the potential contribution of the FCTC in this regard. Therefore, the book will be useful to researchers, students, academics, policy-makers, civil society groups, and personnel of national and regional human rights bodies. The focus on Africa is especially important in filling a gap in literature related to a human rights approach to NCDs, and specifically the FCTC in the African region. The book provides a scholarly reference point for students and researchers on the right to health, human rights, socio-economic rights, humanities and related subjects. The subject matter of this edition will also attract the attention of international and regional institutions and bodies working to eradicate health-related challenges, especially NCDs.

Bibliography

African Union, The Protocol to the African Charter on the Rights of Women in Africa adopted by the African Union in 2003, entered into force on 27 November 2005

Drope, J (ed) *Tobacco control in Africa: People, politics and policies* (Anthem Press, 2011)

General Comment 3 on the African Charter: The right to life (article 4), adopted during the 57th Ordinary Session of the African Commission on Human and Peoples' Rights held from 4–18 November 2015 in Banjul, The Gambia

Gispen, ME & Toebes, B *Human rights and tobacco control* (Edward Elgar 2020)

International Covenant on Economic, Social and Cultural Rights, adopted 16 December 1966, Preamble, GA Res 2200A (XXI), UN GAOR, Supp No 16, UN Doc A/6316 (1966), entered into force 2 September 1990

International Pen on Behalf of Saro Wiwa v Nigeria (1998) AHRLR 212 (ACHPR 1998); Communications 137/94, 139/94, 154/96 and 161/97

McManaman, L 'Social engineering: The legal philosophy of Roscoe Pound' (1958) 33 *St John's Law Review* 1

Organisation of African Unity, African Charter on Human and Peoples' Rights, adopted 27 June 1981, OAU Doc CAB/LEG/67/3 rev 5, 21 ILM 58 (1982), entered into force 21 October 1986

Organisation of African Unity, African Charter on the Rights and Welfare of the Child, adopted 11 July 1990, art 5, OAU Doc CAB/LEG/24.9/49, entered into force 29 November 1999

Social and Economic Rights Action Centre (SERAC) v Nigeria (2001) AHRLR 60 (ACHPR 2001)

UN General Assembly, Convention on the Elimination of All Forms of Discrimination Against Women, 18 December 1979, United Nations, Treaty Series, vol 1249, p 13, entered into force 3 September 1981

UN General Assembly, Convention on the Rights of the Child, 20 November 1989, United Nations, Treaty Series, vol 1577, p 3, adopted 20 November 1989, UN Doc A/44/49 (1989), entered into force 2 September 1990

UN General Assembly, Convention on the Rights of Persons with Disabilities (24 January 2007) UN Doc A/RES/61/106, adopted 13 December 2006, art 10, GA Res A/RES/61/106, UN GAOR, 61st Sess, UN Doc A/61/6111, entered into force 3 May 2008

UN General Assembly 'Political Declaration of the High-Level Meeting of the General Assembly on the Prevention and Control of Non-Communicable Diseases' Doc A/66/L.1 (2011)

Universal Declaration of Human Rights, adopted 10 December. 10, 1948, art 1, GA Res 217A (III), UN Doc A/810 (1948)

Van Loggerenberg, J *Tobacco wars: Inside the spy games and dirty tricks of southern Africa's cigarette trade* (Tatelberg, 2019)

WHO 'Fact sheet on tobacco' (2019) https://www.who.int/news-room/fact-sheets/detail/tobacco (accessed 26 April 2021)

WHO 'WHO framework convention on tobacco control' (2003)

2 The role of the African human rights system in promoting tobacco control and addressing related non-communicable diseases

Ebenezer Durojaye and Lucyline Nkatha Murungi

2.1 Introduction

According to the World Health Organization (WHO), non-communicable diseases (NCDs; or chronic diseases) are not passed from person to person and are clustered into four categories.[1] These include cardiovascular diseases, cancers, chronic respiratory diseases and diabetes. In addition, it is noted that NCDs are the leading cause of death globally, accounting for 41 million (71 per cent) of the world's 56 million deaths in 2016.[2] Furthermore, it is noted that about 15 per cent of NCD-related deaths are premature (between ages 30 and 70), while the burden of NCDs is disproportionately borne by low- and middle-income countries.[3] The WHO estimates that these deaths will increase by 17 per cent in 2025, with a 27 per cent increase arising from Africa.[4] It is also worth noting that in Mauritius, Namibia and Seychelles, NCDs cause over 50 per cent of all reported adult deaths.[5] While there was a decline in tobacco use from 27 per cent in 2000 to 20 per cent at the end of 2016, the rates of decline are still very slow in low- and middle-income countries.[6]

The African Commission on Human and Peoples' Rights is the oldest human rights body charged with the responsibility of monitoring the implementation of the African Charter on Human and Peoples' Rights and the Protocol to the African Charter on Human and Peoples' Rights on the Rights of Women in Africa (Maputo Protocol). This puts it in a pivotal position to hold African governments accountable for the realisation of human rights in general and the right to health

1 WHO 'Non-communicable diseases' (13 April 2021) https://www.who.int/news-room/fact-sheets/detail/noncommunicable-diseases (accessed 1 November 2020).
2 WHO 'Non-communicable diseases: Country profiles 2018' (2018).
3 As above.
4 WHO 'Africa: Non-communicable diseases' https://www.who.int/nmh/ncd-tools/who-regions-african/en/ (accessed 1 November 2020).
5 As above.
6 WHO (n 2).

DOI: 10.4324/9781003264248-3

in particular. It should be noted that other human rights bodies in the region, such as the African Court on Human and Peoples' Rights and the Committee of Experts on the Rights and Welfare of the Child (the Committee), can play an important role in addressing NCDs in the region. However, this chapter focuses mainly on the potential of the African Commission. This delimitation does not discount the potential contribution of the other mechanisms, particularly the Committee. However, a combination of the exclusive focus on children in the African Charter on the Rights and Welfare of the Child (African Children's Charter), and the general approach to tobacco use which precludes use by children, limits the role of the Committee in related to tobacco control and related NCDs. Accordingly, the jurisprudence of the Committee thus far has not engaged with the question of tobacco use and related NCDs.

Furthermore, the fact that the African Charter, as compared to other instruments, is nearly universally ratified by African countries (the only exception being Morocco) gives further impetus for the focus on the Commission in this assessment. The implication of the wide ratification is that almost all African states are obligated under the Charter to respect, protect and fulfil the realisation of the right to health as guaranteed in article 16 of the Charter. This duty is echoed in articles 14 of the Maputo Protocol and the African Children's Charter.

Against this backdrop, this chapter examines the promotional and protective mandate of the African Commission with a view to ascertain the opportunities that exist to hold African governments accountable for addressing NCDs in general and those associated with tobacco use in particular. Drawing on the work of the Commission, the chapter argues that very little has been done so far to ensure that African governments live up to their obligations to realise the right to health of individuals in the context of NCDs in general and tobacco use in particular. It further proposes that the African Commission can draw experiences from other human rights bodies at the UN level and from other jurisdictions.

2.2 Continental efforts at addressing NCDs

As noted above, NCDs have had a disproportionate effect on the African region. Millions of people die yearly due to NCDs, and many more have suffered morbidity.[7] The African Union on various occasions has acknowledged the negative impact of NCDs on Africans and has committed to addressing this serious health and human development challenge. For instance, the Africa Health Strategy 2007–2015 recognises the serious implications of NCDs for the well-being of Africans. It acknowledges that

> Africa's people face a huge burden of preventable and treatable health problems whose solutions are known, proportionately far beyond Africa's share of the world's population. The triple burden from communicable and

7 WHO (n 1).

non-communicable diseases and injury and trauma, including the social impact of these, has adversely affected development in Africa.

In addition, paragraph 8 is emphatic.[8]

The Health Strategy further acknowledges the alarming rate of deaths and burdens caused by NCDs in the region linking these to 'demographic, behavioural and social changes and urbanization'.[9]

One of the main objectives of the revised Health Strategy 2016–2030 is to reduce morbidity and preventable mortality from communicable and non-communicable diseases. In this regard, the Strategy lays emphasis on programmes that address risk factors and premature deaths from 'diabetes, cancer, cardiovascular diseases, respiratory infections, mental health, injuries and other non-communicable diseases, with a particular focus on combatting tobacco use, substance abuse and other risk factors'.[10]

During the commemoration of the Healthy Life Day 2019, the secretariat of the African Union issued a statement noting that adopting unhealthy lifestyles results in metabolic changes that increase the risk of NCDs. The statement further encourages the people to 'maintain good nutrition, have regular physical exercise, stop tobacco use and substance abuse, control alcohol use, manage stress, and ensure regular health check-ups'.[11]

The African Children's Committee has also articulated, as one of its aspirations under the African Union Agenda for Children (2040), a commitment to the reduction of premature mortality of children through NCDs.[12] Unfortunately, while this aspiration has the potential to encompass measures aimed at addressing NCDs related to tobacco use, the scope of measures envisaged under the implementation framework of the Agenda are limited to prevention and treatment focused on mental health. Nevertheless, there is potential for expansion of this scope in the review implementation plan for the next phase of implementation, which covers 2021–2025.

The foregoing developments are in consonance with the African Union's Agenda 2063, whose Aspiration 1 envisages '[a] prosperous Africa, based on inclusive growth and sustainable development'. Certainly, unless Africans are free from the burden of communicable and non-communicable diseases, sustainable development would not be possible.

Despite these commitments, however, it has been noted that many African countries still lag behind in ensuring the effective implementation of the WHO-led

8 See paras 6–7 of the Africa Health Strategy 2007–2015 reported in E Durojaye & G Mirugi-Mukundi *Compendium of documents and cases on the right to health under the African human rights system* (2013).

9 As above.

10 See Objective Strategy 2 of the Africa Health Strategy 2016–2030.

11 See African Union 'African union commemorates the Africa healthy lifestyle day 2019 healthy lifestyle prolongs life' (7 March 2019) https://au.int/sw/node/36029 (accessed 25 November 2021).

12 African Union 'Africa's agenda for children 2040: Fostering an Africa fit for children' (2015) 133.

NCDs Global Action Plan 2013–2020.[13] It is further noted that progress in addressing NCDs in Africa remains uneven and at a slow pace.[14] According to the study, 'some gains were made in implementing national public awareness programmes on diet and/or physical activity, however limited progress was made on guidelines for management of NCDs and drug therapy and counselling'.[15] This calls for a rights-based approach, which requires African governments to ensure that all measures adopted towards addressing NCDs must be grounded in respect for the fundamental rights of the people.

2.3 Making the link between human rights and NCDs

The enjoyment of the right to health requires the state to take appropriate measures that will not only facilitate access to healthcare services for all but also require the state to engage in activities that will promote the health and well-being of the individuals. This may include adopting laws and policies and embarking on education and awareness campaigns. The right to health is guaranteed in international and regional human rights instruments. The first reference to this right was in articles 55 and 56 of the United Nations Charter,[16] where the international community commits to finding solutions to international economic, social, health and related problems. This is followed by the Preamble to the Constitution of the WHO, where the term 'health' was defined broadly to include not merely absence of infirmity but rather a complete state of mental and physical well-being.[17] It further explains that the enjoyment of the highest attainable standard of health is a fundamental right of all. With regard to earlier human rights instruments, article 25 of the Universal Declaration guarantees the right to an adequate standard of living, including health.[18]

By far, the most authoritative provision on the right to health is found in article 12 of the International Covenant on Economic, Social and Cultural Rights (ICESCR).[19] It provides that states shall recognise the enjoyment of the highest attainable standard of health for everyone. The Committee on Economic, Social

13 GN Nyaaba 'Tracing Africa's progress towards implementing the non-communicable diseases global action plan 2013–2020: A synthesis of WHO country profile reports' (2017) 17 *BMC Public Health* 1.

14 As above.

15 As above.

16 Preamble to the Constitution of the WHO as Adopted by the International Health Conference, New York, 19–22 June 1946.

17 The Charter of the United Nations is the founding document of the United Nations. It was signed on 26 June 1945, in San Francisco, at the conclusion of the United Nations Conference on International Organisation, and came into force on 24 October 1945.

18 Universal Declaration of Human Rights, Adopted 10 December 1948, art 1, GA Res 217A (III), UN Doc A/810 (1948).

19 UN General Assembly, International Covenant on Economic, Social and Cultural Rights, 16 December 1966, United Nations, Treaty Series, vol 993, p 3 (16 December 1966) UN Doc A/6316 (1966) (entered into force 2 September 1990).

and Cultural Rights (CESCR) has provided clarification on the meaning and content of the right to health under article 12 of the ICESCR in its General Comment 14.[20] The Committee explains that the right to health does not mean the right to be healthy. Rather it implies that states should take adequate measures to ensure an enabling environment where people can have access to treatment.[21] It further explains that the enjoyment of the right to health requires states to take preventive and curative measures.[22] According to the Committee, the right to health intersects with other rights such as life, privacy, dignity, non-discrimination and freedom from cruel, inhuman and degrading treatment.[23]

Having clarified the content of the right to health, the Committee notes that the realisation of the right to health requires various measures from the state. It explains that states have the obligations to respect, protect and fulfil the right to health. In this regard, states are expected to take concrete measures towards the realisation of the right to health. This could include formulating policies or implementing programmes or norms developed by the WHO. Implicit in this is that states must adopt policies or programmes to address NCDs in general and those related to control of tobacco use in particular. Indeed, the Committee notes that a state will be in violation of the duty to realise the right to health if it fails to protect the people from practices detrimental to their health through activities of third parties in relation to tobacco use.[24]

In addition, states are obligated to adopt a legislative framework that will enable individuals to enjoy their right to health. This is particularly important in the context of tobacco control. It implicitly requires states to adopt a legislative framework to address tobacco use.[25] The Committee explains that a state will be in violation of the right to health where there is 'failure to discourage production, marketing and consumption of tobacco, narcotics and other harmful substances'.[26] States are also obligated to provide health-related information on sexual and reproductive health, alcohol, and cigarettes.[27] In its Guidelines for State Reporting, the Committee requires states to provide information on measures taken to prevent abuse of alcohol, tobacco use, illicit drugs and other harmful substances.[28]

The Committee in some of its concluding observations to states has addressed the challenges posed by NCDs including tobacco use. For instance,

20 UN Committee on Economic, Social and Cultural Rights (CESCR), General Comment 14: The Right to the Highest Attainable Standard of Health (art 12 of the Covenant) (11 August 2000) UN Doc E/C.12/2000/4 (2000).
21 As above.
22 General Comment 14 para 53.
23 General Comment 14 para 11.
24 General Comment 14 para 51.
25 See D Patterson & others 'Identifying a human rights-based approach to obesity for states and civil society (2019) 20 *Obesity Reviews* 45.
26 General Comment 14 para 51.
27 General Comment 14 para 36.
28 See para 57 of the Reporting Guidelines.

in its concluding observations to Mauritius, the Committee expressed deep concern about the incidence of NCDs in the country and recommended that the government

> take effective measures to reduce the risk factors of non-communicable diseases, to improve the early detection of such non-communicable diseases, to provide effective and timely treatment, and to prevent complications.[29]

The Committee has also expressed concerns with the level of tobacco consumption in Cameroon despite efforts by the government to control it.[30] Thus, the Committee enjoined the government to

> design effective policies to combat tobacco consumption, strengthen its prohibition on tobacco product advertising, enact legislation imposing a strict ban on smoking in all closed public areas, and intensify public awareness-raising campaigns.[31]

The UN Committee on the Rights of the Child has also noted that states are obligated to ensure that they adopt international norms and standards for the protection of the right to health of children at the national level.[32] According to the Committee, this would include the FCTC.[33] Moreover, the Committee enjoins states to address obesity in children and its attendant consequences, such as hypertension and other health-related diseases, as these could lead to adult obesity and premature death.[34] Expressing concerns on this issue, the Committee notes as follows:

> Children's exposure to 'fast foods' that are high in fat, sugar or salt, energy-dense and micronutrient-poor, and drinks containing high levels of caffeine or other potentially harmful substances should be limited.[35]

Thus, states are obligated to take preventive measures to address all diseases, both communicable and non-communicable. States are further enjoined to adopt preventive measures to address all communicable and non-communicable diseases.[36] The Committee urges states to protect children from the effect of tobacco use

29 See Concluding Observations on the Fifth Periodic Report of Mauritius, CESCR (April 2019) UN Doc E/C.12/MUS/CO/55 (2019).

30 See Concluding Observations to Cameroon, CESCR (23 January 2012) UN Doc E/C.12/CMR/CO/2–3 (2012) para 31.

31 As above.

32 General Comment 15 (2013) on the right of the child to the enjoyment of the highest attainable standard of health (art 24), Committee on the Rights of the Child (17 April 2013) UN Doc CRC/C/GC/15 (2013) para 44.

33 As above.

34 General Comment 15 para 47.

35 As above.

36 General Comment 15 para 64.

and urges states that are yet to do so to ratify the FCTC. Echoing this sentiment, the Special Rapporteur on the right to health has requested states to 'ban the advertising, promotion and sponsorship of all children's sporting events, and other sporting events which could be attended by children, by manufacturers of alcohol, tobacco and unhealthy foods'.[37]

In some of its concluding observations to states, the Committee has expressed concerns about the impact of NCDs on the well-being and right to health of children. For instance, in its concluding observations to South Africa, the Committee expressed concerns about the prevalence of obesity among children caused by marketing of unhealthy food. It therefore urged the government to 'regulate the marketing of unhealthy foods to children in order to address the rise in child obesity, and introduce strategies that enable poor households to access healthy food'.[38] Expressing a similar concern to the Brazilian government, the Committee expressed concern about the high level of obesity among children, exacerbated by unregulated advertising that promotes unhealthy food in the country.[39] Thus, the Committee urged the government to 'take all necessary measures to address obesity among children, including by promoting healthy lifestyles and raising awareness of healthy nutrition'.[40]

The foregoing statements are a clear indication that the Committee expects states to take concrete measures with a view to mitigating the negative impact of NCDs on children. The fact that the Committee engages with states on this issue reinforces the need for actions to be taken from a rights-based perspective.

Under the African Human Rights System, various rights that are crucial to addressing NCDs, including those related to tobacco use, are recognised in the African Charter, the Maputo Protocol and the African Children's Charter. These include the rights to health, life, dignity, non-discrimination, privacy, and freedom from torture, inhuman and degrading treatment. While there is no express reference to NCDs in these instruments, the obligation can be derived from the foregoing provisions. For instance, the duty to safeguard the health and well-being of children from secondary tobacco use which can undermine their well-being and dignity can be inferred from the overall right to health. Similarly, in some of its decisions, the Commission has affirmed that exposing an individual to suffering or harm (as in the case of tobacco use) would amount to a violation of the right to dignity guaranteed in the Charter.[41]

37 Report of the Special Rapporteur on the right of everyone to the enjoyment of the highest attainable standard of physical and mental health 'Sport and Healthy Lifestyles and the Right to Health' (4 April 2016) UN Doc A/HRC/32/33 (2016) paras 32–33.

38 See Concluding Observations on the Second Periodic Report of South Africa, CRC Committee (27 October 2016) UN Doc CRC/C/ZAF/CO/2 (2016) paras 53(e) and 54(d).

39 Concluding Observations on the Combined Second to Fourth Periodic Reports of Brazil, CRC Committee (30 October 2015) UN Doc CRC/C/BRA/CO/2-4 (2015) para 58.

40 As above.

41 See for instance, *Doebbler v Sudan* (Communication 236/2000) [2003] ACHPR 42 (29 May 2003).

2.4 The African Commission and NCDs

The African Commission on Human and Peoples' Rights is the oldest regional human rights body in Africa, having being established in 1987 pursuant to article 30 of the African Charter to oversee the implementation of the Charter. Consequent upon the entry into force of the Maputo Protocol, the Commission was also assigned the responsibility of overseeing its implementation pending the establishment of the African Court on Human and Peoples' Rights.[42] By virtue of article 31, the Commission consists of 11 members chosen from among African personalities of highest reputation, known for their morality, integrity and competence in matters of human and peoples' rights. Members of the Commission are to be elected by the General Assembly of the African Union, and not more than one person may be elected from a single country. The tenure of members of the Commission is six years; however, members may be eligible for re-election.

The mandate of the commission can broadly be classified into two; promotional and protective. Article 45(1) of the African Charter spells out the promotional mandate of the Commission, which includes the following:

1 To collect documents, undertake studies and researches on African problems in the field of human and peoples' rights, organize seminars, symposia and conferences, disseminate information, encourage national and local institutions concerned with human and peoples' rights, and should the case arise, give its views or make recommendations to Governments.
2 To formulate and lay down, principles and rules aimed at solving legal problems relating to human and peoples' rights and fundamental freedoms upon which African Government may base their legislation.
3 To co-operate with other African and international institutions concerned with the promotion and protection of human and peoples' rights.[43]

The protective mandate of the Commission can be found in articles 47 to 55. While articles 47 to 52 relate to communication filed by states to the Commission, articles 54 and 55 relate to communication filed by non-state parties. This section examines the potential of the African Commission to address NCDs, including those attributable to tobacco use in Africa. It opines that the Commission can develop norms and standards for African governments to address NCDs through its protective and promotional mandate.

2.4.1 The promotional mandate of the Commission

Over the years, the decisions, recommendations, resolutions and general comments of the Commission have influenced governments, non-governmental

42 While the Court has since been established, the Commission has remained to oversee the implementation of the Maputo Protocol.
43 African Charter art 45.

organisations (NGOs) and human rights advocates throughout the continent. As the first human rights body to be established in the region, the Commission occupies a pivotal position in developing norms and standards on human rights in general and the right to health in particular.[44] While the Commission has a great potential to develop norms and standards on NCDs including tobacco control, it is yet to clearly address this issue in its promotional mandate.[45]

In particular, the Commission is yet to adopt any resolution, guidelines or general comments specifically addressing the impact of NCDs, including tobacco use, on the enjoyment of human rights in the region. It should be noted, however, that in its Resolution on Access to Medicines, the Commission urges states to prevent unreasonably high costs of medicines in both private and public sectors.[46] This statement is very important, given the prohibitive cost of treating NCDs in many parts of the region, and can serve as a clarion call to African governments to take appropriate measures with a view to ensuring access to treatment for NCDs.

In its resolution on the right to food and nutrition in Africa, the Commission expressed concerns about malnutrition, under-nutrition, obesity and diet-related NCDs affecting the health and well-being of individuals in Africa.[47] It further called on states to adopt policy, institutional and legislative measures to ensure the full realisation of the right to food. Although this resolution is not directly related to tobacco use, it is important nevertheless in the sense that it demonstrates the potential of the African Commission to address NCD-related challenges in Africa. It further indicates that states are to adopt appropriate measures to address all forms of NCDs, including tobacco-related NCDs.

In both General Comments 1 and 2 on article 14 of the Maputo Protocol, the Commission missed a great opportunity to address NCDs that may affect the sexual and reproductive health and rights of women. This is surprising given the high incidence of NCDs and its attendant consequences in the region. The Principles and Guidelines on the Implementation of Economic, Social and Cultural Rights in the Charter also fail to directly address NCDs and tobacco use.[48] However, the document contains some important provisions to hold states accountable to adopt laws and policies that are able to holistically address every aspect of an individual's right to health. These provisions could be interpreted to mean that states must adopt laws and policies to address NCDs and tobacco use.

44 See E Durojaye 'The approaches of the African commission to the right to health under the African Charter' (2013) 17 *Law Democracy and Development* 393.

45 See O Nnamuchi 'Tobacco use, exploitation and vulnerability in Africa: A human rights analysis' in Marie E Gispen & B Toebes (eds) *Human rights and tobacco control* (2020) 119.

46 See ACHPR/Res 141 (XXXXIIII) 2008: Resolution on Access to Health and Needed Medicines in Africa.

47 ACHPR/Res.431(LXV) 2019: Resolution 431 on the Right to Food and Nutrition in Africa.

48 See para 67(i) of the Principles and Guidelines on the Interpretation of Economic, Social and Cultural Rights in the African Charter on Human and Peoples' Rights, ACHPR (November 2011).

For instance, the Guidelines define vulnerable groups to include persons with terminal illnesses or persistent medical challenges and urge government to pay special attention to their situation. This could be interpreted to include persons suffering from tobacco-related NCDs. Equally, it might be interpreted to require states to adopt measures towards the prevention and treatment of NCDs in general and tobacco use in particular.

Furthermore, the Guidelines require states in accordance with article 1 of the Charter to take measures towards realising socio-economic rights through 'constitutional rights and institutions, legislative, administrative and budgetary measures'.[49] The Guidelines further note that the obligation 'to take steps' towards realising socio-economic rights is immediate and not subject to progressive realisation. This statement implicitly requires African governments to develop the legal framework that will address tobacco use. This is more so when one considers the negative impact of NCDs on the enjoyment of the right to health as guaranteed under the Charter. The Guidelines identify some of the minimum core obligations to realise the right to health to include prevention, treatment and control of epidemics and pandemics and provision of information and health-related education concerning major health challenges facing the community.[50] These provisions are important in holding African governments to account for inaction or failure to address tobacco use through public awareness campaigns or educational programmes.

In terms of the African Charter, the Commission is charged with, amongst other functions, promoting and protecting human and people's rights in Africa. The Commission embarks on promotional state visits during which it gathers information on human rights issues. During such visits, the Commission often meets with government officials, NGOs and the general public to raise awareness on pertinent human rights issues. The Commission also uses the opportunity to urge state parties to protect, promote, respect and fulfil human rights by implementing its obligations under the Charter. These visits create a good opportunity for the Commission to engage states on issues such as NCDs and tobacco use. The Commission could use the forum to raise concerns about the human rights implications of NCDs and tobacco use with policymakers and NGOs. It is not certain to what extent the Commission has engaged with States parties' on the need to adopt a rights-based approach to addressing NCDs, including tobacco use at the national level.

As a way of strengthening its mandate to promote and protect human rights, the Commission has resorted to the use of special mechanisms. This approach borrows greatly from the UN human rights system, where experts are appointed as special rapporteurs or members of working groups to assist in the promotion and protection of human rights. The Commission is empowered to create subsidiary mechanisms such as special rapporteurs, committees and working

49 See para 2 of the Guidelines and Principles.
50 See para 67(d) and (e) of the Guidelines and Principles.

groups. Usually, the Commission determines the mandate and terms of reference of each subsidiary mechanism. While the Commission does not currently have a special mechanism specifically devoted to the realisation of the right to health, three of the current mechanisms can play an important role in addressing NCDs, including tobacco use. These include the Working Group on Economic, Social and Cultural Rights; the Special Rapporteur on the Rights of Women in Africa (SRRWA); and the Committee on the Protection of the Rights of People Living with HIV (PLHIV) and those at Risk, Vulnerable to and Affected by HIV (the HIV Committee).[51]

Currently, these mechanisms have not paid much attention to the human rights implications of NCDs, including those associated with tobacco use. This raises the point that perhaps it is time for the Commission to consider the need for a special mechanism that will be devoted to addressing the human rights in the context of health. This will ensure that better attention is given to health challenges confronting the region. Thus far, the Commission's response to major epidemics and diseases such as Ebola, NCDs and COVID-19 has been reactionary. The Commission would need to adopt a more proactive and pragmatic approach to addressing these health challenges. Creating a special mechanism on the right to health will help in this regard. A special mechanism will not only raise the profile of this right in the region but also ensure that studies are conducted and actions taken to address some of the major health challenges facing the continent.

It may be argued that the Working Group on Economic, Social and Cultural Rights and the Special Rapporteur on the Rights of Women are well placed to do this. However, the truth remains that so far the Working Group has not paid much attention to health-related issues confronting the continent. It should be noted that the Guidelines on the implementation of the socio-economic rights in the Charter contain some provisions that may indirectly apply to NCDs from a rights-based perspective. However, these are not strongly worded enough to make it imperative for states to take concrete measures in addressing NCDs. Besides, as mentioned earlier the Commission is yet to develop norms and standards specifically in relation to NCDs. This is a gap that requires the immediate attention of the Commission.

Also, while the office of the Special Rapporteur on the Rights of Women has done considerable work on women's health, including sexual and reproductive health, the impact of its activities are limited to women and do not address the needs of men in the region. The SRRWA could focus more on the impact of NCDs, including tobacco use on women and girls in the region. Breast cancer and the effects of tobacco use have remained a serious challenge to the health and lives of women across the region. The SRRWA can play an important role in not

51 Resolution ACHPR/Res.163 (XLVII) 10, Adopted at the 47th Ordinary Session of the African Commission on the Establishment of a Committee on the Protection of the Rights of People Living with HIV (PLWHIV), and Those at Risk, Vulnerable to and Affected by HIV.

only raising awareness on these issues but also urging states to adopt appropriate measures to address them.

The challenges posed by NCDs, including those associated with tobacco use, cut across gender and age. Thus, it is important that the Commission gives special attention to addressing these challenges. It might be necessary for these special mechanisms to consider integrating issues relating to NCDs, including tobacco control, in their activities. While there is a link between HIV/AIDS and NCDs including tobacco use, so far the Committee on HIV has not addressed this link. It is a known fact that persons living with HIV are more susceptible to NCDs; conversely, NCDs and tobacco use can exacerbate the health of people living with HIV. The HIV Committee is mandated to address human rights issues in the context of HIV focusing on marginalised and vulnerable groups.[52] While this is no doubt an important mandate, it is argued that there is need for a holistic approach to the mandate of the Committee in such a way as to address crucial health issues affecting the region. In this regard, the Commission may consider expanding the mandate and focus of the HIV Committee to include addressing human rights in the context of health broadly. This may require renaming the Committee so that it covers issues beyond HIV/AIDS. Given the serious threats to lives posed by NCDs in the region, including those associated with tobacco use, broadening the mandate of the HIV Committee to include the right to health will go a long way in ensuring that the Commission focuses more on the negative impact of NCDs and tobacco use in Africa.

2.4.2 Protective mandate of the African Commission

Under its protective mandate, the African Commission can potentially address the issue of NCDS and tobacco use through the state reporting process and its communication procedure.

The African Commission has 106 sessions since its inception, 35 of which were extra-ordinary and 71 ordinary sessions. The extraordinary sessions do not entail any engagements on the state party reports, though concluding observations on some of the state party reports considered in earlier ordinary sessions were adopted at the subsequent extraordinary sessions.

The Commission had received about 128 States Reports as of the 68th Ordinary Session, and had provided its analysis of the report through concluding observations for most of these reports.[53] Overall, States parties' to the Charter fall in one of three clusters: those that have never submitted a report, those that have

52 For a detailed discussion on the mandate of the HIV Committee, see E Durojaye 'The role of the African commission on human and peoples' rights in developing norms and standards on HIV and human rights' (2017) 17 (3) *Global Jurist* 1.

53 This information is available online at ACHPR 'Sessions' https://www.achpr.org/sessions (accessed 2 November 2019).

submitted reports but have not received concluding observations,[54] and those that have submitted reports and received concluding observations.

2.4.2.1 States parties' reporting on NCDs

There are a few States parties' that have reported on steps to deal with NCDs. For instance, with regard to the right to the highest attainable standard of health, Algeria's report stated that

> the health-care system is expected to be adapted to the new requirements of the preventive and curative plan dealing with the burden of morbidities regarding emerging pathologies (such as heart and cardiovascular diseases, combating cancer and other diseases). Towards this end, the concern to ensure equitable access to highly specialized health-care will be translated into the 2014 sector plan development framework, through the establishment of regional specialized centres and national referral centres in the above-mentioned specialities. For instance, the Anti-Cancer Centres (CAC), seven (7) of which are currently operational, should reach 22 by the end of the period and should cover all parts of the country.[55]

Although no specific reference is made to tobacco use, this approach represents a holistic attempt to deal with NCDs generally.

Botswana followed suit, reporting that

> in an effort to address the issue of cervical cancer among the HIV positive women, the Government is implementing a five Year Comprehensive Cervical Cancer Prevention and Control Strategy (2012–2016). This strategy introduces screening and outpatient treatment of cervical pre-cancer in one single visit, commonly referred to as 'See and Treat'.[56]

In addition, the report stated:

> Community Home Based Care is a programme meant to provide basic amenities for people who suffer from terminal illnesses such as cancer, HIV/AIDS, sugar diabetes and physical traumas and cannot do anything for

54 According to the African Commission website, the States parties' that have not submitted any reports are six in number, but a manual count indicates that there are seven: Comoros, Equatorial Guinea, Guinea-Bissau, São Tomé and Príncipe, Somalia, South Sudan and Morocco. See ACHPR 'State parties to the African Charter' https://www.achpr.org/states (accessed 2 November 2019).

55 Algeria's 5th and 6th Report to the ACHPR at the 57th session 4–18 November 2015, Gambia, para 276.

56 Botswana's 2nd and 3rd Report to the ACHPR at the 63rd session 24 October–13 November 2018, Gambia, page 52.

themselves due to poor health. As at July 2014, the country had One Thousand Two Hundred and Twenty-One (1,221) registered Community Home Based patients.[57]

This shows the use of an integrated system that engages both HIV/AIDS and NCDs. Other States parties', such as Togo, Democratic Republic of the Congo, Libya, Mali and Angola, also report on the steps they are taking to deal with NCDs.[58] These are concluding observations to applaud or seek particulars on these measures by States parties'.

2.4.2.2 NCDs in the concluding observations of the Commission

The African Commission applauds States parties' that have taken steps to deal with NCDs. This is a welcome development and is evident in some of its concluding observations. For instance, with respect to Angola, the African Commission stated that it 'welcomed the measures adopted to give effect to the right to the best attainable state of health, including . . . the provision of free medical assistance to women with cervical cancer'.[59]

A juxtaposition of the States parties' that have given insights on dealing with NCDs, against which the African Commission applauds steps taken by States parties' to address NCDs, reveals a lack of a consistent requirement or commitment to provide more detailed information from states on measures taken to address NCDs.

Indeed, although the Commission in some of its concluding observations has urged states to take measures with a view to addressing NCDs, such engagement has been neither consistent nor meaningful enough to respond to the growing concerns on this issue and the effectiveness of the measures adopted by states.

The lack of engagement with States parties' on NCDs and tobacco use may be attributed to three factors. The first is the absence of a specific requirement to address the issue in the reporting guidelines, hence no particular attention is paid to it in the reports. The second is the possibility that civil society groups are not raising the issue when they submit shadow reports to the African Commission. The third factor is that it could also be an indication that the Commission does not view NCDs and tobacco use as serious enough to warrant engaging with states about them.

Reporting on efforts to address NCDs and tobacco use should form part of the reporting guidelines for states. The WHO Guidelines on NCDs and the FCTC could serve as an inspiration in this regard. The Commission can draw lessons from

57 Botswana's 2nd and 3rd Report (n 56) page 70.

58 Togo's Periodic Report to the ACHPR at the 62nd session 25 April–9 May 2018, Mauritania, paras 231–234. See also Angola's Report to the ACHPR at the 62nd session 25 April–9 May 2018, Mauritania, para 89.

59 Angola's 4th and 5th Report at the 51st session of the ACHPR 12th Extraordinary Session 30 July–4 August 2012, Algiers, Algeria para 19.

the work of the treaty monitoring bodies such as the CESCR and the CRC Committee, which have consistently engaged with states on this issue during the state reporting process. As discussed above, these bodies have expressed concerns about the human rights implications of NCDs and tobacco use and have urged states to take concrete measures to address them. In addition, the Commission can draw experience from its counterpart in the Inter-American System, which has shown the willingness towards ensuring accountability by states to address NCDs in general and tobacco use in particular (see the chapter by Barbosa and Cina in this volume).[60]

Two conclusive positions can be deduced from this analysis: to begin with, NCDs were not mentioned by States parties' in the first 47 sessions of the Commission. Instead, references to disease during that period were largely limited to HIV/AIDS or tuberculosis. Subsequently, there has been some traction with regard to NCDs from the 48th to the 65th sessions, with some States parties' reporting on what was being done to deal with particular NCDs, such as cancer. The reason for this development can be attributed to the growing prevalence of NCDs in recent times as compared to the past.

In summary, it is apparent that the concluding observations of the Commission are either largely silent on calling on States parties' to indicate what has been done to deal with NCDs or acknowledging the efforts by the states in dealing with NCDs.

2.4.3 *Jurisprudence of the African Commission and NCDs*

While the African Commission has not addressed issues in relation to NCDs and tobacco use in its communication procedures, some of its decisions have the potential to address NCDs and tobacco use. For instance, the decisions in the *Purohit*[61] and the *Free Legal Assistance*[62] cases point to the fact that the right to health should be interpreted broadly to cover all aspects of human well-being including preventive methods towards addressing communicable and non-communicable diseases.

In the *Purohit* case, the Commission, echoing General Comment 14 of the CESCR, reasoned that the enjoyment of the right to health is vital to all aspects of human well-being and crucial to the realisation of all other rights.[63] It further noted that the right to health implies more than preventing ailments or diseases but also encompasses access to health goods and facilities.[64] In finding the Gambian government in violation of article 16 of the Charter, the Commission noted

60 For a detailed discussion on this, see O Cabrera & A Constantin 'Tobacco control in the inter-American human rights system' in ME Gispen & B Toebes *Human rights and tobacco control* (2020).

61 *Purohit v The Gambia* (2003) AHRLR 96 (ACHPR 2003).

62 *Free Legal Assistance Group v Zaire* (Communication 25/89, 47/90, 56/91, 100/93) [1995] ACHPR 9; (11 October 1995).

63 See *Purohit* para 80.

64 As above.

that states are 'to take concrete and targeted steps' towards the realisation of the right to health. Implicit in this statement is that states must take concrete measures towards addressing tobacco use within their jurisdictions.[65]

This would obviously require more than adoption of a legislative framework. It would also require education and awareness activities warning the public about the dangers of tobacco use. This purposive interpretation gives the Commission the leeway to require states to adopt measures that will address the impact of NCDs and tobacco use. The progressive approach of the Commission in this case is commendable given that NCDs and tobacco use pose serious threats not only to the health of the people but also to their lives and well-being.[66] In some of its jurisprudence relating to the right to health, the Commission has adopted the interdependence and indivisibility of rights approach to holding states accountable for violation of this right.[67] It is hoped that when the Commission has the opportunity to entertain any communications on NCDs and tobacco use in future, it will not shy away from applying a purposive approach to the right to health.

With regard to the right to life, the Commission has adopted a broad and purposive interpretation of this right to require states to take positive measures to prevent the loss of life. In the *International Pen* case, the African Commission affirmed that denying access to life-saving medication to a prisoner would amount to a threat to the enjoyment of the right to life.[68] Similarly, in the *SERAC* case, the Commission applied the indivisibility and interrelatedness of human rights to affirm that the Nigerian government was in breach of the rights to health, food, housing, clean environment and life when it failed to prevent oil pollution caused by the activities of multinational companies in Ogoniland.[69] This interpretation, inspired by the decisions of the European and Inter-American Courts,[70] could apply to failure by African governments to control tobacco use among the public in general and vulnerable groups in particular. Given the high mortality rate associated with tobacco use in developing regions, including Africa, it will amount to a violation of the right to life if African governments fail to adopt legislative framework to combat tobacco use among the population, especially amongst vulnerable groups.

65 As above.

66 For a detailed analysis of the approaches of the Commission to the right to health in the Charter, see Durojaye (n 52).

67 See for instance, *Social and Economic Rights Action Center (SERAC) v Government of Nigeria* (2001) AHRLR 60 (ACHPR 2001); *International Pen on behalf of Saro Wiwa v Nigeria* AHRLR 212 (ACHPR 1998); Communications 137/94, 139/94, 154/96 and 161/97.

68 *International PEN on behalf of Saro-Wiwa v Nigeria*, Decision on Merits, Communication 137/94.

69 *SERAC* case (n 67).

70 See for instance, *VO v France* [GC] judgment of 8 July 2004, 53924/00, ECHR 2004; see also *Case of the 'Street Children' (Villagran-Morales) v Guatemala* Merits, IACHR Series C 63 [1999] IACHR 17, IHRL 1446 (IACHR 1999), 19 November 1999.

Furthermore, the right to non-discrimination presents a good opportunity for the Commission to address the incidence of tobacco use among vulnerable groups such as women and children in the region. In the *Dauda Jawara* case,[71] the African Commission affirmed that the rights to equal protection of law and non-discrimination are fundamental and crucial to the enjoyment of all other rights in the Charter. According to the Commission, states are not permitted to derogate from this right. This interpretation provides a strong basis to require states to take adequate measures to prevent tobacco-related diseases or deaths among vulnerable groups in the region. The Commission has reiterated this point in the *Purohit* case, where it held that the legislative framework relating to persons with mental disabilities in the Gambia was discriminatory and inconsistent with articles 2 and 3 of the Charter.

Another important right in the Charter that is relevant to addressing tobacco use is the right to information guaranteed in article 9. States are obligated to ensure access to information in general and health-related information in particular in order to prevent the outbreak of diseases or epidemics. Access to information is crucial to the prevention of NCDs associated with tobacco use. In *Media Rights Agenda v Nigeria*,[72] the African Commission affirmed that any attempts by the state to stifle access to information is inconsistent with the African Charter. The Commission reasoned that the right to information under the Charter imposes both positive and negative obligations on states. In other words, states are to ensure that people enjoy access to relevant information; at the same time, states are to restrain from taking steps that will hinder access to information. This interpretation of the Commission is fundamental to the prevention of tobacco-related NCDs. Millions of people in Africa still engage in tobacco use due to lack of information and awareness.

2.5 Conclusion

While the African Union has shown concern about the incidence of NCDs and the threats they pose to lives in the region, the African Commission is yet to address this challenge from a human rights perspective. Given its mandate to promote and protect human rights, the African Commission has a great potential to ensure accountability of African countries to address NCDs, including tobacco use. So far, the Commission has given adequate attention to the incidence of NCDs and tobacco use. This serious gap needs the urgent attention of the Commission. The Commission could require states to give more attention to the human rights issues posed by NCDs and tobacco use when submitting their periodic reports. Also, the Commission could engage with states to give more attention to the incidence of NCDs and tobacco use during mission visits. Given the serious threats posed by NCDs and tobacco use to the lives and well-being

71 *Dauda Jawara v The Gambia* (Communication 147/95, 149/96) [2000] ACHPR 17 (11 May 2000).

72 ACHPR, Communication Nos 105/93, 128/94, 130/94 and 152/96 (1998).

of many Africans, the Commission may consider broadening the mandate of the HIV Committee to include the right to health in general and NCDs in particular. This will ensure more attention to human rights issues in relation to NCDs in the region.

Bibliography

ACHPR/Res 141 (XXXXIIII) 2008: Resolution on Access to Health and Needed Medicines in Africa

ACHPR/Res 431 (LXV) 2019: Resolution 431 on the Right to Food and Nutrition in Africa

ACHPR 'Sessions' https://www.achpr.org/sessions (accessed 2 November 2019)

ACHPR 'State parties to the African Charter' https://www.achpr.org/states (accessed 2 November 2019)

African Union 'Africa's agenda for children 2040: Fostering an Africa fit for children' (2015) 133

African Union 'African union commemorates the Africa healthy lifestyle day 2019 healthy lifestyle prolongs life' (7 March 2019) https://au.int/sw/node/36029 (accessed 25 November 2021)

Angola's 4th and 5th Report at the 51st Session of the ACHPR 12th Twelfth Extraordinary Session 30 July–4 August 2012, Algiers, Algeria

Algeria's 5th and 6th Report to the ACHPR at the 57th session 4–18 November 2015, Gambia

Angola's Report to the ACHPR at the 62nd session 25 April–9 May 2018, Mauritania

Botswana's 2nd and 3rd Report to the ACHPR at the 63rd session 24 October–13 November 132018, Gambia

Cabrera, O & Constantin, A 'Tobacco control in the inter-American human rights system' in Gispen, ME & Toebes, B (eds) *Human rights and tobacco control* (Edward Elgar Publishing 2020)

Case of the 'Street Children' (Villagran-Morales et al) v Guatemala Merits, IACHR Series C 63

Concluding Observations on the Combined Second to Fourth Periodic Reports of Brazil, CRC Committee (30 October 2015) UN Doc CRC/C/ BRA/CO/2-4 (2015) [1999] IACHR 17, IHRL 1446 (IACHR 1999), 19 November 1999

Concluding Observations on the Fifth Periodic Report of Mauritius, CESCR (April 2019) UN Doc E/C.12/MUS/CO/55 (2019)

Concluding Observations on the Second Periodic Report of South Africa, CRC Committee (27 October 2016) U Doc CRC/C/ZAF/CO/2 (2016), United Nations, 27 October 2016, paras 53(e) and 54(d)

Concluding Observations to Cameroon, CESCR (23 January 2012) UN Doc E/C.12/CMR/CO/2–3 (2012)

Dauda Jawara v The Gambia (Communication 147/95, 149/96) [2000] ACHPR 17; (11 May 2000)

Doebbler v Sudan (Communication 236/2000) [2003] ACHPR 42; (29 May 2003)

Durojaye, E 'The approaches of the African commission to the right to health under the African Charter' (2013) 17 *Law, Democracy and Development* 393

Durojaye, E 'The role of the African commission on human and peoples' rights in developing norms and standards on HIV and human rights' (2017) 17(3) *Global Jurists* 1

Durojaye, E & Mirugi-Mukundi, G *Compendium of documents and cases on the right to health under the African human rights system* (Berkeley Law 2013)

Free Legal Assistance Group v Zaire (Communication 25/89, 47/90, 56/91, 100/93) [1995] ACHPR 9; (11 October 1995)

General Comment 15 (2013) on the Right of the Child to the Enjoyment of the Highest Attainable Standard of Health (art 24), CRC Committee (17 April 2013) UN Doc CRC/C/GC/15 (2013)

International Pen on behalf of Saro Wiwa v Nigeria AHRLR 212 (ACHPR 1998); Communications 137/94, 139/94, 154/96 and 161/97

Media Rights Agenda v Nigeria ACHPR, Communication Nos 105/93, 128/94, 130/94 and 152/96 (1998)

Nnamuchi, O 'Tobacco use, exploitation and vulnerability in Africa: A human rights analysis' in Gispen, ME & Toebes, B (eds) *Human rights and tobacco control* (Edward Elgar Publishing 2020)

Nyaaba, GN 'Tracing Africa's progress towards implementing the non-communicable diseases global action plan 2013–2020: Aa synthesis of WHO country profile reports' (2017) 17 *BMC Public Health* 1

Patterson, D; Buse, K; Magnusson, R & Toebes, B 'Identifying a human rights-based approach to obesity for States and civil society (2019) 20 *Obesity Reviews* 45

Preamble to the Constitution of the WHO as Adopted by the International Health Conference, New York, 19–22 June 1946

Principles and Guidelines on the Interpretation of Economic, Social and Cultural Rights in the African Charter on Human and Peoples' Rights, ACHPR (November 2011)

Purohit v The Gambia (2003) AHRLR96 (ACHPR 2003)

Report of the Special Rapporteur on the Right of Everyone to the Enjoyment of the Highest Attainable Standard of Physical and Mental Health 'Sport and Healthy Lifestyles and the Right to Health' (4 April 2016) UN Doc A/HRC/32/33 (2016)

Resolution ACHPR/Res.163 (XLVII) 10, Adopted at the 47th Ordinary Session of the African Commission on the Establishment of a Committee on the Protection of the Rights of People Living with HIV (PLWHIV), and Those at Risk, Vulnerable to and Affected by HIV

Social and Economic Rights Action Center (SERAC) v Government of Nigeria (2001) AHRLR 60 (ACHPR 2001)

Togo's Periodic Report to the ACHPR at the 62nd Session 25 April–9 May 2018, Mauritania

UN Committee on Economic, Social and Cultural Rights (CESCR), General Comment 14: The Right to the Highest Attainable Standard of Health (art 12 of the Covenant) (11 August 2000) UN Doc E/C.12/2000/4 (2000)

UN General Assembly, International Covenant on Economic, Social and Cultural Rights, 16 December 1966, United Nations, Treaty Series, vol 993, p 3 (16 December 1966)

Universal Declaration of Human Rights, Adopted 10 December 1948, art 1, GA Res 217A (III), UN Doc A/810 (1948)

VO v France [GC], Judgment of 8 July 2004, no. 53924/00, ECHR 2004

WHO 'Africa: Non-Communicable Diseases' https://www.who.int/nmh/ncd-tools/who-regions-african/en/ (accessed 1 November 2020)

WHO 'Non-communicable diseases' (13 April 2021) https://www.who.int/news-room/fact-sheets/detail/noncommunicable-diseases (accessed 1 November 2020)

WHO 'Non-communicable diseases: Country profiles 2018' (2018)

Part II

Country case studies

3 The implementation of the WHO FCTC

Lessons from Ghana

Bright Nkrumah

3.1 Introduction

Tobacco consumption remains one of the principal causes of death and health risks globally.[1] It remains a growing health concern in the Global South and results in the death of more than 8 million people yearly.[2] Considering that tobacco use in the Global North has witnessed a considerable drop since the turn of the millennium, the tobacco industry has shifted its target to the Global South as a new arena for profit-making.[3] To this end, hypertension and other NCD-related mortality are bound to increase in the coming years. With over 80 per cent of 1.3 billion global tobacco users living in middle- and low-income countries (MLICs), the figure of smokers has been projected to grow to 1.7 billion in the next five years.[4]

Despite its financial and health burden, tobacco is used by a disproportionate percentage of Ghanaians. To be specific, 9.7–10 per cent of the population engages in tobacco consumption.[5] This relatively low number, or 'few tobacco users', may somewhat indicate the existing gap in the empirical evidence on the (socio-economic) drivers of tobacco consumption at the (sub)national level. Yet, regardless of the figure, any percentage of the population involved in smoking is a cause for public concern, as the associated health burden transcends the direct tobacco user.[6] Whereas the figure of primary smokers may be relatively low, the health ramifications for passive smokers may be as bad as those for primary users. This phenomenon is concerning, as tobacco use has been linked to the surge

1 S Thiagarajan 'Tobacco use among adolescent school-going children: Extent of problem and solutions for the future' (2019) 2 *Cancer Research, Statistics and Treatment* 124.

2 WHO 'Tobacco' (2020) https://www.who.int/news-room/fact-sheets/detail/tobacco (accessed 24 September 2021).

3 M Serrano-Alarcón & others 'Tobacco control policies and smoking among older adults: A longitudinal analysis of 10 European countries' (2019) 114 *Addiction* 1077.

4 WHO (n 2).

5 E Owusu-Dabo & others 'Smoking uptake and prevalence in Ghana' (2009) 18 *Tobacco Control* 365.

6 Especially in light of the (socio-economic) ramifications and negative externalities (impact of SHS) tied to its uptake.

DOI: 10.4324/9781003264248-5

in non-communicable diseases (NCDs), including tuberculosis, diabetes, cancer, cardiovascular diseases and related chronic respiratory ailments. Therefore, it is not ironic that diabetes and hypertension have emerged as the top causes of institutional admissions and deaths in contemporary Ghana.[7]

To this end, understanding the driving forces of tobacco use, policy response and institutional mechanisms are essential in weighing the country's level of commitment to NCDs and the right to health more broadly. By adopting an iterative approach, the chapter uses (inter)national instruments, tobacco industry documents, published works and internet sources to unearth the country's smoking pattern, prevalence and measures most feasible to work in this environmental setup. In the end, the chapter will make key recommendations for future action to support tobacco control operationalisation. It will outline the particular local issues, focusing on major structural impediments and priority setting in tobacco control governance.

3.2 Right to health and NCDs

Over the last two decades, the notion of human rights has evolved and become one of the cardinal pillars of Ghana's democratic dispensation. Like many regimes in (West) Africa, the country's 1992 Constitution explicitly affirms the right of all citizens to basic rights without exclusion.[8] To attain long-term progress and human development, the Constitution enjoins the state to adopt reasonable measures to safeguard the right to health.

The history of the right to health in Ghana can be traced back to 1957, when the socialist regime of Kwame Nkrumah established a free healthcare system for all citizens. Unfortunately, following his overthrow in the 1966 coup d'état, successive regimes aborted this policy, leading to the introduction of user fees at all public health facilities. Amidst increasing national debt, this practice was formalised with the adoption of the 1971 Hospital Fees Act, which legitimised the cash and carry system (upfront payment of fees before the provision of medical assistance).[9] As could be expected, this practice resulted in the deaths of many disadvantaged persons, thereby inciting outrage in many poor communities. This unrest, coupled with new leadership and ideological shift in the early 1990s, somewhat shaped the content of the 1992 Constitution.

To be exact, article 34(2) of the Constitution affirms that the 'President shall report to Parliament at least once a year all the steps taken to ensure the realization of the . . . *right to good health care* and the *right to education*'. Paradoxically, this provision falls under the rubric of Chapter 6, 'The Directive Principles of State Policy' (DPSP), which some academics and experts have argued as

7 DE Okai & others 'Patient-level factors influencing hypertension control in adults in Accra, Ghana' (2020) 123 *BMC Cardiovascular Disorders* 1 at 1–2.

8 See art 12(2).

9 Hospital Fees Act 387 of 1971.

constituting a set of aspirations rather than a binding obligation on states. This position was affirmed by the Supreme Court when it placed the stamp of non-justiciability on the DPSP (under which the right to health is located), arguing the provisions remain mere principles.[10] The doubts surrounding the justiciability of the right to health are exacerbated by the lack of emphasis and/or detailed description of its content. For instance, the Constitution dedicates article 25 to the right to education, where it stipulates free basic education, accessible higher and vocational training, and functional literacy.[11] The right to health, however, is stripped of this clarity. Nonetheless, if one draws from the interrelatedness of rights, it will be ironic to assume that an important entitlement such as access to healthcare will be excluded from the Constitution. In this regard, the ruling of the Supreme Court was a landmark when it overturned its initial decision and concluded that to some extent, the rights under the DPSP could be construed as justiciable unless an interested party comes forward and disproves them otherwise.[12]

Having said that, one could claim that the contention surrounding the (non) justiciability is somewhat addressed by article 30 of the Constitution. Titled 'Rights of the Sick' (RoS), the provision emphasises that under no circumstance shall a sick person 'be deprived by any other person of medical treatment'. Still, for nearly two decades, the exact meaning of this provision has not been tested in local courts. Perhaps the dearth of litigation around this right might be tied to its vagueness and lack of clarity on what it encompasses. As an illustration, section 27(1)(a) of the Constitution of the Republic of South Africa, 1996 makes explicit reference to the right to 'health care services, including reproductive health care', thereby making one's claim to the right explicit. In the case of Ghana, the content of the right to health and/or RoS remains ambiguous, thereby making litigation around it quite unattractive for litigators.

Despite these lingering constraints, the state in 2012 set up the Public Health Act (PHA) as a means of forestalling and safeguarding the health of Ghanaians.[13] Aside from speaking to labelling and packaging of tobacco products, articles 58 to 68 of the PHA set out minimum age restrictions for the sale of tobacco products and proscribe tobacco sponsorship, advertising, promotion and smoking in public spaces.[14] Five years later, the state adopted the Tobacco Control Regulations (TCR), which set out several restrictions for curbing tobacco consumption.[15] Following the entry into force of the TCR in 2007, the Food and Drugs Board (FDB) assumed responsibility for their enforcement and compliance.

10 *New Patriotic Party v Attorney General* [1993–1994] 2 GLR 35.

11 Constitutional Review Commission *Report of the constitutional review commission of Ghana: From a political to a developmental constitution* (2011) 687.

12 *Ghana Lotto Operations v National Lotto Authority* (2007–2008) SCGLR 1088 1106.

13 Public Health Act 851 of 2012.

14 Arts 58–68 of the PHA.

15 2016 (LI 2247).

As its name indicates, the FDB has a broad mandate of overseeing the safety of all food and drugs, thus stretching its resources to fully commit to issues arising out of tobacco production, import and sale, and consumption. To this end, it continues to supervise the reinforcement of textual health warnings on cigarette packs, monitor (in)direct cigarette promotional activities, scrutinise permits of importers and periodically update the information of producers and importers. Having said that, a bleak picture emerges if one weighs these gains against the provisions of the Framework Convention on Tobacco Control (FCTC) established by the World Health Organization (WHO).

At the regional and international levels, Ghana is a party to a number of instruments containing provisions that (in)directly call on the state to promote and safeguard the right to health of its citizenry. Still, while fragments of this right can be traced to several international documents, the International Covenant on Economic, Social and Cultural Rights (ICESCR) could be earmarked as the most authoritative document in the present discussion.[16] Ghana ratified the ICESCR on 7 September 2000. Its article 12 imposes a responsibility on Ghana to recognise the right of its citizens to the 'enjoyment of the highest attainable standard of physical and mental health'.[17] Ghana is also a party to several treaties that implicitly or explicitly proscribe it from taking any action which might militate against the health and well-being of its people. These include, but are not limited to, the International Covenant on Civil and Political Rights; the Convention against Torture and Other Cruel, Inhuman or Degrading Treatment or Punishment; the Convention on the Rights of the Child; the Convention on the Rights of Persons with Disabilities; and the Convention on the Elimination of Discrimination against Women.[18]

At the regional level, the African Charter on Human and Peoples' Rights (the Charter) equally imposes an obligation on Ghana to safeguard the health needs of Ghanaians. Article 16 of the Charter was unequivocal when it highlighted that state parties ought to adopt all necessary interventions to ensure that their citizens enjoy the best attainable state of physical and mental health. This obligation is further reinforced in article 40 of Ghana's Constitution where the government is obliged to comply with its obligation under international instruments and decisions of monitoring bodies. Still, being a dualist jurisdiction, article 75 of the 1992 Constitution calls for the domestication of regional and international treaties before their contents could take effect in Ghana. It is against this backdrop that the next sections survey the content of the FCTC and to what extent its provisions have been domesticated in Ghana's legal regime.

16 B Nkrumah *Seeking the right to food: Food activism in South Africa* (2021) 82.

17 UN 'Treaty body database: Ghana' (2021) https://tbinternet.ohchr.org/_layouts/15/TreatyBodyExternal/Treaty.aspx?CountryID=67&Lang=EN (accessed 24 September 2021).

18 As above.

3.3 Framework Convention on Tobacco Control

The year 2020 marked the 15th anniversary since the entry into force of the FCTC.[19] The treaty, which seeks to avert the (inter)national burden of tobacco-related disability and death, may be considered as one of the most successfully endorsed WHO instruments. As of May 2020, it has attracted 182 state parties, covering more than 94 per cent of the world population.[20] The instrument contains a series of guidelines that oblige member states to adopt and operationalise specific tobacco regulatory measures to forestall premature deaths. The treaty specifically calls for the proscription of promotional and advertisement of tobacco products to safeguard future and present generations from the adverse socio-economic, ecological and health impact of tobacco consumption.

Although the treaty, which is the first to be negotiated under the auspices of the WHO, has noble intents, there remain policy and institutional deadlocks which militate against its effective domestication in developing countries. As illustrated in Table 3.1, the operationalisation of the FCTC in Ghana has not been all that successful.[21] This development is worrying, as big tobacco aggressively turns its attention to Africa in light of the decline in demand in the Global North.[22] It is against this backdrop that the WHO bemoans that over the next decade, sub-Saharan Africa (SSA) might be plagued by millions of premature deaths resulting from NCDs. The organisation specifically cautions that between 2010 and 2030, the region might witness a surge in smoking prevalence by over a third, from 15.8 per cent to 21.9 per cent, if it fails to effectively operationalise tobacco control initiatives. The percentage of NCD-related deaths in MLICs is projected to increase by over 50 per cent to a projected 43 million in 2030 (from an estimated 28 million in 2008) among persons aged 15 to 59 years.[23] In echoing concerns of the WHO, Dalal and others moot that by 2030, NCDs such as diabetes and hypertension will be the leading cause of death in SSA.[24] As an illustration, in contrast to an estimated global average increase of 54 per cent from 2010 to 2030 in the figures of persons with diabetes (20–79 years), SSA is projected to witness 98 per cent over the same duration.[25]

19 World Health Assembly *World health organization framework convention on tobacco control* (2003) https://www.who.int/fctc/text_download/en/ (accessed 24 November 2021).

20 FCTC 'Parties to the WHO framework convention on tobacco control' (2020) https://www.who.int/fctc/cop/en/ (accessed 24 September 2021).

21 S Asare & others 'Effects of prices on youth cigarette smoking and tobacco use initiation in Ghana and Nigeria' (2019) 16 *International Journal of Environmental Research and Public Health* 2.

22 WHO 'WHO report on the global tobacco epidemic' (2017) https://www.who.int/tobacco/global_report/2017/en/ (accessed 24 September 2021).

23 IA Nikolic, AE Stanciole & M Zaydman 'Chronic emergency: Why NCDs matter' (2011) *Health, Nutrition and Population (HNP) Discussion Paper* 2.

24 S Dalal & others 'Non-communicable diseases in sub-Saharan Africa: What we know now' (2011) 40 *International Journal of Epidemiology* 889.

25 As above.

Table 3.1 Level of Ghana's compliance

FCTC	*PHA*	*TCR*	*Application*	*State compliance*
Article 6 Taxation and increase in price to deter consumption	–	–	A lower tax percentage has been imposed	Relatively conforms to the obligation
Article 8 Forestall second-hand smoke	–	Articles 2–4 Creation of specific smoking areas	Banning of smoking in designated areas	Relatively conforms to obligations
Article 9 Scrutinise the information inscribed on cigarettes	Article 70 Establish a monitoring directorate	–	Has not been fully complied with	Violates obligations
Article 11 Indicate the health impact of the product on labels and packaging	Article 62 Use labelling and packaging to raise awareness around the health impact of the product	–	Imposes an obligation on producers to allocate half of their packaging to raising health concerns of their product	Relatively conforms to obligations
Article 12 Regularly undertake advocacy campaigns to conscientize citizens of the negative effect of tobacco	Article 66 Embark on intensive tobacco awareness campaigns	Article 10 Raise awareness around the health implications of tobacco use	Bans all forms of advertisement of the product	Conforms to obligations
Article 15 Avert unlawful trade in cigarette and other tobacco products	Article 74 The state has the mandate to detain and imprison violators	Articles 14–16 Proscribe trade in unlawful tobacco products	There is no substantive monitoring agency to enforce these regulations	Violates obligations

Source: Author.

Whereas conventional book chapters are often anti-state and, thus, begin with strong criticism of state policies and programmes, this chapter will not steer that course. It rather adopts a careful approach, by navigating between the gains and losses of existing interventions to frame a comprehensive and feasible remedy for the crisis at hand. For as far back as 1982, Ghana issued its first ban on smoking advertising, making it a key player in the launch of the anti-tobacco directive.[26] Two decades later, it evolved to become an instrumental actor in the drafting of the FCTC. It subsequently became one of the first five countries in SSA to sign and ratify the instrument on 20 June 2003 and 29 November 2004, respectively. Since then, Ghana has been active in several international tobacco control programmes, such as engaging in the 2008 Intergovernmental Negotiating Body on the Protocol on Illicit Trade in Tobacco Products and chairing the first and second Conferences of the Parties (CoP) in 2006 and 2007.

3.4 An assessment of the effectiveness of efforts to implement FCTC/national laws on tobacco use

In an attempt to forestall the prevalence of tobacco use, the WHO in 2008 launched MPOWER, which entreats member states to operationalise a list of cost-effective measures at the state, population and healthcare delivery levels.[27] These recommendations not only seek to reinforce the provisions of the FCTC but also may be considered feasible mechanisms for scaling up the reduction of demand and usage of tobacco. At the state level, it calls for an increase in tobacco taxes, enforcement of tobacco bans, increases in the visibility of advertisements on hazardous effects of smoking, safeguards for non-smokers from second-hand smoke (SHS), monitoring consumption, and increasing resources to tobacco control programmes. At the more technical healthcare level, it recommends (1) beta-2 agonists and inhaled corticosteroids for the treatment of persistent asthma; (2) aspirin therapy for acute myocardial infarction; (3) glycaemic control for diabetic patients; and (4) multidrug therapy and counselling. To safeguard the youth from taking up the habit of tobacco consumption, the organisation recommends (1) increasing taxes on tobacco; (2) enforcing compliance with a ban on tobacco promotion, sponsorship and advertisement; (3) actively disseminating information on the hazards of smoking; and (4) proscribing public smoking. In light of these recommendations, the next sections will survey Ghana's level of compliance in light of the six benchmarks listed in the MPOWER: (1) increasing taxes; (2) averting secondary smoking; (3) creating awareness; (4) monitoring; (5) enforcing the ban; and (6) providing assistance in quitting smoking.

3.4.1 Taxation

Article 6 of the FCTC entreats member states to impose high taxation on tobacco products to deter their demand. In light of this, the global health organisation

26 E Owusu-Dabo & others 'Support for smoke-free policy, and awareness of tobacco health effects and use of smoking cessation therapy in a developing country' (2011) 11 *BMC Public Health* 2.

27 WHO 'Global status report on non-communicable diseases' (2010) https://www.who.int/nmh/publications/ncd_report2010/en/ (accessed 24 September 2021).

calls for the imposition of more than 75 per cent taxation on tobacco retail prices.[28] On the ground, it must be noted that since the entry into force of the FCTC, the country's tax system has undergone significant transformations, specifically due to regime change and demand for capital injection. With no domestic producer and a lack of comprehensive guidelines on liaising with stakeholders in the tobacco industry, most importers generally lobby political actors to cut rates or forestall hikes in import duties and related taxes. In its 2015 Excise Duty Act, parliament approved an amendment to the first schedule of the Excise Duty Act 878 of 2014, in which it increased the excise duty on tobacco to 31.3 per cent of the total tax on value added tax (VAT), import duty, and excise and other minor taxes.[29] This figure, which is far below the threshold set by the WHO, may be attributed to interference by major tobacco players in the tax system. To discourage cigarette consumption and provide free treatment to patients of tobacco-related diseases, it is imperative that the state increases taxes on tobacco and reinvests the revenue in the public health sector, as well as security agencies, for strict enforcement of the PHA. This objective could be attained by safeguarding the tax regime from external manipulation, strengthening tax administration, regularly adjusting the tobacco tax for inflation and periodically reviewing the tobacco import duty.

3.4.2 Smoking spaces

Article 8 of the FCTC obliges member states to frame and operationalise legislation that proscribes tobacco consumption in workplaces and indoor public spaces. It is against this backdrop that section 58 of the PHA states that a 'person shall not smoke tobacco or a tobacco product or hold a lighted tobacco product' in places of collective use, restaurants, bars, offices, transport terminals, children's playgrounds and entertainment facilities. This provision was reinforced with section 2 of the TCR, which states that a designated smoking area shall not be adjacent to walkways or entrances to premises, or allow smoke to seep into non-smoking zones. Suffice to note that these provisions fall short of nicotine consumption, as all forms of designated smoking areas and ventilation do not (in practical terms) safeguard one against SHS. As smoke cannot be contained in a specific perimeter, a disproportionate percentage of young adults report exposure to nicotine in public spaces and homes.[30] Perhaps the ideal provision would have been a complete proscription of smoking, without exemption.

28 WHO 'A policy package to reverse the tobacco epidemic policy' (2008) http s://www.who.int/tobacco/mpower/mpower_english.pdf (accessed 24 September 2021).

29 WHO 'Report on the global tobacco epidemic, 2019: Country profile – Ghana' https://www.who.int/tobacco/surveillance/policy/country_profile/gha.pdf?ua=1 (accessed 24 September 2021) 1.

30 Asare & others (n 21).

3.4.3 Smoking and knowledge of its health implications

The instrument, under article 11, stipulates that member states must operationalise full-colour pictograms or pictures which communicate the health hazards of tobacco to their consumers. It also calls for large rotational warnings on all tobacco products, labelling and packaging. As a response, the PHA has obliged the tobacco industry to allocate 30 per cent of cigarette packs (front and back) to pictorial health hazards.[31] Yet, unlike other disease control interventions for immunisation, malaria and AIDS, there is still no effective and multi-sectorial structure established by the state to oversee compliance with article 11 and safeguarding people from tobacco consumption. At the institutional level, cigarette use remains outside the bracket of national and district health services. Without a designated individual at the local level to strategise, frame, operationalise and evaluate tobacco initiatives, it will be a challenge to safeguard primary and passive smokers from the adverse impact of cigarettes. This constraint is exacerbated by the limited funds and professional staff, particularly as donors and national budgets are generally channelled towards diseases such as malaria, tuberculosis (TB) and AIDS. As an illustration, while the performance of the National Tuberculosis Programme, established in 1994, has undergone several assessments by international evaluators, the performance of the NCD Control Programme (NCDCP) has been overlooked since its establishment in 1990.[32] The latter still lacks comprehensive channels or mechanisms to examine the (in)effectiveness of ongoing programmes and industry compliance.

3.4.4 Risk assessment of tobacco consumption

One of the key provisions of the FCTC (article 12) is that member states must regularly evaluate the ramifications of nicotine on their population as well as the (in) effectiveness of existing interventions.[33] Since 2006, three key surveys have been conducted to trace cigarette consumption among different age groups, as well as the increasing/decreasing number of cigarette consumers. These are the Global Health Professional Students Survey, Global School Personnel Survey and Global Youth Tobacco Survey (GYTS).[34] As an illustration, the GYTS demonstrates that a disproportionate percentage of individuals begin smoking before 18 years and that those who experiment with few cigarettes ultimately become chain smokers. Yet, after nearly two decades since the entry into force of the FCTC, the country

31 Art 11(1)(b).

32 I Law, K Floyd & the African TB Prevalence Survey Group 'National tuberculosis prevalence surveys in Africa, 2008–2016: An overview of results and lessons learned' (2020) 25(11) *Tropical Medicine and International Health* 1309.

33 Art 12.

34 P Baiden & others 'Bullying victimization as a predictor of suicidal ideation and suicide attempt among senior high school students in Ghana: Results from the 2012 Ghana global school-based health survey' (2019) 18(2) *Journal of School Violence* 300.

has not established an overarching mechanism for epidemiological surveillance of the impact of cigarette usage. For this reason, contemporary data on the socio-economic determinants of cigarette consumption has remained scanty over the last three years. Also, while the PHA has been in existence for nearly a decade, there are neither funds set aside for its enforcement nor a complaint mechanism to investigate and prosecute alleged breaches.[35] Regional and district assemblies still lack the mandate to adopt legislation that proscribes tobacco smoking in educational facilities, healthcare facilities, government establishments, workplaces, indoor offices, restaurants, bars, pubs and cafes.[36]

3.4.5 Advertising bans

Ghana is obliged under FCTC article 13 to adopt overarching legislation proscribing the tobacco industry from using electronic or print media to announce new products, create a need for their products, improve the image of their products, and convince and/or inform consumers that their brands are the best. This provision partially complied with the imposition of a ban on tobacco-related promotions and advertisements in the PHA. The Act specifically prohibits the use of newspapers, magazines, radio and television to promote and advertise cigarettes. As indicated in Table 3.1, the FCTC also calls for the imposition of a fine on the violation. In the area of operationalisation, the country was given 8 out of 10 for good compliance with promotional bans on electronic and print media.[37] Suffice to note that this score may not be a direct reflection of the situation on the ground, particularly as a disproportionate percentage of youth are taking up smoking. The practical challenge may be reinforced by the lack of empirical data to demonstrate that tobacco advertisement bans have not been infringed upon at the point of sale, bars, spaza shops, or kiosks.

3.4.6 Treatment of tobacco dependence

In its bid to help many refrain from tobacco use, article 14 of the FCTC obliges member states to establish health facilities with personnel capable of providing therapy and counselling to individuals willing to quit. It further calls for provision of medication, treatment, mobile cessation services and toll-free telephone helplines to assist callers unable to afford medical services. This obligation may be grouped into two camps: treatment and awareness creation. In the first camp, there are insufficient medical supplies and professional staff. At the district and local levels, designated community health workers are assigned to provide some guidance on substance abuse (steroids, cannabis, heroin and cocaine) but not specifically on tobacco consumption. Whereas the country's health service launched

35 WHO (n 29).
36 As above.
37 On a compliance scale of 0–10, where 10 is the highest; WHO (n 29).

smoking cessation clinical guidelines three years ago, basic and more complex treatment remains unavailable, especially as the national health insurance scheme (NHIS) does not cover this intervention. More specifically, there is a limited number of health promotion specialists, physiotherapists, dieticians, psychologists and pathologists available at the local level to provide counselling and diagnose diseases related to smoking. Also, whereas there is some level of cessation support in private clinics and major healthcare facilities, one is expected to bear the cost of treatment as the NHIS does not cover this expense.[38]

Moreover, other pharmacological replacement therapies and products such as varenicline and bupropion (Zyban, Wellbutrin) are equally unavailable in the country to assist in self-help efforts. In the second camp, the country occasionally hosts awareness programmes in local communities to assist smokers to quit the practice. Knowledge of the debilitating health impact of tobacco is essential in containing the menace, especially if campaigners could successfully influence the perception that the substance truly has health repercussions. Nonetheless, education around the cigarette and resultant NCDs remain low among the general populace, as 58 per cent of hypertension patients assumed that their condition is curable. [39] The group also believed that dizziness and joint pain is triggered by hypertension, with high blood pressure being a condition caused by excessive blood in one's organs.[40]

Unless coerced by employers, educational or travel requirements, the norm of seeking periodic health check-ups is lacking among a disproportionate percentage of the Ghanaian community. In such an environment, mass screening or self-referral of people will be essential, particularly as 17 per cent of patients with high blood pressure had not gone for a medical check-up in half a decade, and only about 30 per cent of hypertensive or diabetic patients are aware of their condition.[41] The lack of awareness, exacerbated by traditional healers' claims that there is a cure, has played a primary role in the neglect of pursuing a healthy lifestyle and seeking regular treatment for many diabetic patients.[42] Aside from limited funds to seek medical treatment, patients postpone or skip medical treatment due to sociocultural factors, including spiritual deliverance at prayer camps, recourse to health treatment, apprehension of mastectomy and widespread ignorance. This culture of nonchalance is exacerbated by the non-visibility of screening

38 WHO (n 27).

39 J Spencer, E Philips & G Ogedegbe 'Knowledge, attitudes, beliefs, and blood pressure control in a community-based sample in Ghana' (2005) 15 *Ethnicity & Disease* 748.

40 As above.

41 NCDCP 'Ghana STEPS survey 2006: Fact sheet' https://search.yahoo.com/search?fr=mcafee&type=E210US91105G0&p=Ghana+STEPS+Survey+Fact+Sheet%3A+Greater+Accra+Region+2006 (accessed 24 September 2021); AGB Amoah, SK Owusu & S Adjei 'Diabetes in Ghana: A community-based prevalence study in Greater Accra' (2002) 56 *Diabetes Research and Clinical Practice* 198.

42 GN Nyaaba & others 'Factors hindering hypertension control: Perspectives of front-line health professionals in rural Ghana' (2020) 181 *Public Health* 17.

interventions at the district levels coupled with the limitation of the NHIS which does not make provision for medical examination except for urgent treatment. In conformity with the FCTC, the state should fast-track the launch of screening centres across the 260 districts to enable regular walk-in check-ups.[43] In some areas, the programme could be dedicated specifically to the weekly assessment of hypertension and diabetes by rural and urban residents 18 years and older. Such regular visits will enable tobacco consumers to know their health status and how to manage it.

This section has assessed the national response to countering tobacco use in Ghana. It showed that whereas some strides have been achieved in realising the objectives of the FCTC, much remains to be done. It is in light of this backdrop that the next section turns to reviewing some of the best remedies to safeguard passive smokers while assisting tobacco users to quit.

3.5 Case law

Forestalling tobacco uptake and experimentation should remain a government priority in light of the growing concern and an increasing number of youths indulging in cannabis and shisha (water pipe). An important conduit within this context is litigation. Yet, perhaps due to limited resources, victims of smoke-related illnesses, civil service organisation (CSOs) and the government have been unable to file lawsuits against major companies for the human suffering and health risks triggered by the substance. To break this cycle, it might be useful for relevant actors to draw from jurisdictions where the state has successfully litigated and enabled affected citizens to receive compensation for their medical conditions.

One ground-breaking case worth citing is *United States v Philip Morris USA, Inc.*[44] On 22 September 1999, the US government filed an application in the District Court for the District of Columbia against major global tobacco companies for using coordinated, deliberate and deceitful campaigns to entice vulnerable citizens to take up smoking. The applicant sought, among others, to recoup billions of dollars incurred for the treatment of federal employees, veterans and Medicare patients suffering from tobacco-related illnesses. Ultimately, the court concurred with the applicants and ruled that for over half a decade, the tobacco industry has used deceptive practices towards targeting adolescents and has misled the government and consumers about the tobacco's addictiveness. Therefore it ordered the companies to channel a considerable amount of funds to marketing and promotional programmes to rectify these past deceptive beliefs about smoking.[45]

43 P Lujala, C Brunnschweiler & I Edjekumhene 'Transparent for whom? Dissemination of information on Ghana's petroleum and mining revenue management' (2020) 56 *The Journal of Development Studies* 2135 at 2136.

44 *Complaint About Damages and Injunctive and Declaratory Relief, the United States v Philip Morris Inc* 99-CV-02496 (DDC 22 Sept 1999).

45 CL McCall 'Equity up in smoke: Civil RICO, disgorgement, and *United States v Philip Morris*' (2006) 74 *Fordham Law Review* 2461.

Since this case, several victories have been recorded across the globe. First, by making specific reference to article 13 of the FCTC, Panama's Supreme Court upheld a decree proscribing point-of-sale displays. It highlighted that the instrument flouts neither consumers' rights to access information nor the intellectual property rights of British American Tobacco (BAT).[46] Second, following an application filed by a BAT affiliate, the Argentine Supreme Court held that in light of the harm caused by smoking, a subnational law that proscribes tobacco promotion, advertisement and sponsorship is not unconstitutional, as it imposes a reasonable limitation on commercial freedoms.[47]

Third, in 2016 the UK's High Court of Justice dismissed BAT's application on the packaging of tobacco products. It reaffirmed that plain packaging restrictions were legitimate, as they were supported by the FCTC and did not infringe on the company's property rights. Three years later, following an application filed by a leading health organisation, the UK's Advertising Standards Authority ruled that BAT can no longer use social media (its public Instagram account) to advertise or market in the jurisdiction.[48] It also ordered the producer to remove unlawful e-cigarette promotional content currently on social media.

Fourth, in Brazil, the Supreme Federal Tribunal affirmed the right of the government's Health Regulatory Agency to control tobacco company's operations. It also upheld a 2012 regulation that bans flavours and additives in tobacco products.[49] Closer to home, Kenya's Supreme Court dismissed BAT's appeal, asking the court to declare the Tobacco Control Regulations (TCRs) null and void.[50] It dismissed the petition in its entirety, as the company's appeal had no merits.

In adopting similar reasoning, Uganda's Constitutional Court dismissed BAT's petition challenging the constitutionality of the country's 2015 TCR.[51] The court awarded costs to the government and condemned the petition as a part of the brand's strategy to subvert national attempts towards zero-tobacco consumption. Ultimately, tobacco litigation has the potential to transform the prospects of curbing the operations of tobacco companies in Ghana and across the (West) African region. It will generally put the industry on the political defensive by coercing them to sit at the bargaining table with anti-tobacco advocates and reimburse the state for healthcare costs caused by tobacco.

46 *Rodriguez Robles & Espinosa on behalf of British American Tobacco Panama, SA v The Ministry of Health*, Docket 192–11, Supreme Court of Justice (2014).

47 *Nobleza Piccardo v Provincia de Santa Fe* (2015) CSJ 188/2006 (42-N)/CSI.

48 'ASA Ruling on British American Tobacco UK Ltd t/a Vype' *ASA.org* 1 May 2019.

49 *National Confederation of Industry (Confederação Nacional da Indústria) v ANVISA* (2018) Unique Number: 9984745-20.2012.1.00.0000.

50 *British American Tobacco Kenya, PLC v Ministry of Health* (Supreme Court of Kenya Petition 5 of 2017) (2019).

51 *British American Tobacco Ltd v Attorney General* (Constitutional Petition 46 of 2016) [2019] UGCC 4 (28 May 2019).

3.6 Recommendations

Ghana continues to be a major player in the arena of tobacco control, particularly in terms of ratifying the treaty, adopting national legislation, raising taxes and abolishing publicity of this product. Nonetheless, the number of citizens who consume the substance abounds. In light of the urgency to flatten the curve, the state must direct its attention to six main channels.

The first is the provision of capital and human resources for in-depth research into drivers which exacerbate smoking habits and how to overcome these tendencies. Understanding the driving forces of tobacco use, policy response and institutional mechanisms are essential in weighing the country's level of commitment to safeguarding its population from adverse health conditions. Since the complexity of tobacco consumption transcends the field of medicine, researchers from the field of economics, sociology, anthropology and political science should equally be consulted to provide insight into the underlying factors which incite the poor to barter their scarce resources for tobacco, and how to neutralise such elements. This consultation may take the form of a community-based health survey to understand the local dynamics of cigarette use, gender and age determinants, and unearth local (un)healthy diets and activities which may avert NCDs such as diabetes, hypertension and related cardiovascular diseases. The underlying notion is that there is a need for a paradigm shift in the conventional idea that remedies for cardiovascular diseases are outside the remit of non-surgeons, which is quite incorrect. By all indications, experienced dieticians and physical trainers play vital roles in improving heart health by reversing the progression of atherosclerosis (coronary artery disease) and stabilising plaques in the arteries. Additionally, through tobacco cessation counselling, psychologists play a key role in cutting down on cardiovascular hospital admissions. As demonstrated by the placement of monographs on alcohol by the British Medical Association, the research capacity of the NCDCP could be complemented with scientific reports and journals generated by academics on the adverse effect of tobacco use and what supplements should be taken to enhance one's blood circulation.[52] Ultimately, to frame a feasible solution to address the unique Ghanaian problem, there is a need for a regular and nationally informed survey to be conducted. By drawing inspiration from the 2019 WHO Global Survey, a locally informed survey will provide a clear indication of the regional, tribal, social and religious factors which enable or hinder people's access to and usage of tobacco.[53] An understanding of these dynamics will be instrumental in shaping feasible interventions to address the specific needs of Ghanaian consumers.

Second, on the question of low taxes and smuggling, it is imperative for human rights activities to partner with the state in framing overarching guidelines to

52 BMA Board of Science 'Alcohol misuse: Tackling the UK epidemic' (2008) http://www.dldocs.stir.ac.uk/documents/Alcoholmisuse.pdf (accessed 24 September 2021).

53 WHO (n 29).

eliminate undue influence exerted by actors in the tobacco industry while averting smuggling at the borders. There is also a need to reinforce security at the country's porous borders as smuggling undermines the financial base of the country and undermines socio-economic development at the local and national levels. Yet, considering the sophisticated network of cross-border smuggling, provision of technical support, up-to-date technology and periodic training will be useful in assisting customs officials to intercept and/or halt cigarette contraband from its eastern neighbour.[54] The state should reinforce the powers of the Ghana Committee on Tobacco Control (GCTC) to hand down binding sanctions against retailers who sell cigarettes to underage children and against smokers who expose third parties to nicotine, as well as to advise the government on tobacco-related taxes. The state should also have a research division responsible for studying existing policies, monitor the level of compliance by producers and enhance surveillance on the borders to avert smuggling.

Third, there should be continuous advocacy and lobbying of policymakers to adopt legislation proscribing the use of tobacco, especially in light of its hazardous effect on the population. This is more the case as 18 million people have been projected to become TB patients in half a century, with 40 million deaths triggered by this disease. This statistic is relevant as tobacco consumers, both active and passive, are more likely to develop TB than their non-smoking compatriots.[55] But, to every legislation, there is a need for a (well-resourced) institution to enforce and monitor its compliance. So is the TCA which requires a strong partnership between (non)state actors in mobilising human and financial resources for tobacco control interventions at the (sub)national levels. This collaboration could take the shape of (1) periodic donation to the government's ongoing programmes; (2) pro bono training of government officials on the FCTC and MPOWER; (3) combating smuggling; and (4) forestalling corruption at the borders.

Fourth, an effective CSO-government partnership could scale up rural screening programmes by ensuring high compliance with treatment, access to self-help medications, and early diagnosis and reporting. Resources could equally be channelled towards training, sharpening the skills of primary healthcare providers to enhance screening, helping tobacco users quit and containing cardiovascular diseases, especially as prehypertension detection could avert one's risk of stroke. As asserted by the MPOWER, overcoming tobacco use at the local level requires a considerable amount of financial and human capital to be channelled towards forging an effective mechanism responsible for enforcement and monitoring complaints. To this end, there should be a concerted effort towards vaccination against cervical and liver cancers and improved self-help programmes,

54 Owusu-Dabo & others (n 5).

55 S Basu & others 'Projected effects of tobacco smoking on worldwide tuberculosis control: Mathematical modeling analysis' (2011) 343 *British Medical Journal* 1.

particularly healthier lifestyle choices. This may include quitting the use of alcohol and tobacco, engaging in physical activity and following a nutritious diet.

Fifth, in light of the non-enforcement of the treaty provisions, there is a need to restructure the GCTC, and perhaps make it an autonomous monitoring institution away from the Ghana Health Service (GHS). Their multidisciplinary expertise and perspective on tobacco could be instrumental in holding both public and private actors accountable for a breach of tobacco-related violations. An autonomous GCTC should have a reporting section responsible for receiving complaints from GHS or ordinary citizens who witness any breach of the provisions set out in the FCTC or PHA. This function may only be effective if the people are aware of the existence of such instruments, what they purport and the committee's visibility in local communities. To that end, the GCTC may also take up the role of awareness creation to broadly disseminate information among the population. The content of their educational campaign, among others, may include the rules governing cigarette consumption, its health ramifications, where (not) to consume the substance and the penalties for violating such guidance. The committee must use simple language to convey its message, as cigarette consumption is prevalent among the poor and less educated. Policymakers ought not to overlook this recommendation, as education campaigns around smoking have been sparse, if any, in the various (electronic and print) media used by the state. The mandate of the new committee should be extended to oversee the operations of the NCDCP, conduct a regular review of the operations of the board, and advise the government on setting targets, particularly within the realm of curbing uptake of tobacco use. The NCDCP will remain the foot soldier of the GCTC by coordinating the daily operations of tobacco interventions. The former may thus be responsible for creating awareness at the (sub)national level, assisting customs in countering cross-border smuggling, monitoring compliance and coordinating interventions from different stakeholders. It may equally have a unit responsible for building horizontal and vertical partnerships with domestic and external (healthcare) agencies on the one hand, and relevant government departments towards accelerated screening, counselling and complete prohibition of tobacco on the other.

Finally, awareness of one's condition is paramount in (re)shaping one's lifestyle, as a healthy body and mind are crucial in forestalling cardiovascular diseases such as cancer and stroke. Engaging in healthy eating habits may encompass the consumption of whole grains, legumes, vegetables and fruits while eschewing trans-fatty acids, salt and oil. This aspiration could only be achieved through information dissemination and raising awareness of the health detriments they stand to suffer if they do not alter their eating habits or way of life. Apart from churches, pictorial warnings of smoking could be launched in mosques, marketplaces, on the streets, football fields, campuses and on social media. Advocating for a healthy lifestyle by known figures such as community leaders, imams, pastors, teachers, traditional healers, opinion leaders, actors and musicians will be deemed instructive and trigger compliance by the majority of the population. These actors could integrate healthy living into sermons, curriculums, local songs and campaign manifestos. These opinion leaders should 'walk the talk' by engaging in regular exercises and eschewing a lavish lifestyle that might undermine their message. More so, the state should utilise national media to run commercials on the harmful effects of smoking while giving tax reprieves to private television, radio and newspaper outlets which undertake this issue as a social responsibility. Cigarette experimentation and uptake may be considerably reduced through active 'stop smoking' campaigns and support services in common places of assemblage, such as markets, churches, mosques, clinics, schools and taxi ranks. To this end, the state must reinforce and extend its universal access to education to older adults, as education has the potential to stimulate necessary awareness about the health effects of tobacco. Whereas the free junior/senior high programmes may play a considerable role in this regard, there is a need to extend such interventions to adult education or night school for school dropouts or workers willing to take up studies after their daily struggles.

In sum, the section was guided by one overarching question: what actions are needed for an improved national response to smoking? It identified six entry points: (1) enhancing awareness creation around smoking and related NCDs; (2) involving community leaders in encouraging healthy lifestyles; (3) resourcing health facilities to manage NCDs; (5) improving screening programmes; (5) tightening security at borders to avert smuggling; and (6) calling for a complete ban on tobacco consumption. Attention may be paid to a periodic survey of how many citizens are experimenting and/or taking up smoking, the sociocultural drivers enhancing tobacco consumption, the (in)effectiveness of its current policy and institutional regime and ultimately the prohibition of tobacco use. As the FCTC approaches its second decade, it provides a sober reminder to Ghana to comply with its obligation of adopting effective and urgent intervention to curb the epidemic of smoking among the population. It is believed that with best practices from the Global North, including the United States and New Zealand, the state may raise enough resources and effective cessation programmes to assist smokers to quit cigarette uptake and forestall non-smokers from experimenting.

3.7 Conclusion

On the global platform of tobacco control, it could be said that Ghana could rightly raise its head high in terms of steps taken to safeguard its citizens from the adverse environmental, health and socio-economic effects triggered by cigarette consumption and exposure. It has made considerable strides within the arena of legislative and institutional setup needed to help consumers quit and prevent non-smokers from becoming consumers. Yet, much remains to be done. Safeguarding young people from tobacco uptake and experimentation is essential as cigarette usage and resultant mortality/morbidity are projected to increase over the next decade in the Global South. Nearly two decades after it ratified the FCTC, Ghana still has not framed a comprehensive enforcement/monitoring mechanism to ensure that the tobacco industry and smokers conform to the standards set out by the instrument. It also found that a chain of determinants, including region of residence, educational background, economic condition, age and gender, are key covariates of tobacco usage in the country. Youth are often prone to SHS, with older men more inclined to consume greater quantities than their younger counterparts. Likewise, those in economically viable regions (better educated, residing in urban areas, belonging to the wealthy class) have a lower proclivity to tobacco than their non-elite counterparts. To this end, an important policy directive should incorporate increasing employment opportunities, assistance to rural farmers, adequate salaries for workers and social safety nets to reduce the daily apprehension of the poor. In particular, taxes on cigarettes remain low, thereby making the commodity accessible to the poor and the young. Despite considerable advancement in the adoption of tobacco control legislation, there is still no overarching cessation intervention in the public health system to assist smokers seeking to quit.

Also, contemporary national data on the uptake of consumption, sociocultural factors, and institutional mechanisms which enable or disable uptake of tobacco remains sparse, if not unavailable. Aside from investing in research into the aforementioned gaps, similar support could be directed towards a re-evaluation of contemporary national legislations as to whether they address the specific needs of the Ghanaian tobacco consumer, and what lessons could be drawn from other jurisdictions to reinforce domestic practices. Of priority should be novel means of intersecting tobacco smuggling, the feasibility of criminalising tobacco use and what remedies are best suited to assist consumers to quit the practice. Experts selected to conduct this assessment may also consider the present tax structure to determine the right margin for increased taxation on tobacco use, as well as effective means of forestalling the tobacco industry's interference to this end. Considering the proliferation of media outlets, it is imperative the state optimises its use of newspapers, radio and TV networks across the regions to raise awareness and disseminate information about the harmful impact of tobacco use on primary and passive smokers. Ultimately, human rights activists, CSOs, students and relevant (inter)national institutions should continue to campaign towards a complete ban on tobacco use in Ghana.

Bibliography

Amoah, AGB; Owusu, SK & Adjei, S 'Diabetes in Ghana: A community-based prevalence study in Greater Accra' (2002) 56 *Diabetes Research and Clinical Practice* 197

'ASA ruling on British American Tobacco UK Ltd t/a Vype' *ASA.org* 1 May 2019

Asare, S; Stoklosa, M; Drope, J & Larsen, A 'Effects of prices on youth cigarette smoking and tobacco use initiation in Ghana and Nigeria' (2019) 16 *International Journal of Environmental Research and Public Health* 1

Baiden, P; Kuuire, VZ; Shrestha, N; Tonui, BC; Dako-Gyeke, M & Peters, KK 'Bullying victimization as a predictor of suicidal ideation and suicide attempt among senior high school students in Ghana: Results from the 2012 Ghana global school-based health survey' (2019) 18(2) *Journal of School Violence* 300

Basu, S; Stuckler, D; Bitton, A & Glantz, SA 'Projected effects of tobacco smoking on worldwide tuberculosis control: Mathematical modeling analysis' (2011) 343 *British Medical Journal* 1

BMA Board of Science 'Alcohol misuse: Tackling the UK epidemic' (2008) http://www.dldocs.stir.ac.uk/documents/Alcoholmisuse.pdf (accessed 24 September 2021)

British American Tobacco Kenya, PLC v Ministry of Health (Supreme Court of Kenya Petition 5 of 2017) (2019)

British American Tobacco Ltd v Attorney General (Constitutional Petition 46 of 2016) [2019] UGCC 4 (28 May 2019)

Complaint about Damages and Injunctive and Declaratory Relief, the United States v Philip Morris, Inc 99-CV-02496 (DDC 22 September 1999)

Constitution of Ghana, 1992

Constitutional Review Commission 'Report of the Constitutional Review Commission of Ghana: From a Political to a Developmental Constitution' (2011)

Dalal, S; Beunza, JJ; Volmink, J; Adebamowo, C; Bajunirwe, F; Njelekela, M; Mozaffarian, D; Fawzi, W; Willett, W; Adami, HO & Holmes, MD 'Non-communicable diseases in sub-Saharan Africa: What we know now' (2011) 40 *International Journal of Epidemiology* 885

FCTC 'Parties to the WHO framework convention on tobacco control' (2020) https://www.who.int/fctc/cop/en/ (accessed 24 September 2021)

Ghana Lotto Operations v National Lotto Authority (2007–2008) SCGLR 1088 2007

'The global school personnel survey: A cross-country overview' https://www.ncbi.nlm.nih.gov/pmc/articles/PMC2563538/(accessed 24 September 2021)

Hospital Fees Act 387 of 1971

Law, I; Floyd, K & the African TB Prevalence Survey Group 'National tuberculosis prevalence surveys in Africa, 2008–2016: An overview of results and lessons learned' (2020) 25(11) *Tropical Medicine and International Health* 1309

Lujala, P; Brunnschweiler, C & Edjekumhene, I 'Transparent for whom? Dissemination of information on Ghana's petroleum and mining revenue management' (2020) *The Journal of Development Studies* 2135

McCall, CL 'Equity up in smoke: Civil Rico, disgorgement, and *United States v Philip Morris*' (2006) 74 *Fordham Law Review* 2461

National Confederation of Industry (Confederação Nacional da Indústria) v ANVISA (2018) Unique Number: 9984745–20.2012.1.00.0000

NCDCP 'Ghana STEPS survey fact sheet: Greater Accra region 2006' https://search.yahoo.com/search?fr=mcafee&type=E210US91105G0&p=Ghana+STEPS+Survey+Fact+Sheet%3A+Greater+Accra+Region+2006 (accessed 24 September 2021)

New Patriotic Party v Attorney General [1993–1994] 2 GLR 35

Nikolic, IA; Stanciole, AE & Zaydman, M 'Chronic Emergency: Why NCDs matter' (2011) *Health, Nutrition and Population (HNP) Discussion Paper*

Nkrumah, B *Seeking the right to food: Food activism in South Africa* (Cambridge University Press 2021)

Nobleza Piccardo v Provincia de Santa Fe (2015) CSJ 188 / 2006 (42-N)/CSI

Nyaaba, GN; Masana, L; Aikins, AG & Beune, E 'Factors hindering hypertension control: Perspectives of front-line health professionals in rural Ghana' (2020) 181 *Public Health* 16

Okai, DE; Manu, A; Amoah, EM; Laar, A; Akamah, J & Torpey, K 'Patient-level factors influencing hypertension control in adults in Accra, Ghana' (2020) 123 *BMC Cardiovascular Disorders* 1

Owusu-Dabo, E; Lewis, SA; McNeill, A & Gilmore, A 'Smoking uptake and prevalence in Ghana' (2009) 18 *Tobacco Control* 365

Owusu-Dabo, E; Lewis, SA; McNeill, A; Gilmore, A & Britton, J 'Support for smoke-free policy, and awareness of tobacco health effects and use of smoking cessation therapy in a developing country' (2011) 11 *BMC Public Health* 1

Public Health Act 851 of 2012

Serrano-Alarcón, M; Kunst, AE; Bosdriesz, JR & Perelman, J 'Tobacco control policies and smoking among older adults: A longitudinal analysis of 10 European countries' (2019) 114 *Addiction* 1076

Spencer, J; Philips, E & Ogedegbe, G 'Knowledge, attitudes, beliefs, and blood pressure control in a community-based sample in Ghana' (2005) 15 *Ethnic Disease* 748

Rodriguez Robles & Espinosa on behalf of British American Tobacco Panama, SA v The Ministry of Health Docket 192–11, Supreme Court of Justice (2014)

Thiagarajan, S 'Tobacco use among adolescent school-going children: Extent of problem and solutions for the future (2019) 2 *Cancer Research, Statistics and Treatment* 124

Tobacco Control Regulations 2016 (LI 2247)

UN General Assembly, Convention Against Torture and Other Cruel, Inhuman or Degrading Treatment or Punishment, 10 December 1984, United Nations, Treaty Series, vol 1465

UN General Assembly Convention on the Elimination of All Forms of Discrimination Against Women 18 December 1979, United Nations, Treaty Series, vol 1249

UN General Assembly Convention on the Rights of Persons with Disabilities: Resolution/Adopted by the General Assembly, 24 January 2007, A/RES/61/106

UN General Assembly, Convention on the Rights of the Child, 20 November 1989, United Nations, Treaty Series, vol 1577

UN General Assembly International Covenant on Civil and Political Rights, 16 December 1966, United Nations, Treaty Series, vol 999

UN 'Treaty body database: Ghana' (2021) https://tbinternet.ohchr.org/_layouts/15/TreatyBodyExternal/Treaty.aspx?CountryID=67&lang=EN (accessed 24 September 2021)

WHO 'A policy package to reverse the tobacco epidemic policy' (2008) http s://www.who.int/tobacco/mpower/mpower_english.pdf (accessed 24 September 2021)

WHO 'Framework convention on tobacco control' https://www.who.int/fctc/text_download/en/ (accessed 24 September 2021)

WHO 'Global status report on non-communicable diseases 2010' https://www.who.int/nmh/publications/ncd_report2010/en/ (accessed 24 September 2021)

WHO 'Global Youth Tobacco Survey' https://www.who.int/teams/noncommunicable-diseases/surveillance/systems-tools/global-youth-tobacco-survey (accessed 24 September 2021)

WHO 'Report card on the WHO framework convention on tobacco control' https://www.afro.who.int/sites/default/files/2017-09/Ghana_report_card_0.pdf (accessed 24 September 2021)

WHO 'Report on the global tobacco epidemic, 2019: Country profile – Ghana' https://www.who.int/tobacco/surveillance/policy/country_profile/gha.pdf?ua=1 (accessed 24 September 2021)

WHO 'Tobacco' (2020) https://www.who.int/news-room/fact-sheets/detail/tobacco (accessed 24 September 2021)

WHO 'WHO report on the global tobacco epidemic' (2017) https://www.who.int/tobacco/global_report/2017/en/ (accessed 24 September 2021)

World Health Assembly *World Health Organization framework convention on tobacco control* (2003) https://www.who.int/fctc/text_download/en/ (accessed 24 November 2021)

4 Challenges and opportunities in the implementation of the FCTC in South Africa

Robert D Nanima

4.1 Introduction

The main non-communicable diseases (NCDs) in South Africa include cardiovascular diseases, diabetes, cancer, chronic respiratory diseases and mental illness.[1] According to the World Health Organization (WHO), NCDs account for 51 per cent of all deaths in South Africa.[2] Approximately 19 per cent of deaths are due to cardiovascular diseases, 10 per cent to cancer, 4 per cent to chronic respiratory diseases, 7 per cent to diabetes and 11 per cent to other NCDs.[3] It is instructive to note that while 40 per cent of deaths are due to communicable diseases, injuries like assaults, murders and accidents only account for 9 per cent.[4]

A closer look at tobacco consumption shows a rising trend. A 2012 study showed that 16.8 per cent of adult South Africans as smokers of tobacco, with males at 29.4 per cent and females at 8.2 per cent. This rose to 17.6 per cent of adult South Africans as smokers of tobacco, with slightly lower percentages of males at 29.2 per cent and females at 7 per cent.[5] There was a decrease in the deaths from 53,000 in 2012 to 44,000 in 2014. A closer look at the rate of consumption placed the Western Cape at the helm with 32.9 per cent, the Northern Cape at 31.2 per cent and the Free State at 27.4 per cent.[6]

The mode in which tobacco consumption is socially punctuated is worrying.[7] First, 21.5 per cent of children between the ages of 13 and 15 consume tobacco products, with boys at 24.3 per cent and girls at 19 per cent. Second, 28 per cent of learners between grades 8 and 11 have admitted to the consumption

1 BM Mayosi & others 'The burden of non-communicable diseases in South Africa' (2009) 374 *Lancet* 934 at 935.
2 WHO 'South Africa: Risk of premature death due to NCDs' https://www.who.int/nmh/countries/zaf_en.pdf (accessed 9 September 2021).
3 As above.
4 As above.
5 P Reddy & others 'Prevalence of tobacco use among adults in South Africa: Results from the first South African national health and nutrition examination survey' (2015) 105 *South African Medical Journal* 648.
6 As above.
7 As above.

DOI: 10.4324/9781003264248-6

of tobacco products. This is evident in the social practices of youth who smoke hookah or use hubbly bubbly and e-cigarettes.[8] More dangers have been identified in the consumption of hookah, whereby sharing of the pipes results in the transmission of other infections like tuberculosis and hepatitis. In addition, the smoking of hookah amounts to inhaling approximately 100 times the volume of a normal cigarette.[9] E-cigarettes enhance the habit to start smoking actual tobacco-based products.[10] These other methods, while habit-forming, still present dangers that may increase the current statistics of the global mortality of 7 million deaths and the 900,000 deaths from second-hand inhalation.[11] This chapter contextualises South Africa's state of NCDs and discusses the link between the right to health and NCDs. This is followed by how the Framework Convention on Tobacco Control (FCTC) may be used to realise the right to health at the national level. An assessment of the effectiveness of the efforts to implementing the FCTC under South Africa's national laws is conducted. Finally, the chapter concludes with an analysis of emerging case law and recommendations.

4.2 Right to health and NCDs

The right to health in the context of tobacco use in South Africa has taken a developmental trajectory informed by the shift from apartheid to a democratic dispensation. The current legal framework encapsulates the right to health and accords stringent effects of the laws on the control of tobacco use.

4.2.1 The right under the current legal framework

The South African Constitution provides for the right to access to healthcare.[12] This is seen in the need for access to healthcare services, like sexual and reproductive health and rights, primary healthcare for children, and emergency services and medical services for detained persons and prisoners.[13] The Constitution provides for universal access to healthcare services, and the state has the obligation to take reasonable legislative and other measures, within its available resources, to achieve the progressive realisation of that right.[14] The Constitution identifies groups of people that should not be denied access to healthcare, like children and

8 MA Moreno 'Risks of hookah smoking' (2015) 169 *JAMA Pediatrics* 196.

9 As above.

10 Cancer.Net 'Health risks of e-cigarettes, smokeless tobacco, and waterpipes' https://bit.ly/2Ob8p3i (accessed 9 September 2020).

11 Smoking and tobacco: Health effects, centre for disease control https://www.cdc.gov/tobacco/basic_information/health_effects/index.htm (accessed 9 September 2021).

12 The Constitution of the Republic of South Africa, 1996, secs 27(1)(a)–(b); 27(3); 28(1)(c); 35(2)(e); 24(a); and 12 (c).

13 Constitution secs 27(1)(a)–(c); 28(1)(c); 35(2)(e).

14 Constitution secs 27(1)(a)–(c).

detained persons.[15] The obligation on the state extends to the protection of the right to an environment that is not harmful to one's health or well-being.[16] Other health-related constitutional provisions include the obligation of both state and non-state actors to protect the right to bodily and psychological integrity of patients.[17]

In the context of tobacco control, the Tobacco Products Control Amendment Act was introduced to deal with the harmful effects of tobacco on the health of people.[18] It prohibits the advertising and promotion of tobacco, the free distribution of tobacco products and the smoking of tobacco products in any public place or workplace. It prohibits smoking in public places, and manufacturers have to place particular information on the packaging of tobacco products.

The Constitution provides for the application of international law that has been ratified by the Republic.[19] The Universal Declaration of Human Rights provides for the right of everyone to the adequate standard of health.[20] Although it is not binding, it has become part of customary international law as an authoritative interpretation of international human rights.[21] Most of its provisions have been incorporated as legally binding provisions in various human rights treaties.[22]

Furthermore, the right to health is provided for in article 12 of the International Covenant on Economic, Social and Cultural Rights (ICESCR).[23] The obligation to attain the right to the highest attainable standard of health in international public health is reiterated by the WHO Constitution.[24] It is supposed to be enjoyed as a fundamental human right without distinction of race, religion, political belief, economic or social condition.[25] All States parties' have a role to play in ensuring that they protect the public from health emergencies

15 Constitution secs 28(1)(c) and 35(2)(e).
16 Constitution sec 24(a).
17 Constitution sec 12(c).
18 Act 12 of 1999.
19 Constitution sec 232.
20 See art 25 of the UDHR.
21 K Moyo 'Realising the right to health in South Africa' in Foundation for Human Rights *Socio-economic rights: Progressive realisation?* (2016) 375 http://www.fhr-mirror.org.za/files/7215/1247/1732/Health.pdf (accessed 12 September 2021).
22 As above. The other international human rights laws include the Convention on the Elimination of Discrimination against Women (CEDAW); the Convention on the Rights of the Child (CRC); the American Declaration on the Rights and Duties of Man; the European Social Charter (ESC); the African Charter on Human and Peoples' Rights (African Charter); the Protocol to the African Charter on Human and Peoples' Rights on the Rights of Women in Africa; and the African Charter on the Rights and Welfare of the Child, among others.
23 International Covenant on Economic and Social Rights 966 UNTS 3, art 12. It is referred to as the highest attainable standard of health.
24 Constitution of the WHO, art 1 (1946) 14 UNTS 185. The achievement of this objective is done largely through coordination and collaboration.
25 Constitution of the WHO, para 3 of the Preamble.

like pandemics and epidemics and provide better health and well-being.[26] The Committee on Economic, Social and Cultural Rights (CESCR) has clarified the normative framework concerning the interpretation of this right.[27] The General Comment places an obligation on the government to ensure the accessibility of public health services and information.[28] It requires that public and private health service providers engage the needs of all persons including both vulnerable and marginalised groups.[29] The normative content of the right to health is informed by four cardinal principles: availability, accessibility, acceptability and appropriate quality.[30]

The right to health has to be interpreted as an inclusive right that requires the government to consider all the underlying determinants of health, without regard to underpinning the public health challenges to limit the enjoyment of the right.[31] It is argued that a national health policy that links the promotion, protection and prevention of human rights violations creates a crucial link between the normative context of the right to health and obligation on the state to ensure its protection.[32]

Under international law, the state has to use civil and political rights as a platform to further the right to health of the public and the individual.[33] This is through the fulfilment of socio-economic rights through the provision of civil and political rights.[34] The provision of the enjoyment of the right to health has to intrinsically link to other rights like the right to life, human dignity, equality and non-discrimination.[35] On the other hand, the use of the economic, social and cultural rights approach would require that the state emphasises the enjoyment of the highest attainable standard of health[36] of all persons affected by the adverse impacts of the consumption of tobacco.

26 WHO 'What we do' https://www.who.int/about/what-we-do (accessed 3 September 2021). The WHO was instituted following the adoption of the Constitution of the WHO at the International Health Conference, New York 19 June–22 July 1946, signed on 22 July 1946 by representatives of 61 states and entered into force on 7 April 1948. Subsequently amended by the Twenty-sixth, Twenty-ninth, Thirty-ninth and Fifty-first World Health Assemblies (resolutions WHA26.37, WHA29.38, WHA39.6 and WHA51.23) came into force on 3 February 1977, 20 January 1984, 11 July 1994 and 15 September 2005.

27 CESCR General Comment 14: The Right to the Highest Attainable Standard of Health (Art 12) (2000) UN Doc E/C.12/2000/4 Dated 11 August 2000.

28 As above para 26.

29 As above.

30 Moyo (n 21).

31 General Comment 14 (n 27) paras 23 and 28.

32 General Comment 14 (n 27) para 12(a).

33 HJ Steiner, P Alston & R Goodman *International human rights in context: Law, politics, morals* (2008) generally.

34 ICESCR (n 23) art 12(2)(d).

35 General Comment 14 (n 27) para 11.

36 Committee on Economic, Social and Cultural Rights 'Statement on the coronavirus disease (COVID-19) pandemic and economic, social and cultural rights' (6 April 2020).

State-adopted policies are cost-effective and they present interventions to deal with societal challenges like epidemics and poverty.[37] As indicated earlier, the WHO recognised the consumption of tobacco as a global epidemic that kills up to half of its users, which is more than 8.2 million people each year. Over 7 million of these deaths are directly due to tobacco, and 1.2 million are due to exposure to second-hand smoke. It is reported that over 80 per cent of the world's 1.3 billion tobacco users are in low and middle-income countries (LMIC). Policies that address the consumption of tobacco have to engage both a preventive and a protective approach.

4.2.2 The effect of the current laws on tobacco use

South Africa has enacted principal legislation and several regulations to deal with various aspects of controlling the use of tobacco products. The Regulations relating to the labelling, advertising and sale of tobacco products deal with the packaging and labelling of the products, other than the compliance of packaging and labelling with descriptors depicting flavours, ban the display of quantitative information on emission yields.[38] They do not speak to the mandated display of qualitative information on the constituents and emissions of tobacco products on the packaging, prevention of the display of expiry dates on tobacco packaging or mandate plain packaging.[39]

Also, the Regulations relating to smoking in public places and certain outdoor public places offer a description of a 'public place' without a corresponding prohibition to ensure enforcement of sanctions for prohibited conduct on the part of both the person smoking and the owner of the premises. Besides, the Regulations Relating to the Point of Sale of Tobacco Products defeat compliance with the FCTC by allowing adverts of the forms of existing tobacco products. This allows the purchase and subsequent use of the tobacco products by a person above 16 years of age.[40]

4.3 The FCTC as a treaty to realise the right to health at the national level

The effectiveness of the FCTC as a treaty needs to be done against the history of tobacco law in South Africa. An analysis of the tobacco law in the apartheid era and the democratic transition is done, followed by an analysis of the effectiveness in the FCTC under national law.

37 P Farmer 'Challenging orthodoxies: The road ahead for health and human rights' (2008) 10 *Health and Human Rights* 5 at 6.

38 WHO 'Report on the global tobacco epidemic, 2019: Offer help to quit tobacco use' (2020) 4.

39 As above.

40 Regulations Relating to the Point of Sale of Tobacco Products (GN R976 in GG 21610 of 29 September 2000) reg 2.

4.3.1 An analysis of the history of tobacco law in South Africa

The apartheid era relates to the tobacco laws from the 1970s to 1993, and the democratic dispensation takes on the mantle from 1994 to 2003. During the apartheid era, the government did not consider the control of tobacco as a crucial issue.[41] Between 1970 and 1990, it did little to implement excise taxes, as they fell from 50 per cent in the 1970s to 20 per cent in 1990.[42] The control of tobacco as a critical aspect in the protection of the right to health was not prioritised by the apartheid regime. First, there was no requirement for the display of health warning on the tobacco products, and second, there were no restrictions on tobacco adverts. This was partly due to the political weight that the tobacco industry enjoyed. Other than the major prohibitions on smoking in cinemas and on domestic flights in the 1970s, there was little engagement from the government.[43] The political weight was evident in the strong links that the industries and manufacturers had on government, such as Rembrandt between the 1940s and 1960s and British American Tobacco in the 1960s.[44]

As indicated, the point of departure was in the government's heightened involvement between 1993 and 2003. The first step was the enactment of the Tobacco Control Act in 1993.[45] This was furthered by the subsequent adoption of the Tobacco Control regulations by the African National Congress (ANC) government in 1994.[46] The government took on the control of the consumption of cigarettes as a racial equity issue[47] and sought to reduce their consumption as part of the improvement of public healthcare.[48] This campaign started within the confinement of government business spaces, where there was a call for smoke-free cabinet meetings. The Tobacco Act of 1993 regulated smoking in public places, prohibited tobacco sales to minors under the age of 16 and regulated some aspects of advertising like labelling.[49] The legislation required tobacco companies to display health warnings on cigarette packs, and it introduced a 50

41 C van Walbeek 'Effective development policies require political will: The example of tobacco control in South Africa' *Economics of Tobacco Control Project* (2001) https://bit.ly/3iMRWAp (accessed 12 September 2021).

42 As above. It is reported that the fluctuations in the inflation between 1970 and 1990 was between 10 and 20 per cent per year. The government never re-adjusted the excise tax to maintain its value in relation to the increasing rate of inflation.

43 D Swart & S Panday *The surveillance and monitoring of tobacco control in South Africa* (2003) https://bit.ly/2OhRxIe (accessed 10 September 2021).

44 As above.

45 Tobacco Products Control Act 83 of 1993.

46 C Ndinda & others 'The evolution of non-communicable diseases policies in post-apartheid South Africa' (2018) 18 *BMC Public Health* 1.

47 JP Wisdom & others 'Influence of the WHO framework convention on tobacco control on tobacco legislation and policies in sub-Saharan Africa' (2018) 1 *BMC Public Health* 954.

48 Van Walbeek (n 41).

49 Tobacco Products Control Act. See also P Reddy & others 'A decade of tobacco control: The South African case of politics, health policy, health promotion and behaviour change' (2013) 103 *South African Medical Journal* 835.

per cent tax on the retail price of cigarettes.[50] However, it did not engage other intricate aspects, like radio advertising and a ban in public places.[51] These shortfalls were engaged in subsequent amendments in 1999 that included a ban on all adverts and the promotion of tobacco products through sponsorship and the free distribution thereof. Also, there was a restriction on smoking in public places, such as workplaces and public transport, and a prescription of penalties for violating these prohibitions.[52]

There was a decrease in the prevalence of smoking from 32 to 28 per cent among blacks between 1993 and 2000, though it remained constant at 36 and 49 per cent among whites and coloureds.[53] There was a sharp decrease among males from 51 in 1993 to 43 per cent in 2000.[54] It is also important to note that there was a higher reduction in prevalence among the poor than among the rich.[55] These benefits are worth highlighting to show how they are interpreted in the post-implementation era of 2003. To this end, while the strides following the democratic dispensation were instructive in mitigating the consumption of tobacco products, it is instructive to see how the FCTC has been domesticated in South Africa.

4.3.2 Compliance with the FCTC

The FCTC was adopted to establish an international regulatory strategy to deal with addictive substances concerning demand reduction strategies issues of supply.[56] It offers guiding principles and obligations concerning the control of,[57] and advice on, the adoption of measures to reduce the demand[58] and supply of tobacco.[59] Other aspects include protection of the environment and the health of people,[60] issues of liability,[61] and matters of scientific and technical cooperation and communication concerning information.[62] The adoption of the FCTC in 2003 and the subsequent entry into force in 2005 underscored the need to govern the production,

50 Tobacco Products Amendment Act 12 of 1999.
51 Swart & Panday (n 43).
52 Tobacco Products Amendment Act, 1999 Regulations (GN 6689 in GG19962 of 23 April 1999).
53 C van Walbeek 'Recent trends in smoking prevalence in South Africa – Some evidence from AMPS data' (2002) 92 *South African Medical Journal* 468.
54 As above.
55 As above.
56 WHO Framework Convention on Tobacco Control https://www.who.int/fctc/text_download/en/ (accessed 12 September 2021).
57 Part II of the FCTC.
58 Part III of the FCTC.
59 Part IV of the FCTC.
60 Part V of the FCTC.
61 Part VI of the FCTC.
62 Part VII of the FCTC.

sale, distribution, advertisement and taxation of tobacco.[63] As a consequence, the FCTC would aid the reduction of the impact of tobacco on health.[64] South Africa ratified the FCTC on 19 April 2005, and it came into force on 18 July 2005.[65] The development and implementation of the treaty informed South Africa's response to the call for action on tobacco control. The extent of compliance is addressed below. It evaluates South Africa's use of the MPOWER principles on tobacco control and use. Prior to this, a juxtaposition is provided concerning the developmental trajectory informed by the dispensation from apartheid to the democratic dispensation. This is followed by a discussion of how the FCTC may be engaged.

A comparative assessment of the implementation of the FCTC in South Africa is highlighted in Table 4.1.

Table 4.1 Level of South Africa's compliance

FCTC Provision	*Equivalent Provision in South Africa (Tobacco Products Control Act 83 of 1993)*	*Compliance (Full [F], Partial [P], Not Complied [NC])*
Article 6 on Price and tax measures to reduce the demand for tobacco	Sec 2 (Tobacco Products Control Act 83 of 1993) – tax and price policies on tobacco products	Full
Article 8 on Protection from exposure to tobacco smoke	Sec 2 (Tobacco Products Control Act 83 of 1993) – complete ban on smoking in ground public transport	Partial
Article 9 on Regulation of the contents of tobacco products	Regulating the contents of tobacco products, and regulations on the emissions of tobacco products – Reg 974, notice relating to the maximum permissible yield of tar, nicotine and other constituents in tobacco products	Partial
Article 11 on Packaging and labelling of tobacco	Reg 4 – regulations relating to the labelling, advertising and sale of tobacco products. Requires that the warnings be in the principal language or languages of the country, but no ban on misleading language	Partial

63 Wisdom & others (n 47) 954.

64 As above.

65 The FCTC Implementation Database: South Africa https://untobaccocontrol.org/impldb/south-africa/ (accessed 5 August 2021).

FCTC Provision	*Equivalent Provision in South Africa (Tobacco Products Control Act 83 of 1993)*	*Compliance (Full [F], Partial [P], Not Complied [NC])*
Article 12 on Education, communication, training and public awareness	Use of full education, communication, training and public awareness	Full
Article 13 on Tobacco advertising, promotion and sponsorship	Sec 3 (Tobacco Products Control Act 83 of 1993) – no ban on cross-border tobacco advertising, promotion and sponsorship	Partial
Article 14 on Demand reduction measures concerning tobacco dependence and cessation	Diagnosis and treatment of tobacco-related diseases	Full
Article 15 on Illicit trade in tobacco products	Confiscation of proceeds derived from illicit trade. No legislation against illicit trade.	Partial
Article 16 on Sales to and by minors	Sec 4 (Tobacco Products Control Act 83 of 1993) – prohibition on sale to minors	Full
Article 17 on Provision of support for economically viable alternative activities	No promotion on economically viable alternative activities	Not compliant
Article 18 on Protection of the environment and the health of persons	No protection of the environment and the health of persons	Not compliant
Article 19 on Liability	Sec 3 (Tobacco Products Control Act 83 of 1993) – no criminal liability against tobacco companies. Liability on individuals. See also Reg 977, regulations relating to provision for exemption for unintended consequences and the phasing out of existing sponsorship or contractual obligations.	Not compliant

4.4 An assessment of the effectiveness of efforts to implement the FCTC

An assessment of the effectiveness of the laws is informed by the use of the WHO MPOWER initiative. The introduction of this mode of engaging the FCTC speaks to six aspects: (1) to monitor tobacco use and prevention policies; (2) to protect people from tobacco smoke; (3) to offer users help to quit tobacco use; (4) to warn about the dangers of tobacco; (5) to enforce bans on tobacco advertising, promotion and sponsorship; and (6) to raise taxes on tobacco.[66] A discussion of these six aspects follows (there are seven sub-paragraphs).

4.4.1 Ensuring accountability in tobacco use and prevention policies

The extent to which South Africa has engaged the MPOWER policies to deal with the six wide matters concerning the control of tobacco is instructive. As of 2020, South Africa has reported steps on its implementation five times (in 2009, 2010, 2012, 2014 and 2018).[67] The prevalence of smoking stands at among 37 per cent among males and 6.8 per cent among females.[68] However, these statistics show a greater effect on school-going children who have adopted the vice of smoking. Children are introduced to the consumption of tobacco at an early age in the family and community.[69] This invalidates the effectiveness of legislation that bans adverts that promote the use of tobacco products, restricts smoking in public places and provides penalties that follow the violation of these prohibitions.[70]

4.4.2 Protection of people from tobacco smoke

The Tobacco Products Control Act 83 of 1993 (as amended by Act 63 of 2008) (TPCA) accords people protection from tobacco smoke. First, it prohibits the smoking of any tobacco product in four instances: a public place; any area close to a window, ventilation inlet, doorway to or entrance to a public place; in a vehicle where a child under the age of 12 years is present; or any other places as prescribed by the minister.[71] Second, the TPCA places a duty on the owner or person in control of a public place or area contemplated as such to ensure that

66 WHO 'MPOWER: Six policies to reverse the tobacco epidemic' https://bit.ly/3eiGzN1 (accessed 12 September 2021).

67 Tobacco Tactics 'FCTC compliance in Africa' https://tobaccotactics.org/wiki/fctc-compliance-in-africa/ (accessed 11 September 2021).

68 As above.

69 As above.

70 Tobacco Products Amendment Act, 1999 Regulations (n 52).

71 Tobacco Products Control Act, secs 3(1) and (3).

no person smokes in the aforementioned area.[72] Third, the minister's discretion to prohibit smoking at any other prescribed outdoor public place may extend to areas where there are hazards.[73] Fourth, the owner or person in control of a public place is mandated to display signs and make prescribed public announcements on the prohibition on smoking.[74]

This position is reinforced by the regulations that govern smoking areas. To this end, the Regulations prepared under section 2 of the TPCA are called the Regulations relating to smoking in public places and certain outdoor public places.[75] They identify a public place to include stadiums, arenas, sports facilities, playgrounds, zoos,[76] schools or child care facilities,[77] health facilities,[78] and outdoor eating or drinking areas.[79] Public areas include venues when outdoor events take place,[80] covered walkways and covered parking areas,[81] and service areas and service lines. Others include beaches where public bathing is permitted, not less than 50 metres away from the closest person near the demarcated swimming area.[82] These examples are in line with the FCTC-designated places.[83] However, the description or definition of these public places is not sufficient if the laws on the protection of people from the dangers of tobacco in these areas are not effective.

It is further argued that the existence of ventilation or the use of designated smoking rooms does not protect one from the harms of second-hand tobacco smoke.[84] The Regulations state:

> No person shall smoke any tobacco product within a 10 metre distance from a window of, ventilation inlet of, doorway to or entrance into a public place.

This prohibition does not apply to any person who is temporarily within the area while actively passing through such area.[85]

72 Tobacco Products Control Act, secs 3(2).
73 Tobacco Products Control Act, secs 3(3).
74 Tobacco Products Control Act, secs 3(4).
75 Regulations relating to smoking in public places and certain outdoor public places (GR 264 GN 35198 in GG 35198 of 30 March 2012).
76 Regulation 2(2)(a).
77 Regulation 2(2)(b).
78 Regulation 2(2)(c).
79 Regulation 2(2)(d).
80 Regulation 2(2)(e).
81 Regulation 2(2)(f).
82 Regulation 2(2)(g).
83 WHO report (n 38) 3.
84 As above.
85 Regulations relating to smoking in public places and certain outdoor public places (n 75) reg 4(a) and (b).

While the regulation provides a prohibition, it is tainted with a self-defeating clause that does not apply to the person who is actively passing through the area. It is argued that this means that enforcing this law to prosecute a person who is simply passing through the public area is very subjective and prone to human error or abuse. The simple prohibition not to smoke in a public place should be sufficient without the need for qualification in the application of the regulation.

Besides, there is no law concerning fines for smoking on the establishments and the smoker, exacerbated by lack of funds for enforcement.[86] According to the regulations under review, the closest form of an iota of liability is in the format of this warning:

> The sign referred to in sub-regulation (3) shall: . . . (b) carry the warning: 'ANY PERSON WHO FAILS TO COMPLY WITH THIS NOTICE SHALL BE PROSECUTED AND MAY BE LIABLE TO A FINE'. written in black letters, at least 2 cm in height and 1,5 cm in breadth, on a white background.[87]

The provision of the format of a warning and a possible legal sanction without a corresponding provision that unpacks the criminal conduct and the punishment is a silence of the Regulations relating to smoking in public places and certain outdoor public places.

A reconciliation of the TPCA and the Regulations reveals promising legislation that has challenges in implementation. The FCTC requires States parties' to enact and enforce completely smoke-free environments in various designated places.[88] These include healthcare and educational facilities, and indoor public places like workplaces, restaurants and bars.[89] It is argued that the protection of people from tobacco smoke has received minimal compliance with the FCTC. While South Africa has placed complete smoke-free laws in specifically designated places,[90] the term 'complete' means that smoking is not permitted, with no exemptions allowed.[91] This points to the need to evaluate to which extent this is implemented. There is a lot of smoking in public places and on public transport, and there is very minimal implementation to counter it, leading to weak policy engagement on the protection of people from tobacco smoke and non-compliance on the part of South Africa.[92]

86 WHO report (n 38) 3.

87 Regulations relating to smoking in public places and certain outdoor public places (n 75) reg 3(4)(b).

88 WHO MPOWER (n 66) 12.

89 As above.

90 WHO report (n 38) 3.

91 As above.

92 As above.

4.4.3 Offer to help quit tobacco use

The TPCA and the various regulations are silent on the offer to help quit smoking. However, there are national policies that call for an inclusion of smoke cessation advice to persons who smoke.[93] This initiative requires a strengthening of health systems to enable them to provide tobacco cessation advice as part of primary healthcare.[94] This has been heightened through the use of support quit-lines and societal initiatives that are accessible and affordable.[95] There is treatment of tobacco dependence through the listing of nicotine replacement therapy as essential drugs and its use through items like gum, lozenges and patches.[96] While some of the essential available drugs include bupropion and varenicline, they are not covered by the national insurance scheme.[97] To this end, there is a moderate policy engagement on the offer to help quit tobacco use.[98]

4.4.4 Warning about the dangers of tobacco

The TPCA does not provide substantive information about the placing of warnings on the dangers of tobacco. However, it provides that the minister may make regulations concerning health warnings that ought to appear on the packaging, their size, format, location of the signs and the legal age at which tobacco products may be purchased.[99] As such, the Regulations relating to the labelling, advertising and sale of tobacco products provide the enabling provisions on the engagement of warnings about tobacco.[100] They require that the warning should be in the wording in column A of Annexure 1 to the Regulations, positioned in a manner described in column B of Annexure 1.[101] In addition, the warning shall be for the duration described in column C of Annexure 1 and position and fill the area indicated in column D of Annexure 1.[102]

93 For instance, the National Council Against Smoking offers various initiatives. See National Council Against Smoking 'Quit smoking' https://bit.ly/33ys3Pu (accessed 7 September 2021).

94 WHO MPOWER (n 66) 12.

95 As above.

96 For more information on nicotine replacement therapy, see J Hartmann-Boyce & others 'Nicotine replacement therapy versus control for smoking cessation' (2018) 5 *Cochrane Database of Systematic Reviews* 1. WHO report (n 38) 3.

97 WHO report (n 38) 3.

98 WHO report (n 38) 6.

99 The Tobacco Products Control Act, sec 6(1).

100 Regulations relating to the labelling, advertising and sale of tobacco products provide the enabling provisions on the engagement of warnings about tobacco (GN 2063 in GG 16111 of 2 December 1994, as amended by GN R1148 in GG 16588 of 4 August 1995) regs 2, 3 and 4.

101 Regulation 2(1)(a) and (b) generally.

102 Regulation 2(1)(c) generally.

It is argued that South Africa's current Regulations on warnings, labelling, advertising and sale of tobacco do not deal with the compliance of packaging and labelling with descriptors depicting flavours, or a ban on display of quantitative information on emission yields.[103] There is no law on the mandated display of qualitative information on the constituents and emissions of tobacco products on the packaging, prevention of the display of expiry dates on tobacco packaging or mandate plain packaging.[104] There are no reported anti-tobacco mass media campaigns from July 2016 to June 2018.

The FCTC expects a triple approach that engages effective package warning labels, implementation of counter-tobacco advertising and the use of free media coverage of anti-tobacco activities.[105] South Africa's stance on warnings about the dangers of using tobacco also shows a weak policy engagement. South Africa has registered some compliance in this area in various aspects.[106] It has been indicated that the legally mandated health, unobscured warning in principal languages cover about 20 per cent of the packaging, at the top, in the required font size, and around the pack.[107] However, there is a lack of compliance concerning the omission of a photograph or graphic of the dangers of the use of tobacco.[108] From an overall perspective, there is weak policy engagement on the issues of warnings on the dangers of tobacco.[109]

4.4.5 *Enforcement of bans on tobacco advertising, promotion and sponsorship*

The TPCA provides for bans of various forms of advertising, promotion and sponsorship, stating:

> No person shall advertise or promote, or cause any other person to advertise or promote, a tobacco product through any direct or indirect means, including through sponsorship of any organisation, event, service, physical establishment, programme, project, bursary, scholarship or any other method.[110]

103 WHO report (n 38) 4.
104 As above.
105 WHO MPOWER (n 66) 12.
106 Regulations relating to the labelling, advertising, and sale of tobacco products deal with the packaging and labelling of the products (n 100) regs 2, 3 and 4.
107 As above.
108 WHO report (n 38) 4.
109 As above.
110 The Tobacco Products Control Act, sec 3(1)(a).

It states further:

> No manufacturer, importer, distributor or retailer of tobacco products shall –
>
> (a) organise or promote any organised activity that is to take place in whole or in part in the Republic;
> (b) make any financial contribution to any organised activity that is to take place, or is taking place, or has taken place in whole or in part in the Republic;
> (c) make any financial contribution to any person in respect of –
>
> (i) the organisation or promotion of any organised activity in the Republic by that person;
> (ii) the participation, by that person, in any organised activity that is to take place, or is taking place in whole or in part, in the Republic.[111]

In addition:

> No person shall package or label a tobacco product in any way that is false, misleading, deceptive or likely to create any erroneous, deceptive or misleading impression about its characteristics, properties, health effects, toxicity, composition, merit, safety, hazards or emissions, including any term, descriptor, trade mark, figurative or other sign that directly or indirectly creates the impression that a particular tobacco product is less harmful than another tobacco product.[112]

These provisions point to the holistic attempt to curb the mode of adverts, promotions or forms of sponsorship that may be used to extend the dangers of smoking. It is argued that this is in part in line with the FCTC's requirement that a state enacts and enforces effective legislation that systematically bans any form of direct tobacco advertising, promotion and sponsorship on the one hand, and enacts and enforces effective legislation to ban indirect tobacco advertising, promotion and sponsorship on the other.[113]

Without prejudice to the foregoing, the use of bans on direct tobacco advertising was missing on international television, radio, magazines, newspapers and points of sale.[114] The bans on tobacco promotion and sponsorship did not extend to sponsorship contributions, their publicity or corporate social responsibility activities.[115]

111 The Tobacco Products Control Act, sec 3(2).
112 The Tobacco Products Control Act, sec 3(6).
113 The FCTC, art 11; WHO MPOWER (n 66) 12.
114 WHO report (n 38) 6.
115 As above.

In addition, there are no laws that ban the display of tobacco products at the points of sale or tobacco vending machines.[116] To this end, South Africa's laws actively provide for adverts at the points of sale. The Regulations Relating to the Point of Sale of Tobacco Products state:

> A retailer of tobacco products may indicate the availability of tobacco products and their price only by means of signs at the point of sale that –
>
> (a) do not exceed one square metre in size; and
> (b) are placed within one metre of the point of sale.[117]
>
> All signs that indicate the availability of tobacco products and their price must contain the following messages in letters that are at least two cm in height and 1,5 cm in width – (a) 'WE CANNOT, BY LAW, SELL TOBACCO PRODUCTS TO ANYONE UNDER THE AGE OF 16 YEARS'; this message must appear at the top of the sign and across its full width; and (b) a health message as contained in Annexure A of these Regulations.[118]

This provision to advertise the forms of existing tobacco products notwithstanding the prohibition to sell to persons below 16 years of age is also self-defeating, as it allows the purchase and subsequent use of tobacco products by a person above 16 years of age.

However, the effective bans on national television, radio, magazines, newspapers, billboards and outdoors, the internet and the existence of a law providing for fines showed progress on this front.[119] This was further evident in the existence of bans on free distribution, promotional discounts, non-tobacco products associated with tobacco names and the appearance of tobacco products on television and in movies.[120] Other areas of compliance included the complete ban on sponsorships.[121] This is evident in the provisions for the exemption for unintended consequences and the phasing out of existing sponsorship or contractual obligations.[122] However, South Africa opted for a more systematic phasing out of existing sponsorship and contractual obligations.[123] Despite the moderate engagement of this principle, this is a good practice that other countries may emulate.[124]

116 As above.
117 Regulations Relating to the Point of Sale of Tobacco Products, reg 2.
118 Reg 3.
119 WHO report (n 38) 6.
120 As above.
121 As above.
122 Regulations relating to provision for exemption for unintended consequences and the phasing out of existing sponsorship or contractual obligations (GN R977 in GG 21610 of 29 September 2000).
123 Regs 2, 3, 4, 5, 6 and 7.
124 WHO report (n 38) 6.

4.4.6 Raising taxes on tobacco

State parties have to increase tax rates for tobacco products and ensure periodic adjustment to keep pace with inflation and rise faster than the consumer purchasing power.[125] In addition, it is expected that the state strengthens tax administration to reduce the illicit trade in tobacco.[126] South Africa has achieved moderate policy compliance, as it has collected 54.6 per cent on taxes from the retail price of tobacco products, in the form of 41.6 per cent in excise tax and 13 per cent in value added tax.[127] While the taxes on tobacco are effective in reducing or stopping the use of tobacco, there has been an escalation in the consumption of tobacco despite the increase in tobacco prices. This is because the increase in the excise taxes has not been matched to the increase in inflation.[128] The increase in the use of tobacco is also associated with the increase in illicit trade in tobacco-related products.[129]

It should be added that the use of raising taxes as a means of controlling the use of tobacco is a good practice that other countries may emulate.[130] The major challenge that follows the attempts to control tobacco includes the adoption of the WHO MPOWER strategy without tailoring it to the needs of the country. For instance, enforcement of bans is greatly targeted to public areas like places of work and public transport. It should be recalled that these places usually involve adults. The children who form 23 per cent of the learners who consume tobacco are not adequately targeted. As such, the social setting where caregivers allow youth and children to consume tobacco products exacerbates the situation.[131] A systematic policy review carried out across the world using data from the Global Youth Tobacco Survey indicates that most national policies have been guided by WHO MPOWER strategies. However, the policies are not necessarily targeted at the youth.[132]

4.4.7 Monitor tobacco use and prevention policies

South Africa, like other signatories to the FCTC, monitors tobacco use and preventive policies through obtaining nationally representative and population-based

125 WHO MPOWER (n 66) 12.

126 As above.

127 As above 12.

128 For more details on excise tax and tobacco use in South Africa, see DJ Linegar & C van Walbeek 'The effect of excise tax increases on cigarette prices in South Africa' (2018) 27 *Tobacco Control* 65.

129 N Vellios, C van Walbeek & H Ross *Illicit cigarette trade in South Africa: 2002–2017* (2019).

130 WHO report (n 38) 6.

131 CL Ranabhat & others 'Situation, impacts and future challenges of tobacco control policies for youth: Systematic policy review' (2019) 10 *Frontiers in Pharmacology* 1.

132 As above 1–13.

periodic data on key indicators of tobacco use for youth and adults.[133] While the data indicates a recent survey of the adults, the same cannot be said of the youth. The tobacco use prevalence indicates that 30.4 of males and 6.3 per cent of females smoke tobacco daily.[134] The data also show that 6.4 of males and 1.3 per cent of females use smokeless tobacco.[135] The point of departure is in the lack of data on tobacco use, smoking and e-cigarette use among the youth. In addition, the shortfall is in the lack of similar desegregated data concerning the youth. According to the South African National Youth Risk Behaviour Survey of 2011,[136] 15.3 per cent of male youths smoke cigarettes and 9.1 per cent use smokeless tobacco.[137] As to female youths, 11.0 per cent smoke cigarettes and 6.9 use smokeless tobacco.[138] These figures lack data on tobacco use and cigarette smoking and e-cigarettes daily.[139] As of 2019, there is minimal policy engagement on this initiative.[140]

4.5 The court's approach to tobacco control

Before looking at the decisions, it is important to appreciate the methodology used to arrive at the decisions that inform this research. The study uses the major website that provides for a great number of decisions from the South African courts.[141] A search on the website with South African documents using the term 'tobacco' returned 470 results.[142] A look at the cases from South Africa from the superior courts (the High Court, the Supreme Court of Appeal and the Constitutional Court) and the labour courts returned 283 cases.[143] This still offered a very high number of cases to be engaged in the study. The author then opted to use key terms such as 'tobacco FCTC', 'British American Tobacco', 'monitoring tobacco use', 'protection from tobacco' and warnings about the dangers of tobacco and employment. Other terms that the author uses to identify the cases

133 WHO 'MPOWER: A policy package to reverse the tobacco epidemic' https://www.afro.who.int/publications/mpower-policy-package-reverse-tobacco-epidemic (accessed 13 September 2021).

134 WHO report (n 38); Country Profile: South Africa at 2. This data is as per the Demographic and Health Survey as at 2016.

135 As above.

136 WHO report (n 38) 2.

137 As above.

138 As above.

139 A look at the emphasis of South Africa's policies is available here: Tobacco Control Laws 'Legislation by country: South Africa' https://www.tobaccocontrollaws.org/legislation/country/south-africa/summary (12 September 2021).

140 WHO report (n 38) 2.

141 The study engages a search on google.com at https://bit.ly/303rNEQ, and the results indicate that the major site South African cases is saflii.org (all accessed 13 September 2021).

142 SAFLII results on 'tobacco' https://bit.ly/30drU0w (accessed 13 September 2021).

143 As above. The labour court is included because of cases that emanate from employers and employees.

included enforcement of bans on and raising taxes on tobacco.[144] As will be shown, this led to the identification of four cases.[145] The cases relate to the enforcement of bans on tobacco use and the protection of people from tobacco smoke.

4.5.1 Protection of people from tobacco smoke

Protection of people from tobacco smoke occurs in all public spaces. The decisions that have been handed down primarily stem from the Commission of Conciliation, Mediation and Arbitration (CCMA). One may argue that the CCMA only deals with labour disputes. It is stated that where some of the disputes question the extent to which employers as third parties have a role to ensure the protection of employees from tobacco smoke, this falls squarely within this research. To this end, the Labour Relations Act 66 of 1995 establishes the CCMA that is at the level of the High Court and mandates it to resolve disputes referred to it.[146] Some of the disputes include alleged unfair dismissal or suspension and other work-related grievances.

In *National Union of Metalworkers of SA on Behalf of Bhulwana and Boardman Brothers (Pty) Ltd*, the factory owners banned smoking on the factory premises without consulting the workers or the workers' union.[147] As a result, one of the workers who was found smoking on the premises was suspended for 17 days. The union took the matter to the CCMA for unlawful dismissal, stating that the imposition of the rule without consultation was a unilateral change to the terms and conditions of employment.[148] The union engaged a factual analysis that indicated that the smoking policy was inconsistently used at the workplace, as senior staff smoked at will whereas low-end employees could only do so during lunch breaks.[149] The respondent argued that smoking was not a term of employment, and their decision to impose restrictions on smoking in the workplace was justified by the law.[150] In addition, the respondent added that the rule to restrict smoking in the workplace related to the corporate responsibility towards the health of its workers.[151]

144 With regard to key terms a search using the keywords 'tobacco FCTC' https://bit.ly/32i0idi (accessed 13 September 2021) led to the identification of *British American Tobacco South Africa v Minister of Health*. The results returned on the search on monitoring tobacco use, protection of people from tobacco use, and help to quit tobacco use did not yield any usable results.

145 Other cases on British American Tobacco were not related to the study. A look at the results' search at https://bit.ly/2WoFHQO (accessed 13 September 2021) related to the competitions' tribunal, pension fund, trademarks and intellectual property and distribution agreements.

146 Sec 112.

147 (2004) 25 ILJ 2258 (BCA).

148 *National Union of Metalworkers of SA* (n 147) 2259.

149 As above 2260.

150 As above.

151 As above.

The main issues that the arbitrator had to decide were: first, whether the imposition of a no-smoking rule for the respondent's entire factory premises without prior consultation or agreement with the employees or the union constitutes a unilateral change to a term or condition of employment; and second, whether the respondent acted fairly by suspending the applicant for allegedly smoking on the respondent's premises.[152] While these issues at face value do not speak to the protection of people from tobacco, the findings do. The arbitrator found that the total ban on smoking in the workplace was not a unilateral variation or change to working conditions because of the lack of a contractual entitlement to smoke at the workplace, and more importantly, the employer has the discretion to either designate a portion of a public place as a smoking area or to prohibit smoking in that place.[153] It appears that other than using the labour laws as a guide to determine the right of the worker in the workplace, the arbitrator chose the primary legislation and policies that govern the protection of people from tobacco smoke.[154] By implication, the arbitrator engaged the right to equality for all workers by ensuring that no smoking would take place, and more importantly, if it deemed fit it would create a special section in its discretion for the smokers to do so. The reiteration that smoking is not a contractual aspect of employment underscored the resolve to concretise the government's efforts to deter the habit in the public spaces.[155]

In *Coetzee v Sinakho Staff Shop (Pty) Ltd*,[156] after the applicant's tenure as a consultant for the respondent, she resigned and took the matter to the CCMA on grounds that the respondent was liable for the deterioration of her health due to the failure to enforce rules on non-smoking in the public place.[157] She claimed that due to the laxity with which other members of staff smoked around her office and the lack of a no-smoke policy, the applicant contracted asthma.[158] The respondent claimed that he did not know about the applicant's deteriorating health due to smoking in the workplace because she did not file a grievance.[159] He added that he was not aware of other members of staff who used to smoke at the front door.[160] The arbitrator established that the applicant never called the medical doctor to testify to substantiate her documentary evidence. First, this is an indication that the failure of the applicant in informing the employer about the effects of the smoke from other members of staff could not amount to

152 As above.
153 As above.
154 See sec 3 of the Tobacco Control Act 1993.
155 For a detailed analysis of this case from the context of smoking in the workplace, see generally JD Mujuzi 'Smoking in the workplace in South Africa: Law and practice relating to the rights and obligations of employers and employees' (2010) 3 *South African Journal of Bioethics and Law* 79.
156 *Coetzee v Sinakho Staff Shop (Pty) Ltd* (2009) JOL 24414 (CCMA).
157 As above 2.
158 As above 3.
159 As above 6.
160 As above 7.

constructive dismissal. Second, for the applicant's allegations to stand, she had to adduce medical evidence to prove the adverse effects of smoking on her health. It is argued that this case was not decided correctly because the CCMA placed an evidentiary burden on the applicant to prove the dangers she suffered despite the clear position that the government has to take initiatives to protect people from tobacco smoke. While the need for proof is important, it does not take away from the fact that the CCMA could have on its own accord called the author of the medical letter to testify. It is argued further that the negation of employee liability without clear proof of implementation of a non-smoking policy is something that the CCMA could have gone to lengths to test its veracity.[161] If the court had engaged the human right to health as a preventive measure that protects people from tobacco, it would have arrived at a different conclusion.

In the similar case of *Naudi v Stealth Marine*,[162] the applicant was employed by the respondent as a receptionist. Unlike the facts in *Coetzee*, where the employee was diagnosed with asthma, Naudi had respiratory problems and other serious health conditions like asthma attacks due to smoking. These underlying problems caused her to stop smoking.[163] The appellant argued that there were no designated smoking areas on the premises, and the constant smoking led to health complications on her part.[164] Despite her complaints to the senior managers, the latter continued to condone the practice themselves by smoking on the premises.[165] Attempts at filing formal complaints were not adhered to, and she had to terminate her employment.[166] She brought this matter before the CCMA to establish whether the conduct of the employer amounted to constructive dismissal. As indicated earlier, this study looks at whether the CCMA engaged the Tobacco Control Act or a human rights approach in its decisions. It was established that save for the conduct of the respondent, the applicant would not have resigned.[167] In addition, the respondent had a duty to designate smoking areas and ensure that the law was complied with. As such, despite the ill health of the applicant as a previous smoker, the respondent made the working conditions of the applicant unbearable, and as such his actions were unlawful and unfair.[168] From a holistic perspective, the conduct of the respondent amounted to unlawful dismissal. In the context of this case, it can be argued that where an employee receives information about the lack of protection from tobacco smoke, and he does nothing or condones it, he is liable. Besides the right to health, dignity is implicitly echoed strongly.

161 As above.
162 (2004) 25 ILJ 2402 (BCA).
163 As above 2403.
164 As above.
165 As above.
166 As above 2404.
167 As above.
168 As above 2405.

4.5.2 *Enforcement of bans on tobacco advertising, promotion and sponsorship*

In *British American Tobacco South Africa (Pty) Ltd v Minister of Health*,[169] the Supreme Court of Appeal was tasked to offer guidance on the interpretation of section 3(1)(a) of the Tobacco Products Control Act 83 of 1993 (as amended by Act 63 of 2008) concerning the definitions of 'advertise' and 'promotion'. It was argued by the appellant that the prohibition of 'advertising' and 'promotion' in the Act was overly broad and that an interpretation that extended to one-to-one communications was unconstitutional.[170] The appellant also argued that the prohibition limited freedom of speech as guaranteed by section 16(1) of the Constitution.[171] For purpose of context, section 3(1)(a) of the Act states:

> No person shall advertise or promote, or cause any other person to advertise or promote, a tobacco product through any direct or indirect means, including through sponsorship of any organisation, event, service, physical establishment, programme, project, bursary, scholarship or any other method.

Also, advertisement

> means any commercial communication or action brought to the attention of any member of the public in any manner with the aim, effect or likely effect of – promoting the sale or use of any tobacco product, tobacco product brand element or tobacco manufacturer's name in relation to a tobacco product; or . . . (c) excludes commercial communication between a tobacco manufacturer or importer and its trade partners, business partners, employees and shareholders and any communications required by law.[172]

Promotion refers to

> the practice of fostering awareness of and positive attitudes towards a tobacco product, brand element or manufacturer for purposes of selling the tobacco product or encouraging tobacco use, through various means, including direct advertisement, incentives, free distribution, entertainment, organised activities, marketing of brand elements by means of related events and products through any public medium of communication including cinematographic film, television production, radio production or the internet.[173]

169 *BATSA v Minister of Health* [2012] 3 All SA 593 (SCA).
170 *BATSA* (n 169) para 12.
171 As above.
172 Tobacco Products Control Act, sec 1.
173 As above.

The appellant, British American Tobacco, was concerned that the amendment had an impact on its ability to communicate one-to-one with consenting adult consumers of tobacco products and would greatly affect its businesses.[174] Furthermore, this amendment limited the appellant's right to engage in commercial expression on one hand, and the consumers' (tobacco users') freedom of expression through the denial of the right to receive information concerning tobacco products on the other.[175]

The respondent argued that the Department of Health was committed to the government's stance at limiting and preventing the spread of tobacco usage among South Africans since 1994. This was informed by the global growth concerns about the extremely harmful effects of tobacco on both smokers and those exposed to secondary smoke. This gradual trend from restricting smoking in public places and certain forms of tobacco advertising[176] extended to further restrictions on tobacco usage and advertising.[177] The respondent argued further that these restrictions sought to prevent the use of tobacco, especially by the youth, and reduce the number of existing smokers.[178] The government also sought to ensure that those who stop smoking do not revert to the practice and to protect non-smokers from exposure to second-hand smoke.[179]

The issue that the Court ultimately had to decide was whether the right to freedom of speech by the appellant and the right to receive information by the tobacco users could be limited under section 36 of the Constitution.[180] One point that comes across strongly is the fact the respondent's call for justification was not based on facts before the court, but rather policy considerations that sought to mitigate and control the effects of tobacco use. It would appear this potentially dangerous situation was engaged using similar principles concerning the limitation analysis. In *Minister of Home Affairs v Nicro*,[181] Chaskalson CJ stated:

> This [meaning the limitation analysis] calls for a different enquiry to that conducted when factual disputes have to be resolved. In a justification analysis facts and policy are often intertwined. There may for instance be cases where the concerns to which the legislation is addressed are subjective and not capable of proof as objective facts. A legislative choice is not always subject to courtroom fact-finding and may be based on reasonable inferences

174 *BATSA* (n 169) para 6.
175 As above para 12. The appellant relied on *City of Cape Town v Ad Outpost (Pty) Limiteds* 2000 (2) SA 733 (C) at 749D–E and *North Central Local Council and South Central Local Council v Roundabout Outdoor (Pty) Ltd* 2002 (2) SA 625 (D) at 633D–E. It was held that the right to freedom of expression can be interpreted as 'commercial speech' protected under sec 16(1) of the Constitution.
176 Tobacco Products Control Act.
177 As above.
178 *BATSA* (n 169) para 20.
179 As above.
180 As above para 21.
181 2005 (3) SA 280 (CC).

> unsupported by empirical data. When policy is in issue it may not be possible to prove that a policy directed to a particular concern will be effective. It does not necessarily follow from this, however, that the policy is not reasonable and justifiable. If the concerns are of sufficient importance, the risks associated with them sufficiently high, and there is sufficient connection between means and ends, that may be enough to justify action taken to address them.[182]

On this basis, the court found that in light of the dangers of smoking, the limitation on the right to freedom of speech was reasonable and justifiable in an open and democratic society based on human dignity, equality and freedom, taking into account the relevant factors, including the nature of the right, the importance of the limitation and its nature and extent.[183] The balancing was based on the weighing of the hazards of smoking against the interests of the smokers as a group.[184]

The Court adopted an interpretational approach that aided the evaluation of the limitation. The court found that as long as the interpretation was not fanciful and far-fetched, it was prudent to evaluate the effect of what the appellant sought to communicate to the purchasers of its product.[185] To this end, all the communications that the appellant sought to make were designed to promote the sale of its product and to maintain the mischief which the Act was designed to combat.[186] This entrenched the call to find the limitation as reasonable and justified under section 36(1) of the Constitution. It would appear from this decision that the Court took a human rights approach that recognised the existence of a constitutional right in favour of corporations that deal in tobacco, but found that the limitations outweigh the dangers from the consumption of tobacco.

Concerning the enforcement of bans on tobacco advertising, promotion and sponsorship, there is a snail-paced engagement between the state and the courts. While the state places reliance on the legislative provisions, it would appear that the evaluation of the constitutionality of the provisions brings to the fore the issue of limitation of rights. It suffices to state that until a matter is brought to court, legislation that condones the continued adverts of use of tobacco products in other places like the points of sale will continue undeterred. In addition, the cases reflect a limited engagement on other aspects, like monitoring tobacco use and prevention policies, warning about the dangers of tobacco and raising taxes on tobacco. The author is not aware of court direction on deliberate policies that offer to quit tobacco use on the part of tobacco users other than engaging this from the position of the manufacturers of tobacco products.

182 Para 35.
183 *BATSA* (n 169) para 26.
184 As above.
185 As above para 28.
186 As above.

4.6 Conclusion and recommendations

The transition from apartheid to democracy foresaw a government take deliberate efforts to control the consumption of tobacco products. This was greatly informed by the lack of government links to the manufacturers of tobacco products and the adoption of various amendments to the Tobacco Control Act of 1993 from 1994 to date. The ratification of the FCTC and the use of the MPOWER initiative has foreseen the creation of a bar that South Africa has to adhere to or exceed. It is apparent following the recent reports to the FCTC that there is little compliance with these standards.

This is evident in the weak policy engagement of monitoring tobacco use and prevention policies, protection of people from tobacco smoke and issues of warnings on the dangers of tobacco. However, there is moderate compliance with the offer to help quit tobacco use, enforcement of bans on tobacco advertising promotion and sponsorship and the raising of taxes. A look at selected decisions shows that the courts have offered insights on the protection of people from tobacco smoke and enforcement of bans on tobacco advertising, promotion and sponsorship. The executive, legislative and judicial arms of government have jointly registered successes on the protection of people from tobacco smoke and enforcement of bans on tobacco advertising, promotion and sponsorship.

It is recommended that there should be a shift from the erstwhile known dangers of tobacco that are reiterated by the government, stakeholders and the companies that produce it, to an emphasis on the human being. To develop this recommendation further, earlier research shows that when dealing with a human subject, it is prudent to ask not just the question but the right question to the subject.[187] They argue that in the development of jurisprudence on the rights of women, one should not just ask the 'woman question' but the 'African woman question'.[188] A look at these decisions presents various human principles. First, the court is always ready to apply the constitutional limitation clause, even in instances where it is faced with matters of policy other than the usual factual issues. Second, when courts are faced with matters of tobacco (ab)use, they should use a three-step approach: (1) identify the human rights that are violated, (2) relate them to the FCTC principles and (3) balance the findings with any other relevant matters. This will inform the use of a human rights–centred approach in engaging the FCTC and MPOWER initiatives.

Much remains to be done for this approach to be viable. A deliberate empirical study that identifies the extent of the danger of tobacco smoke to vulnerable persons like children, women and the elderly needs to be done on a national

187 For instance, Durojaye and Oluduro conduct research on improving the person of the African woman, and they argue that one has to ask not just the woman but the right woman question. See E Durojaye & O Oluduro 'The African commission on human and peoples' rights and the woman question' (2016) 24 *Feminist Legal Studies* 315.

188 Durojaye & Oluduro (n 187) 315.

level to inform the directions of policy development. Besides, there should be a shift of emphasis from the dangers that the producers of tobacco present to the dangers that people face. This will aid the deliberate development and tailoring of policies that lead to compliance with the FCTC in South Africa's situational setting.

Bibliography

BATSA v Minister of Health [2012] 3 All SA 593 (SCA)

Cancer.Net 'Health risks of e-cigarettes, smokeless tobacco, and waterpipes' https://bit.ly/2Ob8p3i (accessed 27 September 2021)

CESCR General Comment 14: The Right to the Highest Attainable Standard of Health (Art 12) (11 August 2000) UN Doc E/C.12/2000/4 (2000)

City of Cape Town v Ad Outpost (Pty) Limited 2000 (2) SA 733 I

Coetzee v Sinakho Saff Shop (Pty) Ltd (2009) JOL 24414 (CCMA)

Committee on Economic, Social and Cultural Rights 'Statement on the coronavirus disease (COVID-19) pandemic and economic, social and cultural rights' (6 April 2020)

Constitution of the Republic of South Africa, 1996

Constitution of the WHO, Art 1 1 (1946) 14 UNTS 185

Durojaye, E & Oluduro, E 'The African commission on human and peoples' rights and the woman question' (2016) 24 *Feminist Legal Studies* 315

Farmer, P 'Challenging orthodoxies: The road ahead for health and human rights' (2008) 10 *Health and Human Rights* 6

FCTC 'Implementation Database: South Africa' https://bit.ly/2Xabsqy (accessed 27 September 2021)

Hartmann-Boyce, J; Chepkin, SC; Ye, W; Bullen, C & Lancaster, T 'Nicotine replacement therapy versus control for smoking cessation' (2018) 5 *Cochrane Database of Systematic Reviews* 1

International Covenant on Economic and Social Rights 966 UNTS 3

Linegar, DJ & Van Walbeek, C 'The effect of excise tax increases on cigarette prices in South Africa' (2018) 27 *Tobacco Control* 65

Mayosi, BM; Flisher, AJ; Lalloo, UG; Sitas, F; Tollman, SM & Bradshaw, D 'The burden of noncommunicable diseases in South Africa' (2009) 374 *Lancet* 935

Minister of Home Affairs v Nicro 2005 (3) SA 280 (CC)Moreno, MA 'Risks of hookah smoking' (2015) 169 *JAMA Pediatrics* 196

Moyo, K 'Realising the right to health in South Africa' in *Socio-economic rights – Progressive realisation?* (Foundation for Human Rights 2016) http://www.fhr-mirror.org.za/files/7215/1247/1732/Health.pdf (accessed 27 September 2021)

Mujuzi, JD 'Smoking in the workplace in South Africa: Law and practice relating to the rights and obligations of employers and employees' (2010) 3 *South African Journal of Bioethics and Business Law* 79

National Council Against Smoking 'Helping you quit' https://bit.ly/33ys3Pu (accessed 27 September 2021)

National Union of Metalworkers of SA on behalf of Bhulwana and Boardman Brothers (Pty) Ltd (2004) 25 ILJ 2258 (BCA)

Naude v Stealth Marine (2004) 25 ILJ 2402 (BCA)

Ndinda, C; Ndhlovu, TP; Juma, P; Asiki, G & Kyobutungi, C 'The evolution of non-communicable diseases policies in post-apartheid South Africa' (2018) 18 *BMC Public Health* 1

North Central Local Council and South Central Local Council v Roundabout Outdoor (Pty) Ltd 2002 (2) SA 625 (D)

Ranabhat, CL; Kim, CB; Park, MB & Jakovljevic, MM 'Situation, impacts and future challenges of tobacco control policies for youth: systematic policy review' (2019) 10 *Frontiers in Pharmacology* 1

Reddy, P; James, S; Sewpaul, R; Yach, D; Resnicow, K; Sifunda, S; Mthembu, Z & Mbewu, A 'A decade of tobacco control: The South African case of politics, health policy, health promotion and behaviour change' (2013) 103 *South African Medical Journal* 835

Reddy, P; Zuma, K; Shisana, O; Jonas, K & Sewpaul, R 'Prevalence of tobacco use among adults in South Africa: Results from the first South African national health and nutrition examination survey' (2015) 105 *South African Medical Journal* 648

Regulations Relating to the Labeling, Advertising, and Sale of Tobacco Products Deal with the Packaging and Labeling of the Products (GN 2063 in GG 16111 of 2 December 1994 as Amended by GN R1148 in GG 16588 of 4 August 1995)

Regulations Relating to the Point of Sale of Tobacco Products (GN R976 in GG 21610 of 29 September 2000)

Regulations Relating to Smoking in Public Places and Certain Outdoor Public Places (GR 264 in GG 35198 of 30 March 2012)

Steiner, HJ; Alston, P & Goodman, R *International human rights in context: Law, politics, morals* (Oxford University Press 2008)

Swart, D & Panday, S *The surveillance and monitoring of tobacco control in South Africa* (World Health Organization) https://bit.ly/2OhRxIe (accessed 12 September 2021)

Tobacco and your health https://https://bit.ly/2VY8YS3 (accessed 12 September 2021)

Tobacco Control Laws 'Legislation by country: South Africa' https://www.tobaccocontrollaws.org/legislation/country/south-africa/summaryhttps://bit.ly/3eiIMrX (12 September 2021)

Tobacco Products Amendment Act, 1999 Regulations (GN 6689 in GG19962 of 23 April 1999)

Tobacco Products Control Act 83 of 1993

Tobacco Products Control Act 63 of 2008

Tobacco Tactics 'FCTC compliance in Africa' https://tobaccotactics.org/wiki/fctc-compliance-in-africa/ (accessed 11 September 2021)

Van Walbeek, C 'Effective development policies require political will: The example of tobacco control in South Africa' (2001) *Economics of Tobacco Control Project* https://bit.ly/3iMRWAp (accessed 12 September 2021)

Van Walbeek, C 'Recent trends in smoking prevalence in South Africa-some evidence from AMPS data' (2002) 92 *South African Medical Journal* 468

WHO 'Framework convention on tobacco control' https://www.who.int/fctc/text_download/en/ (accessed 27 September 2021)

WHO 'MPOWER: Six policies to reverse the tobacco epidemic' https://bit.ly/3eiGzN1 (accessed 27 September 2021)

WHO 'South Africa: Risks of premature deaths dues to NCDs' https://www.who.int/nmh/countries/zaf_en.pdf (accessed 27 September 2021)

WHO 'What we do' https://www.who.int/about/what-we-do (accessed 27 September 2021)

Wisdom, JP; Juma, P; Mwagomba, B; Ndinda, C; Mapa-Tassou, C; Assah, F; Nkhata, M; Mohamed, SF; Oladimeji, O; Oladunni, O & Oluwasanu, M 'Influence of the WHO framework convention on tobacco control on tobacco legislation and policies in sub-Saharan Africa' (2018) 1 *BMC Public Health* 954

5 An overview of Nigeria's efforts in addressing non-communicable diseases within the WHO FCTC

Adetoun T Adebanjo

5.1 Introduction

Tobacco use remains one of the leading epidemics in the world and does not appear to be going away anytime soon. Tobacco can be used in different forms, both smoked or smokeless. Smoked tobacco is any product made entirely or partly of leaf tobacco which is intended to be lit and the produced smoke inhaled (e.g. cigarettes, cigars and pipes). Smokeless tobacco is any product that consists of cut, ground, powdered or leaf tobacco that is intended to be placed loose or in sachet in the oral or nasal cavity (e.g. snuff and chewing tobacco).[1] Smoked and smokeless tobacco are extracted from the tobacco plant, which has leaves containing high levels of nicotine, a highly addictive chemical.[2] Cigarettes are the most common types of smoked tobacco in Nigeria; popular brands include Benson & Hedges, Rothmans, Pall Mall, Marlboro and St Moritz. The Zip brand is an example of packaged smokeless tobacco in Nigeria. Locally made smokeless tobacco products which can be found in different regions of the country include Asa, Taba, Utaba, Uwong, Unguru and Mandira.[3] Shisha has become increasingly popular in Nigeria as well. With shisha (also known as water pipe or hookah), the user inhales tobacco through a tube.

The health dangers of tobacco have been established and documented. According to the World Health Organization (WHO), tobacco kills up to half its users, with more than 8 million deaths recorded annually.[4] While more than 7 million of those are from direct tobacco use, a staggering 1.2 million estimated deaths are

1 WHO 'Tobacco and cancer treatment outcomes' (July 2018) https://apps.who.int/iris/bitstream/handle/10665/273077/WHO-NMH-PND-TKS-18.1-eng.pdf?ua=1/ (accessed 30 September 2021).

2 National Cancer Institute at the National Institute of Health *NCI dictionary of cancer terms* https://www.cancer.gov/publications/dictionaries/cancer-terms/def/tobacco (accessed 28 September 2021).

3 I Agaku, A Akinyele & A Oluwafemi 'Tobacco control in Nigeria – policy recommendations' (2012) 10 *Tobacco Induced Diseases* 1 at 3.

4 WHO 'Fact sheet: Tobacco' (2020) https://www.who.int/news-room/fact-sheets/detail/tobacco (accessed 30 September 2021).

DOI: 10.4324/9781003264248-7

from non-smokers' exposure to second-hand smoke.[5] It is noteworthy that the WHO had as far back as 2008 projected the possibility of 8 million tobacco-related deaths annually by 2030, if the rate of tobacco use was sustained.[6] Unfortunately, that figure has already been well and truly surpassed, with a decade still to go. By 2012, an estimated 4.5 million adults 15 years or older used tobacco in Nigeria, with nearly a third of the adult population exposed to second-hand smoke.[7] An estimated 2.7 million people working indoors were exposed to tobacco smoke at their workplace, while as many as 6.4 million were exposed in restaurants.[8] This goes against the requirement in article 12(b) of the International Covenant on Economic, Social and Cultural Rights (ICESCR) of the improvement of all aspects of environmental and industrial hygiene.

An estimated 19–21 billion cigarettes are produced annually in Nigeria, 12 million of these are sold in Nigeria and the rest sold to other West African markets.[9] Nigeria, with a population of over 200 million, is a major market for tobacco products. Apart from population size, its access to other markets makes it a major player in tobacco distribution.

Tobacco use has been linked to a host of non-communicable diseases (NCDs), such as lung cancer, lip cancer, nasopharyngeal carcinoma, emphysema, chronic bronchitis and gum disease. It has been identified as the single greatest preventable cause of death globally.[10] Usually, the mode of administration is directly linked with the type of medical condition that a user would suffer from. For instance, a user who smokes tobacco is more susceptible to medical issues like lung cancer, emphysema and chronic bronchitis. On the other hand, those who use tobacco in smokeless form are more likely to suffer from oral and pharyngeal medical complications such as dental and gum disease, oral cancers involving the soft palate of the tongue, nasopharyngeal carcinoma and lip cancer. Be that as it may, there can be an overlap of these diseases from smoked and smokeless tobacco use. Medical conditions like lip cancer, gum disease, gingivitis and dental caries can be caused by both. It is therefore confounding to note that notwithstanding these and other diseases linked to tobacco, its use has continued to thrive in endemic proportions.

In 2013, Nigeria developed a national policy on the prevention and control of NCDs.[11] The policy noted that NCDs had become a major cause of morbidity

5 As above.

6 WHO 'MPOWER: A policy package to reverse the tobacco epidemic' (2008). As of 2008, annual tobacco-related deaths were put at over more than 5 million.

7 WHO (n 2).

8 As above.

9 F Owoeye 'Product review: The Nigerian cigarette market has only one winner' *Nairametrics* 13 December 2018 https://nairametrics.com/2018/12/13/product-review-the-nigerian-cigarette-market-has-only-one-winner/ (accessed 29 September 2021).

10 WHO (n 8).

11 Federal Ministry of Health, Nigeria *National policy and strategic plan of action on prevention and control of non-communicable diseases* (2013).

and mortality in Nigeria.[12] The prevalence of hypertension had jumped from 11.2 per cent in 1990–1992 to over 20 per cent in 2013.[13]

The WHO continues to advocate against tobacco use; it has designated 31 May as World No Tobacco Day.[14] The health body noted that rates of tobacco use decreased from 27 to 20 per cent between 2010 and 2016.[15] Notwithstanding, much still needs to be done in the global tobacco fight.

5.2 The right to health and NCDs

The connection between the right to health and NCDs will now be examined. A right to health approach can help to put the fight against tobacco in the proper perspective. Achieving tobacco control aligns with protecting the right to health guaranteed under various human rights instruments. As previously stated, tobacco use interferes with the health of not only tobacco users but also millions of innocent third parties by way of second-hand smoke; it must therefore be viewed as one of the obstacles to achieving the right to health. Legislating on and implementing tobacco control is a step towards protecting people's right to health. A reduction in tobacco use will lead to a reduction in the incidence of NCDs and death, which will work in favour of achieving the right to health objective.

The right to health is a fundamental right guaranteed in various human rights instruments, including the Universal Declaration on Human Rights (UDHR; article 25), the ICESCR (article 12) and the African Charter on Human and Peoples' Rights (the Banjul Charter; article 16).

Article 25(1) of the UDHR recognises the right to a standard of living which is adequate for the health and well-being of the individual and their family, including medical care and other necessary social services, among other things.

Article 12(1) of the ICESCR recognises the right of every individual to the enjoyment of attainable standards of physical and mental health. The dangers of tobacco have been well established, judging by the millions of people affected by NCDs globally. Tobacco users are themselves interfering with their fundamental right to health. Of note also is article 12(2)(b), which enjoins States parties' to take steps towards the improvement of all aspects of environmental and industrial hygiene. So not only does this treaty guarantee the right to health, but it also advocates that governments work to improve environmental hygiene. Part of improving environmental hygiene would be working to eliminate pollution from tobacco. The poisonous effect of tobacco on air quality can be seen in the high number of people who are estimated to die from second-hand smoke annually.

12 As above 13.

13 As above.

14 WHO 'World no tobacco day 2019' https://www.who.int/campaigns/world-no-tobacco-day/world-no-tobacco-day-2019 (accessed 30 September 2021).

15 WHO 'Don't let tobacco take your breath away' https://apps.who.int/iris/bitstream/handle/10665/312260/WHO-NMH-PND-2019.3-eng.pdf(accessed 30 September 2021).

In effect, tobacco pollutes the air and tampers with the right to health of all who unfortunately inhale it second-hand, even though they do not use tobacco.

Likewise, article 16 of the Banjul Charter reaffirms the right to health. It recognises every individual's right to the best attainable state of physical and mental health and enjoins States parties' to take measures to protect citizens' health and provide medical attention when required. According to Durojaye, the manner in which article 16 is couched suggests a focus on the real enjoyment of rights by the individual, and the African Commission's method is to hold states accountable in this regard.[16] Resolution 141 on Access to Health and Needed Medicines in Africa also reaffirms the right to health, which it stressed was not confined to a right to healthcare but rather covering all underlying aspects of health.[17] Here, the Commission went beyond an umbrella statement on the right to health to emphasise that access to needed medicines was a fundamental component of the right to health, and to stress the importance of access to needed medicine for treatment, prevention and palliative care as a necessary condition for a healthy and dignified life.[18] It enjoined state parties to provide needed medicines or facilitate access to them. Resolution 141 calls on state parties to ensure availability, accessibility, acceptability and quality of medicines.[19] The Commission enjoined countries to refrain from actions which negatively impact access to medicines,[20] to protect access to needed medicines from actions by third parties through good regulatory systems, and to fulfil access to medicines by adopting all necessary and appropriate positive measures to the maximum of its available resources to promote, provide and facilitate access to medicines.[21]

Factors mitigating against the realisation of the right to health in the African region include a lack of political will to follow through with state obligations, poor healthcare systems, corruption, non-availability of health workers and non-justiciability of the right to health.[22] Non-justiciability of the right to health should be considered especially problematic, as it invariably weakens the right as conferred by treaties and legislative instruments, ultimately affecting the outcome for the prevention and handling of NCDs. As observed by Durojaye, the right to health though a fundamental right has not been recognised as legally enforceable in the Nigerian Constitution, but rather as a directive principle of government policies. Indeed, section 6(6)(c) is to the effect that the socio-economic

16 E Durojaye 'The approaches of the African commission to the right to health under the African Charter' (2013) 17 *Law, Democracy & Development* 397.

17 The African Commission on Human and Peoples' Rights at its 44th Ordinary Session in Abuja, Nigeria 10–24 November 2008, ACHPR/Res 141 (XXXXIIII) 2008.

18 As above.

19 As above.

20 Such as denying or limiting access to medicines for marginalised groups.

21 Including by meeting minimum core obligations of ensuring availability and affordability to all, and by promoting meaningful participation by affected individuals and groups in decisions that affect access to medicines.

22 Durojaye (n 18) 400.

rights recognised under Chapter II of the Constitution cannot be the subject of adjudication. This will make it difficult for people with NCDs to enforce their constitutionally guaranteed right to health.

The Committee on Economic, Social and Cultural Rights (CESCR) in its General Comment 14[23] recognised health as a fundamental right indispensable with other rights.[24] It also recognised that the right to health could be realised through such means as the formulation of health policies and the implementation of WHO programmes.[25] The Committee also significantly pointed out that the spread of diseases such as cancer was an obstacle to the realisation of the right to health.[26]

The Committee recognised four essential elements to the right to health: availability, accessibility, acceptability and quality. The element of availability presupposes that functioning public healthcare facilities, programmes, and goods and services have to be available in sufficient quantity.[27] The element of accessibility presupposes that these have to be accessible to all without discrimination.[28] The element of acceptability in clause 12(c) requires health facilities to be respectful of medical ethics and to be culturally appropriate. The element of quality in clause 12(d) requires health facilities and services to be scientifically and medically appropriate, and of good quality. In effect, General Comment 14 stresses the importance of the right to health in addressing NCDs.

The National Tobacco Control Regulations introduced in Nigeria in 2019 also stressed as their objective the realisation of the people's right to health, life, physical integrity, safe and healthy workplaces and other rights adversely affected by tobacco.[29]

NCDs, or chronic diseases, are medical conditions or diseases that are non-infectious and non-transmissible among people.[30] The main types of NCDs are cardiovascular diseases (heart attacks and stroke), cancers, chronic respiratory disease and diabetes.[31] NCDs kill an estimated 41 million people every year, 15 million of whom are in the 30–69 age range.[32] Of these 15 million deaths, 85 per cent occur in low- and middle-income countries.[33] In 2018, the human and economic costs of NCDs over the following 15-year period were projected to

23 Twenty-second session, Committee on ESCR Geneva 25 April–12 May 2000. E/C.12/2000/4.

24 Clause 1.

25 As above.

26 Clause 10.

27 Clause 12(a).

28 Clause 12(b). This factor encompasses the issues of non-discrimination, physical accessibility, affordability and information accessibility.

29 Clause 1(b).

30 HC Kim & SM Oh 'Non-communicable diseases: Current status of major modifiable risk factors in Korea' (2013) 46 *Journal of Preventive Medicine & Public Health* 165.

31 WHO 'Fact sheet: Non-communicable diseases' (1 June 2018) https://www.who.int/news-room/fact-sheets/detail/noncommunicable-diseases (accessed 30 September 2021).

32 As above.

33 As above.

exceed $7 trillion in developing countries alone.[34] NCDs remain a major threat to health globally.

There are metabolic risk factors[35] and modifiable behavioural risk factors for NCDs. Modifiable behavioural risk factors include tobacco use, physical inactivity, unhealthy diet and harmful use of alcohol.[36] With an estimated 7.2 million deaths annually as of 2018, and 8 million at present, tobacco remains a leading cause of death from modifiable behavioural risk factors.[37]

It therefore became a top priority to develop initiatives aimed at tackling NCDs. The high-level meetings of the UN General Assembly (UNGA) on NCDs in 2011 and 2014 were in furtherance of this objective.[38] The third high-level meeting in 2018 was a follow-up on the progress made in reducing risks of premature deaths from NCDs and to consecrate plans for the 2018–2030 period.[39] The WHO also developed a Global Action Plan for the prevention and control of NCDs 2013–2020. This contains nine global targets aimed at preventing and managing NCDs, one of which is a 30 per cent relative reduction in prevalence of current tobacco use in people over 15 years of age.[40] The WHO noted that NCDs undermined the achievements of the Millennium Development Goals (MDGs) and established a link between poverty and hunger and NCDs.[41] The Global Action Plan proposes preventive 'best buy' interventions, which the WHO identified as highly cost-effective, feasible and culturally acceptable for achieving improved results for public health within low- and middle-income countries in the prevention of NCDs.[42] These 'best-buy' interventions include raising tobacco and alcohol taxes; making indoor workplaces and public spaces smoke-free; enforcing bans on tobacco and alcohol advertising, promotion and sponsorship; implementing plain packaging and/or large graphic health warnings on all tobacco packaging; and implementing effective mass media campaigns that educate the public about the dangers of tobacco use and second-hand smoke.[43]

34 WHO 'Time to deliver: Third UN high-level meeting on non-communicable diseases' (27 September 2018) https://www.who.int/ncds/governance/third-un-meeting/brochure.pdf?ua=1 (accessed 30 September 2021).
35 WHO (n 34), e.g. elevated blood pressure, overweight/obesity, hyperglycaemia (high blood glucose) and hyperlipidaemia (high levels of fats in the blood).
36 WHO (n 34).
37 As above.
38 UNGA 2011 High level meeting on prevention and control of non-communicable diseases, New York 19–20 September 2011; UNGA 2014 High level meeting on the comprehensive review and assessment of the 2011 political declaration on NCDS, New York 11–12 July 2014.
39 WHO (n 37) 3.
40 WHO 'Global action plan for the prevention and control on noncommunicable diseases 2013–2020' (2013) 5 www.who.int/publications/i/item/9789241506236 (accessed 30 September 2021).
41 As above.
42 As above.
43 WHO 'Tackling NCDs: "Best buys" and other recommended interventions for the prevention and control of non-communicable diseases' (2017) 7.

In September 2011, Nigeria was a signatory to the political declaration at the UNGA High-Level Meeting on NCDs. Two years later, Nigeria developed its national policy on the prevention and control of NCDs, mentioned above. The WHO had put the projected cumulative annual economic loss for the period 2005–2015 from deaths due to heart disease, stroke and diabetes at $7.6 billion (at an average annual loss of $800 million).[44]

The national policy set out a host of policy actions to achieve its goal of prevention and control of NCDs. The discussion of the policy in this chapter will be mostly restricted to its coverage of tobacco. These included establishing a sustainable framework to facilitate prevention, early detection and management of NCDs in Nigeria; reducing risk factors arising from tobacco use and exposure to tobacco smoke and other modifiable risk factors; establishing units to train health professionals in tobacco cessation and alcohol and drug addiction; and establishing sustainable research framework to facilitate research in prevention and control of NCDs.[45] The policy also firmly reiterates the importance of implementing the demand reduction strategies of the WHO Framework Convention on Tobacco Control (FCTC) through the MPOWER strategy, as a means of achieving a reduction in tobacco use in Nigeria.[46] It advocates smoking cessation as the main method of controlling tobacco use in a health facility setting and recognises the major role to be played by health workers in identifying smokers for initiation, providing psychosocial support and medication.[47]

The policy also encourages research into tobacco control programmes to cover such areas as pricing and taxation, supply and demand measures, sales and advertising, the relationship between tobacco and poverty, and the prevalence of tobacco use among adults, women and children.[48] It is submitted that if implemented, this document will aid Nigeria's war on NCDs in general and combat tobacco use in the process.

Juma and others have identified lack of government funding as a major challenge to policy formulation and implementation, oftentimes as a result of inadequate political will to tackle NCDs, while more focus has been put on communicable diseases and other health challenges.[49] This leads to a disproportionate reliance on non-governmental organisations (NGOs), which unfortunately also grapple with low funding.[50]

44 D Abegunde & A Stanciole 'An estimation of the economic impact of chronic non-communicable diseases in selected countries' WHO Working Paper (2006) 11 www.who.int/chp/working_paper_growth%20model29may.pdf (accessed 30 September 2021).

45 FMH Nigeria (n 13) 30–31.

46 As above 34.

47 As above 33–34.

48 As above 37.

49 P Juma & others 'Non-communicable disease prevention policy process in five African countries' (2018) 18 *BMC Public Health* 1 at 12.

50 As above 12.

In 2012, Nigeria became the first African country to successfully implement the Global Adult Tobacco Survey (GATS). It was the first nationally representative survey of adults in Nigeria to monitor adult tobacco use and track key tobacco control indicators,[51] in line with article 20 of the WHO FCTC, which required countries to develop tobacco surveillance programmes to monitor things like tobacco laws, consumption and tobacco control. The survey was a joint effort of major players including the Federal Ministry of Health, the National Bureau of Statistics, the Centres for Disease Control and the WHO regional and country offices.

Multi-sectoral action (MSA) has been proposed in the global fight against NCDs.[52] MSA is action by sectors other than the health sector that aims to achieve health-related outcomes or to influence health determinants.[53] It recognises that socio-economic factors affecting health can also be found in other sectors apart from the health sector.[54] Adopting MSA in policy formulation where such policy's coverage extends beyond the health sector is believed to be critical to its success.[55] The WHO Global Action Plan gives a perfect example of how MSA comes into play in a situation where tobacco taxes are increased and restrictions or bans are placed on tobacco advertisement.[56]

As already stated, Nigeria has a high rate of tobacco use. Interestingly, even though there was a high rate of electronic media campaign and pictorial health warnings on cigarette packs, this did not significantly impact on awareness and behavioural change. Only 4 out of 10 adults took notice of anti-smoking campaigns in the media, yet almost 50 per cent did not believe that smoking caused strokes. Nigeria's efforts in undertaking GATS should be applauded, as it provided evidence to improve the country's tobacco control programmes and fulfilled its obligation under the FCTC to generate comparable data. Interestingly, more recent studies have findings which differ from those above. In their study, Adeloye and others focused on the 20-year period between 1995 and 2015, observing that even though the prevalence of ever smokers[57] had increased

51 WHO (n 2).

52 WHO 'Background paper: Non-communicable diseases in low-and middle-income countries' Regional High-Level Consultation in the Eastern Mediterranean Region on the Prevention and Control of Non-communicable Diseases in low-and Middle-Income countries, hosted in Tehran 25–26 October 2010 https://www.who.int/nmh/events/2010/Tehran_Background_Paper.pdf?ua=1 (accessed 30 September 2021).

53 M Arora & others 'Multisectoral action for addressing social determinants of non-communicable diseases and mainstreaming health promotion in national health programmes in India' (2011) 36 *Indian Journal of Community Medicine* S43.

54 P Juma & others 'Multisectoral action in non-communicable disease prevention policy development in five African countries' (2018) 18 *BMC Public Health* 953 at 16.

55 O Oladepo, M Oluwasanu & O Abiona 'Analysis of tobacco control policies in Nigeria: Historical development and application of multi-sectoral action' (2018) 18 *BMC Public Health* 78.

56 WHO (n 43).

57 People who have always smoked.

during this period, there had been a decline in current smokers, and even though smoking prevalence had declined in Nigeria, one in ten people were daily smokers.[58] They found the decline in Nigeria to be different from the experience in some other countries in sub-Saharan Africa that had instead recorded increased smoking rates.[59] The estimated number of current smokers was put at 11 million people, while an estimated 20 million people were ever smokers. It should be borne in mind that the GATS figures quoted above were for adult smokers only. The authors conceded that disparities in estimated figures from different studies could be attributable to challenges with sampling and case ascertainment, and that pooling of figures from a range of studies conducted over a 27-year period (1990–2017), like they had done, could affect reliability.[60]

5.3 The FCTC as a treaty to realise the right to health at the national level

The WHO has been at the forefront of the global tobacco fight. In 2003, at the 56th World Health Assembly in Geneva, the WHO adopted the FCTC, which came into force in February 2005. The FCTC has been ratified by 181 countries.

The objective of the FCTC is to protect people from the devastating health, social, economic and environmental consequences of tobacco consumption by providing a framework for tobacco control measures to be implemented by parties at all levels.[61] Article 4 sets out some means to achieve this objective. They include creating awareness on the health consequences and addictive nature of tobacco; putting in place adequate legislative, executive and administrative measures to protect all from exposure to tobacco smoke; committing to developing comprehensive multi-sectoral measures and coordinated responses; and providing technical and financial assistance to help persons whose livelihoods have been affected by the introduction of tobacco control programmes.

The FCTC encouraged parties to impose even stricter standards than its own.[62] It encouraged using pricing and taxation as a means of checkmating consumers,[63] since higher price and tax regimes should ideally act to discourage buyers or drastically reduce demand. The Convention importantly recognised the dangers of exposure of non-smokers to second-hand smoke,[64] banned misleading advertising and required that each tobacco package carries a warning.[65] Article 12 required parties to create public awareness on the health risks and addictive

58 D Adeloye & others 'Current prevalence pattern of tobacco and smoking in Nigeria: A systemic review and meta-analysis' (2019) 19 *BMC Public Health* 1.

59 As above 10.

60 As above 10–11.

61 Art 3, FCTC.

62 Art 2.

63 Art 6.

64 Art 8.

65 Art 11.

nature of tobacco. It encouraged a comprehensive ban on advertisement, promotion and sponsorship (or at least a reduction where this is not possible) as a means of reducing tobacco consumption.[66]

As part of the drive to end tobacco use, countries were required among other things to develop programmes promoting cessation of tobacco use in places like schools, workplaces, healthcare facilities and sports centres, and include diagnosis and treatment of tobacco dependence in national health and educational programmes.[67] Sale of tobacco to minors is prohibited, as is the distribution of free tobacco.[68] Individual sale, or sale of small packs, is prohibited to discourage affordability. The FCTC advocated the commissioning of research and training on tobacco control.[69]

To further help in implementing the provisions of the FCTC, the WHO introduced MPOWER measures in 2008.[70] There are six MPOWER measures through which countries are expected to implement the WHO's policies on tobacco: (1) monitor tobacco use; (2) protect people from tobacco use; (3) offer help to quit tobacco use; (4) warn about the dangers of tobacco; (5) enforce bans on tobacco advertising, promotion and sponsorship; and (6) raise taxes on tobacco. These measures have been set in motion across countries, with tangible results. For instance, countries have made rules banning smoking in indoor public facilities like workplaces, restaurants and bars and a total ban on smoking in certain places like healthcare facilities and educational institutions.

Although fraught with various challenges, Nigeria has attempted to implement the MPOWER measures. Its National Tobacco Control Act of 2015 replaced the Tobacco Smoking (Control) Act of 1990. The evolution of Nigeria's legislation on tobacco will be traced below to show efforts at compliance with FCTC provisions.

5.3.1 History of tobacco control in Nigeria

Nigeria was one of the first African countries to attempt tobacco control, with the introduction of the Tobacco Smoking (Control) Decree in 1990.[71] However, the start of its tobacco control regime has been traced as far back as the early 1950s, with the introduction of the Nigeria (Revenue Allocation) Order-in-Council 1951, the Nigeria (Constitution) Order-in-Council 1954; and the Tobacco (Licences and Returns) Ordinance 1958,[72] which basically provided for licencing of all tobacco imports in Nigeria and payment of duties thereon.[73]

66 Art 13.
67 Art 14.
68 Art 16.
69 Art 20.
70 WHO (n 8).
71 Decree 20 of 1990.
72 Cap 198 Laws of the Federation of Nigeria 1958.
73 Secs 3–4, however, exempts tobacco imported for personal use from such licence.

The Act restricted the importation of tobacco without a licence. In Nigeria, the major players in the tobacco industry were the Nigerian Tobacco Company (NTC)[74] and the International Tobacco Company (ITC). In 1979, both companies formed the Tobacco Advisory Council of Nigeria (TACON), which was Nigeria's version of a national manufacturer's association (NMA).

Meanwhile, in the 70s, the WHO and the World Conferences on Smoking and Health (WCSH) had become increasingly vocal on the need for tobacco control and to curb the aggressive marketing strategies targeting the developing world.[75] The tobacco industry countered this growing discontent with activism of its own; such as establishing NMAs in countries with a tobacco presence to represent industry interests, and deflecting attention from the dangers of tobacco in developing countries to other health issues like malaria and reproductive health.[76] This appears to have consistently been the ploy used by the tobacco industry to quash or distract from the global fight against tobacco. As Van der Eijk and others noted in their study using the Truth Tobacco Industry Documents library (an online collection of previously secret tobacco industry documents), the tobacco industry, feeling threatened by UNICEF's activism in the area of tobacco control in the late 1990s and early 2000s, had subsequently inserted itself in the middle of UNICEF's efforts, thereby weakening these efforts.[77] This it did by partnering with UNICEF on youth smoking prevention initiatives and making efforts purporting to combat child labour, among others.

Propelled by the WHO's growing calls for tobacco control, Nigeria took definite steps towards greater awareness and control. The Ministry of Health had inaugurated a national anti-smoking campaign on World Health Day 1980[78] and hosted a conference for health commissioners which approved submission of a tobacco control bill to the National Assembly.[79] The government thereafter established a committee with representatives from different federal ministries and – curiously – the two major tobacco companies to deliberate on the introduction of some restrictions on tobacco in Nigeria.[80] It is also interesting to note that an anti-tobacco bill, the Cigarette Smoking (Injury) Bill, had also been tabled before the National Assembly but had been defeated.[81]

74 Although government owned, BAT had controlling shares of 60 per cent in NTC.

75 CO Egbe, SA Bialous & SA Glantz 'Avoiding "a massive spin-off effect in West Africa and beyond": The tobacco industry stymies tobacco control in Nigeria' (2017) 19 *Nicotine & Tobacco Research* 878.

76 As above.

77 Y van der Eijk, SA Bialous & S Glantz 'The tobacco industry and children's rights' (2018) 141 *Pediatrics* e20174106. The industry's methods included partnering with UNICEF on youth smoking prevention initiatives and combatting child labour.

78 Egbe & others (n 78) 878.

79 As above.

80 As above.

81 As above.

The Tobacco Smoking (Control) Decree 1990 – which subsequently became known as the Tobacco Smoking (Control) Act 1990,[82] to reflect Nigeria's return to democratic rule – introduced significant changes to the position of the law on tobacco use. Importantly, it took action to prevent and reduce the incidence of second-hand smoke by prohibiting smoking in certain public spaces: cinemas, theatres, stadia, public transport, lifts, medical establishments and schools.[83] The decree also, for the first time, placed restrictions on the advertisement of tobacco products. Section 2 prohibited advertisement of tobacco to the general public through newspapers, magazines, radio and television, cinemas, billboards and handbills, except if it carried the specific warnings crafted under section 3(1) thus: 'The Federal Ministry of Health warns that tobacco smoking is dangerous to health' and 'Smokers are liable to die young'. The tar and nicotine content of each unit of tobacco product for sale was also required to be stated on the packaging.[84] There were penalties attached for non-compliance in the form of a fine, imprisonment or both.[85]

To protect persons authorised to enforce the decree, no action could be instituted against them for anything done in the course of their job, and in furtherance of this objective, the fundamental rights provisions of the Constitution could not be invoked.[86]

The 1990 Act was supposed to a big step forward in Nigeria's journey to better tobacco control. However, it did not achieve much of its intended purpose. This is attributable to a number of factors. First of all, the tobacco industry's interference posed a major threat to the success of the Act. Its war on the Act could be traced as far back as two years before its enactment, when it obtained a copy of the proposed Decree 20, labelled it 'anti-business' and instead proposed wording that ultimately led to the passage of a weaker version.[87] Egbe and others concluded that the influence of the tobacco industry could be glimpsed from provisions (see Table 5.1) which ostensibly weakened the final law. For example, hospitality venues were not part of smoke-free areas; minimal restrictions were placed on marketing of tobacco products, and the supposed health warnings were tempered by vague and confusing clauses with no guidance on details (e.g. print size and positioning) of health warnings to be carried by tobacco products.[88] Despite the watered-down provisions, the tobacco industry still made attempts to influence a review a few years later.[89]

82 Cap T16.
83 Sec 1.
84 Sec 3(2).
85 Secs 4–5.
86 Sec 6(1)–(2).
87 Egbe & others (n 78) 877–887.
88 As above 880 & 882.
89 As above 882–883.

Table 5.1 Level of Nigeria's compliance

FCTC Provisions	*NTCA Provisions*	*Remarks*
1 Protection from exposure to tobacco smoke (art 8).	Prohibits smoking in indoor and enclosed spaces, and in public places (sec 9). The National Tobacco Control Regulations (NTCR) 2019 go further to demand action from managers of public spaces (clause 9), e.g. displaying 'No Smoking' signs, and in designated smoking areas (DSAs), displaying a warning on the dangers of tobacco in DSAs (clause 11(9)).	Partial compliance, as exception was made for DSAs (sec 9(2)–(4)). Notably, NTCR introduced extensive restrictions for DSAs. For example, a DSA must not be a passageway between spaces; must be located not less than 10 m away from an entrance, must have floor-to-ceiling walls if indoors, and must have a completely separate system of ventilation and air filtration (clause 11). DSAs not actively enforced.
2 Regulation of contents of tobacco products (art 9). States to adopt measures for testing and regulating contents and emissions of tobacco products.	Prohibits manufacture, distribution and sale of tobacco which does not conform to prescribed standard and quality. Substandard tobacco to be confiscated (sec 17) and penalties attached (sec 19).	Full compliance.
3 Regulation of product disclosures (art 10). Manufacturers/ importers to disclose product content and emissions to the government. The government is to implement measures for public disclosure.	Manufacturers/importers to submit reports on product content and emissions to Standards Organisation of Nigeria (sec 18(1)).	Partial compliance. Limited by sec 18(2), which gives government power to withhold public access to reports.
4 Packaging and labelling of tobacco products (art 11). Tobacco products to carry health warnings which describe harmful effects of tobacco. Pictures or pictograms could be used.	Requires health warning in English covering not less than 50% of surface area (sec 20). Non-compliance attracts fine or jail term. NTCR 2019 has extensive provisions on display of health warnings (Part II).	Full compliance. Requirement of health warning being only in English is a limitation, however.

(*Continued*)

Table 5.1 (Continued)

FCTC Provisions	*NTCA Provisions*	*Remarks*
5 Education, training, public awareness (art 12). Parties to adopt measures to promote awareness on health risks of tobacco, train health and allied workers. Encourages public access to information on the tobacco industry.	Provides for public awareness campaigns on the dangers of tobacco, including second-hand smoke section (38(1)). Silent on public access to information on tobacco industry.	Partial compliance.
6 Ban on advertising, promotion and sponsorship of tobacco products (art 13).	Bans advertising, promotion and sponsorship, with fines and jail terms attached for non-compliance (sec 12).	Full compliance.
7 Parties to develop and pursue measures which promote cessation of tobacco use and treatment for dependence (art 14).	Provides for implementation of demand reduction measures in its objectives (sec 1). Namely, discouraging initiation of smoking, encouraging cessation, informing consumers of health consequences of tobacco, ensuring packaging is not misleading or does not undermine warnings.	Full compliance.
8 Provides comprehensive measures to combat illicit trade in tobacco (art 15).	Extensive provisions on illicit trade (secs 29–32). Harsh penalties for non-compliance (imprisonment and fine). Police and other officials given broad powers to enforce these provisions.	Full compliance.
9 Prohibits sale to minors (art 16).	Prohibits sale to and by minors (sec 15). Retailer to display signage to that effect and check identification prior to sale.	Full compliance.
10 States to promote alternative means of livelihood for persons involved in the tobacco industry.	No provision in this regard.	Non-compliance.

Implementation was a major problem. In the WHO 2008 Report on the Global Tobacco Epidemic, the Act was deemed weak and poorly implemented.[90] The new law had been vague in many respects, including its effective date, the areas designated as smoke-free spaces, and whether in fact it imposed a total ban on smoking. In the absence of clear-cut instructions, the tobacco industry resorted to continue business on the periphery of the law, choosing to 'take advantage of the vagueness of Decree 20'.[91]

Based on the perceived failure of the 1990 law, Nigeria attempted a review in 1995. The Ministry of Health had held a workshop specifically for this purpose and had come up with an MSA plan for tobacco control in Nigeria.[92] The agenda included designing an action plan for tobacco control and addressing core details like specifying public places, advertisement of tobacco, sale of tobacco to minors, penalties and presentation of a draft amendment of Decree 20. The 1990 Act remained in force until the introduction of the National Tobacco Control Act of 2015 (the NTCA).

5.3.2 Nigeria's current law on tobacco control

The NTCA is Nigeria's post-FCTC tobacco control law. Although acknowledged as an improvement on the 1990 Act, it is still not fully compliant with FCTC standards.[93] For example, in their study on the prevention of NCDs in five African countries, Juma and others note that of the five focus countries, none had met the WHO recommended tobacco product taxation of 75 per cent of products' retail price. At 20.63 per cent, Nigeria was at the bottom of the compliance ladder in 2015.[94]

Nigeria ratified and signed the WHO FCTC in 2005. By 2009, there was agitation for a new tobacco law.[95] This led to the development of the National Tobacco Control Bill of 2009, which unfortunately did not see the light of day. British American Tobacco (BAT) was fingered in this turn of events. The company went as far as taking out a full-page post in the *Guardian* newspaper, claiming there was an aggressive propaganda campaign against the tobacco industry in Nigeria.[96] The Bill was signed by the national legislative houses and sent for presidential assent in 2013. Unfortunately, assent was not given due to a combination of factors. Top on this list was increased pressure from the tobacco industry and

90 WHO *WHO report on the global tobacco epidemic 2008: The MPOWER package* (2008).
91 Egbe & others (n 78) 880–881.
92 As above 882.
93 As above 884.
94 Juma & others (n 52) 9. Other countries in the focus group were South Africa (52 per cent), Kenya (35 per cent) and Cameroon (34.6 per cent).
95 Oladepo & others (n 58) 80.
96 'Increasing aggressive propaganda against the tobacco industry' *The Guardian* (Nigeria) 14 July 2014 at 34 http://ntcang.org/wp-content/uploads/2014/08/BAT-advert.pdf (accessed 30 September 2021).

government bureaucracy.[97] Another version of the Bill was eventually approved by the Senate and forwarded for presidential assent. Owing to immense pressure from the tobacco industry, assent was delayed until President Goodluck Jonathan's final days in office. Although the sustained pressure from anti-tobacco activists was a major catalyst for the introduction of NTCA, President Jonathan's last-minute decision to sign the Bill into law was seen as a calculated attempt to score political points as he left office.[98]

BAT's action targeting tobacco control described above is not an isolated one. In June 2020, the company was caught interfering with tobacco control efforts in the UK. It had hired a public relations company to issue press releases attacking the National Health Service and council stop-smoking services (which was part of government's efforts at helping tobacco users to quit smoking), without any disclosure as to its involvement.[99] The press release stressed the cost per taxpayer of stop-smoking services but refused to mention the money saved as a result of the reduced burden from smokers needing treatment. It had instead tried to encourage vaping, in which BAT has vested interests. In summing up BAT's actions, the head of a UK anti-smoking charity said:

> This covert ad for e-cigs purports to be public information and has been covered as such by unsuspecting journalists. BAT has an appalling and shameful track record going back generations. In just the last year, BAT has been found to have broken advertising rules by promoting its Vype e-cigs to young people on social media.[100]

The company's meddlesome tactics continue to be a source of concern in the global anti-tobacco movement. Its unique position as the leader in the Nigerian tobacco market makes this an even bigger concern. The delay in introducing the NTCA of 2015 has been attributed not only to a lack of funding but also to the conflict of interest presented by the need to protect the Nigerian people from the harmful effects of tobacco and the economic implications of restricting the tobacco industry.[101] Keen observers note the tobacco industry's interference with the formulation of the 2015 Act. This interference was believed to have led to the Jonathan government foot-dragging on introducing the law, with the president waiting until the final moments of his term in office before signing it.[102]

The Act also attempts to reduce the influence of the tobacco industry on tobacco policy. Section 25 requires transparency in the dealings between the government

97 Oladepo & others (n 58) 81.

98 As above.

99 M Busby 'Tobacco firm funded attack on council quit-smoking services' *The Guardian* (Australia) 3 July 2020 https://www.theguardian.com/business/2020/jul/02/tobacco-giant-behind-attack-on-quit-smoking-services (accessed 30 September 2021).

100 As above.

101 Oladepo & others (n 58) 77.

102 As above 81.

and the tobacco industry. Interactions between both parties are to be done in public by way of public hearings, except where this would not be possible, for example in litigation. Hence, government institutions are prohibited from accepting donations from the tobacco industry.[103] The Act also bars persons with links to the tobacco industry from taking up a role involving tobacco control in any capacity in Nigeria.[104] These provisions are commendable and much needed. The government's involvement in the tobacco industry has evolved over the years, considering that the Nigerian government had been an initial co-owner of the Nigerian Tobacco Company (with a 40 per cent stake) for several years until it sold its stake to BAT. Significantly, the Act also bars the tobacco industry or any of its members from involvement in, or providing funding for, any tobacco control activity.[105]

The NTCA of 2015 has no doubt made significant improvements on its predecessor, with provisions like its comprehensive and hard-line stance on smoke-free indoor and public spaces, penalties for non-compliance and the creation of the National Tobacco Control Committee and the Tobacco Control Fund. However, there is room for improvement. Certain provisions of the Act have proved problematic. For example, section 39(1) empowers the Minister of Health to make regulations in furtherance of the objectives of the Act. However, section 39(2) requires the approval of the National Assembly before such regulations can be effective. The rationale for this clause is unknown and it interferes with the inherent powers reposed in the Minister. As has been rightly observed, this requirement slows down the process of implementing the Act and provides the tobacco industry with the opportunity to interfere.[106] Indeed, the conclusion could be reached that this clause was inserted into the law for the purpose of benefiting the tobacco industry, as it is not a secret in Nigeria that business owners like the tobacco companies have friends in high places, such as Nigeria's legislative houses. This is another potential case of giving something with one hand and taking it away with the other; namely, the Act by way of sections 25–29 prohibits undue influence from the tobacco industry while leaving room for the very same thing under section 39(2). It is suggested that this provision should be reviewed in the interest of transparency and seamless implementation of the law.

The Act also bequeaths on the Standards Organisation of Nigeria (SON) the power to make guidelines for regulating tobacco. Egbe and others are quick to point out that the tobacco industry dominates the processes of the SON, and that representatives of the tobacco industry outnumber those from other agencies on the Committee tasked with writing these guidelines.[107] This is another issue than needs to be addressed if the Act is to achieve effective tobacco control.

103 Sec 27.
104 Sec 28.
105 Sec 38(2).
106 CO Egbe & others 'Nigeria isn't doing enough to reduce tobacco use. Here's why' *The Conversation* 8 January 2019 https://theconversation.com/nigeria-isnt-doing-enough-to-reduce-tobacco-use-heres-why-108695 (accessed 30 September 2021).
107 As above.

Table 5.1 highlights the FCTC provisions on tobacco and the corresponding degree of compliance in Nigeria. These FCTC provisions can be grouped into demand-reduction provisions (articles 6–14) and supply-reduction provisions (articles 15–17).

5.4 An assessment of the effectiveness of efforts to implement FCTC/national laws on tobacco use

The NTCA is the most FCTC-compliant Nigerian tobacco legislation to date, addressing all five WHO best-buy interventions: (1) increasing tax on tobacco; (2) enforcing smoke-free indoor workplaces and public places; (3) banning tobacco advertising, promotion and sponsorship; (4) including health information and warnings on tobacco packs; and (5) running media campaigns on the harmful effects of tobacco and second-hand smoke.[108]

The objectives of the Act included protecting people from the devastating health, social, economic and environmental consequences of tobacco use or exposure, in compliance with Nigeria's obligations under the FCTC and other regional and international treaties to which Nigeria is a party.[109] The Act established the National Tobacco Control Committee[110] and the Tobacco Control Fund.[111] The Tobacco Control Committee is to advise and make recommendations on the implementation of tobacco control policies in Nigeria in accordance with FCTC guidelines and protocols; coordinate national youth smoking prevention programmes; and develop strategies for counselling and rehabilitating smokers, among other things.[112]

Even though Nigeria has recorded progress in the fight against tobacco, there are legitimate concerns about achieving effective implementation of policies. Not only is Nigeria a key market for the tobacco industry owing to its population size, it also facilitates access to other markets within the region.[113] Shedding more light on Nigeria's strategic position in the West African sub-regional tobacco industry is the fact that BAT chose to situate its manufacturing plant and head office, which service the sub-region, in Ibadan and Lagos states, respectively. This poses a problem for the fight against tobacco.

One of the most basic challenges to tobacco control in Nigeria, and indeed globally, is its addictive nature. Nicotine, the main ingredient in tobacco, is highly addictive, and smokers feed their habit even with limited funds. This is comparable to attempts to quit other highly addictive consumables like caffeine and sugar. Despite efforts and resources funnelled into sensitisation programmes on the dangers of tobacco, it remains widely used.

108 WHO (n 46) 1–5, respectively.
109 Sec 1(a) NTCA 2015, which was framed from art 3 of the FCTC.
110 Sec 2.
111 Sec 8.
112 Sec 2.
113 Egbe & others (n 109).

Further, enforcement of rules and policies remain problematic in Nigeria, so much so that even in the face of the coronavirus pandemic, people openly flouted government measures like lockdown, social distancing and the compulsory wearing of masks.[114] This could make for a better understanding of the indifference shown towards sensitisation on the dangers of tobacco.

Although Nigeria has put in place a system to oversee the country's tobacco control policy, measures which support proper implementation must be put in place. For this purpose, it has been suggested that implementation language be clear, simple and should not leave any room for misinterpretation.[115] This would help to avoid the mistakes of the 1990 Act and the problems that came with it.

The tobacco industry's interference with policymaking processes remains a major challenge to firm state control over tobacco use.[116] Referring to the tobacco industry as 'the greatest obstacle to ending the tobacco epidemic', Dr Vera Luiza da Costa e Silva, the head of the FCTC Secretariat, noted that the industry makes vast profits from making people dependent on tobacco and does not want the situation to change.[117] Representatives of Nigeria's tobacco industry were involved in the development of the Nigerian Industrial Standard for Tobacco and Tobacco Products – Specifications for Cigarettes of 2014 (NIS 463:2014).[118] This contradicts the WHO's recommendations, cannot be said to comply with best practices and could defeat the aim of formulating the Standards in the first place.

Lack of proper or detailed documentation of consultations with relevant stakeholders has also been identified as a deficiency in the process. As Juma and others noted from their study on the NCD prevention process in five African countries, one of which was Nigeria, although policies are usually developed after engaging relevant stakeholders, proper records of these were not usually kept, thereby making it difficult to determine their actual contributions to the cause.[119]

Illiteracy (including in urban areas) and ignorance on the dangers of tobacco also constitute a big problem to the tobacco fight in Nigeria. Illiteracy, or a lack of formal education, presumes ignorance or limited knowledge on a wide array of issues. It could manifest in different ways. For instance, the message in media jingles on the dangers of tobacco could be lost on an illiterate smoker. As already mentioned, the fact that health warnings on packets of tobacco are in the English language only is a limiting factor based on the assumption that smokers speak and

114 R Maclean 'COVID-19 outbreak in Nigeria is just one of Africa's alarming hotspots' *New York Times* (New York) 17 May 2020 (updated 29 June 2020) https://www.nytimes.com/2020/05/17/world/africa/coronavirus-kano-nigeria-hotspot-html (accessed 30 September 2021).

115 Egbe & others (n 78) 885.

116 WHO *WHO Report on the Global tobacco Epidemic 2019: Offer help to quit tobacco use* (2019) 19; Juma & others (n 52) 12.

117 WHO (n 119) 19.

118 Several staff of British American Tobacco (BAT) and one from International Tobacco Company (ITC) were members of the Technical Committee which worked on the document.

119 Juma & others (n 52) 9.

read English. To an illiterate, the words 'The Federal Ministry of Health warns that tobacco smokers are liable to die young' might not have any effect. It is also doubtful that such a person would look for an interpreter before purchasing or lighting a cigarette. Unfortunately, it will be tedious to ask the government to mandate that health warnings in local languages be included on tobacco packaging, and it is doubtful that tobacco companies would be willing to commit to such a venture. It is suggested that to address this problem, a leaflet carrying the stipulated health warning in the major local languages be introduced on tobacco packaging in Nigeria. This wording should be done in big lettering, making it hard to miss. It must be acknowledged that this suggestion will only work with packaged tobacco, such as cigars and cigarettes, and not other forms of tobacco like shisha.

Another challenge to tobacco control in Nigeria is the prevalence of locally made tobacco, as many people resort to 'home-made', 'locally made' or 'rolled' tobacco in Nigeria. It would be difficult if not futile to estimate the number of people who 'improvise' due to illiteracy, poverty, ease of access to materials and the absence of regulations. Since they are not manufactured and are not subject to any form of control or restriction, users indulge without the hassles attached to manufactured tobacco. There are different factors mitigating against the control of home-made tobacco. Not only will it be difficult to come up with accurate figures, but it also could prove challenging to reach many users who are located in remote or far-flung areas. The Nigerian government can partner with NGOs and other anti-tobacco campaigners to deal with the problem of home-made tobacco. Strategies can include tailor-made campaigns. These could take the form of sensitisation trips to villages, identifying places with high incidence of use, and door-to-door information or question-and-answer sessions in the local language and dialect.

Yet again, the ridiculously cheap pricing of tobacco in Nigeria works against the country's tobacco control efforts. As of October 2020, the price of the Marlboro brand of cigarettes was given to be under a dollar ($0.91) per a pack of 20.[120] This makes it affordable for anyone, including young people, to purchase and share cigarettes. Home-made tobacco is expected to be even cheaper. To combat this problem, there is an urgent need to upwardly review the prices of tobacco products. A steep increase in price is expected to result in a reduction in the number of users purchasing and the number of products sold.

The tobacco industry in Nigeria is seen as an all-important contributor to the economy. It is believed that BAT Nigeria has good salary packages for its staff and is a major source of revenue from tax. While it is true that thousands of people

120 K Buchholz 'Cigarettes: Where smoking breaks the bank' *Statista* 9 October 2020 www.statista.com/chart/15293/price-for-cigarettes-per-country/ (accessed 30 September 2021). In comparison during the same period, a pack of Marlboro cigarettes cost $25.12, $21.13, $15.90 and $14.25 in Australia, New Zealand, Ireland and the UK, respectively.

will be affected by a collapse of the tobacco industry, it is submitted that the damage to lives and the pressure on the country's health negates any so-called contribution to the economy. What the tobacco industry gives with one hand (jobs, contribution to the economy) it takes with the other (dependency, diseases and death). The economic contributions of the tobacco industry are not worth the toll that tobacco use takes on the fabric of the society it claims to benefit. The government, in conjunction with NGOs and other volunteers, could organise information sessions, workshops and the like, where the devastating effects of tobacco are juxtaposed with the industry's contribution, to show that any benefit is illusory. In the long run, the Nigerian government must focus on job creation. It must focus on encouraging and supporting the creation of other small- and medium-scale businesses to cushion the effects of projected losses of income.

The allowance made in the NTCA for designated smoking areas (DSAs) in places where smoking is otherwise banned is also problematic. Bars, lounges and outdoor recreation areas are known for the high incidence of tobacco use. Allowing DSAs has enabled operators to get away with not enforcing the stipulated restrictions. For the purpose of this chapter, individuals living in Nigeria were asked whether they were familiar with DSAs in places of relaxation. Most responses indicated no knowledge of DSAs. Some indicated that it was a 'free-for-all' in the clubs that they had been to, meaning smoking patrons were allowed to mingle freely with non-smoking patrons, and there was no restriction on smoking to begin with. In a study of 1,000 patrons of outdoor relaxation spots in Ibadan, Lasebikan and others stress the importance of smoke-free rules in outdoor spaces, as these venues may create unique opportunities for the prevention of NCDs.[121]

It must be noted that the National Tobacco Control Regulations (NTCR) of 2019 take the DSA provisions in the 2019 Act further. Clauses 11 and 12 extensively cover the requirements for DSAs, some of which have been set out in Table 5.1. Although attempts by the NTCR 2019 to hold DSAs to a strict standard must be commended, it must be added that with these rules must come mechanisms for enforcement.

Also, cessation of tobacco use can unfortunately not be forcefully achieved. To uphold the enjoyment of the right to health, the government in partnership with relevant stakeholders such as healthcare providers and NGOs can promote smoking cessation programmes to offer support to users who wish to quit. Primary healthcare providers can be trained to discourage tobacco use/encourage (not force) cessation during consultations and provide helpful information on the dangers of tobacco to patients and to refer users and their families (or carers) to mental health workers. The services of mental health workers (psychiatrists, psychologists and mental health nurses) can be offered to identified smokers.

These are some of the challenges posed to the tobacco efforts in Nigeria. Addressing these challenges will take the country closer to resolving its tobacco crisis.

121 V Lasebikan, T Lasebikan & S Adepoju 'Outdoor smoking in Nigeria: Prevalence, correlates and predictors' (2019) 19 *BMC Public Health* 1313.

5.5 Case law

There is not much to report by way of tobacco litigation in Nigeria. The federal government and some state governments instituted legal proceedings against leading tobacco companies in the country around 2007. The Lagos, Kano, Gombe, Oyo, Akwa Ibom and Ogun state governments sued tobacco companies for the costs of treating tobacco-related illnesses over a 20-year period, among other reliefs. The federal government's suit was instituted in response to an advertising campaign targeting young people. It sought $42.4 billion as damages for the dangers posed by tobacco on the health of Nigerians ($34.4 billion of this was for the future cost of treating patients with tobacco-related illnesses). The Lagos state government subsequently withdrew its suit,[122] and generally, not much has come out of these cases. In the *Ogun State* case,[123] BAT had delayed proceedings by challenging the court's jurisdiction, and it appealed upon dismissal of its notice of preliminary objection.[124] The appeal court had found the appeal to be 'grossly lacking in merit and substance' and dismissed it in its entirety.[125]

In the absence of any Nigerian case law on tobacco, guidance can be drawn from other jurisdictions. In the South African case of *British American Tobacco South Africa (Pty) Ltd v Minister of Health*,[126] the bone of contention was the proper interpretation of section 3(1)(a) of the Tobacco Control Act,[127] which prohibited the advertisement or promotion of tobacco products. The appellant deemed this prohibition as a limitation on its right to engage in commercial expression and the freedom of expression of tobacco users.[128] Having failed at the trial court, proceedings were brought before the Supreme Court of Appeal to determine if the provision was unconstitutional, and if one-on-one communication between the appellant (the tobacco manufacturer) and consenting adult consumers could be excluded from this prohibition.[129]

In its judgment, the Court reaffirmed that any right found in the Bill of Rights could be limited by a law of general application to the extent that such limitation is reasonable and justifiable in an open and democratic society based on human dignity, equality and freedom, duly taking into account factors including the nature of the right and the nature and extent of the limitation.[130] According to the Court, determining justification requires an overall assessment on a case-by-case

122 'Nigerian state withdraws $23 bln tobacco suit' *Reuters* 25 February 2008 https://www.reuters.com/article/nigeria-tobacco/nigerian-state-withdraws-23-bln-tobacco-lawsuit-idukl2545558120080225 (accessed 30 September 2020).

123 *Attorney General of Ogun State v British American Tobacco (Nigeria) Limited* Suit No AB/61/2008.

124 *British American Tobacco PLC v Attorney General of Ogun State* Suit No CA/I/254/2010.

125 As above.

126 (2012) 3 All SA 593 (SCA).

127 Act 83 of 1993 (as amended by the Tobacco Product Amendment Act 63 of 2008).

128 Para 9.

129 Para 10.

130 Para 15.

basis, based on proportionality.[131] In this instance, smokers' rights to receive information on tobacco products will be balanced against the government's obligation to protect citizens from the dangers of tobacco.[132] The Court found the powerful public health considerations addressed by the Act and the FCTC to be adequate justification for the policy.[133] The Court agreed with the submission of the National Council Against Smoking as amicus curiae that the right to communicate with consumers, which the appellant sought, amounted to an avenue for promoting the sale of its product, thereby circumventing the purpose of the prohibition in the first place.[134] The appeal was accordingly dismissed.[135]

Also of significance is South Africa's alcohol and tobacco ban during the COVID-19 pandemic. The South African government had effected the ban on health grounds under the Disaster Management Act.[136] The ban had been hailed as a heroic move, aimed at protecting citizens,[137] with organisations such as the Cancer Association of South Africa and the Heart and Stroke Foundation of South Africa lending their voices in support.[138] The tobacco industry had challenged the ban, however, labelling it bizarre and unconstitutional.[139] The ban on alcohol had been lifted temporarily but was re-imposed following a spike in COVID-19 cases in the country and what the president termed a burdening of the health system with related injuries, violence and trauma.[140]

The Fair Trade Independent Tobacco Association (FITA) had instituted legal proceedings against the Minister for Cooperative Governance and Traditional Affairs, alleging there was no rational connection between the ban and the government's aim of preventing the spread of the virus.[141] The court ruled that the Minister had acted reasonably, in order to save lives, and dismissed the proceedings.[142] With the ban on tobacco having been lifted in August 2020, FITA has changed direction towards an order prohibiting the government from re-imposing a ban down the line.[143]

131 Para 16.
132 As above.
133 Para 22.
134 Para 28.
135 Para 29.
136 Act 57 of 2002.
137 CO Egbe & SP Ngobese 'COVID-19 lockdown and the tobacco product ban in South Africa' (2020) 18 *Tobacco Induced Diseases* 39.
138 M Swart 'Tobacco companies sue South African government over smoking ban' *Al Jazeera* 19 August 2020 https://www.aljazeera.com/news/2020/8/19/tobacco-companies-sue-south-african-government-over-smoking-ban (accessed 30 September 2021).
139 As above.
140 'Return of alcohol ban stirs debate in South Africa' *Al Jazeera* 14 July 2020 https://www.aljazeera.com/news/2020/07/return-alcohol-ban-stirs-debate-south-africa-200714061421613.html (accessed 30 September 2021).
141 *Fair Trade Independent Tobacco Association v President of the Republic of South Africa* 2020 (6) SA 513 (GP).
142 As above paras 53 & 99.
143 Swart (n 141).

The Australian case of *McCabe v British American Tobacco Australia Services Limited*[144] is one of the biggest cases on tobacco and sheds light on the unwholesome practices of tobacco companies. It inspired changes nationally and internationally. Following her lung cancer diagnosis, Rolah McCabe, 51, instituted proceedings against BAT Australia in 2001.[145] McCabe sought damages from BAT, alleging that its negligence in manufacturing and marketing its cigarettes had caused her cancer. She argued that the defendant knew that cigarettes were addictive and dangerous to health, yet did nothing to reduce the risks of these happening, and had instead targeted children in its advertising and had publicly discredited research which showed the dangers of smoking.[146] The defendant alleged that they did not have any knowledge about lung cancer risks or difficulty in quitting smoking beyond what was in the public domain.[147] Instead, it asserted that for several decades, the Australian public had been made aware of the health dangers of tobacco and its addictive nature, and insisted the plaintiff should be deemed to have had that knowledge.[148]

The court was satisfied that as far back as 1985, BAT had anticipated 'a wave of litigation' and had allocated vast resources in readiness for this threat.[149] It was also satisfied that BAT understood the importance of documents to litigation, and appreciated the danger that their discovery posed,[150] as its lawyers provided advice on enhancing legal professional privilege so as to minimise a plaintiff's prospects of gaining the benefit of damaging documents.[151]

The court held that the process of discovery had been subverted by the defendant and its solicitors, with the sole aim of denying the plaintiff a fair trial, and the strategy used to apply their aim had been successful. Judgment was given in the plaintiff's favour, with $700,000 subsequently awarded as damages.[152]

On appeal, however, the judgment was overturned and sent back for trial.[153] McCabe had, unfortunately, passed away before the ruling of the Court of Appeal.[154] Proceedings were instituted again in 2006, which progressed all the way to the Supreme Court of Victoria. Eventually, in 2011, the McCabe family and BAT Australia reached a confidential settlement which was believed to have set the tobacco company back significantly.[155]

144 [2002] VSC 73.
145 Para 4.
146 Para 7.
147 Para 10.
148 Para 11.
149 Para 17.
150 As above.
151 Para 20.
152 Para 385.
153 *British American Tobacco Services Limited v Roxanne Joy Cowell as Representing the Estate of Rolah Ann McCabe deceased* [2002] VSCA 197 paras 191–192.
154 *Cowell* (n 156) para 3.
155 M Hawthorne 'McCabe family reaches settlement with tobacco giant over landmark case' *Sydney Morning Herald* 31 March 2011 https://www.smh.com.au/business/

The *McCabe* case significantly led to the Victorian government passing new legislation to address a major issue that had been raised in this case. A new section 254(1)(a) was inserted into the Victorian Crimes Act 1958 by the Crimes (Document Destruction) Act of 2006. Section 3 of the Victoria Evidence (Document Unavailability) Act of 2006 also expanded on the court's discretion in cases where evidence is concealed or destroyed. Significantly too, BAT's lawyers Clayton Utz announced it was undertaking an internal review, parted ways with one of its partners who had been involved in the *McCabe* case, and stopped representing the tobacco industry.[156] The judgment of Justice Eames, even though it had been reversed, and the *McCabe* case generally had a profound effect on discussions around tobacco and the actions of industry players.

The preceding cases show that a connection can be established between tobacco use and NCDs, violence and disorderly conduct. These can open the door for holding tobacco companies accountable for these issues in Nigeria and beyond.

5.6 Recommendations

It is possible to reverse the devastating effects of NCDs in Nigeria. However, this will require a synergy of efforts from the government and Nigerian society. Fifteen years on from Nigeria signing the FCTC, it has remained an attractive market for the tobacco industry for a combination of reasons, including its population size, its strategic positioning as a gateway to other markets, and the lax implementation system. Hence tobacco control has been a challenge. Unfortunately, with the prevalence of NCDs and deaths from NCDs, it has become expedient to double down on efforts at tobacco control. The NTCA of 2015 can be said to be FCTC compliant. However, more still needs to be done to make it fully compliant; for instance, the tax on tobacco is significantly low compared to the WHO-recommended level.

Recommendations made in this chapter include significantly increasing the prices of tobacco and tobacco tax to make tobacco less affordable for most people; developing aggressive information and sensitisation programmes, with wide coverage on the dangers of tobacco and the connection to NCDs; introducing warnings in all the main local languages in tobacco packaging to reach a wider array of people; including graphic imagery on packaging, showing the devastating effects of tobacco; and training healthcare providers to better provide cessation support for tobacco users. More comprehensive measures and strict anti-tobacco law targeting tobacco production and marketing have also been recommended.[157]

---

mccabe-family-reaches-settlement-with-tobacco-giant-over-landmark-case-20110331-1ch9z.html (accessed 30 September 2021).

156 W Birnbauer 'Justice denied: How lawyers set out to defeat a dying woman' *The Age* 29 October 2006 https://www.theage.com.au/national/justice-denied-how-lawyers-set-out-todefeat-a-dying-woman-20061029-ge3ux3.html (accessed 30 September 2021).

157 Adeloye & others (n 61).

In conclusion, even though Nigeria has taken steps in implementing tobacco control policies, there remains a lot that can be done to strengthen its position. To resolve these challenges to tobacco control in Nigeria, the government must collaborate with the health sector, NGOs, tobacco users themselves and other relevant stakeholders, as addressing the 'epidemic' of tobacco will strengthen the realisation of the right to health.

Bibliography

Abegunde, D & Stanciole, 'An estimation of the economic impact of chronic non-communicable diseases in selected countries' WHO Working Paper (2006) www.who.int/chp/working_paper_growth%20model29may.pdf (accessed 30 September 2021)

Adeloye, D; Auta, A; Fawibe, A; Gadanya, M; Ezeigwe, N; Mpazanje, RG; Dewan, MT; Omoyele, C; Alemu, W; Harhay, MO & Adewole, IF 'Current prevalence pattern of tobacco and smoking in Nigeria: A systemic review and meta-analysis' (2019) 19 *BMC Public Health* 1719

African Union *African charter on human and peoples rights* CAB/LEG/67/3 rev 5, 21 ILM 58 (1982)

Agaku, I; Akinyele, A & Oluwafemi, A 'Tobacco control in Nigeria – Policy recommendations' (2012) 10 *Tobacco induced Diseases* 1

Al Jazeera 'Return of alcohol ban stirs debate in South Africa' (14 July 2020) https://www.aljazeera.com/news/2020/07/return-alcohol-ban-stirs-debate-south-africa-200714061421613.html (accessed 30 September 2021)

Alli, YO 'Tobacco usage and Nigerian laws' https://www.yusufali.net/articles/Tobacco_Usage_And_Nigerian_Laws.pdf (accessed 30 September 2021)

Arora, M; Chauhan, K; John, S & Mukhopadhyay, A 'Multisectoral action for addressing social determinants of non-communicable diseases and mainstreaming health promotion in national health programmes in India' (2011) 36 *Indian Journal of Community Medicine* S43

Attorney General of Ogun State v British American Tobacco (Nigeria) Limited Suit No AB/61/2008

Birnbauer, W 'Justice denied: How lawyers set out to defeat a dying woman' *The Age* 29 October 2006 https://www.theage.com.au/national/justice-denied-how-lawyers-set-out-todefeat-a-dying-woman-20061029-ge3ux3.html (accessed 30 September 2021)

British American Tobacco South Africa (Pty) Ltd v Minister of Health (2012) 3 All SA 593 (SCA)

Buchholz, K 'Cigarettes: Where smoking breaks the bank' *Statista* 9 October 2020 www.statista.com/chart/15293/price-for-cigarettes-per-country/ (accessed 30 September 2021)

Busby, M 'Tobacco firm funded attack on council quit-smoking services' *The Guardian* (Australia) 3 July 2020 https://www.theguardian.com/business/2020/jul/02/tobacco-giant-behind-attack-on-quit-smoking-services (accessed 30 September 2021)

British American Tobacco PLC v Attorney General of Ogun State Suit No CA/I/254/2010CA

British American Tobacco Services Limited v Roxanne Joy Cowell as Representing the Estate of Rolah Ann McCabe Deceased [2002] VSCA 197

Committee on Economic, Social and Cultural Rights, General Comment 14, Twenty-Second Session, Geneva 25 April–12 May 2000, E/C.12/2000/4

Constitution of the Federal Republic of Nigeria, 1999

Durojaye, E 'The approaches of the African Commission to the right to health under the African Charter' (2013) 17 *Law, Democracy & Development* 393

Egbe, C; Bialous, SA & Glantz, SA 'Avoiding "a massive spin-off effect in West Africa and beyond": The tobacco industry stymies tobacco control in Nigeria' (2017) 19 *Nicotine & Tobacco Research*

Egbe, CO; Glantz, S & Bialous, SA 'Nigeria isn't doing enough to reduce tobacco use: Here's why' *The Conversation* 8 January 2019 https://theconversation.com/ealiza-isnt-doing-enough-to-reduce-tobacco-use-heres-why-108695 (accessed 30 September 2021)

Egbe, CO & Ngobese, SP 'COVID-19 lockdown and the tobacco product ban in South Africa' (2020) 18 *Tobacco Induced Diseases* 39

Fair Trade Independent Tobacco Association v President of the Republic of South Africa 2020 (6) SA 513 (GP)

Federal Ministry of Health, Nigeria *National Policy and Strategic Plan of Action on Prevention and Control of Non-Communicable Diseases (NCDs)* (2013)

Guardian (Nigeria) 'Increasing aggressive propaganda against the tobacco industry' (14 July 2014) http://ntcang.org/wp-content/uploads/2014/08/BAT-advert.pdf (accessed 30 September 2021)

Hawthorne, M 'McCabe family reaches settlement with tobacco giant over landmark case' *Sydney Morning Herald* 31 March 2011 https://www.smh.com.au/business/mccabe-family-reaches-settlement-with-tobacco-giant-over-landmark-case-20110331–1ch9z.html (accessed 30 September 2021)

Itanyi, IU; Onwasigwe, CN; Ossip, D; Uzochukwu, BSC; McIntosh, S; Aguwa, EN; Wang, S; Onoka, CA & Ezeanolue, EE 'Predictors of current tobacco smoking by adolescents in Nigeria: Interaction between school location and socioeconomic status' (2020) 18 *Tobacco Induced Diseases* 13

Juma, P; Mapa-Tassou, C; Mohamed, SF; Matanje Mwagomba, BL; Ndinda, C; Oluwasanu, M; Mbanya, J-C; Nkhata, MJ; Asiki, G & Kyobutungi, C 'Multi-sectoral action in non-communicable disease prevention policy development in five African countries' (2018) 18 *BMC Public Health* 953

Juma, P; Mohamed, SF; Matanje Mwagomba, BL; Ndinda, C; Mapa-Tassou, C; Oluwasanu, M; Oladepo, O; Abiona, O; Nkhata, MJ; Wisdom, JP & Mbanya, J-C 5 'Non-communicable disease prevention policy process in five African countries' (2018) 18 *BMC Public Health* 961

Kim, HC & Oh, SM 'Non-communicable diseases: Current status of major modifiable risk factors in Korea' (2013) 46 *Journal of Preventive Medicine & Public Health* 165

Lasebikan, V; Lasebikan, T & Adepoju, S 'Outdoor smoking in Nigeria: Prevalence, correlates and predictors' (2019) 19 *BMC Public Health* 1313

Maclean, R 'COVID-19 outbreak in Nigeria is just one of Africa's alarming hotspots' *New York Times* (New York) 17 May 2020 (updated 29 June 2020) https://www.nytimes.com/2020/05/17/world/africa/coronavirus-kano-nigeria-hotspot-html (accessed 30 September 2021)

National Cancer Institute, National Institute of Health *NCI dictionary of cancer terms* https://www.cancer.gov/publications/dictionaries/cancer-terms/def/tobacco (accessed 28 September 2021)

National Tobacco Control Act (Nigeria) 9 of 2015

National Tobacco Control Bill (Nigeria), 2009

National Tobacco Control Regulation (Nigeria), 2019

Nigeria (Constitution) Order-in-Council, 1954

Nigeria (Revenue allocation) Order-in-Council, 1951

Oladepo, O; Oluwasanu, M & Abiona, O 'Analysis of tobacco control policies in Nigeria: Historical development and application of multi-sectoral action' (2018) 18 *BMC Public Health* 959

Owoeye, F 'Product review: The Nigerian cigarette market has only one winner' *Nairametrics* 13 December 2018 https://nairametrics.com/2018/12/13/product-review-the-nigerian-cigarette-market-has-only-one-winner/ (accessed 29 September 2021)

Oyewole, BK; Animasahun, VJ & Chapman, HJ 'Tobacco use in Nigerian youth: A systematic review' (2018) 13 *PLOS ONE* e0196362

Reuters 'Nigerian state withdraws $23 bln tobacco suit' (25 February 2008) https://www.reuters.com/article/nigeria-tobacco/nigerian-state-withdraws-23-bln-tobacco-lawsuit-idukl2545558120080225 (accessed 30 September 2021)

Swart, M 'Tobacco companies sue South African government over smoking ban' *Al Jazeera* 19 August 2020 https://www.aljazeera.com/news/2020/8/19/tobacco-companies-sue-south-african-government-smoking-ban (accessed 30 September 2021)

Tobacco (Licences and Returns) Ordinance 1958 cap 198 Laws of the Federation of Nigeria 1958

Tobacco Smoking (Control) Decree (Nigeria) 20 of 1990

UN General Assembly *International covenant on economic, social and cultural rights* 16 December 1966, United Nations, Treaty Series, vol 993

UN General Assembly *Universal Declaration of Human Rights* 10 December 1948 217 A (III)

Van der Eijk, Y; Bialous, S & Glantz, S 'The tobacco industry and children's rights' (2018) 141 *Pediatrics* e20174106

WHO *Background paper: Non-communicable diseases in low-and middle-income countries* Regional High-Level Consultation in the Eastern Mediterranean Region on the Prevention and Control of Non-Communicable Diseases in Low-and Middle-Income Countries, Held in Tehran, 25–26 October 2010 https://www.who.int/nmh/events/2010/Tehran_Background_Paper.pdf?ua=1 (accessed 30 September 2021)

WHO 'Don't let tobacco take your breath away' https://apps.who.int/iris/bitstream/handle/10665/312260/WHO-NMH-PND-2019.3-eng.pdf (accessed 30 September 2021)

WHO 'Fact sheet: Non-communicable diseases' (1 June 2018) https://www.who.int/news-room/fact-sheets/detail/noncommunicable-diseases (accessed 30 September 2021)

WHO 'Fact sheet: Tobacco' (2020) https://www.who.int/news-room/fact-sheets/detail/tobacco (accessed 30 September 2021)

WHO 'Global action plan for the prevention and control on non-communicable diseases 2013–2020' (2013)

WHO 'Global adult tobacco survey in Nigeria: A success story in the African region' www.knowledge-action-portal.com/en/content/global-adult-tobacco-survey-nigeria-success-story-african-region (accessed 30 September 2021)

WHO *MPOWER: A policy package to reverse the tobacco epidemic* (WHO 2008)

WHO 'Tackling NCDs: "Best buys" and other recommended interventions for the prevention and control of non-communicable diseases' (2017)

WHO 'Time to deliver: Third UN high-level meeting on non-communicable diseases' https://www.who.int/ncds/governance/third-un-meeting/brochure.pdf?ua=1 (accessed 30 September 2021)

WHO 'Tobacco and cancer treatment outcomes' July 2018 https://www.who.int/tobacco/publications/knowledge-summaries/cancer-treatment-outcomes/en/ (accessed 30 September 2021)

WHO *Report on the global tobacco epidemic 2019: Offer help to quit tobacco use* (WHO 2019)

WHO *Report on the global tobacco epidemic 2008. The MPOWER package* (WHO 2008)

WHO 'World no tobacco day 2019' https://www.who.int/campaigns/world-no-tobacco-day/world-no-tobacco-day-2019 (accessed 30 September 2021)

6 Tobacco control and the right to health in Kenya

Implementation of the WHO FCTC

Emma Wanyonyi, Rachel Kitonyo and Belice Odamna

6.1 Introduction

During the United Nations General Assembly third high-level meeting on non-communicable diseases (NCDs),[1] the main NCDs contributing to the high mortality rates were identified to be cardiovascular diseases, chronic respiratory diseases, cancer, diabetes and mental health conditions. It was also noted that NCDs are responsible for 71 per cent of all deaths worldwide (41 million people), and each year the lives of 15 million people are cut short due to NCDs. Nearly 800,000 people die from suicide. Poorer people are disproportionately affected by NCDs and mental health conditions. The five factors considered as risks fuelling NCDs are unhealthy diets, tobacco use, air pollution, harmful use of alcohol and physical inactivity. Some of the above-mentioned risk factors can be regulated and eradicated by reducing exposure to tobacco and alcohol, taking up healthy diets and increasing physical activity.[2]

In Kenya, 50 per cent of patients admitted to hospitals and over 55 per cent of deaths occurring in hospitals are accounted for by NCDs.[3] The Kenya Demographic and Health Survey (2014) found that the use of tobacco is more rampant in men than women in Kenya.[4] The Global Adult Tobacco Survey (GATS) 2014, which is part of the Global Tobacco Surveillance System (GTSS), shows that 11.6 per cent (2.5 million) of Kenyan adults, including 19.1 per cent men and 4.5 per cent women, use tobacco products, while 9.5 million adults are exposed to second-hand smoke.[5] The Global Youth Tobacco Survey (GYTS) 2013 found that 9.9 per cent overall (12.8 per cent boys and 6.7 per cent girls) used tobacco products, with 4.9 per cent overall (7.4 per cent boys and 2.6 per cent girls) smoking cigarettes and 3.9 per cent overall (4.3 per cent boys and 3.3 per cent

1 Third United Nations General Assembly High-level meeting on NCDs, 27 September 2018, New York.
2 National Council for Population and Development *Policy Brief 57* (June 2017).
3 As above.
4 Kenya National Bureau of Statistics 'Kenya demographic and health survey' (2014).
5 Global Adult Tobacco Survey (GATS) Factsheet, Kenya 2014.

DOI: 10.4324/9781003264248-8

girls) using smokeless tobacco.[6] These figures show how rampant the use of tobacco is, therefore raising the risk of health complications, in particular NCDs, due to tobacco use.

Further, on expenditures for health issues arising out of tobacco use, it is estimated that for every dollar that the tobacco industry in Kenya gives in revenue, the country uses approximately three dollars to address the health effects of tobacco use through individual and government expenditure. On the environmental impact through farming, tobacco growing has led to environmental degradation and food insecurity due to reduction of the soil quality in the tobacco growing areas in Kenya, as well as deforestation caused by massive cutting of trees to be used for the curing of tobacco leaf.[7] In tobacco growing areas in Kenya, women and children provide most of the labour, leading to adverse effects on their socio-economic development including malnutrition, children's education levels and women's reproductive health.[8] Studies have found that the labour force in tobacco farms is prone to green tobacco sickness because of exposure to the tobacco leaf, and that further, women have reported increased miscarriages, especially during the tobacco harvest and curing periods.[9]

6.2 Right to health and NCDs

6.2.1 Understanding the right to health

The right to health was first articulated in the 1946 Constitution of the World Health Organization (WHO), whose Preamble defines health as a 'state of complete physical, mental and social well-being and not merely the absence of disease or infirmity'. The Preamble goes further to state that 'the enjoyment of the highest attainable standard of health is one of the fundamental rights of every human being without distinction of race, religion, political belief, economic or social condition'.[10] In 1948, the Universal Declaration of Human Rights (UDHR) also mentioned health as part of the right to an adequate standard of living.[11] The International Covenant on Economic, Social and Cultural Rights (ICESCR) in 1966 recognised health as a human right.[12]

6 Global Youth Tobacco Survey (GYTS) Factsheet, Kenya 2013.

7 Ministry of Health 'National tobacco control action plan (2010–2015)'.

8 As above.

9 International Tobacco Control Public Health Institute 'Women in tobacco farming: Health, equality and empowerment – A study conducted in China, Tanzania and Kenya' (2016).

10 Preamble to the Constitution of WHO. The WHO Constitution Was Adopted by the International Health Conference held in New York from 19 June to 22 July 1946, Signed on 22 July 1946 by the Representatives of 61 States.

11 Art 25, Universal Declaration of Human Rights, proclaimed on 10 December 1948, GA Resolution 217 A (III).

12 Art 12 International Covenant on Economic, Social and Cultural Rights, adopted on 16 December 1966.

The development of the right to health has grown, with pronouncements of the Committee on Economic, Social and Cultural Rights (CESCR) in General Comment 14. CESCR emphasised that enjoyment of the right to health ought to extend to the four elements of availability, accessibility, acceptability and quality.[13] On availability, functioning public health and healthcare facilities, goods and services as well as programmes have to be available in sufficient quantity: for tobacco control and management, the government must ensure both preventive and curative services within the public health system including education on tobacco use and treatment for the illnesses that occur as a result of tobacco use. On accessibility, health facilities, goods and services have to be accessible to everyone without discrimination: the government must ensure that they are physically and economically accessible, and users must be able to seek and receive information regarding health issues. Health facilities, goods and services must also be accessible to all without fear of discrimination. In terms of acceptability, all health facilities, goods and services must be respectful of medical ethics and be culturally appropriate and be of good quality, including the availability of skilled medical personnel, approved drugs, hospital equipment and adequate sanitation.[14]

6.2.2 The right to health and NCDs

At the emergence of NCDs at the global health and development agenda, human rights guiding principles were not adopted. The WHO Global Action Plan for the Prevention and Control of NCDs 2013–2020 in its NCD Global Monitoring Framework – objectives, targets and indicators – did not take into account aspects of human rights. The contribution of human rights, including the right to health, has not been fully utilised in NCD prevention and control as has been done for HIV, tuberculosis and reproductive health. The promotion of the right to health ensures conditions in which people can lead healthy lives by defining legal obligations of governments and putting in place accountability mechanisms to public health strategies.[15]

Tobacco use is one of the modifiable behavioural risk factors that cause NCDs and could be addressed through timely intervention and lifestyle modification to avert or delay the progression of disease. For instance, the cessation of smoking or no use of tobacco could delay the onset of tobacco-related NCDs or prevent them altogether. The 2014 Global Status on NCDs proposed cost-effective interventions for tobacco control to include reducing affordability of tobacco products by increasing tobacco excise taxes; creating by-laws to restrict tobacco

13 CESCR General Comment 14: The Right to the Highest Attainable Standard of Health (Art 12 of the Covenant) (2000) UN Doc E/C.12/2000/4 Dated 11 August 2000.

14 Art 12 (n 12).

15 S Gruskin & others 'Noncommunicable diseases and human rights: A promising synergy' (2014) 104 *American Journal of Public Health* 773 https://doi.org/10.2105/AJPH.2013.301849 (accessed 29 September 2021).

sale and use, completely smoke-free environments in all indoor workplaces, public spaces and public transport; warning people of the dangers of tobacco and tobacco smoke through effective health warnings and mass media campaigns; and banning all forms of tobacco advertising, promotion and sponsorship.[16]

The law, human rights and specifically the right to health are important in addressing NCDs and their effects. The implementation of the law and actualization of human rights is an important aspect in addressing NCDs – this includes fiscal policies like raising taxes or regulations that prescribe standards and mandate actions to be followed by government agencies to monitor enforcement. This may include addressing all NCD risk factors like unhealthy diets by regulating the marketing of foods and beverages and introducing proper food labelling standards; controlling the use of tobacco and its products; regulating alcohol to avoid its harmful use; preventing pollution; and putting in place measures to promote physical activity. It is however important to note that the law alone cannot effectively deal with the complex issues brought about by NCDs; a comprehensive approach to encourage healthier lifestyles includes community-based programmes, health promotion and a focus on prevention. Prevention is vital to the control of NCDs, and law and promotion of rights are important tools for achieving this goal.[17]

In arguing for human rights, including the right to health in prevention and control of NCDs, Sofia Gruskin and others[18] identify four areas in which the congruence of public health and human rights can enhance the response to NCDs. First, policies, laws, strategies and practices in areas including environmental, food, tobacco, pharmaceutical industries and the educational sector can promote healthy diets and lifestyles by imposing stringent, evidence-based standards. Second, as was evidenced in the HIV response, facilities, goods and services are required at every stage of risk factor and disease management, including appropriate technologies and essential medicines and vaccines that are available, accessible, acceptable and of optimal quality. The protection of human rights in identifying predictors of vulnerability to NCDs, as well as their detection and treatment, must take into account and support marginalised populations directly affected by NCDs. Third, while the WHO's NCD Global Monitoring Framework has included monitoring of national policies relating to food and tobacco industry, among others, attention needs to also shift to the degree to which such policies are implemented, including accountability mechanisms to monitor and review progress and the necessity of remedial action in relation to relevant actors. Finally, advancing accountability at the subnational, national and international

16 WHO *Global status report on noncommunicable diseases* (2014).

17 RS Magnusson & D Patterson 'The Role of law and governance reform in the global response to non-communicable diseases' (2014) 10 *Global Health* 44 https://doi.org/10.1186/1744-8603-10-44 (accessed 29 September 2021).

18 Gruskin & others (n 15).

levels through mechanisms specifically established to address NCDs and the use of the existing United Nations UN human rights machinery.

Social determinants of health,[19] which are to a great extent non-medical, also have an impact on health and well-being of individuals and society at large. While low income and sometimes low levels of education could be the main social determinants of health that can determine increased tobacco use, unequal distribution of resources and services can also lead to inequities in tobacco prevention and control and disparities in tobacco use.[20] It is important that tobacco control takes into account the social determinants approach by changing the environmental context and ensuring equal distribution of resources and services to eliminate tobacco use and related disparities. The right to health therefore extends to regulation of the production, manufacture, sale and use of tobacco and its products, provision of information on tobacco and ensuring adequate health facilities, goods and services to treat illnesses that occur as a result of tobacco use.

6.2.3 Kenya's legal framework on the right to health

Kenya's health policy after independence in 1963 was founded on the Sessional Paper 10 on African Socialism and its Application to Kenya of 1965, which emphasised the elimination of disease, poverty and illiteracy.[21] In 1994, the first Kenya Health Policy Framework[22] was put in place, and it guided the health sector until 2010 when the current Constitution was promulgated.

One of the effects of the promulgation of the 2010 Constitution was that through article 2(5)–(6), general rules of international law now form part of the laws of Kenya. The Article recognises ratified international conventions, treaties and principles of international law as part of Kenyan law and being applicable to Kenya. Some of the international treaties and declarations, general comments and recommendations from treaty bodies that have a bearing on tobacco control and the right to health that Kenya has signed and ratified include the Interna-

19 The World Health Organization defines social determinants of health as the non-medical factors that influence health outcomes. They are the conditions in which people are born, grow, work, live and age and the wider set of forces and systems shaping the conditions of daily life. These forces and systems include economic policies and systems, development agendas, social norms, social policies and political systems.

20 KT Brady 'Social determinants of health and smoking cessation: A challenge' (2020) 177 *American Journal of Psychiatry* 1029.

21 RG Wamai 'The Kenya health system: Analysis of the situation and enduring challenges' (2009) 52 *Japan Medical Association Journal* 134.

22 Government of Kenya 'The first National Health Sector Strategic Plan (NHSSP1) 1999–2004' Ministry of Health, Health Sector Reform Secretariat, Nairobi (1999).

tional Covenant on Civil and Political Rights,[23] ICESCR,[24] the African Charter on Human and Peoples' Rights (African Charter),[25] the African Charter on the Rights and Welfare of the Child (ACRWC),[26] the United Nations Convention on the Rights of the Child (CRC),[27] the Convention on the Elimination of Discrimination against Women (CEDAW),[28] and the World Health Organization Framework Convention on Tobacco Control (FCTC).

The Constitution of Kenya, 2010 guarantees the right to health under article 43(1)(a), which states: 'Every person has the right to the highest attainable standard of health which includes the right to health care services, including reproductive health care'.

However, the foregoing provision is read together with and subject to article 20(5), which states:

> In applying any right under Article 43, if the state claims that it does not have the resources to implement the right, a court, tribunal or other authority shall be guided by the following principles –
>
> a. It is the responsibility of the State to show that the resources are not available.
> b. In allocating resources, the State shall give priority to ensuring the widest possible enjoyment of the right or fundamental freedom having regard to prevailing circumstances, including the vulnerability of particular groups or individuals.
> c. The court, tribunal or other authority may not interfere with a decision by a state organ concerning the allocation of available resources, solely on the basis that it would have reached a different conclusion.

The Constitution further provides for implementation of rights and fundamental freedoms in article 21(2), which provides that the state shall take legislative, policy and other measures, including setting of standards, to achieve the progressive realisation of the rights guaranteed under article 43. The Constitution of Kenya

23 Arts 2, 3, 6 & 19, UN General Assembly, International Covenant on Civil and Political Rights, 16 December 1966, United Nations, Treaty Series, vol 999, 171.

24 Art 12, UN General Assembly, International Covenant on Economic, Social and Cultural Rights, 16 December 1966, United Nations, Treaty Series, vol 993, 3.

25 Art 16, Organisation of African Unity (OAU), African Charter on Human and Peoples' Rights (Banjul Charter), 27 June 1981, CAB/LEG/67/3 rev 5, 21 ILM 58 (1982).

26 Art 14, Organisation of African Unity (OAU), African Charter on the Rights and Welfare of the Child, 11 July 1990, CAB/LEG/24.9/49 (1990).

27 Art 24, UN General Assembly, Convention on the Rights of the Child, 20 November 1989, United Nations, Treaty Series, vol 1577, 3.

28 Art 12 & 14, UN General Assembly, Convention on the Elimination of All Forms of Discrimination Against Women, 18 December 1979, United Nations, Treaty Series, vol 1249, 13.

advances the justiciability of the right to health, among other rights, through the provisions of article 23 which gives the courts authority to uphold and enforce the Bill of Rights.

In terms of statutes, the Health Act 21 of 2017 is an important legislative framework to operationalise the right to health entrenched in the Constitution and also to unbundle functions of both the national and county governments in relation to health. First, the Act seeks to protect, respect, promote and fulfil the health rights of all persons in Kenya to the progressive realisation of their right to the highest attainable standard of health, including reproductive healthcare and the right to emergency medical treatment.[29] Second, the Act seeks to respect, protect, promote and fulfil children's rights to basic healthcare services and nutrition as advanced in articles 53(1)(c) and 43(1)(c) of the Constitution. Third, in all matters regarding health, the Act seeks to respect, protect, fulfil and promote the rights of vulnerable members of the society by virtue of article 21[30] of the Constitution. The Public Health Act,[31] originally promulgated in 1940, concerns itself with aspects of public health, including enforcement of tobacco control regulations.

6.3 The FCTC as a treaty to realise the right to health at the national level

In understanding how tobacco production, manufacture, sale and use is linked to the right to health, the Office of the High Commissioner for Human Rights (OHCHR), in explaining what the right to health is, notes that it includes not only appropriate and timely healthcare but also the fundamental determinants and contributors of health. Growing and use of tobacco and its products causes adverse health effects that occur in the short run as well as chronic ailments such as lung cancer that occur in the long term. Such threats to health and well-being should also be considered by governments in their duty to guarantee the right to health. The right to health is an inclusive right, which includes a wide range of factors that can help individuals to lead a healthy life, including receiving health-related education and information which is an important aspect in tobacco control.

States have the primary onus to protect and promote human rights, including the right to health, as is demonstrated in the Government of Kenya's continued action on tobacco control. These obligations generally fall into three categories: to protect, respect and fulfil.[32] The duty to respect demands that states desist

29 Sec 3 of the Health Act 21 of 2017.

30 Art 21 of the Constitution defines the vulnerable groups to include women, older members of society, persons with disabilities, children, youth, members of minority or marginalised communities, and members of particular ethnic, religious or cultural communities.

31 Cap 242 Laws of Kenya.

32 Office of the High Commissioner for Human Rights, CESCR General Comment 14: The Right to the Highest Attainable Standard of Health (art 12) (2000) UN Doc

from directly or indirectly interfering with a person's right to health. The duty to protect obligates states to prevent third parties from meddling with one's right to health. The onus to fulfil demands that states adopt necessary administrative, legislative, judicial, budgetary and promotional measures so as to adequately guarantee this right.

The World Health Assembly adopted the FCTC in 2003, and it became international law on 27 February 2005. Kenya signed and ratified the FCTC on 25 June 2004. The Treaty in its Preamble gives priority to the right to protect public health and also draws from article 12 of the ICESCR,[33] which provides for the right of everyone to the enjoyment of the highest attainable standard of health. The Preamble further draws from the WHO Constitution, CEDAW[34] and the CRC.[35] The Treaty has provisions geared towards reducing the demand for and supply of tobacco. The Convention also has provisions on tax and price measures to decrease tobacco demand,[36] protection of public health policies from industry interference,[37] protection from exposure to tobacco smoke,[38] packaging and labelling of tobacco products,[39] tobacco promotion, sponsorship and advertising,[40] and surveillance, research and information exchange.[41]

The FCTC was invaluable in providing guidelines that strengthened the tobacco control legislation, by setting minimum requirements for the content and scope of the law. The Convention accelerated adoption of the Tobacco Control Act, 2007. Additionally, fundamental social and environmental rights reaffirmed by the FCTC are entrenched in the Constitution of Kenya. The FCTC and the Tobacco Control Act, 2007, though both enacted before the promulgation of the Constitution of Kenya, sought to promote and protect the lives of the public by warning against tobacco use, educating the public about the dangers of tobacco use, regulating tobacco advertising and putting in place public health measures that the tobacco industry could not interfere with.

Table 6.1 summarises the provisions of the FCTC and corresponding provisions of the Tobacco Control Act, 2007 and the subsequent Tobacco Control Regulations, 2014 and an analysis of the level of compliance.

E/C.12/2000/4 dated 11 August 2000. See also R Lencucha & others 'Tobacco, trade, and the right to health' (2019) 2 *Canadian Human Rights Yearbook* 175.

33 International Covenant on Economic, Social and Cultural Rights (n 23).

34 Convention on the Elimination of Discrimination against Women (n 27).

35 Convention on the Rights of the Child (n 26).

36 Art 6 FCTC.

37 Art 5(3) FCTC.

38 Art 8 FCTC.

39 Art 11 FCTC.

40 Art 13 FCTC.

41 Art 20 FCTC.

Table 6.1 Level of Kenya's compliance

FCTC Provision	*Relevant Provision in the Tobacco Control Act*	*Level of Compliance*
Article 8: Protection from exposure to tobacco smoke	Part VI – Involuntary exposure to tobacco smoke The Tobacco Control Act restricts smoking in all indoor public spaces and workplaces. Other places where smoking is restricted include all forms of public transport, government facilities, hospitals, educational facilities, restaurants and public areas in hotels, amongst others.[42]	The country has complied with this provision and continues to ensure enforcement of the provisions of the law. Smoking has been permitted in designated smoking areas.[43] This is contrary to the spirit of article 8[44] of the FCTC and to its guidelines because it does not provide universal (100%) protection from exposure to tobacco smoke. [45]
Article 13: Tobacco advertising, promotion and sponsorship	Part V: Promotion The Tobacco Control Act avails a broad ban on all forms of promotion and advertising of tobacco products.[46] Specifically, the Act explicitly bans advertising on print and electronic media, be it domestic,[47] international,[48] or through internet communications and sales.[49] The ban also covers advertising through telephone, cellular phones, conventional mail[50] and sales through vending machines[51] complying with article 13 on promotion, advertising and sponsorship and to article 16 on sales by and to minors.	While the Kenyan law has been found to be comprehensive, some gaps have been identified, therefore making compliance with the FCTC only partial. The law does not cover reverse brand stretching, brand sharing and sponsorship through direct contributions to individuals, governments and events, falling short of the obligations under article 13 of FCTC.

42 Secs 33(1)–(2) Tobacco Control Act 2007.
43 Secs 33(2) & 35 Tobacco Control Act.
44 Art 8 FCTC.
45 Arts 5(3), 8, 9, 10, 11, 12, & 13 FCTC.
46 Secs 22–26 Tobacco Control Act.
47 Sec 25 Tobacco Control Act.
48 Sec 31 Tobacco Control Act.
49 Secs 22 & 26 Tobacco Control Act.
50 Sec 25 Tobacco Control Act.
51 Sec 17 Tobacco Control Act.

FCTC Provision	*Relevant Provision in the Tobacco Control Act*	*Level of Compliance*
	Outdoor and point-of-sale advertising are also banned,[52] as is the free distribution of any form of tobacco products with or without the purchase of other products, as well as free distribution of other products with the purchase of a tobacco product.[53] Similarly, toys, snacks and sweets resembling tobacco products are banned.[54] Organising, promoting and sponsoring of activities such as competitions and raffles in exchange for a tobacco product is also prohibited.[55] Use of brand marking (words, designs, images, logos and colour) on physical structures not owned, leased or used by a manufacturer,[56] on non-tobacco products[57] and brand stretching[58] are all prohibited. Additionally, promotion by sponsorship (of sporting, cultural, artistic, recreational, and educational or entertainment programs or events)[59] and false promotion are banned in compliance with article 13 of the FCTC and its guidelines.	The Act is also not explicit on addressing retail incentive programmes as well as paid and unpaid placement in film, TV and other media even though a broad interpretation of the general provisions on Tobacco advertising, promotion and sponsorship under sec 25 and other related sections would cover them.[60] Finally, the Act does not define 'sponsorship', making the scope of prohibitions unclear.

(*Continued*)

52 Secs 25 & 19 Tobacco Control Act.
53 Sec 30 Tobacco Control Act.
54 Sec 16 Tobacco Control Act.
55 Sec 26 Tobacco Control Act.
56 Sec 27 Tobacco Control Act.
57 Sec 29 Tobacco Control Act.
58 Sec 25 Tobacco Control Act.
59 Sec 26 Tobacco Control Act.
60 Tobacco Control Act.

Table 6.1 (Continued)

FCTC Provision	*Relevant Provision in the Tobacco Control Act*	*Level of Compliance*
Article 11: Packaging and labelling of tobacco products	Section 21: Information required on packages The Tobacco Control Act requires every tobacco package to have at least two text warning labels of the same health message in both English and Kiswahili, comprising not less than 30% of the total surface area of the front panel and 50% of the total surface area of the rear panel.[61] The warning must be in conspicuous and legible text with even rotation and distribution of all the messages for a 12-month period. These features align the Kenyan law and with article 11 of the FCTC. Through the Tobacco Control Regulations 2014, the Minister of Health prescribes that warnings under this Act, be in the form of pictures, further compliance with article 11 of the FCTC that provides that health warnings may take the form of pictograms. Section 21 of the Act prescribes that health warnings be placed on the packaging just beneath the cellophane or any other form of clear wrapping used but does not explicitly require that they may not be placed in a manner that they may result to them getting permanently destroyed or hidden once the pack has been opened as provided in article 11 guidelines.	The country has partially complied with the provisions of the FCTC on packaging and labelling. With regard to the message content, the text warnings as provided in the Act are aligned with the FCTC article 11 in describing the health impacts and effects of the use of tobacco on family and friends. Although the Act does not unequivocally ban certain terms such as 'mild', 'light' and 'low tar', it does (in sec 23) prohibit promotion of tobacco products by any means, including but not limited to the means of the packaging, that are or may be misleading, deceptive or false or as may be prescribed by the relevant Minister. This subject section is interpreted as prohibiting false, misleading descriptors, terms, figuratives, trademarks or other representations on tobacco packaging.[62] complied with the provisions of the FCTC on packaging and labelling. With regard to the message content, the text warnings as provided in the Act are aligned with

61 Sec 21 Tobacco Control Act.
62 Tobacco Control Act.

FCTC Provision	*Relevant Provision in the Tobacco Control Act*	*Level of Compliance*
	Alignment to the FCTC is, however, addressed through the Regulations which ban devices that may be used to obscure, cover, alter and obstruct from the display of the indicated health messages or warning. It also bans the design and use of packages with covers that may obstruct the given health messages and warnings and requires that health messages be printed on both wrapper and package in the event that the wrapper is likely to obscure or obliterate the prescribed health warning.[63]	the FCTC article 11 in describing the health impacts and effects of the use of tobacco on family and friends. Although the Act does not unequivocally ban certain terms such as 'mild', 'light' and 'low tar', it does (in sec 23) prohibit promotion of tobacco products by any means, including but not limited to the means of the packaging, that are or may be misleading, deceptive or false or as may be prescribed by the relevant Minister. This subject section is interpreted as prohibiting false, misleading descriptors, terms, figuratives, trademarks or other representations on tobacco packaging.[64] Furthermore, section 8 of the Tobacco Control Regulations 2014 does provide greater clarity by banning use of packaging that carries a brand name, pictorial, trademark or any other form of representation or a sign that implies the tobacco product is or could be less harmful to health as compared any other tobacco product in accordance with article 11 of the FCTC.

(*Continued*)

63 Tobacco Control Regulations, 2014.
64 Tobacco Control Act.

Table 6.1 (Continued)

FCTC Provision	*Relevant Provision in the Tobacco Control Act*	*Level of Compliance*
		Additional content prescribed under the Act includes a declaration as to the nicotine, tar and any other constituents which should directly be placed, conspicuously and prominently on the right side or part of the packaging, beneath the cellophane or any form of clear wrapping. In line with article 11 of the FCTC, this is only limited to the revelation of the contents and not their quantity.
Article 13: Tobacco advertising, promotion and sponsorship Article 15: Illicit trade in tobacco products Article 16: Sales to and by minors	Sections 15–20: Restriction of sales of tobacco products Section 18(1) of the Tobacco Control Act 2007 forbids the sale of cigarettes except in a set containing a minimum of 10 sticks of cigarettes or at least 10 units of other products. Other sale restrictions include a ban of sale by vending machines (section 17(1)). In 2017, the Minister of Health banned the importation, manufacture, sale, and offer for sale, use, advertising, promotion and distribution of shisha or water pipes.[65] Section 15(1) of the Act forbids the sale of any kind of tobacco products to anyone under the age of 18 as per article 16 of the FCTC and requires that signs are posted by every retailer to inform the public that sale to persons under the age of 18 is prohibited.[66]	However, the Act and its Regulations are inconsistent with the FCTC in areas including provision of advice on cessation, a quit-line phone number and/or website as advanced in the guidelines to article 11 of the FCTC. Additionally, the law does not directly address the possible obstruction of prescribed health messages and warnings by other required labelling and packaging marks, such as tax stamps (as required by article 15 of the WHO FCTC) or commercial inserts and onserts.[67]

65 The Public Health (Control of Shisha Smoking) Rules 2017.

66 Sec 15(3) Tobacco Control Act.

67 Arts 5(3), 8, 9, 10, 11, 12 & 13 FCTC.

FCTC Provision	*Relevant Provision in the Tobacco Control Act*	*Level of Compliance*
		Restrictions provided in the Act are largely compliant with the FCTC including article 16 that prohibits the sale of single sticks of cigarettes and sale to and by minors and article 13 on ban on advertising and sale by mail. The Act and its regulations do not restrict the sale of tobacco products based on location, meaning that sale is permitted in public places described above as places where smoking is prohibited or restricted. The law also does not require a specific license for the sale of tobacco products as provided under Article 15 of the WHO FCTC.
Article 9: Regulation of the contents of tobacco products Article 10: Regulation of tobacco product disclosures	Section 4(a–d): Regulation of contents and disclosures The Minister is empowered to regulate emissions and contents of tobacco products by prescribing permissible levels of tar, nicotine and other constituents.[68] This includes ingredients that could facilitate or cause nicotine uptake, those that create or have an impression of health benefits and those linked to vitality and strength.[69] The Minister also has the powers to prescribe methods to test tobacco products and emissions and prescribe information to be declared by the tobacco manufacturers.	The powers provided to the Minister of Health align with obligations under articles 9 and 10 of the FCTC and their guidelines, therefore making the country partially compliant. The Minister is yet to make Regulations to actualise these obligations.

(*Continued*)

68 Sec 4(a)–(b) Tobacco Control Act.
69 Art 9–10 FCTC.

Table 6.1 (Continued)

FCTC Provision	*Relevant Provision in the Tobacco Control Act*	*Level of Compliance*
Article 6: Price and tax measures to reduce the demand for tobacco	Under the Tobacco Control Act, the Minister of Finance is empowered to develop and implement price and tax policies on tobacco products so as to advance tobacco control goals.[70] Tax policies in Kenya are released annually as an Act of Parliament in the form of Regulations usually gazetted by the Finance Minister.[71]	Over the years, there have been frequent changes in the tobacco excise tax policy in Kenya, culminating in the Excise Duty Act 23 of 2015.[72] This Act was an effort towards aligning Kenya's tobacco tax measures to the FCTC article 6 and its guidelines by, amongst other things, simplification of the tobacco tax structure by introducing a specific, uniform tax rate for all types of cigarettes and an equal rate for all products, progressive increase of the excise tax rate towards the WHO recommended 70% of retail selling price, application of inflation to avoid eroding of the real value of the excise tax and greater strengthening of tax administration. However, the Excise Duty Act has been amended severally with the latest change being the re-introduction of a two-tiered system based on product characteristics and price as announced through the Minister of Finance in his budget statement of the financial year 2017/ 2018. This falls short of the FCTC recommendations.

70 Sec 12 Tobacco Control Act.

71 WHO 'Joint national capacity assessment on the implementation of effective tobacco control policies in Kenya' (2012).

72 Institute of Legislative Affairs 'Tax campaign case study: Successful passage of the Kenya Excise Duty Act, 2015' (2016).

6.4 An assessment of the effectiveness of efforts to implement the FCTC through the Tobacco Control Act, 2007 and other national laws

There has been a mixed level of enforcement and success for different policy areas in implementation of tobacco law in Kenya. This assessment will be based on the WHO's MPOWER package of six proven policies developed to expand the fight against the tobacco epidemic: (1) monitoring tobacco use and prevention policies; (2) protecting people from tobacco use; (3) offering help to quit tobacco use; (4) warning about dangers of tobacco; (5) enforcing bans on tobacco advertising, promotion and sponsorship; and (6) raising taxes on tobacco.

6.4.1 Monitoring and evaluation (article 20)

The Ministry of Health takes leadership in tobacco control epidemiological surveillance often in collaboration with other institutions including the National Campaign Against Drug Abuse (NACADA), Kenya Medical Research Institution (KEMRI), universities and civil society organisations.[73] Kenya is part of the GTSS and has so far participated in the GYTS in 2001, 2007 and 2013, the GATS in 2014 and the Global Health Professions' Students Survey (GHPSS) in 2009. Tobacco consumption data has also been collected through the Kenya Demographic and Health Survey in 2008/2009. Other institutions have carried out smaller-scale research and monitoring studies on different aspects of tobacco control, including implementation and compliance studies some of which are referenced in this chapter. Civil society organisations in particular have taken up monitoring the tobacco industry, for example through the documented research on tobacco industry interference in Kenya carried out by the International Institute for Legislative Affairs in 2017 which uncovered tobacco industry interference strategies used since the 1970s.[74]

The joint national capacity assessment of 2012 found that mechanisms and capacity for national tobacco control surveillance and reporting are not fully in place. The national surveys are not carried out as regularly as they should be and are highly donor dependent, making them unsustainable.

6.4.2 Protection from tobacco smoke/smoke-free environments (article 8)

In smoke-free environments, while there has been good compliance in most government buildings, public offices and other workplaces, tobacco smoke exposure is still observed in the entertainment and hospitality sectors.[75] This is corroborated by a study by Karimi and others which showed that observance of

73 WHO (n 69).

74 Centre for Tobacco Control in Africa 'Smoking out lies: Documents research on tobacco industry interference in Kenya' (2017).

75 WHO (n 69).

the smoke-free provisions in the tobacco control law in restaurants and within Nairobi County is partial.[76]

With regard to designated smoking area requirements, there is uneven compliance.[77] The Tobacco Control Regulations provide for further regulations including expanding the scope of a 'public place' by including walkways and verandas adjacent to public places, private vehicles when children are on board and streets,[78] the size and text of 'no smoking' signs[79] to be displayed at premises, and placing obligations for supervision of smoking regulations at premises on managers.[80] If these are enforced, implementation of smoke-free policy will be strengthened.

6.4.3 *Offering help to quit tobacco use (article 14)*

The GATS 2014 showed 77.4 per cent of current smokers planned to or were thinking about quitting. However, there is little counselling offered in public health facilities to assist tobacco users to quit.[81] In 2017, Kenya adopted its national guidelines for tobacco dependence, treatment and cessation which aim to integrate tobacco dependence treatment and cessation interventions into the healthcare services, provide opportunity for tobacco users to quit, create standards and tools for tobacco dependence treatment and cessation support and interventions, and establish a monitoring and evaluation framework. Furthermore, one of the objectives of the National Tobacco Control Strategic Plan 2017–2022 is to establish tobacco cessation services within primary healthcare by establishing regional cessation clinics, disseminating the tobacco cessation guidelines and establishing a national quit-line for tobacco cessation.

To finance cessation services, the TCA creates a Tobacco Control Fund to be used for among other things, promotion of national cessation and rehabilitation programmes.[82]

6.4.4 *Warning about the dangers of tobacco use (articles 11 and 12)*

Under section 9 of the Tobacco Control Act, the government should

> promote public awareness about the health consequences, addictive nature and mortal threat posed by tobacco consumption and exposure to second-hand smoke and the harmful effects of tobacco growing and handling

76 KJ Karimi, R Ayah & T Olewe 'Adherence to the tobacco control act, 2007: Presence of a workplace policy on tobacco use in bars and restaurants in Nairobi, Kenya' (2016) 6 *BMJ Open* 1.

77 WHO (n 69).

78 Reg 15(a)–(b), Tobacco Control Regulations 2014.

79 Reg 16.

80 Reg 17.

81 Tobacco Control Regulations.

82 As above.

through a comprehensive nationwide education and information campaign through the relevant Ministries, departments, authorities and other agencies.

The government is also obligated to provide training, sensitisation and awareness programmes for different cadres of actors, including community, social workers and the media. Currently, tobacco control awareness and sensitisation are part of the overall public health education conducted through the Department of Health promotion.

Implementation of graphic health warnings[83] has been ongoing since 2016. Currently, three out of the 15 pictures that are provided in the Regulations have appeared on cigarette packs. Enforcement of the Regulations[84] will increase the effectiveness of the graphic health warnings.

6.4.5 *Enforcing advertising promotion and sponsorship bans (article 13)*

Compliance with the tobacco advertising, promotion and sponsorship (TAPS) ban is high, though it is limited for direct advertising and moderate for indirect[85] and point-of-sale advertising. A TAPS ban compliance study carried out in 2018 in select counties in Kenya showed that advertising and promotion is still prevalent at points of sale in Kenya.[86] This happens in the form of product displays, poster/signs/stickers, banners, flyers, window packs, toys and sweets resembling tobacco products, brand marking and stretching, video screens and illuminated ads. Promotional activities observed included discount coupons (e.g. buy one, get one free), free samples of tobacco products, competitions associated with tobacco products and brands, and free gifts with purchase of tobacco products. Tobacco placement in entertainment and media is largely unchecked.[87]

Compliance with sponsorship restrictions is problematic. The tobacco industry has on several occasions been involved in sponsorship of activities and events resulting in favourable action from the government and other actors. For instance, a top Kenyan tobacco company has made contribution to the COVID-19 pandemic response through manufacture and distribution of hand sanitisers, resulting in the listing of tobacco products in the essential products list by the National Emergency Response Committee on Coronavirus.[88]

83 Reg 3, Tobacco Control Regulations.

84 Reg 6(1)–(3), Tobacco Control Regulations.

85 Tobacco Control Regulations (n 76).

86 Kenya Tobacco Control Alliance 'Tobacco advertising, promotion and display at points-of-sale in Kenya: A compliance monitoring study carried out in Nairobi, Kakamega, Vihiga and Tharaka Nithi Counties' (2018).

87 WHO 'Joint national capacity assessment on the implementation of effective tobacco control policies in Kenya' (2012).

88 P Vidija 'Kenya lists alcohol, tobacco among essential products' *The Star* (Nairobi) 8 April 2020.

6.4.6 *Raising tobacco prices and taxes (article 6)*

Implementation of tobacco tax and price measures in Kenya has had mixed outcomes. Kenya's excise tax system has been a complex transition between different structures (ad valorem, specific and various tier-based formulae based on retail selling price, product characteristics and packaging characteristics) from the 1980s to 2012.[89] In 2012, the Finance Act simplified the tax structure by reducing the four-tiered specific tax system to a single-tier system and provided for automatic adjustment for inflation, the first step towards compliance with article 6 of the FCTC and its guidelines.[90] This was followed in 2015 with the enactment of the Excise Duty Act, which was expected to 'deepen tax Administration Reforms and ease compliance',[91] and it introduced a uniform specific rate. This was implemented for two years before the Act was amended to re-introduce a two-tier system based on product characteristics (plain and filtered cigarettes), which prevails to date. The Finance Act of 2019 introduced a 15 per cent increase in the excise rate for all cigarettes.[92]

In May 2020, Kenya ratified the Protocol to Eliminate Illicit Trade in Tobacco Products,[93] an essential step towards greater cross-border collaboration in the control of illicit tobacco products. However, Kenya had already established a strong system to address illicit trade within its borders. In 2010, the country introduced digital tax stamps, licensing of tobacco manufacturers and an electronic cargo tracing system and set up tax enforcement units[94] to strengthen tax administration. In 2014, the Kenya Revenue Authority (KRA) introduced the Electronic Goods Management System (EGMS) which provides for a strong tracking and tracing system.

6.5 Litigation against tobacco control measures in Kenya

Since 2006, the tobacco industry in Kenya has filed numerous lawsuits challenging the constitutionality of the Tobacco Control Act and Regulations[95] developed thereunder. The intention of the litigation has been to deflect attention from tobacco use as a public health problem requiring government intervention in the form of regulation, and the tobacco industry as the vector of the problem,

89 Institute for Legislative Affairs 'Tax adjustment proposals for the financial year 2019/20' (2019).
90 WHO 'Technical manual on tobacco tax administration' (2013).
91 Ministry of Finance 'Republic of Kenya budget statement for the fiscal year 2015–2016' (2015).
92 Finance Act of Kenya 2019.
93 J Muchangi 'Kenya ratifies treaty to end tobacco smuggling' *The Star* (Nairobi, Kenya) 9 May 2020.
94 M Stoklosa 'International Community welcomes Kenya to the Protocol to eliminate illicit trade in tobacco products' *Tobacco Atlas* 9 May 2020.
95 Tobacco Control Regulations, 2014 (Legal Notice 169, Legislative Supplement 161).

and to focus instead on constitutional arguments about the commercial rights of corporations. The litigation in essence has been pitting the right to health against rights to intellectual property and procedural justice. This section shall focus on litigation between 2015 and 2020.

6.5.1 British American Tobacco Kenya (Ltd) *case*

In 2015, British American Tobacco Kenya (Ltd), hereinafter referred to as BAT (K), challenged the constitutionality of the Tobacco Control Regulations, 2014 that had been made pursuant to section 53 of the Tobacco Control Act. BAT (K) challenged both the procedure followed in enactment of the Regulations as well as the measures in the Regulations.[96]

With regard to procedure, BAT (K) alleged that as a stakeholder who would be affected by the Regulations, it had not been (sufficiently) consulted during the formulation of the Regulations and its representations had not been taken into account and therefore stakeholder engagement was limited and unsatisfactory. These arguments centred around articles 10 and 118 of the Constitution, which provide inter alia for the participation of the people as one of the national values and principles of governance, and for public access and participation in parliamentary proceedings, where Parliament is required to facilitate public participation and involvement in the legislative business of Parliament and its committees. Further, they argued that the Ministry of Health had not published a regulatory impact statement contrary to the provisions of section 6 of the Statutory Instruments Act 23 of 2013 or tabled the regulatory impact statement or compliance certificate as required by law before Parliament.

With regard to substantive provisions of the regulations, BAT (K) challenged:

1 The imposition of a sum of 2 per cent of the total worth of all tobacco products imported or manufactured in Kenya as compensation, and the limitation of contact between tobacco industry players and public officers based on article 5(3) of the FCTC as discriminatory, since such strictures did not apply to any other industries.
2 The introduction of graphic health warnings as being arbitrary, unnecessary, unproportioned and infringing on their intellectual property rights insofar as it affected the use of their trademarks.
3 The requirement for the tobacco industry to disclose certain information on tobacco products, on the grounds that these were trade secrets, could lead to counterfeiting by illicit manufacturers resulting in loss of tax revenue to the government and could mislead the public as to the relative safety of one product over another.

96 *British American Tobacco Kenya Ltd v Cabinet Secretary for the Ministry of Health* [2016] eKLR.

4 That the provisions of the ban on smoking in public areas were ultra vires the ministerial powers in the Tobacco Control Act.
5 That the Minister for Health did not have power to domesticate or even to implement article 5(3) of the FCTC and the Guidelines thereto.

BAT (K) therefore sought that the entire set of regulations be declared null and void. In the course of submissions, BAT (K) also averred that the harmful effects of tobacco were not relevant to 'the narrow inquiry on the constitutionality of the measures challenged' which the court was required to undertake.

The court ruled:

> Having mulled over the intentions of the legislation and the implications of tobacco consumption on public health and the health of the individual . . . that the effects of a product on the health rights of others cannot be divorced from the process and need for its regulation.[97]

The court therefore proceeded to evaluate the constitutionality of the Regulations with regard to Kenya's public health system and its needs vis-à-vis the commercial interests and rights of stakeholders in the tobacco industry, while simultaneously balancing the rights of BAT (K) with the rights of others, including but not limited to the consumers of tobacco products, as well as the general public that is exposed to tobacco and its products.

The court readily dismissed the arguments on the inadequacy of the procedure during adoption of the regulations. The court found that it was not necessary for every person or professional to be invited to every forum convened for public participation and that there could be various means of facilitating an appropriate degree of participation in the law-making process, so long as a reasonable opportunity is offered to members of the public and all interested parties to know about the issue and have an adequate say. Since BAT (K) had attended some of the public participation fora and submitted written representations, the fact that their representations did not prevail was no basis for impugning the Regulations for lack of participation. In essence, the court ruled that public participation was a right to be heard, not a right to get one's way.

With regard to the Minister failing to publish a regulatory impact statement, it was held that it was not necessary to do so, as there was an exception under the Statutory Instruments Act 23 of 2013 that where the anticipated law arises under a statue that is significantly complementary or uniform with the parent act, then no regulatory impact assessment is required.

In determining whether the *solatium* compensatory contribution, limitation of contact between tobacco industry players and public officers, the requirements for labelling and packaging of tobacco products plus the requirements for tobacco products disclosure were unconstitutional for being arbitrary, unreasonable or

97 As above.

discriminatory, the court decided them as one issue and considered the legal status of the FCTC and the Guidelines adopted thereunder. The court rejected BAT's arguments that the subject provisions of the FCTC are not binding or that the government of Kenya cannot make Regulations to implement them. The court also noted that article 2(5) and (6) of the Constitution of Kenya recognised that the general rules of international law, as well as any international conventions and treaties to which Kenya is party to, shall form part of Kenyan law. Further, the court advanced that the Tobacco Control Act was adopted in 2007 after Kenya had ratified the FCTC and that this appeared to have been an intention to comply with the FCTC.

The Court also considered the mandate of the WHO as provided in article 2 of its Constitution:

> To propose conventions, agreements and regulations, and make recommendations with respect to international health matters and to perform such duties as may be assigned thereby to the Organization and are consistent with its objective . . .

and ruled

> that the guidelines for the Implementation of Article 5(3) of the WHO FCTC enacted pursuant to powers granted under the WHO FCTC were 'regulations' formulated by the WHO under Article 2 of the WHO Constitution and therefore binding upon State Parties to the WHO.

The Court then noted that paragraph 5 of the Guidelines to article 5(3) provided that 'parties are encouraged to implement these guidelines to the extent possible in accordance with their national law'. The court found that the Guidelines to article 5(3) did not in any way contravene either the Constitution of Kenya or the Tobacco Control Act. With regard to whether the limitation of contact between public officers and tobacco industry players was discriminatory, the court found that

> BAT(K) and other players in the tobacco industry were a peculiar industry whose products had been scientifically implicated in debility, disease and death . . . and that given the nature of the industry, the differential treatment with other industries is permissible.

For this ruling, the court relied on *State of Kesata v NM Thomas*,[98] where it was observed that

> the principle of equality does not mean that every law must have universal application for all persons who are not by nature, attainment or circumstances

98 (1976) AIR 490, SCR (17906).

> in the same position and the varying needs of different classes of persons require special treatment. . . . Equality means parity of treatment under parity of conditions. Equality does not connote absolute equality. A classification in order to be constitutional must rest upon distinctions that are substantial and not merely illusory. The test is whether it has a reasonable basis free from artificiality and arbitrariness embracing all and omitting none naturally falling into that category.

With regard to the *solatium* compensatory contribution, BAT (K) had argued that this amounted to unlawful denial and limitation of BAT's right to own property. The court determined that the reason behind the creation of the Tobacco Control Fund into which the *solatium* compensator contribution would be paid was in fact to assist the state in addressing the negative effects of tobacco consumption, and that it was provided for in the Tobacco Control Act and therefore did not amount to a limitation of BAT (K)'s right to property.

In light of the debilitating effects of tobacco consumption, the court upheld the Regulations (save for the requirement to disclose information relating to their market share) so as to protect the public, both those who smoked and those who did not.

BAT (K) appealed to the Court of Appeal[99] where it once again raised the issue of public participation, the violation of their rights to non-discrimination and to property and whether tobacco products effects on health were of any importance to the court proceedings. The Court of Appeal agreed with the High Court's interpretation of the right to public participation and the finding that the tobacco industry could not be compared to manufacturers of other products and thus could not expect equal treatment given the harmful effects of tobacco products. With regard to the constitutionality of the *solatium* compensatory contribution, the court noted that

> the contribution of 2% of the value of the tobacco products manufactured or imported, does not appear to be too high in the circumstances. It is indeed a small price that the appellant and those in the industry have to pay to mitigate the adverse effects of tobacco products. It is consistent with the State's obligation under Article 43(1)(a) of the Constitution to provide the highest attainable standard of health.

The court found that whatever infringement of intellectual property rights was caused by the requirement for tobacco products disclosure was reasonable and justifiable, as it was intended for counteractive reasons mainly to mitigate and control health problems related to tobacco. Based on the balancing act that the Court of Appeal undertook between the public health interests as well as the

99 *British American Tobacco Ltd v Cabinet Secretary for the Ministry of Health* **Civil Appeal 112 of 2016 [2017] eKLR.**

commercial rights of the tobacco industry and its stakeholders, public health prevailed, and therefore the appeal was dismissed in its entirety.

BAT (K) appealed again to the Supreme Court of Kenya,[100] raising the same procedural and substantive issues. In addition, it also sought a determination of what doctrine was applicable where there were competing rights. The Supreme Court agreed with all the findings of the Court of Appeal and those of the High Court on all the issues raised. With regard to the test where there were competing rights, the court found:

> The limitation of constitutional rights for a purpose that was reasonable and necessary in a democratic society involved the weighing up of competing values, and ultimately an assessment based on proportionality . . . so as to resolve the tension between such rights where it arose. In considering decisions limiting fundamental rights, courts looked at whether the government's decision was reasonably appropriate and adapted to serve a legitimate end. In that context, the phrase 'reasonably appropriate and adapted' did not mean 'essential' or 'unavoidable' but had been said to be closer to the notion of proportionality.

It was established that the tests of proportionality, reasonableness and necessity were correctly applied in weighing between BAT's commercial rights to property, privacy and equality vis-à-vis the need to ensure a clean and safe environment that is free of the dangers of tobacco use for the entire general public. The appeal was dismissed in its entirety on 26 November 2019.

6.5.2 Importance of the British American Tobacco Kenya (Ltd) *case to effective tobacco control in the country*

The BAT (K) case is important because it clearly outlined the binding nature of the obligations upon Kenya as a state party to the FCTC and the Guidelines adopted thereunder. The FCTC contributed to the resolution of the case in favour of the government of Kenya by providing a legal basis for the measures being challenged, demonstrating their public health purpose; the evidence in favour of the measures; international consensus that the measures are necessary, reasonable, proportionate and justifiable; and that the measures promote the right to health. It also indicated that the Kenyan courts prioritise the right to health over the commercial rights of the tobacco industry.

It also exposes, as is their tactic in other jurisdictions globally,[101] the use of litigation by stakeholders within the tobacco industry to delay the implementation of

100 *British American Tobacco Kenya, PLC (Formerly British American Tobacco Kenya Limited) v Cabinet Secretary for the Ministry of Health; Kenya Tobacco Control Alliance (Interested Parties); Mastermind Tobacco Kenya Limited (The Affected Party)* [2019] eKLR.

101 SY Zhou, J Liberman & E Ricafort 'The impact of the WHO framework convention on tobacco control in defending legal challenges to tobacco control measures' (2019) 28

policies on tobacco control. Zhou and others analysed 96 court decisions on legal challenges to tobacco control measures. They noted that since the FCTC's entry into force, the tobacco industry has initiated litigation in order to prevent, delay or weaken implementation of tobacco control measures. In Africa, in addition to Kenya, the governments of South Africa and Uganda have had their tobacco control measures challenged all the way from the High Court to the Supreme Court or the highest court in the land.

In Uganda,[102] British American Tobacco Uganda filed a lawsuit in the Constitutional Court in 2016 challenging the constitutionality of several provisions in the Tobacco Control Act 2015 providing for large graphic health warnings, a ban on smoking in public, a ban on tobacco advertising promotion and sponsorship, prohibiting the sale of tobacco products in specified places and including by vending machines, and prohibiting the import, distribution and sale of electronic nicotine delivery systems and water pipe tobacco. The court dismissed the petition in its entirety and found that the petition appeared to have been brought in bad faith as part of a global strategy to fight tobacco control legislation.

In South Africa,[103] British American Tobacco South Africa challenged a ban on advertisement or promotion of a tobacco product through any direct or indirect means. They sought to have the ban declared unconstitutional for infringing on their right to commercial speech or, in the event that this prayer was denied, to be interpreted as not applying to one-on-one communications between manufacturers, importers, wholesalers and retailers on the one hand and consenting adult tobacco consumers on the other. This case was also dismissed.

As a result, constant litigation by the tobacco industry has been cited as a barrier to the implementation of strong tobacco control measures.[104] Of the measures challenged by BAT (K), the litigation delayed the implementation of the *solatium* compensatory contribution and the limitation of interactions between the public officials and the tobacco industry until the Supreme Court judgment was delivered. The lack of funding for tobacco control programmes occasioned by this delay has impacted effective implementation of tobacco control policies, especially those requiring capacity building of enforcement officers, research and provision of cessation services for those smokers willing to stop. The Ministry of Health is currently developing the policy framework to operationalise collection of the *solatium* contribution.

Tobacco Control s113 https://www.ncbi.nlm.nih.gov/pmc/articles/PMC6589463/ (accessed 29 September 2021).

102 *BAT Uganda Limited v Attorney General and Centre for Health, Human Rights and Development*, Constitutional Petition 46 of 2016, Constitutional Court of Uganda (2019).

103 *British American Tobacco South Africa (Pty) Ltd v Minister of Health* [2012] 3 All SA 593 (SCA).

104 Conference of the Parties to the WHO Framework Convention on Tobacco Control 'Global progress in implementation of the WHO FCTC – A summary report by the Convention Secretariat' FCTC/COP/6/5 (25 June 2014).

6.6 Conclusion and recommendations

Tobacco use is a preventable cause of death in Kenya and the world at large. Kenya has made good progress in enacting tobacco control policies to protect the right to health of its people. Implementation of the FCTC and the Tobacco Control Act and Regulations can reverse the devastating effects of tobacco production, manufacture, sale and use. Kenya's legislative framework including the Constitution of Kenya and the Tobacco Control Act and subsequent Regulations provide a proper framework for advancing tobacco control and the promotion and protection of the right to health. A human rights–based approach to tobacco control is essential as exhibited in legislation and further pronouncements by various courts in Kenya and is key in ensuring that citizens are protected from punitive commercial practices.

The existing legislative framework meets the FCTC obligations, and it is therefore important that the country strengthens compliance with and enforcement of the legislative framework. There is need to broaden the enforcement machinery to ensure that guidelines and regulations provided under the law are adhered to.

In keeping with best practices and the continually evolving nature of the tobacco industry, its products and the epidemic globally, there is still room to further improve the legal and policy measures in the following areas in Kenya:

1 Amend the Tobacco Control Act, 2007 and subsequent regulations to remove the provisions for designated smoking areas, refine the definition of and sections covering sponsorship to cover the areas of reverse brand stretching, brand sharing and direct contributions to individuals, government entities and events.
2 Review the existing graphic health warnings to increase their size and consider plain/standardised packaging for tobacco products.
3 Adopt regulations on contents and emissions of tobacco products.
4 Address the emergence of new tobacco products such as Electronic Nicotine Delivery Systems (ENDS), Electronic Non-nicotine Delivery Systems (ENNDS), smokeless tobacco products and other heated tobacco products.
5 Operationalise the Tobacco Control Fund and allocate more resources to provision of cessation services, capacity building of national and county level staff, enforcement of the tobacco control measures and public education and awareness, especially mass media campaigns.
6 Initiate further reforms to the tobacco taxation policy to bring it in line with the recommendations and guidelines in article 6 of the FCTC.
7 Improve multi-sectoral cooperation and coordination between the national and county governments to ensure that all sectors are involved in implementation and enforcement of existing laws.
8 Frame tobacco-related issues from a right to health and the wider rights-based perspective in order to address other factors that influence health outcomes.

Bibliography

African Charter on Human and Peoples' Rights adopted on 27 June 1981

BAT Uganda Limited v Attorney General and Centre for Health, Human Rights and Development, Constitutional Petition 46 of 2016, Constitutional Court of Uganda (2019)

Brady, KT 'Social determinants of health and smoking cessation: A challenge' (2020) 177 *American Journal of Psychiatry* 1029

British American Tobacco Kenya Ltd v Cabinet Secretary for the Ministry of Health [2016] eKLR

British American Tobacco Kenya, PLC v Ministry of Health Supreme Court of Kenya Petition 5 of 2017 (2019)

British American Tobacco Ltd v Cabinet Secretary for the Ministry of Health Civil Appeal 112 of 2016 [2017] eKLR

British American Tobacco South Africa (Pty) Ltd v Minister of Health [2012] 3 All SA 593 (SCA)

Children's Act 8 of 2001 of the Laws of Kenya

City Council of Nairobi (Environmental Management) Bylaws (2006)

Conference of the Parties to the WHO Framework Convention on Tobacco Control 'Global progress in implementation of the WHO FCTC – a summary: Report by the convention secretariat' FCTC/COP/6/5, 25 June 2014

Constitution of Kenya, 2010

Convention on the Elimination of all forms of Discrimination Against Women, UN General Assembly, 18 December 1979, United Nations, Treaty Series, vol 1249

Convention on the Rights of the Child, UN General Assembly, 20 November 1989, United Nations, Treaty Series, vol 1577

Committee on Economic, Social and Cultural Rights, General Comment 14: The right to the Highest Attainable Standard of Health (art 12) (2000) UN Doc E/C.12/2000/4 dated 11 August 2000

County Council of Kangundo (Environmental Management) Bylaws (2006)

Craig, L; Fong, GT; Chung-Hall, J; Puska, P; & WHO FCTC Impact Assessment Expert Group 'Impact of the WHO FCTC on tobacco control: Perspectives from stakeholders in 12 countries' (2019) 28 *Tobacco Control* s129

Crow, ME 'Smokescreens and state responsibility: Using human rights strategies to promote global tobacco control' (2004) 29 *The Yale Journal of International Law* 209

Finance Act of Kenya, 2019

Government of Kenya 'The first national health sector strategic plan (NHSSP1) 1999–2004' (1999)

Gruskin, S; Ferguson, L; Tarantola, D & Beaglehole, R 'Noncommunicable diseases and human rights: A promising synergy' (2014) 104 *American Journal of Public Health* 773

Institute for Legislative Affairs 'Smoking out lies: Document research on tobacco industry interference in Kenya' (2017)

Institute for Legislative Affairs 'Tax adjustment proposals for the financial year 2019/2020' (2019)

Institute for Legislative Affairs 'Tax campaign case study: Successful passage of the Kenya excise duty act 2015' (2016)

International Covenant on Civil and Political Rights, UN General Assembly, 16 December 1966, United Nations, Treaty Series, vol. 999, 171

International Covenant on Economic, Social and Cultural Rights, UN General Assembly, 16 December 1966, United Nations, Treaty Series, vol 993

International Tobacco Control Public Health Institute 'Women in tobacco farming: Health, equality and empowerment – A study conducted in China, Tanzania and Kenya' (2016)

Karimi, KJ; Ayah, R & Olewe, T 'Adherence to the tobacco control act, 2007: Presence of a workplace policy on tobacco use in bars and restaurants in Nairobi' (2016) 6 *BMJ Open* e012526

Kenya National Bureau of Statistics 'Kenya demographic and health survey' (2014)

Kenya Tobacco Control Alliance 'Tobacco advertising, promotion and points- of-sale display in Kenya: A compliance monitoring study carried out in Nairobi, Kakamega, Vihiga and Tharaka Nithi Counties' (2018)

Kenya Tobacco Control Situational Analysis Consortium 'Situational analysis of tobacco control in Kenya: Report of the baseline assessment carried out by The Kenya Tobacco Control Situational Analysis Consortium' (2008)

Lencucha, R; Drope, J; Labonté, R & Packer, C 'Tobacco, trade, and the right to health' (2019) 2 *Canadian Human Rights Yearbook* 175

Magnusson, RS & Patterson, D 'The role of law and governance reform in the global response to non-communicable diseases' (2014) 10 *Global Health* 44

Ministry of Health 'Kenya stepwise survey for non-communicable diseases risk factors' (2015)

Mohamed, SF; Juma, P; Asiki, G & Kyobutungi, C 'Facilitators and barriers in the formulation and implementation of tobacco control policies in Kenya: A qualitative study' (2018) (18) *BMC Public Health* 960

Muchangi, J 'Kenya ratifies treaty to end tobacco smuggling' *The Star* (Nairobi, Kenya) 9 May 2020

Municipal Council of Eldoret (Environmental Management) By-Laws (2006)

Municipal Council of Nakuru (Environmental Management) By-Laws (2006)

Mwenda, V; Mwangi, M; Nyanjau, L; Gichu, M; Kyobutungi, C & Kibachio, J 'Dietary risk factors for non-communicable diseases in Kenya: Findings of the STEPS survey, 2015' (2018) 18 *BMC Public Health* 1218

National Council for Population and Development (NCPD) (June 2017), Policy Brief 57

National Tobacco Control Action Plan (2010–2015)

Public Health (Control of Shisha smoking) Rules 2017 of Kenya

Reubi, D 'Making a human right to tobacco control: Expert and advocacy networks, framing and the right to health' (2012) 7 *Global Public Health* s176

State of Kesata v NM Thomas (1976) AIR 490, SCR (17906)

Stoklosa, M 'International community welcomes Kenya to the Protocol to eliminate illicit trade in tobacco products' *Tobacco Atlas* 9 May 2020

Tobacco Control Act of 2007 of the Laws of Kenya

Tobacco Control Regulations of 2014 of Kenya

Universal Declaration of Human Rights proclaimed by the United Nations General Assembly on 10 December 1948

Vidija, P 'Kenya lists alcohol, tobacco among essential products' *The Star* (Nairobi) 8 April 2020

Wamai, RG 'The Kenya health system: Analysis of the situation and enduring challenges' (2009) 52 *Japan Medical Association Journal* 134

WHO Constitution, 1948

WHO Framework Convention on Tobacco Control, 2003

WHO 'Joint national capacity assessment on the implementation of effective tobacco control policies in Kenya' (2012)

WHO 'Technical manual on tobacco tax administration' (2013)

WHO 'Global status of non-communicable diseases' (2014)

Wisdom, JP; Juma, P; Mwagomba, B; Ndinda, C; Mapa-Tassou, C; Assah, F; Nkhata, M; Mohamed, SF; Oladimeji, O; Oladunni, O; Oluwasanu, M; Sanni, S; Mbanya, J-C & Kyobutungi, C 'Influence of the WHO framework convention on tobacco control on tobacco legislation and policies in sub-Saharan Africa' (2018) 18 *BMC Public Health* 954

Zhou, SY; Liberman, J & Ricafort, E 'The impact of the WHO framework convention on tobacco control in defending legal challenges to tobacco control measures' (2019) 28 *Tobacco Control* s113

7 Examining tobacco-related health rights in Zambia in light of the WHO FCTC

Chipo Mushota Nkhata

7.1 Introduction

Zambia has a population of 19,068,102 as of October 2021,[1] with more females than males. More than 46 per cent of its population are young people aged 0–14 years, 20 per cent are aged 15–24 years and 29 per cent are aged 25–54 years.[2] Vulnerable people suffer the disproportionate burden of both communicable and non-communicable diseases (NCDs). Zambia's health system is skewed towards communicable diseases but with a growing realisation that NCDs are posing an even greater threat in Zambia.[3] The prevalence of NCDs in the country is significantly high, with such diseases being responsible for 33 per cent of deaths in 2016 as compared to 23 per cent in 2014.[4] The common NCDs in Zambia include cardiovascular diseases (strokes and heart attacks), diabetes mellitus (type 2), cancers, chronic respiratory diseases, epilepsy, mental illnesses, oral health, eye diseases, injuries (particularly from road traffic accidents and burns) and sickle cell anaemia.[5] Research shows that respiratory infections are the leading NCDs in Zambia.[6] The leading drivers of NCDs are poor diet (particularly low fruit and vegetable intake), lack of exercise, genetics and consumption of dangerous substances such as alcohol and tobacco.[7]

Tobacco use is responsible for numerous NCDs and deaths in Zambia. Although there seems to be disparities in the documented prevalence rate of

1 WorldoMeter 'Zambia population' https://www.worldometers.info/world-population/zambia-population/ (accessed 5 October 2021).
2 IndexMundi 'Zambia population' https://www.indexmundi.com/zambia/population.html (accessed 5 October 2021).
3 B Phiri 'The rise of non-communicable diseases in Zambia and strategies for action' *Medium* 29 August 2017 https://medium.com/amplify/the-rise-of-non-communicable-diseases-in-zambia-and-strategies-for-action-cc45d4db9c9 (accessed 28 September 2021).
4 WHO 'Noncommunicable diseases country profile' (2014) http://www.who.int>zmb_en (accessed 28 September 2021).
5 Government of the Republic of Zambia's *Annual progress report 2014: Revised sixth national development plan* 108 http://www.mndp.gov.zm (accessed 28 September 2021).
6 As above.
7 As above.

DOI: 10.4324/9781003264248-9

tobacco use in the country, research studies have shown a high tobacco-use prevalence rate of 24 per cent in the general population and more than double in the prison population. The disparities in data on prevalence rate is due to the use of varying research methodologies and periods in which studies were undertaken, with some periods overlapping.

A survey undertaken by the World Health Organization (WHO) in 2017 indicates that 23 per cent of males and 2 per cent of females smoke tobacco or tobacco-related products.[8] Goma and others state that approximately 20 per cent of adult males in Zambia use tobacco compared to 1.6 per cent of adult females, which translates to more than 1 million adult smokers and over 56,000 child and youth smokers.[9] Another report suggests that approximately 24 per cent of male Zambians and 3.1 per cent of female Zambians are smokers.[10] The WHO further reports an increase in the prevalence rate compared to a similar surveillance for 2012–2014 undertaken by the International Tobacco Control Policy Evaluation Project. Conversely, a survey conducted in Zambia in 2018 indicates a decrease in the number of tobacco users. Cigarette smoking had reduced among men aged 15–49 from 23 per cent in 2007 to 19 per cent from 2013 to 2018.[11] The survey does not suggest any reasons for the decline but this could be attributed to high inflation that the country has been experiencing since 2013. According to the Zambia Statistical Agency, inflation has negatively impacted the consumer price index (CPI) for tobacco, which in turn has affected its consumption.[12] Despite the inconsistencies, it is evident that the prevalence rate of tobacco use in the country is high and that tobacco use is higher among males than females, with many smokers having smoked their first cigarette before the age of 16 years.[13]

There is also evidence of a shifting tendency towards more female youths consuming tobacco than male youths. Goma and others state that[14]

> in Zambia, tobacco use prevalence in adult males is more than 20%. At 1.6% it is lower in women, but the latest Global Youth Tobacco Survey and the most recent wave of the International Tobacco Control (ITC 2015) Project Survey results indicate that a higher proportion of girls than boys in Zambia now use tobacco products, suggesting a major and potentially catastrophic shift.

8 As above.

9 F Goma & others 'The economics of tobacco farming in Zambia' (Revised version 2017) 2.

10 Trading Economics 'Zambia – cause of death by non-communicable diseases' (accessed 28 September 2021).

11 Government of the Republic of Zambia 'Zambia's Demographic and Health Survey 2018' (2018) 275.

12 Zambia Statistics Agency *Monthly bulletin* (2020) 3.

13 Republic of Zambia 'Zambia's STEPS for non-communicable diseases risk factors' (2017) 80.

14 Goma & others (n 9) 2.

Again, no reasons for the shift in more girls using tobacco are advanced but this could have disproportionate effects on their health and personal development, particularly because girls' health is already disproportionately affected by many social ills. The high prevalence of tobacco use in Zambia is unsurprising considering that the country is one of the leading tobacco leaf producers in Africa.[15] Although it is contended that most tobacco is produced for the global market as opposed to the domestic market, it is arguable that the high production of tobacco influences its consumption at the domestic level.

There is little research on Zambia's health rights response to tobacco use and the effectiveness of Zambia's regulatory framework for addressing tobacco control. This chapter contributes to the literature in this regard. It commences with a discussion on tobacco-related health risks and the right to health in the country. It then examines Zambia's legislative framework on the right to health, focusing on national laws that advance health rights. The chapter further analyses the Framework Convention for Tobacco Control (FCTC) as a treaty for realising tobacco-related health rights in Zambia. The chapter proceeds to assess the implementation of the FCTC and national laws on tobacco use in Zambia. It also analyses local advocacy efforts for advancing the right to health using FCTC-compliant laws. The chapter closes with a conclusion and recommendations for strengthening Zambia's interventions to ensuring FCTC-compliant laws.

7.2 The right to health and tobacco-related NDCs in Zambia

7.2.1 The right to health under international law applicable to Zambia

Tobacco use and production is a threat to the enjoyment of the right to health. Under international human rights law applicable to Zambia, the right to health refers to the right to the highest attainable standard of mental and physical health conducive for living a dignified life.[16] This entails access to healthcare facilities, goods and services, and access to resources and conditions that make it possible for one to enjoy this standard of health.[17] At an international level, Zambia has signed and ratified various human rights instruments that respect, promote and protect the right to health for everyone, including groups most vulnerable to health rights violations such as women, children, persons with disabilities and

15 University of Bath Tobacco tactics 'Zambia – country profile' https://www.tobaccotactics.org (accessed 28 September 2021).

16 Art 12 of UN General Assembly, International Covenant on Economic, Social and Cultural Rights, 16 December 1966, United Nations, Treaty Series, vol 993, p 3.

17 Please provide full citation NCD Alliance 'Non-communicable Diseases (NCDs) and the Rights-based movement' Briefing Paper 16 August 2011 http://www.ncd.alliance.org/resources/non-communicable-diseases-ncds-and-the-rights-based-movment (accessed 28 September 2021).

prisoners. The International Covenant on Economic, Social and Cultural Rights (ICESCR) and its interpretations arguably constitute the most comprehensive international health rights provision applicable to Zambia. The Committee on Economic, Social and Cultural Rights (CESCR) elucidated on the normative content of article 12 of the ICESCR as requiring health facilities, goods and services are available, accessible, acceptable and of good quality.[18] In the context of tobacco-related health responses in Zambia, this includes the following: 'Availability' includes provision of prevention and treatment programmes emanating from tobacco use and production; for example, introducing education programmes that sensitise the public on the dangers of tobacco use on their health and provision of goods and services for preventing and treating tobacco-induced diseases. 'Accessibility' refers to inclusivity of health facilities, goods and services for tobacco prevention and treatment, requiring that all barriers to health programming are eliminated. Examples include provision of tobacco prevention and treatment programmes close to communities that need them, free from cost burdens, language barriers, negative attitudes of service providers and any other encumbrances. 'Acceptability' requires the upholding of medical ethics and cultural values of individual users in the provision of health programmes. In the context of tobacco-related health services in Zambia, acceptability includes consulting tobacco users on services they would require to help them quit tobacco use and health personnel adhering to confidentiality when treating tobacco-related illnesses. 'Good quality' refers to the provision of health goods and services that are scientific and medically appropriate. For instance, provision of tobacco-related health goods and services that are substandard compromises the quality of healthcare and violates one's right to health. Substandard health services may arise as a result of many factors, including focusing on the wrong beneficiaries of health programmes, providing health goods that are of low quality, designing health programmes that are implemented by personnel that are not qualified, establishing health facilities that are under-resourced, and failure to implement a multi-sectoral approach to health where this is necessary to achieving good health outcomes.

The Committee also recognises that for people to enjoy article 12 rights, a state would have to implement several complementary approaches, including formulating health policies, implementing health programmes developed by the WHO, and adopting special legal instruments.[19]

Adherence to legal standards set in article 12 and creation of national laws that give effect to article 12 are cardinal interventions in realising the right to health at the country level. Thus, States parties' are mandated to take legislative and

18 Para 12 of the UN Committee on Economic, Social and Cultural Rights (CESCR), General Comment 14: The right to the highest attainable standard of health (Art 12 of the Covenant) (2000) UN Doc E/C.12/2000/4 dated 11 August 2000.

19 As above.

administrative actions to advance provisions of international human rights treaties, such as the article 12 provision.

Article 12 further imposes a duty on States parties' to the ICESCR to take steps to progressively realise the right, being fully aware that not all States parties' are at the same level of development. In interpreting article 12, the Committee averred that the duty to progressively realise the right to health necessitates states to use their maximum available resources to ensure that costly aspects of the right to health such as healthcare and disease control are incrementally guaranteed to rights holders.[20] This requires Zambia to immediately implement 'deliberate, concrete and targeted' interventions for the full realisation of the right and restrain from retrogressive measures.[21] Retrogressive measures may only be introduced under very strict conditions; that is, 'that they have been introduced after the most careful consideration of all alternatives and that they are duly justified by reference to the totality of the rights provided for in the Covenant'.[22]

The Committee also emphasised that many obligations under the right to health are immediately realisable, including the right to equality and freedom from discrimination in accessing health facilities, goods and services.[23] Thus, if a member state is irresponsible in the manner in which it collects and utilises its resources, it cannot use the argument of insufficient resources to justify its failure to discharge its obligations under the ICESCR. Irresponsibility in this case would include creating a health burden from preventable diseases that further requires states to spend exorbitant resources to contain diseases and their negative socio-economic impact. The Special Rapporteur on the Right to Health augmented this view, stating that States parties' must be accountable in their discharge of health rights obligations, thereby ensuring that 'health systems are improving and the right to the highest attainable standard of health is being progressively realised for all, including disadvantaged individuals, communities and populations' .[24]

Zambia needs, among other things, a robust legal framework on the right to health to effectively respond to tobacco-related health problems in the country. The following section analyses Zambia's national legal framework on the right to health with a view of ascertaining the extent to which it is suited to discharge its tobacco-related health obligations.

20 Para 30 General Comment 14.
21 Paras 30 and 32 General Comment 14.
22 Para 32 General Comment 14.
23 As above.
24 United Nations General Assembly 'Report of the Special Rapporteur on the right of everyone to the enjoyment of the highest attainable standard of physical and mental health' para 12 https://documents-dds-ny.un.org/doc/UNODC/GEN/N08/456/47/PDF/N0845647.pdf? (accessed 7 October 2021).

7.2.2 Zambia's legislative framework on the right to health

The international human rights framework for realising the right to health sets a standard for national implementation of the right to health. At the national level, Zambia has a dual legal system in which it applies African customary law and statutory law. While Zambia's legal framework does not have a comprehensive right to health provision, it has various statutes that guarantee health rights and respond to health determinants. The relevant Zambian health laws include the Public Health Act,[25] the Penal Code Act,[26] the Environmental Management Act,[27] the Anti–Gender Based Violence Act[28] and the Zambian Constitution.

The Public Health Act was enacted to 'prevent and suppress diseases and regulate matters connected to public health in Zambia'.[29] The Act also proscribes the creation of nuisances. The remission of a nuisance is also criminalised in the Penal Code Act.[30] A nuisance is defined to include the remission of offensive smells. Not all tobacco products remit offensive smells; thus, for Zambia, where tobacco control regulations are weak, it may be necessary to redefine what a nuisance is to include any physical and mental discomfort experienced as a result of remission of tobacco products into the environment. This would widen the remedies available to people who are involuntarily exposed to tobacco products. The Penal Code Act also criminalises fouling of water and air as means of proscribing health inconveniences.[31] Similarly, it proscribes the sale of noxious food and drinks and offensive trades, although tobacco production and sale are not considered as threats to health convenience. Notably, however, criminal law is not an effective way of achieving many public health goals. Thus, laws must primarily focus on advancing protective frameworks as guided by articles 6–14 and 15–17 of the FCTC, where penalties are used minimally.

The Environmental Management Act 12 of 2011 provides for integrated environmental management, protection and conservation of the environment and the sustainable management and use of natural resources.[32] It also regulates the conduct of environmental assessments of proposed policies and programmes that are likely to affect environmental management and provides a framework for responding to pollution in Zambia. This Act could strengthen the regulatory and institutional framework for addressing tobacco-based environmental issues envisaged in the FCTC.[33] For gender-based harmful practices affecting physical and mental health, the Anti–Gender Based Violence Act 1 of 2011 is the relevant statute. It prohibits gender-based violence that is economic, sexual and psychological

25 Chapter 295 of the Laws of Zambia.
26 Chapter 87 of the Laws of Zambia.
27 Act 12 of 2011.
28 Act 1 of 2011.
29 Preamble.
30 Sec 172, Chapter 87 of the Laws of Zambia.
31 Secs 188 and 189, respectively.
32 Preamble.
33 Art 18.

among others. It also proscribes violence which occurs in a domestic relationship or a work environment, as tends to be the case with violence against women and girls in tobacco production in Zambia.

Although the Constitution neither guarantees the right to health nor the right to development, it was recently amended to enhance protection of fundamental rights.[34] The amendments prescribe new constitutional values and principles that would enhance health rights.[35] These include human dignity, equity, social justice, equality and non-discrimination, amongst others. These provisions thus enhance the standard for constitutionally protected rights that impact on the enjoyment of good quality life and health.

It is evident from the examination of Zambia's legislative framework that no Zambian law holistically adheres to any aspect of article 12 of the ICESCR or is well suited to comprehensively address the health risks that tobacco use and production pose in the country. National laws contain scarce provisions on health rights and were not drafted with the full understanding on tobacco prevalence and its ramifications. Zambia's ability to discharge its health rights obligations under international and national human rights law is severely impacted by high prevalence of tobacco use, high tobacco-related disease burdens and loss of public income arising from the huge health burdens. The following section discusses the extent of tobacco-related health burden and determinants of tobacco use in Zambia.

7.2.3 Determinants of tobacco use in Zambia

NCDs, including tobacco-related NCDs are affected by many factors. The right to health entails that these factors are considered when formulating responses and discharging health-rights obligations.[36] To adhere to its health rights obligations under article 12 of the ICESCR, the Zambian government must prevent tobacco use and tobacco-related NCDs. It must also improve access to treatment for tobacco-related NCDs and address social impacts of tobacco-related illnesses.[37] This section discusses the factors influencing tobacco use and tobacco-related NCDs.

Although tobacco is responsible for many health risks, many people in Zambia still continue to consume it. Key determinants of tobacco use applicable to Zambia include sex, age, education level, rural-urban divide, employment status and social status. The Zambia Demographic and Health Survey reveals that 'the proportion of men who smoke any type of tobacco generally increases with age; only 3% of men aged 15–19 smoke tobacco, as compared with 33% of those aged 45–49'. This finding was attributed to the relative affordability of cigarettes by

34 Constitution (Amendment) Act 2 of 2016.
35 Art 8.
36 N 18.
37 As above.

this group.[38] Further, in Zambia, cigarette smoking decreases with an increase in education, which signifies that education empowers people to appreciate the dangers of tobacco use and to avoid it. Only 8 per cent of those with higher education smoke, compared to 26 per cent of those with no education.[39] Thus, increasing education of people and raising awareness among communities on the dangers of tobacco is effective in reducing tobacco use and must thus be promoted in line with the FCTC.[40] Further, the response of smokers to tobacco price adjustments is indicative of the effectiveness of price increments on reduction of tobacco use. This is consistent with FCTC standards for tobacco control.[41]

Furthermore, tobacco use in Zambia is prevalent in rural compared to urban areas. Research reveals that prevalence rates in tobacco use rise in rural areas even when there is no rise in urban areas.[42] Another relevant determinant of tobacco use is alcohol. Smokers in Zambia are more likely to be influenced to smoke if they consume alcohol. Thus, targeted messaging for smokers must consider the other factors that influence them to smoke.[43]

There are other ways in which tobacco is used other than through smoking factory-made cigarettes: snuffing, vaping, and smoking roll-your-own (RYO) cigarettes or pipes. Approximately 15 per cent of adults between the ages of 18 and 69 years in Zambia use tobacco in one form or another.[44] This is indicative of target age groups and products for tobacco rehabilitation programmes and taxes.

Because research tends to exclude certain groups of people like persons with disabilities, especially mental disabilities, prisoners, poor people, people in rural areas, or persons with diverse gender and sexual identities or to generalise findings to such groups, it is necessary to generate comparable evidence to ascertain when, why and where these groups use tobacco and to identify effective interventions. For example, it is not an effective intervention to ban tobacco use in a public place when many users are found at home, some living with children and in densely populated areas, thereby exposing family and neighbours to tobacco.

The negative impact of tobacco use on individuals ultimately affects public health and welfare. This is evident from tobacco's effect on individuals' health and mortality, productivity, the environment and government's expenditure on health. The adverse repercussions of tobacco in Zambia include its impact on health and health determinants, such as access to basic necessities including a

38 Government of the Republic of Zambia (n 11).

39 As above.

40 Art 12 of FCTC which promotes education, communication, training and public awareness.

41 See art 6 of FCTC on price and tax measures to reduce the demand for tobacco.

42 P Olowski & C Michelo 'Differential burden and determinants of tobacco smoking: Population-based observations from the Zambia Demographic and Health Survey (2002 and 2007)' (2016) 1 *Journal of Healthcare Communications*.

43 C Zyaambo & others 'Prevalence and predictors of smoking in a mining town in Kitwe, Zambia: A 2011 population-based survey' (2013) 5 *Health* 1021.

44 F Goma, M Ililonga & J Drope *Tobacco control in Africa: People, politics and policies* (2012) 264 https://www.cambridge.org/core/books/tobacco-control-in-africa/CC9DD7E1B839116124A2C65BB9AD8148 (accessed 21 November 2021).

clean environment, food and water and fuels social ills such as child labour and gender inequality. These not only impact personal health but also Zambia's ability to discharge its health rights obligations.

7.2.4 *The impact of tobacco use on health and health determinants in Zambia*

There has been an increase in tobacco-related deaths in Zambia, from approximately 3,000 to 8,000 deaths per year between 1990 and 2015.[45] The 2018 Zambia Demographic and Health Survey states that 'one hundred sixty-seven of every 1000 women and 234 of every 1000 men age 15–49 years are expected to die before age 50'.[46] The WHO identified a similar prevalence rate of tobacco-related illnesses.[47] Lungu augments these findings, stating that[48]

> tobacco production should be discouraged at all cost to prevent the 3300 deaths caused by tobacco-related ailments every year and to also stop more than 56,000 children and 105, 200 adults who continue to use tobacco each day in Zambia . . . tobacco is the most toxic crop that is grown, processed and used legally. It has been scientifically proven that tobacco causes more than 100 diseases and at least 12 cancers, and that it is the only product which, when used as intended, kills half to two-thirds of its consumers.

Tobacco also negatively impacts on people's mental health, especially for adolescents and persons under immense stress. There is little information that shows the effects of using tobacco on mental health in the country. However, neuropsychiatric disorders are a common form of mental illness in Zambia, and tobacco use has been identified as one cause of such disorders. A study conducted in one of Zambia's large correctional facilities indicates that the following factors were partly responsible for cigarette smoking among prisoners:[49]

1 Worry – 54.6 per cent of respondents (55.1 per cent male and 50 per cent female).
2 Stress – 64.9 per cent of respondents (68.2 per cent male and 33.3 per cent female).

45 University of Bath (n 15).
46 Government of the Republic of Zambia (n 11).
47 WHO *Zambia smoking prevalence tobacco economy* https://www.who.int>media>zam (accessed 14 June 2020).
48 F Lungu 'Economic vs health: Experts bash tobacco industry' *Zambia Daily Mail* (Lusaka) 19 March 2018 at www.daily-mail.co.zm (accessed 9 July 2020).
49 K Mwewa, S Siziya & M Kwangu 'Prevalence and correlates of tobacco smoking among prisoners at Kamfinsa correctional facility, Kitwe, Zambia' (2017) 12 *Health Press Zambia Bull* 11.

3 Relaxation – 53.8 per cent of respondents (54.8 per cent male and 44.4 per cent female).
4 Enjoyment – 62.6 per cent of respondents (63.3 per cent male and 55.6 per cent female).

The study further indicates that of all the respondents, 51.6 per cent of male prisoners and 43.9 per cent of female prisoners consumed tobacco in one form or another (i.e. cigarettes, pipe tobacco and smokeless (snuffing)). Of male respondents, 99.4 per cent smoked cigarettes, compared to 22.2 per cent of female respondents, recording a prevalence higher than the general population.[50] A large percentage of respondents attributed their smoking to worry and stress, factors that negatively impact on mental health. It is also noteworthy that 13.3 per cent of respondents started smoking cigarettes after their imprisonment, while 86.7 per cent started smoking beforehand.[51] Mwewa and others put forward that 'the continual use of tobacco by prisoners has been reported to contribute to violence, antisocial personality disorder, psychotic illness and increased effects of licit and illicit drug use'.[52]

Furthermore, the close relationship between tobacco and alcohol use among people in Zambia needs to be examined further to determine health risks and interventions. The Mental Health Conference organised by the Psychology Association of Zambia in 2019 saw many delegates attributing mental health problems, particularly suicide, to substance abuse. Alcohol-induced mental illness exacerbates tobacco use, and in turn tobacco use negatively impacts mental health diagnosis and treatment. Evidence suggests that persons with mental health problems tend to abuse tobacco more than those without.[53] The effects of tobacco use on mental health users are devastating, as it not only interferes with one's treatment but also severely affects mortality. The Centre for Disease Control (CDC) states that 'individuals with serious mental health disorders who smoke die almost 15 years earlier than individuals without these disorders who do not smoke'.[54] The CDC further states that the effect of tobacco on mental health is that it makes it more difficult to diagnose mental illness. This is because 'nicotine has mood-altering effects that can temporarily mask the negative symptoms of mental health disorders, putting people with such disorders at higher risk for cigarette use and nicotine addiction'.[55] With a high prevalence of mental health problems in Zambia and among tobacco users, it is possible for the two to overlap in individuals, causing a negative impact on morbidity and mortality.

50 As above.
51 As above 12.
52 As above 13.
53 CDC 'Tobacco use and quitting among individuals with behavioural health conditions' www.cdc.gov/tobacco/disparities/mental-illness-substance-use (accessed 28 September 2021).
54 As above.
55 As above.

There is no justification for high mortality rates caused by diseases that should not exist in the first place. Zyaambo and others argue that tobacco smoking is a preventable cause of death,[56] making tobacco users one of the primary groups responsible for preventing tobacco-related illnesses and deaths. The government, as primary duty-bearer, ought to put in place measures to discourage tobacco use. Since smoking is a habit that negatively impacts on a person's mortality and quality of life, it must be discouraged, and smokers must be encouraged to seek better health behaviours in the same way behavioural change has been encouraged for addressing HIV-related and COVID-19-related illness and deaths, among others.

Several factors affect the severity of tobacco production and use on growers, users of tobacco and those exposed to it. For tobacco growers, the exposure to tobacco makes them susceptible to diseases like green leaf disease. The longer they are exposed to tobacco fields and products, the more susceptible they are to tobacco-related illnesses. The severity of tobacco-related illnesses is often affected by, among others, the age at which a user or unprotected person is first exposed to tobacco and the frequency of use or exposure. The nicotine in tobacco and tobacco products is one of the most addictive substances on earth, making it difficult to quit and even more difficult to treat.[57] In Zambia almost 50 per cent of men who smoke cigarettes smoke about five cigarettes per day.[58] This, combined with other factors, not only explains the high mortality rate but also the adverse consequences for their quality of life.

There are several health determinants exacerbated by tobacco use and production. It is trite that poor health is induced and worsened by poverty (causing inadequate access to necessities and poor living conditions), inequality and rights violations, among others. Due to the addictive nature of tobacco and tobacco products, the quality of life of tobacco users is severely affected by diversion of resources from essential goods and services that, if accessed, would improve their quality of life and promote their health. Evidence from a household survey conducted in 2014 indicates that non-smoking households allocated more funds to education, personal care, water, food, electricity and alternative power sources than smoking households.[59] The findings also reveal that smoking households spent more funds on alcohol and entertainment. However, it was interesting to note that 'there was no statistically significant differences in health expenditure between the two types of households'.[60]

Other determinants of health affected by tobacco in Zambia include environmental degradation, casualisation of labour, child labour, gender inequality and

56 N 43.
57 Goma & others (n 9) 2.
58 Government of the Republic of Zambia (n 11).
59 G Chelwa & C van Walbeek 'Assessing the causal impact of tobacco expenditure on household patterns in Zambia' ERSA working paper 453 (2014) 10.
60 As above.

food insecurity. Tobacco production causes environmental degradation, as large areas of land are cleared and treated with toxic chemicals for growing tobacco. This in turn impacts the health of tobacco growers who work such fields for long periods. Further, the need for large areas of land demands a large workforce, which many tobacco farmers cannot afford. Casualisation of labour is thus very rife in the tobacco industry in Zambia, with about 40 per cent of total production costs comprising labour costs compared to 10 per cent for maize.[61] Tobacco farmers, who are typically smallholder farmers, rely on their families to provide the services they require to engage in tobacco farming. Thus, it is common to find women and children working tobacco fields without pay and at a very high cost of doubled workload with household chores, which leads to exhaustion, high exposure of illness in the family and missed educational opportunities. About 23 per cent of tobacco farmers from a research study knew that they were not supposed to use children to work in tobacco fields, but they did it anyway because they did not have money to hire workers.[62] The study also indicates that the girl children are disproportionately affected, as they often help their mothers with household chores in addition to working in tobacco fields. The International Labour Organization (ILO) identifies the work females do to include 'stringing, reaping, weeding, ridging, grading, watering nurseries, transplanting, applying fertilizers and harvesting', all of which require them to work long hard hours, carrying heavy loads and exposing them to highly toxic chemicals.[63] This means that health of women and girls is disproportionately affected by tobacco production.

Gender inequality in tobacco farming extends beyond the use of women and children doing the bulk of the work for no pay to their invisibility and lack of protection, including from physical and sexual violence, in and as a result of their provision of labour in the tobacco industry.[64] Considering the increasing numbers of girls and women consuming tobacco in Zambia, it is worth investigating the extent to which tobacco use is influenced by their participation in tobacco farming. Further, tobacco farming seemingly is a very stressful business with a high potential to affect the mental health of families engaged in it. The ILO indicates that after all the hard work that many farmers and their families put into growing tobacco, they are still indebted to tobacco companies, which supply them with farming equipment at exorbitant prices and buy their product at low prices.[65]

Tobacco farming also contributes to food insecurity among farmers in Zambia. When vast areas of land are allocated to tobacco farming, relatively little land

61 ILO 'An integrated strategy to address decent work deficits in the tobacco sector' (11 October 2018) 2 https://www.ilo.org/wcmsp5/groups/public/-ed_norm/-relconf/documents/meetingdocument/wcms_646755.pdf (accessed 1 October 2021).

62 Goma (n 9) 3.

63 ILO (n 61) 4.

64 As above 5.

65 As above 3.

is reserved and utilised for growing food, causing food insecurity. Over 20 per cent of farmers in Eastern Province confirmed not having enough food to feed their families.[66] Even though tobacco is a cash crop, it is not profitable. Instead, it negatively impacts the physical and mental health of farmers and their families and leaves them impoverished and susceptible to human rights abuses. It is not surprising, therefore, that over 60 per cent of tobacco farmers in Zambia are considering abandoning tobacco farming for other crops, and that '51.2% of farmers in the study reported that they do not envisage themselves growing tobacco in the next five years'.[67] This indicates that tobacco farming is not as profitable to the farmers that engage in it as it is to the big companies that make profits off their hard work. The negative impact that tobacco growing has on the farmers is not only a health burden on the farmers but on the public health system and national resources generally, thereby negatively impacting on the realisation of health rights.

Tobacco use and production impacts negatively on the realisation of health rights, as it saps resources from which health rights are protected and fulfilled. When a country's resources dwindle, its outputs suffer:[68]

> Tobacco use causes at least 7000 deaths and costs Zambians 1.2% of GDP. It also suggests that modest investments to stem tobacco use – rather than encouraging it through increased cigarette production will save more than 40,000 lives and K12.4billion [about US$690,000,000] in health costs alone over the next 5–15 years.

In the Zambian context, tobacco use and production have received insignificant attention as an issue that negatively impacts on health. It is often viewed as a matter of personal choice and a source of national income. Even though tobacco use is a bad personal habit with severe consequences on an individual's morbidity and mortality, it has far-reaching consequences for public health and national development. If the government does not implement the FCTC obligations to curtail tobacco use, it not only violates this Treaty but its right to health obligations under the ICESCR and other human rights obligations. The FCTC thus offers an important avenue by which Zambia can realise its right to health obligations and other human rights.

66 Goma & others (n 9) 2.

67 As above 2.4.

68 F Goma, R Zulu & J Drope 'An opportunity for meaningful public health progress: Zambia's pending tobacco control legislation' *Tobacco Atlas* 7 December 2019 https://tobaccoatlas.org/2019/12/07/an-opportunity-for-meaningful-public-health-progress-zambias-pending-tobacco-control-legislation/ (accessed 7 October 2021).

7.3 The FCTC as a treaty to realise the right to health in Zambia

The FCTC is a health-rights law that frames the causes of tobacco-related illnesses, their determinants and impact using the human right lens. It directly impacts on the realisation of the right to health by offering a robust set of norms, defining states' legal obligations and accountability mechanisms that can be used to effectively implement tobacco-related NCD prevention and control.[69] The primary motivation for the enactment of the FCTC was to safeguard people's health by controlling their use and exposure of tobacco and tobacco products among others. The scope of the right to health envisaged in article 12 of the ICESCR is well suited to facilitate the attainment of the objectives of the FCTC through the improvement of all aspects of environmental and industrial hygiene arising from tobacco use and production; the prevention, treatment and control of epidemic, endemic, occupational and other tobacco-related diseases; and the creation of conditions which would assure to all medical services and medical attention in the event of tobacco-related sickness.[70]

Tobacco control interventions that the FCTC introduced are necessary to address the myriad of effects that lead to physical and mental health risks due to tobacco-related environmental degradation and diseases. They also require a health system that offers users health services to enable them to quit tobacco use. The FCTC offers an opportunity for states to set up such a system by addressing tobacco control from both demand and supply sides and providing holistic guidance for appropriate state interventions.

The prevention measures envisaged by the FCTC are stipulated in articles 6–14 targeting use of tobacco and articles 15–17 targeting tobacco production. Treatment of tobacco-related illnesses requires that the Zambian government implements measures to address NCDs. These include conducting research on disease burden and gaps in health frameworks to address health needs, develop health policies and systems and finance health programmes. This is particularly important given Zambia's inept health-rights legal framework and inadequate response to NCDs.[71] The FCTC thus not only sets a standard but also provides a model for how national tobacco control laws should contribute to advancing the right to health. Table 7.1 illustrates the extent of Zambia's domestication or compliance with the FCTC.

69 Sofia Gruskin & others 'Non-communicable diseases and human rights: A promising synergy' (2014) 104 *American Journal of Public Health* 773.

70 Art 12 of CESCR.

71 MM Mukanu & others 'Responding to non-communicable diseases in Zambia: A policy analysis' (2017) *Health Research Policy and Systems* 34 https://health-policy-systems.biomedcentral.com/articles/10.1186/s12961-017-0195-7 (accessed 1 October 2021).

Table 7.1 Level of Zambia's compliance

FCTC Provision	*Equivalent Zambian Provision*	*Comment*
Each party to develop, implement, periodically update and review comprehensive multi-sectoral national tobacco control strategies (article 5(1)).	Yes, partially compliant.	Zambia does not have national policies and strategies on tobacco control.[72] However, it does have a national strategic plan for responding to NCDs. Nevertheless, this strategy inadequately covers the major NCDs in Zambia.[73]
Establish or reinforce and finance a national coordinating mechanism or focal points for tobacco control according to its capacity (article 5(2)(a)).	Yes, partially compliant.	Zambia has a national agency for tobacco control with a lean staff establishment.[74]
Adopt and implement effective legislative, executive, administrative and/or other measures for preventing and reducing tobacco consumption, nicotine addiction and exposure to tobacco smoke (articles 5 (2)(b) and 7).	Yes, partially compliant.	Zambia has a few laws and policies for preventing and reducing tobacco consumption, addiction and exposure to smoke, as discussed below; however, these are not effectively enforced.
Price and tax measures to reduce the demand for tobacco (article 6).	Yes, partially compliant.	Zambia's tobacco taxes are at 44%, while its tax on cigarettes is at 21%, making it one of the lowest in the Southern African Development Community.[75] It is recommended that retail tax on tobacco and tobacco products be increased to at least 70% and 'ensure that they are adjusted periodically to keep pace with inflation and rise faster than consumer purchasing power'.[76]

(*Continued*)

72 Report Card on the WHO Framework Convention on Tobacco Control for Zambia https://www.afro.who.int (accessed 1 October 2021).

73 Mukanu & others (n 71) 79.

74 N 72. Report Card on WHO Framework Convention at page 3–4.

75 AN Moraces 'Tax the smoker, save the smoker! The health and economic benefits of increased tobacco tax in Zambia' (2017) 5 *Health Press Zambia Bull* 5 at 6–8.

76 As above. Report Card on WHO Framework Convention at page 10.

Table 7.1 (Continued)

FCTC Provision	*Equivalent Zambian Provision*	*Comment*
Protection from exposure to tobacco smoke (article 8).	Yes, partially compliant. SI 163 of the Public Health (Tobacco) Regulations of 1992 proscribe smoking in public places including health institutions, educational institutions for children and adolescents, elevators, public transport, cinema halls and nursing homes. This is buttressed by SI 39 of 2008.[77]	Although smoking is prohibited in most public areas in Zambia, enforcement of the law is weak and needs to be strengthened to achieve its objective.
Regulation of the contents of tobacco products (article 9).	Not compliant.	There are no regulations expressly empowering competent national authorities to test and measure contents and emissions of tobacco products.
Regulation of tobacco products disclosure (article 10).	Not compliant.	There are no regulations expressly requiring disclosure of tobacco contents and emissions of tobacco product or toxic constituents.
Packaging and labelling of tobacco products (article 11).	Partially compliant.	The law bans the use of deceitful labelling but does not sufficiently prescribe how health warnings must appear on the package.[78] Only one messaging provision exists in the Public Health (Tobacco) Regulations of 1992, which requires tobacco product package to read 'WARNING: TOBACCO IS HARMFUL TO HEALTH'.[79] Further, SI 39 of 2008 prescribes that the warning message be printed in bold and on contrasting background on the two largest sides of the tobacco product package.

77 Zambia Consumer Association 'Shadow report on the implementation of the framework convention on tobacco control (FCTC): Articles 8 and 13 in Zambia' https://www.fctc.org/wp-content/uploads/2018/05/Zambia_FCTC_Shadow_Report_2012.pdf (accessed 1 October 2021).

78 As above.

79 Goma & others (n 44).

FCTC Provision	*Equivalent Zambian Provision*	*Comment*
Education, communication, training and public awareness (article 12).	Partially compliant.	Evidence exists of information, education and communication programmes on the dangers of tobacco use on health, but more evidence exists for pro-tobacco advertisements and other information and education materials in both urban and rural areas and amongst most vulnerable populations to tobacco use in Zambia.[80]
Tobacco advertising, promotion and sponsorship (article 13).	Partially compliant. Section 10 of SI 163 of the Public Health Tobacco Regulations of 1992 prohibit commercial advertisements of a limited number of tobacco products including cigarettes. Further, section 11 proscribes marketing of tobacco products as beneficial to health on account of its treatment or production process. Further according to section 12, no tobacco product can be offered as a prize in any competition or raffle. Other progressive provisions in this regard are sections 7 and 8, which regulate advertising on billboards, posters and periodicals.	Zambia has a partial ban on tobacco advertising, promotion and sponsorship, which makes it ineffective for dissuading tobacco use. Further, even where tobacco advertising is prohibited, there is a weak enforcement mechanism, as tobacco advertisements are placed in innovative ways, such as attractive point-of-sale advertising in public places such as malls, supermarkets, bars and bus stations.[81]

(*Continued*)

80 As above.
81 As above.

Table 7.1 (Continued)

FCTC Provision	*Equivalent Zambian Provision*	*Comment*
Demand reduction measures concerning tobacco dependence and cessation (article 14).	Yes, partially compliant.	Zambia has not developed and disseminated context-specific and appropriate, comprehensive and integrated guidelines based on scientific evidence and best practice for the promotion of cessation of tobacco. It has, however, introduced limited services to help users to quit tobacco use. These include the availability of nicotine replacement therapy, bupropion and smoking cessation support offered by health professionals and community centres.[82] This can be enhanced by introducing a toll-free quit-line.
Illicit trade in tobacco products (article 15)	Partially compliant.	Zambia is said to have a fairly high incidence of illicit trade in tobacco trade, constituting 5%–10% of tobacco consumption.[83] Zambia has a relatively weak capacity to combat illicit tobacco trade with major challenges arising from 'limited control over tobacco supply chain, under capacitated and inadequately killed government agencies, legal framework that do not reflect contemporary good practice and lack of robust risk management approaches', among others.[84]

82 As above 47 Report Card WHO Zambia Report.

83 A Lester & E Allen, GFA Consulting Group, Hamburg, Germany 'SADC review – study into the illicit trade in excisable products with particular reference to alcohol and tobacco products' (November 2012) 127 https://www.sadc.int (accessed 1 October 2021).

84 The World Bank 'Confronting illicit tobacco trade: A global review of country experiences' (2019) http://pubdocs.worldbank.org (accessed 1 October 2021).

FCTC Provision	*Equivalent Zambian Provision*	*Comment*
Sales to and by minors (article 16).	Yes, partially compliant. The Public Health (Tobacco) Regulations (Statutory Instrument 163 of 1992) of the Public Health Act (Laws of Volume XI Cap 535) banned tobacco sales to minors under the age of 16.	The law proscribes sale of tobacco to minors but there is a weak enforcement of the law. Roadside stores often sell cigarettes in small packets and individually, making them readily accessible and affordable to minors.
Provision of support for economically viable alternative activities (article 17).	Not compliant. No equivalent provision.	Tobacco farmers have expressed interest to switch to alternative crops, but the government has to put measures in place to facilitate this.
Protection of the environment and the health of persons (article 18).	Not compliant. No equivalent provision.	Zambia has environmental protection laws but they do not expressly provide for regulation of environmental protection against tobacco cultivation and manufacture.

7.4 An assessment of the implementation of the FCTC and national laws on tobacco use in Zambia

This section reviews the government's efforts to implement the FCTC using the MPOWER[85] model, a model developed by the WHO to aid in country-level implementation of the FCTC. MPOWER has been developed to help countries build their capacity to implement the demand reduction provisions of the WHO FCTC.[86] The extent to which Zambia has implemented FCTC in the context of MPOWER is examined below.

85 M, monitor tobacco use and prevention policies; P, protect people from tobacco smoke; O, offer help to quit tobacco; W, warn about the dangers of tobacco; E, enforce bans on tobacco advertising, promotion and sponsorship; R, raise taxes on tobacco.

86 WHO 'MPOWER: Advancing the WHO framework convention on tobacco control (WHO FCTC)' https://www.who.int/cancer/prevention/tobacco_implementation/mpower/en (accessed 7 October 2021).

7.4.1 Monitoring tobacco use and prevention policies

Although Zambia has been a state party to the FCTC since 2008, it has not amended its archaic tobacco laws or enacted comprehensive FCTC-compliant laws. Zambia has minimal useful regulations that pre-date the FCTC, notably the Public Health (Tobacco) Regulations enacted in 1992 and regulations of 2008 which ban smoking in public places. There is a paucity of evidence on the extent to which the Public Health Act regulations on tobacco have been implemented. However, one report has shown that regulations concerning the prohibition of sale of tobacco to minors and those proscribing advertising of cigarettes have been inconsistently enforced.[87] The Public Health Act pursuant to which the Regulations were made was repealed and replaced, but the Regulations seemingly survived, as the government has occasionally cited them post repeal of the Act.[88] Arguably, the lack of a comprehensive FCTC-compliant legal framework makes it difficult for Zambia to effectively monitor tobacco use and prevention policies. The absence of a comprehensive legal framework on the right to health coupled with a weak legislative framework for tobacco control negatively impacts on Zambia's tobacco-related health response and ability to monitor the effects of the impact of its interventions.

7.4.2 Protect people from tobacco smoke

Although Zambia has laws that prohibit people from smoking cigarettes in many public places, it is difficult to ascertain the extent to which these laws have effectively protected people in Zambia. This is mostly due to the weak enforcement of such laws and poor local data on the effectiveness of the laws in protecting people from tobacco smoke. The high incidence of tobacco smokers in the country and the lacunas in the legislative and policy frameworks for tobacco control add to the challenges of protecting people from tobacco smoke. The more people smoke tobacco, the more people are exposed to tobacco smoke. To protect people from tobacco smoke thus requires a reduction in the number of smokers. Increasing taxes on cigarettes and other tobacco products is thus an effective strategy for reducing the number of smokers and those exposed to tobacco smoke. The government's failure to significantly increase tobacco taxes has greatly contributed to the increasing number of smokers and those exposed to smoke since 2005 . [89] Further, the government's continued support of tobacco producers compromises the effectiveness of existing progressive provisions aimed at curtailing tobacco

87 N 74.

88 National Assembly of Zambia *Report of the Committee on Health, Community Development and Social Services for the Second Session of the Twelfth National Assembly Appointed on 20th September 2017* http://www.parliament.gov.zm (accessed 7 October 2021).

89 The Tobacco Atlas 'As cigarettes become more affordable, the number of Zambian smokers increases' https://tobaccoatlas.org/2018/04/30/zambia-rolly-your-own-affordability-tobacco-control-itc/ (accessed 7 October 2021).

smoking. For instance, the government's opening of new cigarette manufacturing plants, provision of tax concessions on tobacco and making of policy pronouncements supporting cigarette manufacturing[90] send mixed messages on government's commitment to preventing tobacco use and exposure.

7.4.3 Offer help to quit tobacco use

Although Zambia offers limited tobacco-quitting services to tobacco users, most of these are driven by the private sector and thus costly for the average Zambian.[91] A high number of smokers are willing to quit, but the lack of comprehensive tobacco cessation services in public facilities and failure of the national health insurance scheme to cover such services in private facilities limits accessibility to and impact of such services.[92] With the help of private actors, the government has trained health personnel in some public health institutions to implement tobacco-cessation programmes in routine consultations.[93] The trained staff from various health facilities were supported to develop workplans on how to implement tobacco cessation programmes in their health facilities hoping to regularise cessation practice in the participating health institutions.[94] While the Ministry of Health is supportive of health-promotion initiatives, it has not institutionalised this initiative to ensure sustainability beyond the support of private actors. No evidence exists of the impact of such support and whether such initiatives continue to exist beyond the life of the projects that support them.

7.4.4 Warn about the dangers of tobacco

The 1992 tobacco-related regulations prescribe a singular warning message, written in English, for tobacco product packaging. The lack of local language translations and pictorial warning messaging limits the effectiveness of the warning message, particularly given the high illiteracy levels and existence of various forms of disabilities in the country. It is thus arguable that considering the high prevalence of tobacco use in the country, such caution is ineffective as it is not accessible. The prescription of the messaging provided in SI 39 of 2008 is said to be inadequate, vague and susceptible to abuse.[95]

90 'Global tobacco industry interference index 2020, Zambia' https://globaltobaccoindex.org (accessed 7 October 2021).

91 SC Kaai & others 'Identifying factors associated with quit intentions among smokers from two nationally representative samples in Africa: Findings from the ITC Kenya and Zambia surveys' (2019) 15 *Prevention Medicine Reports* 100951 2.

92 As above 9.

93 Goma & others (n 44).

94 As above 277.

95 As above 266.

7.4.5 Enforce bans on tobacco advertising, promotion and sponsorship

Whereas Zambia has regulations that partially proscribe tobacco advertising and promotions, these are not readily enforced, thus rendering them ineffective. Arguably, because the government's stand against tobacco use and production is inconsistent, it cannot take a firm stance against tobacco advertising, as this is one of the most effective ways of fundraising for the tobacco industry. Some government line ministries and officials have participated in and benefited from activities of tobacco manufacturing companies, such as launches of cigarette factories and commissioning of the clinics and schools they construct or support as part of their corporate social responsibility . [96] Some authors have also argued that government ministries tend to support the tobacco industry because they contribute positively and substantially to Zambia's GDP and employment.[97] If the tobacco industry is curtailed from advertising, it cannot make as much money as it currently does and would not be able to support government in the way that it does. Although this thinking is erroneous, it would explain the government's minimalist approach to regulating tobacco advertising, promotion and sponsorship.

7.4.6 Raise taxes on tobacco

All increments in tobacco taxes since 2007 have effectively remained unchanged, with Zambia having one of the world's lowest excise tax shares for cigarettes.[98] Further, Zambia's tax regime is only partially suitable to address tobacco use, as it focuses mostly on factory manufactured tobacco and not (RYO, which is widely used in the country.[99] The relatively low taxes, coupled with the government's occasional support of the tobacco industry, makes Zambia a desirable investment destination for many international companies. The low taxes payable by the tobacco industry in Zambia largely contribute to the affordability of tobacco products, including by youths and unemployed persons. By failing to increase taxes to the extent where it can effectively respond to the high prevalence of tobacco use and production, and contribute to raising funds for responding the huge health burden that tobacco poses, the government is ultimately failing in discharging its health rights obligations under the ICESCR and FCTC.

96 University of Bath 'Zambia Country profile' http://tobaccotactics.org/wiki/zambia-country-profile (accessed August 2020).

97 R Labonté & others 'The institutional context of tobacco production in Zambia' (2018) 14 *Globalization and Health* 1 at 3–5.

98 M Stoklosa & others 'Price, tax and tobacco product substitution in Zambia: Findings from the ITC Zambia surveys' (2019) 28 *Tobacco Control* s45.

99 As above.

7.5 Local advocacy efforts for advancing the right to health using FCTC-compliant laws

Zambia's civil society has been very active in advocating for tobacco control in the country. Many of their efforts have been supported by the WHO and other cooperating partners to undertake various advocacy and education programmes for enhancing Zambia's response to tobacco control.

Anti-tobacco proponents have concentrated on using sensitisation strategies for key stakeholders to build mass support for pro-FCTC laws as opposed to litigation.[100] This has probably been the best course of action, considering that Zambia has had a relatively weak legislative framework for health rights. A similar approach was taken by mental health rights advocates in Zambia, who for many years invested in sensitisation of key stakeholders and only engaged in litigation after the 2016 constitutional amendments. The litigation was partially successful, but it expedited the legislative process for the now existing Mental Health Act. Evidence abounds in the Southern African Development Community and beyond that strategic litigation of health rights is a useful advocacy tool in holding governments accountable. It may thus now be worthwhile for anti-tobacco proponents to change strategy and seek judicial interventions to hold the state liable for its tobacco-related health-rights obligations.

Another advocacy approach implemented by activists is lobbying for the Tobacco Products and Nicotine Inhalants Control Bill. The Bill was first drafted in 2010 but has been vehemently opposed by many in government and the tobacco industry. The Ministry of Health has conducted an investment assessment and prepared an investment case report for Zambia which recognises the negative impact of tobacco consumption on public and personal health.[101] In spite of this undertaking, neither the Ministry of Health nor any other government department has undertaken any legislative or other measures it proposes in the report to curtail the negative health impact of tobacco in Zambia. Zambia needs to draw some lessons from countries such as South Africa where the Ministry of Health, being aware of the negative impact of tobacco use on health, put in place measures to curb the use of tobacco. Appreciating that health is an evolving concept, advocates for health rights including the ministry responsible for health must constantly review and reform interventions to ensure the negative effects of tobacco on health are averted. In the case of *Fair Trade Independent Tobacco Association v President of the Republic of South Africa* (the *FITA* case),[102] the Minister of Cooperative Governance and Traditional Affairs banned the use of tobacco as a way of mitigating the spread of COVID-19, considering the negative impact of tobacco use on transmission of COVID-19, as well as the

100 Goma & others (n 9).

101 Ministry of Health 'Investment case for tobacco control in Zambia' www.who.int/fctc/implementation/fctc/2030/investment-case-zambia-who-fctc-2030.pdf (accessed 6 October 2021).

102 2020 (6) SA 513 (GP).

exacerbation of the effect of COVID-19 on smokers in comparison to non-smokers. The Minister averred that the ban was primarily introduced to preserve human life and avoid straining the healthcare system.[103] In upholding the Minister's rational for the ban, the court held that[104]

> a vigorous attempt to contain the spread of the virus at all costs had to be made especially bearing in mind the high COVID-19 mortality rates and the fact that, as a developing country with limited resources as well as an already overwhelmed healthcare system, South Africa is ill-equipped to survive the full brunt of the pandemic at its peak if no concerted efforts are made to contain the virus. In line with its constitutionally mandated duties to preserve life and provide adequate health care, the State was under a duty to adopt measures to ensure that the already fragile healthcare system was not overwhelmed even further.

In the same vein, state institutions in Zambia, particularly the Ministry of Health, must ensure that it puts in place measures that mitigate the impact of tobacco use on health and not overburden an already fragile healthcare system. Upholding the Minister's power to pass regulations for tobacco control in response to the threat of COVID-19, the South African Constitutional Court found that the test for limiting constitutional rights is much higher and more stringent than the rationality test used in the *FITA* case.[105] In the case of *British American Tobacco South Africa v Minister of Cooperative Governance and Traditional Affairs* (the *BAT* case)[106] the court held that for administrative actions to pass the constitutionality test, the administrator must show that the infringement of fundamental rights guaranteed in the Constitution is reasonably justified in an open and democratic society, as the courts are required to 'weigh the extent of the limitation of the right against the purpose for which the legislation was enacted'.[107] The court refused to uphold the tobacco ban imposed by the Minister in the *BAT* case because she failed to demonstrate that it was necessary for achieving the purpose and in line with the constitutional parameters for limitation of rights. Thus, careful consideration to evidence-based interventions for responding to tobacco control as a means of enhancing the right to health, among others, is imperative. Other fundamental rights and freedoms should not be arbitrarily violated in the name of upholding health rights, even in public emergencies. Conversely, the right to health as guaranteed in article 12 of ICESCR and the FCTC must be promoted and protected based on context-specific experiences of the impact of tobacco use on health and scientifically sound interventions for mitigating the impact of tobacco.

103 *Fair Trade Independent Tobacco Association* (n 102) para 36.
104 As above.
105 2021 (7) BCLR 735 (WCC) paras 156 and 157.
106 As above.
107 BAT case (n 105) para 174.

7.6 Conclusion and recommendations

Tobacco use is highly prevalent in Zambia. It is particularly common among prisoners, men, young people, persons with disabilities, the unemployed and persons in rural areas. Tobacco use disproportionately affects women, children, persons with disabilities and prisoners. Tobacco negatively impacts on people's health, the economy and social life. Zambia's legal framework on the right to health is weak to respond to tobacco use and production and ensure discharge of its tobacco-related health rights. While efforts have been made by government and civil society to be FCTC compliant, these are inadequate and need to be upscaled. The following recommendations may thus be useful for this purpose.

To address the negative effects of tobacco, Zambia must adhere to its FCTC and health rights obligations and put in place measures to monitor the impact on different sectors and actors. Since it has a strong anti-tobacco civil society movement, efforts should be invested in capacity building to monitor, document and publish efforts for and against tobacco control.

Zambia must also protect people from the harmful effects of tobacco; create a health system that adequately responds to NCDs arising from tobacco use; help tobacco users to quit using tobacco; enforce bans that advertise, promote or sponsor tobacco use and production; and increase the price of tobacco through taxes.

An effective institutional framework supporting a multidisciplinary health-rights approach must be put in place to ensure that data collected on tobacco use and production informs response interventions including law and policy development. Further, all tobacco-related health determinants must be adequately addressed; for example, by enhancing food security and good health among tobacco farmers and their families by helping them switch to less harmful forms of farming and cash crops.

Zambia also needs to invest in implementing its progressive tobacco control provisions,; for example, by establishing an enforcement fund similar to the Anti–Gender Based Violence Fund.

It is evident from the preceding discussion that in many respects, Zambia is non-compliant with the FCTC. This could be attributed to the fact that tobacco laws predate its ratification of the FCTC, having been enacted at a time when the full ramifications of tobacco were not known. This, coupled with the continued ignorance of the negative impact of tobacco use and production in Zambia and the quest to 'grow the Zambian economy', has motivated the maintenance of the status quo and relegated Zambia's health rights obligations to a non-priority. Considering Zambia's commitment to socio-economic development and advancing the welfare of its people,[108] and given the extent of the tobacco problem in Zambia, it is paramount for Zambia to enact FCTC-compliant laws. The

108 See National Health Policy, National Child Policy, National Gender Policy, Non-Communicable Disease Strategic Plan 2013–2016, the Seventh National Development Plan, Vision 2030.

enactment of piecemeal subsidiary legislation to give effect to laws that are mostly non-FCTC compliant does not discharge Zambia of its right to health obligations.

Bibliography

African Union Commission and SAFAIDS 'The impact of tobacco use on health and socio-economic development in Africa: A status report' https://catalogues.safaids.net (accessed 1 October 2021)

Anti-Gender Based Violence Act 1 of 2011

British American Tobacco South Africa v Minister of Cooperative Governance and Traditional Affairs 2021 (7) BCLR 735 (WCC)

Chelwa, G & Van Walbeek, C 'Assessing the causal impact of tobacco expenditure on household patterns in Zambia' ERSA working paper 453 (2014)

Constitution (Amendment) Act 2 of 2016

Environmental Management Act 12 of 2011

Fair Trade Independent Tobacco Association v President of the Republic of South Africa 2020 (6) SA 513 (GP)

Global Tobacco Industry 'Interference index 2020 Zambia' https://globaltobaccoindex.org (accessed 7 October 2021)

Goma, F; Drope, J; Zulu, R; Li, Q; Chelwa, G; Labonté, R & Banda, A 'The economics of tobacco farming in Zambia' (Revised version) (University of Zambia and American Cancer Society 2017)

Goma, F; Ililonga, M & Drope, J *Tobacco control in Africa: People, politics and policies* (Anthem Press 2012)

Goma, F; Zulu, R & Drope, J 'An opportunity for meaningful public health progress: Zambia's pending Tobacco Control Legislation' *Tobacco Atlas* 7 December 2019 https://tobaccoatlas.org/2019/12/07/an-opportunity-for-meaningful-public-health-progress-zambias-pending-tobacco-control-legislation/http://www.tobaccoatlas.org (accessed 7 October 2021)

Government of the Republic of Zambia's *Annual progress report 2014. Revised Sixth National Development Plan* available at http://www.mndp.gov.zm (accessed 1 June 2020)

Government of the Republic of Zambia's *Zambia Demographic and Health Survey* (2018)

Gruskin, S; Ferguson, L; Tarantola, D & Beaglehole, R 'Non-communicable diseases and human rights: A promising synergy' (2014) 1045 *American Journal of Public Health* 773

ILO *An integrated ILO strategy to address decent work deficits in the tobacco sector* 8–22 March 2018 http://www.ilo.org/wcmsp5/groups/public/ednorm/ (accessed 1 July 2020)

IndexMundi 'Zambia population' https://www.indexmundi.com/zambia/population.html (accessed 5 October 2021)

Juveniles Act Chapter 53 of Laws of Zambia

Kaai, SC; Fong, GT; Goma, F; Meng, G; Ikamarie, L; Ong'ang'o, JR & Elton-Marshall, T 'Identifying factors associated with quit intentions among smokers from two nationally representative samples in Africa: Findings from the ITC Kenya and Zambia Surveys Prevention Medicine Reports' (2019) 15 *Preventable Medicine Reports* 100951

Labonté, R; Lencucha, R; Drope, J; Packer, C; Goma, FM & Zulu, R 'The institutional context of tobacco production in Zambia' (2018) 14 *Globalization and Health* 1

Lungu, F 'Debate around proposed tobacco control bill' *Zambia Daily Mail* (Lusaka) 27 June 2018 http://www.daily-mail.co.zm/debate-around-proposed-tobacco-control-bill (accessed 2 July 2020)

Lungu, F 'Economic vs health: Experts bash tobacco industry' *Zambia Daily Mail* (Lusaka) 19 March 2018 www.daily-mail.co.zm (accessed 9 July 2020)

Mental Health Act 6 of 2019

Moraces AN 'Tax the smoker, save the smoker! The health and economic benefits of increased tobacco tax in Zambia' (2017) 5 *Health Press Zambia Bull* 1

Mukanu, MM; Zulu, JM; Mweemba & Mutale, W 'Responding to non-communicable diseases in Zambia: A policy analysis' (2017) 15 *Health Research Policy and Systems* 34 https://health-policy-systems.biomedcentral.com/articles/10.1186/s12961-017-0195-7 www.health-policy-systems.biomedcentral.com (accessed 1 October 2021)

Mwewa, K; Siziya, S & Kwangu, M 'Prevalence and correlates of tobacco smoking among prisoners at Kamfinsa correctional facility, Kitwe, Zambia' (2017) 12 *Health Press Zambia Bull* 11

National Assembly of Zambia *Report of the Committee on Health, Community Development and Social Services for the Second Session of the Twelfth National Assembly Appointed on 20th September 2017* http://www.parliament.gov.zm (accessed 7 October 2021)

NCD Alliance 'Non-communicable diseases (NCDs) and the rights-based movement' Briefing Paper 16 August 2011 http://www.ncd.alliance.org/resources/non-communicable-diseases-ncds-and-the-rights-based-movment

Olowski, P & Michelo, C 'Differential burden and determinants of tobacco smoking: Population-based observations from the Zambia demographic and health survey (2002 and 2007)' (2016) 1 *Journal of Healthcare Communications* http://www.imedpub.com (accessed 2 June 2020)

Penal Code Act Chapter 87 of the Laws of Zambia

Persons with Disabilities Act 6 of 2012

Phiri, B 'The rise of non-communicable diseases in Zambia and strategies for action' *Medium* 29 August 2017 https://medium.com/amplify/the-rise-of-non-communicable-diseases-in-zambia-and-strategies-for-action-cc45d4db9c9 (accessed 28 September 2021)

Plant Pests and Diseases Act Chapter 233 of the Laws of Zambia

Prisons Act Chapter 97 of Laws of Zambia

Public Health Act Chapter 295 of the Laws of Zambia

Report Card on the WHO Framework Convention on Tobacco Control for Zambia https://www.afro.who.int (accessed 1 October 2021)

Republic of Zambia's Zambia *STEPS for non-communicable diseases risk factors* (2017) 80 https://www.afro.who.intel/publications/zambia-steps-survey-non-communicable-diseases-zambia-report-2017 (accessed 1 October 2021)

SADC Review-Study into the Illicit Trade in Excisable Products with Particular Reference to Alcohol and Tobacco Products https://www.sadc.int (accessed 1 October 2021)

Shadow Report on the Implementation of the Framework Convention on Tobacco Control Articles 8 and 13 in Zambia http://www.fctc.org (accessed 1 October 2021)

Stoklosa, M; Goma, F; Nargis, N; Drope, J; Chelwa, G; Chisha, Z & Fong, GT 'Price, tax and tobacco product substitution in Zambia: Findings from the ITC Zambia surveys' (2019) 285 *Tobacco Control* s45

Tobacco Act Chapter 237 of the Laws of Zambia

Tobacco Industry Board (Establishment) Act Chapter 110 of the 1964 Edition of the Laws of Zambia

Tobacco (Levy) Act 238 of the Laws of Zambia

Trading Economics 'Zambia – causes of death by non-communicable diseases' https://tradingeconomics.com (accessed 1 June 2020)

United Nations General Assembly 'Report of the special rapporteur on the right of everyone to the enjoyment of the highest attainable standard of physical and mental health' para 12 https://www.who.int/medicines/areas/human_rights/A63_263.pdf

University of Bath 'Tobacco tactics: Zambia country profile' https://www.tobaccotactics.org (accessed 14 June 2020)

WHO 'MPOWER: Advancing the WHO framework convention on tobacco control (WHO FCTC)' https://www.who.int/cancer/prevention/tobacco_implementation/mpower/en (accessed 7 October 2021)

WHO 'Noncommunicable diseases country profile' Geneva 2014 http://www.who.int>zmb_en (accessed 1 June 2020)

WHO 'Zambia smoking prevalence tobacco economy' https://www.who.int>media>zam (accessed 14 June 2020)

World Bank 'Confronting illicit tobacco trade: A global review of country experiences' (2019)

WorldoMeter 'Zambia population' https://www.worldometers.info/world-population/zambia-population/ (accessed 5 October 2021)

Zambia Statistics Agency *Monthly bulletin* (2020) 3

Zyaambo, C; Babaniyi, O; Songolo, P; Muula, AS; Rudatsikira, E & Siziya, S 'Prevalence and predictors of smoking in a mining town in Kitwe, Zambia: A 2011 population-based survey' (2013) 5 *Health* http://www.researchgate.net (accessed 1 June 2020)

https://pt.tobaccoatlas.org/2018/04/30/zambia-rolly-your-own-affordability-tobacco-control-itc (accessed 7 October 2021)

8 Tobacco smoking and the law in Rwanda

Progress, challenges and perspectives

Christian Garuka

8.1 Introduction

Rwanda has been experiencing a rise in non-communicable diseases (NCDs) in recent years.[1] Regarding the prevalence of the main risk factors in relation to NCDs, findings from a survey conducted in Rwanda in 2015 revealed that tobacco use, the harmful use of alcohol, accident-related injuries and physical inactivity are precursors of NCDs.[2] According to the World Health Organization (WHO), NCDs are estimated to account for 44 per cent of all deaths in Rwanda.[3] As far as the link between tobacco use and NCDs is concerned, the survey indicated that it contributed to 12.9 per cent of NCDs.[4]

It is useful to note that Rwanda has adopted a specific policy on NCDs with the overall goal of alleviating the burden of NCDs and their risk factors and protection of the Rwandan population from premature morbidity and mortality related to NCDs.[5]

In addition to the above, the Health Sector Policy acknowledges NCD prevention and control among challenges faced by the government of Rwanda, as services were not yet available across the healthcare system in terms of human resources capacities, diagnostic and treatment technologies, and more importantly, existing services were not affordable and accessible to all.[6]

1 C Kraef & others 'Fighting non-communicable diseases in East Africa: Assessing progress and identifying the next steps' (2020) 5 *BMJ Global Health* e003325 https://www.ncbi.nlm.nih.gov/pmc/articles/PMC7662421/pdf/bmjgh-2020-003325.pdf (accessed 5 September 2021).
2 Ministry of Health 'Rwanda non-communicable diseases risk factors report' (2015) http://moh.gov.rw/fileadmin/templates/Docs/Rwanda_Non-communicable_Diseases_Risk_Factors_Report.pdf (accessed 15 September 2021).
3 WHO 'Non communicable diseases progress monitor (2020)' https://www.who.int/publications/i/item/ncd-progress-monitor-2020 (accessed 25 September 2021). See also F Nuwagaba & P Williams 'Programs to prevent non-communicable diseases (NDCs) in Rwanda: Improving healthy eating for adolescents and adults' Evidence brief (2018).
4 WHO (n 3).
5 Ministry of Health *Non-communicable diseases policy* (2015).
6 Ministry of Health *Health sector policy* (2015).

DOI: 10.4324/9781003264248-10

Furthermore, Rwanda adopted a Strategic Plan for NCDs with a target of reducing 80 per cent of deaths due to NCDs among persons aged 40 years and younger by 2020.[7] An in-depth analysis of the implementation of policies and plan is beyond the scope of this chapter.

As far as tobacco use is concerned, it must be noted that the Rwanda Demographic Health Survey (RDHS) 2014–2015 revealed that 10 per cent of men aged between 15 and 49 smoke in Rwanda compared to 2 per cent of women of the same age group.[8] There is a decline compared to findings from the RDHS of 2010, which revealed that 14 per cent of men aged between 15 and 49 years smoked tobacco, compared to 4 per cent of women of the same age group.[9]

Finally, from a cultural standpoint, it is useful to note that tobacco plays an important role in the Rwandan culture, especially during traditional weddings where the delegation from the groom gave traditional tobacco (*igikamba*) as a gift to the family of the bride.[10] However, this practice was abolished in the country more than 20 years ago.[11]

8.2 Right to health and NCDs

This section discusses the legal framework relevant to the right to health in Rwanda and makes the link between the right to health and NCDs, including the effects of tobacco use.

The Constitution of 2003 as revised in 2015 guarantees the right to health under articles 21 and 45. According to article 21 of the Constitution of 2003, all Rwandans have the right to good health. It is submitted that 'good health' is difficult to define or assess, but also the right to health as guaranteed under the Constitution falls below the threshold of this right as guaranteed under international and human rights treaties ratified by Rwanda, as these instruments use the superlative 'best' instead of 'good'.

Indeed, the International Covenant on Economic, Social and Cultural Rights (ICESCR), the Convention on the Rights of the Child (CRC), the African Charter on Human and Peoples' Rights (ACHPR) and the African Charter on the

7 Ministry of Health *Strategic plan for non-communicable diseases July 2014–June 2019*.

8 National Institute of Statistics of Rwanda and Ministry of Health *Rwanda demographic and health survey 2014–2015*.

9 National Institute of Statistics of Rwanda and Ministry of Health *Rwanda demographic and health survey 2010*.

10 B Kwizera 'Itabi, umuco wakendereye mu misango y'ubukwe mu Rwanda' *Rwanda Broadcasting Agency* 27 December 2019 https://www.rba.co.rw/post/Itabi-umuco-wakendereye-mu-misango-yubukwe-mu-Rwanda (accessed 20 September 2021); see also Menya Umwanditsi 'Kunyara ku muhanda, imwe mu ngeso mbi nyinshi zacitse burundu mu Banyarwanda' *Kigali Today* 20 June 2008 https://www.kigalitoday.com/amakuru/amakuru-mu-rwanda/article/kunyara-ku-muhanda-imwe-mu-ngeso-mbi-nyinshi-zacitse-burundu-mu-banyarwanda (accessed 27 September 2021).

11 Field interview conducted on 16 August 2021. On file with the author.

Rights and Welfare of the Child (ACRWC) all stipulate that every individual shall have the right to enjoy the *best attainable* state of physical and mental health.

The second constitutional provision, article 45, obligates the state to mobilise the population for activities aimed at good health and to assist them in the realisation of those activities. It is contended that this provision fails to mention how this will be achieved.

In explaining what constituted the state obligation as per article 45(1) of the Constitution in the context of reproductive health, the Supreme Court of Rwanda held, in *National Public Prosecution Authority v Ntibajyinama Esther*:

> It is clear that the State has fulfilled some of its obligations to assist the population to take part in activities aimed at good health in terms of reproductive health as health facilities were built, staff recruitment and supply of equipment based on the available resources of the State and sensitization by the State of pregnant women about attending health facilities for consultation and delivery at health facilities.[12]

It is argued that the Supreme Court missed an opportunity to reiterate that the services had to be of good quality, affordable and accessible.

The second paragraph of article 45 of the Constitution of 2003 as revised in 2015 is quite problematic, as it obligates every Rwandan citizen to take part in activities aimed at good health. The Constitution neither provides a list of what constitutes activities aimed at good health nor suggests the enactment of a law or statute regulating activities aimed at good health. This constitutional provision is premised on the assumption that every citizen is aware of activities aimed at good health.

These instructions do not provide for any administrative or criminal sanctions in case of failure to observe them. It is argued that the omission of custodial sentences as criminal sanctions was rational from an international and regional human rights perspective. Indeed, article 9(1) of the International Covenant on Civil and Political Rights (ICCPR)[13] and article 6 of the ACHPR provide no one shall be deprived of their liberty except on such grounds and in accordance with such procedure as are established by law.[14]

Since the ministerial instructions are not considered law per se, they cannot therefore provide for criminal sanctions such as a custodial measure (imprisonment) as envisaged under the aforementioned international and regional human rights treaties. Doing otherwise would have been in contravention with the right to liberty and security of a person as provided under the aforementioned human rights treaties.

12 RPAA0078/15/CS.

13 Rwanda ratified the ICCPR on 1 March 1975 through the Decree – Law 8/75 of 12 February 1975.

14 Rwanda ratified the African Charter on Human and Peoples' Rights on 1 July 1983 through Decree Law 10/1983 of 1 July 1983.

Prior to the enactment of the Law 08/2013 of 1 March 2013 relating to the control of tobacco, Rwanda criminalised the sale or distribution of tobacco to a child. Indeed, article 219 of the Penal Code of 2012 criminalised the sale or offer of tobacco to a child or encouraging a child to smoke tobacco.

As far as the criminalisation of smoking in public is concerned, the repeal of the Penal Code of 2012 and omission of penalties for smoking in public in the subsequent enacted legal framework has created a legal vacuum. To put it differently, article 26 of the Law 08/2013 of 1 March 2013 relating to the control of tobacco stipulates that anyone who smokes in public shall be liable for sentences as provided for in the Penal Code. It is obvious that article 26 of the Law 08/2013 of 1 March 2013 relating to the control of tobacco was referring to the Penal Code of 2012.

Figures from Tobacco Atlas indicate that Rwanda recorded 4.72 per cent of adult men and 1.57 per cent of women succumbing to tobacco-related deaths in 2016 . [15]

8.3 The WHO FCTC as a treaty to realise the right to health at the national level

8.3.1 From scattered tobacco-related legal provisions to a stand-alone law on tobacco control

Rwanda ratified the FCTC in 2005.[16] By virtue of article 190 of the Constitution of 2003, the FCTC was part and parcel of the legal framework. With the revision of the Constitution in 2015, the ratification and subsequent publication treaties makes them binding to Rwanda by virtue of article 168.

Indeed, article 168 provides that international treaties and agreements which have been duly ratified or approved have the force of law as national legislation in accordance with the hierarchy of laws upon publication in the Official Gazette. As far as the hierarchy of laws is concerned, it must be noted that article 95 of the Constitution provides that ratified treaties come in third position after Organic Laws[17] (second) and the Constitution. One of the obligations stemming from the ratification of the FCTC is the adoption of legislative measures by States parties' to give effect to the FCTC.

In this regard, the first attempt to regulate tobacco use was the issuance of the instructions by the Minister of Health 20/10 of 10 May 2005 relating to the protection of non-smokers and the environment against adverse effects of tobacco. It is quite useful to highlight that the Preamble of these instructions refers to the Presidential Order 13/01 of 25 May 2005 ratifying the FCTC and, more importantly, emphasising the adverse consequences on non-smokers, smokers and to the environment. The second attempt was the criminalisation of the

15 'The Tobacco Atlas: Rwanda' https://tobaccoatlas.org/country/rwanda/ (accessed 12 September 2021).

16 Rwanda ratified the FCTC by the Presidential Order 13/01 of 25 May 2005.

17 Organic Laws are laws which are enunciated in the Constitution.

sale or distribution of tobacco to a child under the Penal Code of 2012. Indeed, article 219(1) of the Organic Law 01/2012/OL of 2 May 2012 instituting the Penal Code[18] stipulated that any person who offers or sells tobacco to a child or involves them in the sale of such products shall be liable to a term of imprisonment of at least three months but less than six months and a fine of 300,000 to 1,000,000 Rwandan francs or one of these penalties.

The second paragraph of article 219 of the then Penal Code of 2012 stipulated that penalties provided under article 219(1) were applicable to any person who encouraged a child to smoke. It must also be noted that article 428(3) of the then Penal Code criminalised any person who smoked in public and in any other place where many people gather with a fine ranging from 10,000 to 50,000 Rwandan francs.

In 2013, Rwanda enacted a law known as Law 08/2013 of 1 March 2013 specifically relating to the control of tobacco (Tobacco Control Act). It is interesting to observe that the Preamble of the Tobacco Control Act makes a clear reference to the FCTC, more specifically articles 3, 5, 11, 12, 13, 15 and 16. The Preambles of other laws only refer to conventions ratified by Rwanda without making specific reference to the provisions of these conventions or treaties. On a different note, it must be emphasised that it took Rwanda eight years to enact a specific law to give effect to the FCTC, despite the fact that the ratification took place in 2005.

Another notable delay to emphasise is the issuance of ministerial orders which are supposed to give effect to the enforcement of the Tobacco Control Act. In this respect, articles 12 and 18 of the Tobacco Control Act of 2013 provide for ministerial orders for the implementation of the Act.

These ministerial orders were promulgated in the Official Gazette two years after the publication of the Tobacco Control Act. Ministerial Order 20/33 of 9 June 2015 determines the characteristics of smoking areas and the content which shall be included in the notice to be displayed in the smoking area, and Ministerial Order 20/34 of 9 June 2015 determines the content and design of the warning to be put on the package of tobacco and tobacco products.

There is no dispute that the delay in promulgating the aforementioned ministerial orders created a legal vacuum, as without these two ministerial orders, articles 12 and 18 of the Tobacco Control Act were not enforceable. As far as reporting is concerned, it should be noted that Rwanda has submitted three reports to the Secretariat of the Conference of the Parties. The most recent report was submitted in 2018,[19] whereas the second report was submitted in 2012[20] and the initial report in 2009.[21]

18 The Penal Code of 2012 was repealed by the Law 68/2018 of 30 August 2018 determining offences and penalties in general.

19 Republic of Rwanda 'Third national report to the Secretariat of the Conference of Parties' https://untobaccocontrol.org/impldb/wp-content/uploads/Rwanda_2018_report.pdf (accessed 12 September 2021).

20 Republic of Rwanda 'Second national report to the secretariat of the conference of parties' https://untobaccocontrol.org/impldb/wp-content/uploads/reports/rwanda_2012_report.pdf (accessed 12 September 2021).

21 Republic of Rwanda 'National report to the Secretariat of the Conference of the Parties' https://untobaccocontrol.org/impldb/wp-content/uploads/reports/Rwanda_report.pdf (accessed 12 September 2021).

8.3.2 *The FCTC and the realisation of the right to health in Rwanda*

The nexus between tobacco and health is explicitly found under article 8 of the FCTC. Indeed, article 8 emphasises the recognition by States parties' of the fact that exposure to tobacco smoke causes death, disease and disability. The FCTC stresses that the scientific recognition of the casual link between the exposure to tobacco smoke and disease is unequivocal, meaning there is no room for further debate on the subject.

Article 8(2) of the FCTC obligates States parties' to

> adopt and implement in areas of existing national jurisdiction as determined by national law and actively promote at other jurisdictional levels the adoption and implementation of effective legislative, executive, administrative and/or other measures, providing for protection from exposure to tobacco smoke in indoor workplaces, public transport, indoor public places and, as appropriate, other public places.

This clearly falls under the obligation of states to protect individuals from the exposure to tobacco smoke and thus uphold their right to health. From the regional and international human rights point of view in the context of health, it must be noted that Rwanda is a party to the following instruments: the International Covenant on Economic, Social and Cultural Rights (ICESCR);[22] the Convention on the Rights of Persons with Disabilities (CRPD);[23] the Convention on the Elimination of Discrimination against Women (CEDAW);[24] the Convention on the Rights of the Child (CRC);[25] the African Charter on Human and Peoples' Rights (ACHPR);[26] the African Charter on the Rights and Welfare of the Child (ACRWC);[27] and the Protocol to the African Charter on Human and Peoples' Rights on the Rights of Women in Africa (Maputo Protocol).[28]

Before embarking on these obligations, it is imperative to examine the provisions which guarantee the right to health under these regional and international human rights instruments to which Rwanda is a party. In its General Comment 14

22 Rwanda ratified the ICESCR on 1 March 1975 by Decree Law 8/75 of 12 February 1975.

23 Rwanda ratified the CRPD on 31 December 2012 by Presidential Order 131/01 of 27 December 2012.

24 CEDAW was ratified by Rwanda on 15 February 1981 by Presidential Order 431/16 of 10 November 1980.

25 The CRC was ratified by Rwanda on 1 November 1990 by Presidential Order 773/16 of 19 September 1990.

26 The ACHPR was ratified by Rwanda on 1 July 1983 by Decree Law 10/1983 of 1 July 1983.

27 This instrument was ratified on 15 November 2001 by Presidential Order 11/01 of 30 May 2001.

28 The Maputo Protocol was ratified by Rwanda on 24 June 2004 by Presidential Order 11/01 of 24 June 2004.

on article 12, the Committee on Economic, Social and Cultural Rights (CESCR) interpreted the right to healthy natural and workplace environments as an obligation to States parties' to discourage tobacco use.[29]

As far as the right of the child to health is concerned, the CRC and ACRWC provide that 'every child has the right to enjoy the highest attainable standard of health and facilities for the treatment of illness and rehabilitation of health'.[30] Besides the aforementioned child-rights instruments, it must be recalled that the right to health guaranteed under regional and international human rights instruments[31] is applicable to the child, as the liberal interpretation of 'person', 'woman' and 'individual' encompasses the child.

With regard to women's rights, it is useful to note that the Preamble of the FCTC clearly states that signatories are alarmed by the increase in smoking and other forms of tobacco consumption by women and young girls worldwide, and that there is a need for full participation of women at all levels of policymaking and implementation and the need for gender-specific tobacco control strategies. In General Recommendation 24, the CEDAW Committee has outlined the responsibility of states that fail to address private practices that put women's health in danger in the following terms:

> [T]he obligation to protect rights relating to women's health requires States parties', their agents and officials to take action to prevent and impose sanctions for violations of rights by private persons and organizations.

From this General Recommendation it is clear that Rwanda has a duty to protect women's health in the context of exposure to tobacco smoke by adopting and implementing measures including laws and policies and impose sanctions on persons and businesses which expose women to tobacco smoke. In this regard, it is submitted that the omission in the current Rwandan national legal framework of sanctions for persons who smoke in public is a failure to protect women, as well as other persons who are exposed to tobacco smoke.

With regard to the right of the child to health in the context of tobacco use, the UN Committee on the Rights of the Child recommended that the government of Rwanda address the issue of drug use and substance abuse by children and adolescents by, inter alia, providing children and adolescents with accurate and objective information on preventing substance abuse, including tobacco and alcohol, and developing accessible and youth-friendly drug dependence treatment and harm reduction services for children and adolescents.[32]

29 CESCR General Comment 14: The right to the highest attainable standard of health (art 12) (2000) UN Doc E/C.12/2000/4 dated 11 August 2000.

30 Art 24(1) of the CRC and art 14 of the ACRWC.

31 The right to health is guaranteed under art 12 of the ICESCR, art 25 of the CRPD, art 12 of CEDAW, art 16 of the ACHPR and art 14 of the Maputo Protocol.

32 Concluding Observations on the combined fifth and sixth periodic reports of Rwanda, CRC Committee (28 February 2020) UN Doc CRC/C/RWA/CO/5-6 (2020) para 36.

This recommendation falls under the obligation imposed on the state to promote the right to health in relation to tobacco.

The right to health is also implicitly protected under article 38 of the Law 36/2012 of 21 August 2012 relating to competition and consumer protection, which prohibits any advertisement that may encourage risky behaviour dangerous for health or safety of persons.

Article 45(1) of the Constitution of 2003 as revised in 2015 obligates the state to mobilise the population for activities aimed at good health and to assist them in the realisation of those activities. As far as the obligation of Rwanda as a state party is concerned in relation to the right to health in the context of tobacco use, it can be argued that the state is under obligation to sensitise the population on negative impacts of tobacco use and more importantly to support those who are willing to quit smoking. The obligation to sensitise the population on either avoiding or quitting smoking falls under the obligation imposed on the state to fulfil and promote the right of citizens to health.

Besides the Constitution, other laws or Acts contain provisions which deal with the right to health. In this regard, article 4(1) of the Law 49/2012 of 22 January 2013 establishing medical professional liability prohibits any form of discrimination in terms of access to consultation and healthcare services, as well as other paramedical procedures. The broad interpretation of this provision implies that individuals have the right to access to consultation and healthcare services in the context of tobacco use, such as information and treatment. The obligation imposed on the state is to protect the individual against discrimination.

Article 15(2) of Law 48/2015 of 23 November 2015 governing the organisation, functioning and management of health insurance reads: 'It is prohibited to deny a person or a group of persons access to health insurance services for any reason based on discrimination of any kind'. It is submitted that this right is applicable to individuals who are addicted to tobacco smoking or just tobacco smokers.

It is worth mentioning that article 5(4) of Law No 49/2012 of 22 January 2013 establishing medical professional liability stipulates that a patient or any other health service user shall have the right to have access to reliable results when subjected to tests, having a prosthesis done or being administered compulsory vaccinations and using medical devices and products. This right is applicable in the context of tobacco use where a patient would seek test results. It must be emphasised that a patient seeking test results or any health services in the context of tobacco use should be treated with dignity without being subjected to any moral judgment based on their smoking habit or addiction.

The obligations stemming from these regional and international human rights instruments require States parties' to protect, respect and promote the right of an individual to health.

As far as the obligation to protect the right to health in the context of tobacco is concerned, some authors have asserted that tobacco-related human rights violations often stem from tobacco companies' activities, although the companies are not directly bound by the international human rights treaty obligations undertaken by their host governments.[33]

As far as the obligation to respect the right to health in the context of tobacco is concerned, it has been rightly argued by some legal scholars that states have the duty to refrain from engaging in activities that directly infringe on the right to health by incentivising tobacco consumption.[34] It was also argued that states' obligation to protect the right to health in the context of tobacco requires states to take measures to prevent third parties from interfering and affecting individual's realisation of human rights through the ban on tobacco advertisement.[35]

The CESCR, in its General Comment 14, observed that the 'failure to discourage production, marketing and consumption of tobacco' constitutes a violation of the obligation imposed on States parties' in relation to protect the right to health as guaranteed under article 12 of the ICESCR.

General Comment 14 clearly states that violations of the obligation to protect follow from the failure of a state to take all necessary measures to safeguard persons within their jurisdiction from infringements of the right to health by third parties. This shall include omissions as the failure to discourage production, marketing and consumption of tobacco.

The CRC has also made general recommendations regarding the need for more effective tobacco information campaigns and the importance of tobacco advertising restrictions. In this regard, the Committee in its General Comment 4 (2003) emphasised the obligation of States parties' to promote cost-effective measures, including through laws, policies, and programmes, with regard to the abuse of alcohol, tobacco and other harmful substances.

It has been argued that tobacco consumption, often by the male members of the family, competes with the purchase of essential food, medicine and education for children and is thus a direct threat to children's and women's right to food, healthcare and education.[36]

Table 8.1 illustrates the extent to which Rwandan national laws comply with the FCTC.

33 ME Crow 'Smokescreens and state responsibility: Using human rights strategies to promote global tobacco control' (2004) 29 *The Yale Journal of International Law* 209 https://digitalcommons.law.yale.edu/cgi/viewcontent.cgi?article=1228&context=yjil (accessed 22 November 2021).

34 OA Cabrera & A Madrazo 'Human rights as a tool for tobacco control in Latin America' (2010) 52 *Human Rights and Tobacco Control* S288 https://www.scielosp.org/pdf/spm/v52s2/a26v52s2.pdf (accessed 16 September 2021).

35 As above.

36 R de Silva de Alwis & R Daynard 'Reconceptualizing human rights to challenge tobacco' (2008–2009) 17 *Michigan State Journal of International Law* 291.

Table 8.1 Level of Rwanda's compliance

Obligations	*FCTC Article*	*National Legal Framework (Laws and Ministerial Orders)*	*Level of Compliance*
Health warning.	Article 11 requires States parties' to ensure that health warnings are displayed on tobacco product packaging.	Article 18 of the Tobacco Control Act requires that all tobacco products for sale in Rwanda must bear health warnings on product packaging. Article 3(1) of Ministerial Order 20/34 of 9 June 2015 determining the content and design of the warning to be put on the package of tobacco and tobacco products, and more importantly, the warning must be clear and in Kinyarwanda and English or Kinyarwanda and French.	Full compliance.
Taxation.	Article 6 obligates state parties to adopt tax measures to reduce the demand for tobacco.	Article 4 of Law 37/2015 of 30 June 2015 modifying and complementing law 26/2006 of 27 May 2006 imposes taxes on Tobacco.	Full compliance.
Protection from tobacco exposure.	Article 8(2) obligates States parties' to provide for protection from exposure to tobacco smoke in indoor workplaces, public transport, indoor public places and, as appropriate, other public places.	Article 26 of the Tobacco Control Act criminalises smoking in public places but stipulates that the penalties are provided for in the Penal Code. The current Penal Code does not contain any specific provision that criminalises smoking in public places.	Partial compliance.

Obligations	*FCTC Article*	*National Legal Framework (Laws and Ministerial Orders)*	*Level of Compliance*
Tobacco reduction measures and cessation support.	Article 14(2) obligates States parties' to include diagnosis and treatment of tobacco dependence and counselling services on cessation of tobacco use in national health and education programmes.	Article 1 of the Tobacco Control Act stipulates that among its purposes are to motivate smokers to quit smoking and provide rehabilitation for those who stop smoking, but there is no specific provision to achieve these goals.	Partial compliance.
Prohibition of illicit trade	Article 15 prohibits the sale of illicit tobacco.	Article 19 of the Tobacco Control Act requires tobacco and tobacco products sold in Rwanda to bear a stamp issued by customs services and with the imprint 'sold in Rwanda'. Article 25 of the Tobacco Control Act provides for an administrative fine that is equal to the value of the confiscated tobacco and tobacco products to any person who imports tobacco and tobacco products and sells them in Rwanda without a stamp and imprints written in languages recognised in Rwanda.	Full compliance.

8.4 Assessment of the effectiveness of efforts to implement FCTC/national laws on tobacco use

This section critically assesses whether efforts by the government to implement the FCTC and national laws on tobacco use has yielded any results. For this purpose, the assessment will be guided by the WHO MPOWER package. MPOWER stands for the following:

- Monitor tobacco use
- Protect people from tobacco use
- Offer help to quit tobacco use
- Warn about the dangers of tobacco
- Enforce bans on tobacco advertising, promotion and sponsorship
- Raise taxes on tobacco

8.4.1 Monitor tobacco use

As far as the monitoring of tobacco use is concerned, it must be highlighted that unlike the previous RDHS of 2014–2015, the latest RDHS 2019–2020 does not provide any information related to tobacco use in Rwanda in the last period. In addition, annual reports from the Ministry of Health do not contain periodic data on key indicators of tobacco use for youth and adults.

8.4.2 Protect people from tobacco use

It is worth mentioning that article 9 of the Tobacco Control Act prohibits the sale of tobacco and other tobacco-related products in healthcare and educational facilities, including nursery, primary and secondary schools, and higher learning institutions, sports and leisure facilities. In addition, article 11 of the Tobacco Control Act prohibits smoking in public and further provides a list of prohibited smoking areas. It should be noted that the list of prohibited smoking areas is not exhaustive, as article 11 allows the Minister of Health to determine other prohibited smoking areas. On a very different note, the prohibition of smoking in public is not absolute, as article 12 of the Tobacco Control Act provides for an exception and thus stipulates the enactment of a ministerial order which shall determine characteristics of smoking areas and the content which shall be included in the notice to be displayed in those areas.

As far as the location of designated smoking areas is concerned, article 4 of Ministerial Order 20/33 of 9 June 2015[37] provides that the smoking area must be situated in an open space area of the premises, with nearby doors and windows having access to open air or installed with suitable ventilation and extraction

37 The official title is Ministerial Order 20/33 of 9 June 2015 determining the characteristics of smoking areas and the content which shall be included in the notice to be displayed in the smoking area.

solutions to ensure that there is no smoke drift from the smoking area into the rest of the premises in accordance with the decision of an inspector. I agree with one author who has argued that a general ban on tobacco smoking is preferential on the basis of the aim to protect the health of non-smoking individuals whose health suffers from second-hand smoke.[38]

With regard to law enforcement, some media outlets reported that some hotels and restaurants were not compliant with the law, and this led the Ministry of Health to issue a public release in 2019 reminding restaurants and hotels owners to abide by the Tobacco Control Act. It was found that most of them did not display visible warning signs of 50 cm × 50 cm informing and restricting smokers that smoking in any given public area in their premises was strictly prohibited.[39] Another challenge which needs to be highlighted in the context of smoking in public is the current legal vacuum as a consequence of legal reform that occurred in 2018. Indeed, article 26 of the Tobacco Control Act criminalises such conduct but stipulates that the penalties are provided for in the Penal Code. It is useful to note that when the Tobacco Control Act was enacted in 2013, the Penal Code was in force. However, the Penal Code was repealed in 2018 by Law 68/2018 of 30 August 2018.[40] To put it differently, Law 68/2018 does not criminalise smoking in public.

In light of the foregoing, it is submitted that the omission of sanctions in case of smoking in public in the current legal framework is a clear violation to the obligation imposed on States parties', Rwanda being one of them, in the context of the right to health which requires them to adopt legislative measures in the realisation of economic, social and cultural rights.[41]

8.4.3 Offer help to quit tobacco use

Although article 1 of the Tobacco Control Act stipulates that one of its purposes of is to motivate smokers to quit smoking and provide rehabilitation for those who want to stop smoking, this law does not indicate how this will be achieved

38 C Borucki 'When healthcare goes up in tobacco smoke: A selective healthcare system from a (European) human rights perspective' (2019) 15 *Utrecht Law Review* 6 https://www.utrechtlawreview.org/articles/10.36633/ulr.539 (accessed 19 September 2021).

39 H Kuteesa 'MoH issues fresh warning against smoking in public' *The Newtimes* 27 May 2019 https://www.newtimes.co.rw/news/moh-issues-fresh-warning-against-smoking-public (accessed 20 September 2021). See also W Buningwire 'How you become [a] second hand smoker in Kigali pubs' *KT Press* 1 September 2019 https://www.ktpress.rw/2019/06/how-you-become-second-hand-smoker-in-kigali-pubs/ (accessed 20 September 2021). See further 'Rwanda's ministry of health issues new warning against practice of smoking in public' *Devdiscourse* 27 May 2019 https://www.devdiscourse.com/article/law-order/539274-rwandas-ministry-of-health-issues-new-warning-against-practice-of-smoking-in-public (accessed 20 September 2021).

40 The official title is Law 68/2018 of 30 August 2018 determining offences and penalties in general.

41 Article 2(1) of the ICESCR.

either in terms of cessation of tobacco use or adequate treatment for tobacco dependence as required under article 14 of the FCTC. In addition, article 3 of Ministerial Order 20/34 of 9 June 2015, determining the content and design of the warning to be put on the package of tobacco and tobacco products, does not require tobacco manufacturers or sellers to provide a hotline number for those who want to quit smoking.

8.4.4 Warning about the dangers of tobacco

Article 3 of Ministerial Order 20/34 of 9 June 2015[42] requires health warnings to mention that 'smoking kills, causes cancer, heart diseases, and other health vices such as impotence, infertility, miscarriage and stroke'; more importantly the warnings shall appear in Kinyarwanda and English or Kinyarwanda and French.[43] In addition, the Ministerial Order requires health warnings to be clear and legible, not be printed in a place where it may be damaged when the packaging is opened, and more importantly shall not be obstructed with other packaging and labelling marks.

8.4.5 Enforcement of bans on tobacco advertising, promotion and sponsorship

The Tobacco Control Act prohibits tobacco advertisement, promotion and sponsorship. But there is no report on enforcement on bans on tobacco advertisement, promotion and sponsorship.

8.4.6 Raising taxes on tobacco

As far as taxation is concerned, article 4 of the Law 37/2015 of 30 June 2015 modifying and complementing law 26/2006 of 27 May 2006 determining and establishing consumption tax on some imported and locally manufactured products as modified and complemented to date provides that 36 per cent of taxes shall be levied on the retail price of a pack (of 20 rods) and 30 Rwandan francs per pack.

With regard to the elimination of illicit trade of tobacco products, it is useful to note that article 19 of the Tobacco Control Act requires tobacco and tobacco products sold in Rwanda to bear a stamp issued by customs services and with imprints 'sold in Rwanda', and article 25 of the Tobacco Control Act provides for an administrative fine that is equal to the value of the confiscated tobacco and tobacco products to any person who imports tobacco and tobacco products and

42 The official title is Ministerial Order 20/34 of 9 June 2015 determining the content and design of the warning to be put on the package of tobacco and tobacco products.

43 Kinyarwanda is among the official languages but more importantly the national language of Rwanda which is spoken by the majority of Rwandan citizens.

sells them in Rwanda without a stamp and imprints written in languages recognised in Rwanda.

8.5 Case law

With regard to court decisions, it must be underscored that court decisions in relation to the allegation of non-compliance of the Tobacco Control Act are in short supply, if not non-existent. Nevertheless, in *Public Prosecution v Saidi Athuman Mohamed*,[44] the Nyarugenge Intermediate Court found Saidi Athuman Mohamed guilty of smoking cigarettes in an aircraft lavatory and sentenced him to a 5-year suspended term and a fine of 5 million Rwandan francs. It is useful to note that Mohamed was prosecuted under Law 21/2018 of 29 April 2018 modifying law 42/2011 of 31 October 2011 relating to civil aviation security.[45]

This case decision clearly indicates that smoking in some designated places like the airport or inside an aircraft attracts heavier punishments compared to others. As far as Law 21/2018 of 29 April 2018 relating to civil aviation security is concerned, this court decision is a good, clear example of effective law enforcement, as the current Law 08/2013 of 1 March 2013 relating to the control of tobacco does not have a specific provision penalties in relation to tobacco smoking on board an aircraft but rather refers to the Penal Code which was later repealed in 2018.

Indeed, the amended article 23 inserted article 41, which stipulates that any person who performs acts or with behaviour that interferes or is likely to interfere with the safe operation of an aircraft or that endangers the aircraft disregarding the safety of human life, commits an offence.

8.6 Conclusion and recommendations

The analysis of the legal framework has revealed that scattered provisions were found in some laws which were enacted after Rwanda's ratification of the FCTC. It took Rwanda eight years to finally enact a stand-alone law on tobacco control and two more years to enact ministerial orders to implement some of the provisions contained in the Tobacco Control Act. Legal reform recently undertaken in Rwanda has created a legal vacuum in terms of penalties or sanctions for smoking in public.

The analysis of the Tobacco Control Act and its implementing ministerial orders or instructions, as well as other laws which have provisions dealing with tobacco use, has revealed that some of them comply fully or partially with various aspects of the FCTC. Aspects which need to be highlighted are taxation where the amended law on consumption tax, promulgated in 2015, has shifted from levying on tobacco generally to retail. The assessment of laws and other strategies

44 RP 00520/2020/TGI/NYGE.

45 The amended law was promulgated in the Official Gazette 18 of 30 April 2018.

in compliance with the FCTC using the WHO MPOWER has identified some gaps which call for concrete recommendations.

As far as recommendations are concerned, legal reform is needed urgently to ensure that Rwanda complies with its obligations under the FCTC. In this regard, the Tobacco Control Act should be amended with a view to including sanctions for persons smoking in public, as currently there is a vacuum as a result of the repeal of the Penal Code. Second, the Tobacco Control Act and Ministerial Order should provide for a general ban on smoking in public without any exception.

Third, Ministerial Order 20/34 of 9 June 2015 determining the content and design of the warning to be put on the package of tobacco and tobacco products should be amended with the view to ensuring that tobacco manufacturers or sellers are required to provide a hotline number for those who want to quit smoking.

Rwanda needs to periodically conduct a study on whether taxation on tobacco contributes to tobacco reduction in Rwanda. Rwanda also needs to develop and implement a robust strategy with clear indicators on smoking cessation and support for those who are willing to quit smoking. Rwanda needs to increase the capacity of agencies responsible for the implementation of laws and strategies related to tobacco control.

Finally, Rwanda needs to collect periodically disaggregated data on gender and age to assess whether its efforts to reduce tobacco use are yielding results.

Bibliography

Borucki, C 'When healthcare goes up in tobacco smoke: A selective healthcare system from a (European) human rights perspective' (2019) 15 *Utrecht Law Review* 6 https://www.utrechtlawreview.org/articles/10.36633/ulr.539 (accessed 19 September 2021)

Buningwire, W 'How you become [a] second hand smoker in Kigali pubs' *KT Press* 1 September 2019 https://www.ktpress.rw/2019/06/how-you-become-second-hand-smoker-in-kigali-pubs/ (accessed 20 September 2021)

Cabrera, OA & Madrazo, A 'Human rights as a tool for tobacco control in Latin America' (2010) 52 Human Rights and Tobacco Control S288 https://www.scielosp.org/pdf/spm/v52s2/a26v52s2.pdf (accessed 16 September 2021)

Concluding Observations on the Combined Fifth and Sixth Periodic Reports of Rwanda, CRC Committee (28 February 2020) UN Doc CRC/C/RWA/CO/5–6 (2020)

Constitution of the Republic of Rwanda of 2003 as Revised in 2015

Crow, ME 'Smokescreens and state responsibility: Using human rights strategies to promote global tobacco control' (2004) 29 *The Yale Journal of International Law* 209 https://digitalcommons.law.yale.edu/cgi/viewcontent.cgi?article=1228&context=yjil https://www.scielosp.org/pdf/spm/v52s2/a26v52s2.pdf (accessed 16 September 2021)

De Silva de Alwis, R & Daynard, R 'Reconceptualizing human rights to challenge tobacco' (2008–2009) 17 *Michigan State Journal of International Law* 291

Decree Law 8/75 of 12 February1975

Decree Law 10/1983 of 1 July 1983

Devdiscourse 'Rwanda's Ministry of Health issues new warning against practice of smoking in public' https://www.devdiscourse.com/article/law-order/539274-rwandas-ministry-of-health-issues-new-warning-against-practice-of-smoking-in-public (accessed 30 September 2021)

Kraef, C; Juma, PA & Mucumbitsi, J 'Fighting non-communicable diseases in East Africa: Assessing progress and identifying the next steps' (2020) 5 *BMJ Global Health* e0033252020 https://www.ncbi.nlm.nih.gov/pmc/articles/PMC7662421/pdf/bmjgh-2020-003325.pdf (accessed 5 September 2021)

Kuteesa, H 'MoH issues fresh warning against smoking in public' *The New Times* (Rwanda) 27 May 2019 https://www.newtimes.co.rw/news/moh-issues-fresh-warning-against-smoking-public (accessed 20 September 2021)

Kwizera, B 'Itabi, umuco wakendereye mu misango y'ubukwe mu Rwanda' *Rwanda Broadcasting Agency* 27 December 2019 https://www.rba.co.rw/post/Itabi-umuco-wakendereye-mu-misango-yubukwe-mu-Rwanda (accessed 20 September 2021)

Law 08/2013 of 1 March 2013 Relating to the Control of Tobacco

Law 37/2015 of 30 June 2015 Modifying and Complementing Law 26/2006 of 27 May 2006 Determining and Establishing Consumption Tax on Some Imported and Locally Manufactured Products as Modified and Complemented to Date

Law 68/2018 of 30 August 2018 Determining Offences and Penalties in General

Law 71/2018 of 31 August 2018 Relating to the Rights of the Child

Law 003/2018 of 9 February 2018 Establishing the Rwanda Food and Drugs Authority and Determining Its Mission, Organisation and Functioning

Ministry of Health 'Health sector policy' (2015)

Ministry of Health 'Non communicable diseases policy' (2015)

Ministry of Health 'Non-communicable diseases risk factors report' (2015) http://moh.gov.rw/fileadmin/templates/Docs/Rwanda_Non-communicable_Diseases_Risk_Factors_Report.pdf (accessed 25 September 2021)

Ministry of Health 'Strategic plan for non- communicable diseases July 2014–June 2019'

Ministerial Order 20/33 of 9 June 2015 Determining the Characteristics of Smoking Areas and the Content Which Shall Be Included in the Notice to Be Displayed in the Smoking Area

Ministerial Order 20/34 of 9 June 2015 Determining the Content and Design of the Warning to be Put on the Package of Tobacco and Tobacco Products

Ministerial Order 004/2016 of 8 January 2016 Determining Rules Governing Code of Conduct of Headmasters, Teachers and Students

National Institute of Statistics of Rwanda & Ministry of Health Rwanda 'Demographic and health survey' (2010)

National Institute of Statistics of Rwanda & Ministry of Health Rwanda 'Demographic and health survey' (2014–2015)

National Public Prosecution Authority v Ntibajyinama Esther (RPAA0078/15/CS)

National Public Prosecution Authority v Saidi Athuman Mohamed (RPA 0787/15/HC/KIG)

Nuwagaba, F & Williams, P 'Programs to prevent non-communicable diseases (NDCs) in Rwanda: Improving healthy eating for adolescents and adults' Evidence brief (2018)

Organic Law 01/2012/OL of 2 May 2012 Instituting the Penal Code (Now Repealed)

Organisation of African Unity (OAU), African Charter on Human and Peoples' Rights (Banjul Charter) (27 June 1981) CAB/LEG/67/3 rev 5, 21 ILM 58 (1982)
Organisation of African Unity (OAU), African Charter on the Rights and Welfare of the Child (11 July 1990) CAB/LEG/24.9/49 (1990)
Presidential Order 431/16 of 10 November 1980
Presidential Order 773/16 of 19 September 1990
Presidential Order 11/01 of 30 May 2001
Presidential Order 11/01 of 24 June 2004
Presidential Order 13/01 of 25 May 2005
Presidential Order 131/01 of 27 December 2012
Republic of Rwanda 'Second national report to the secretariat of the conference of parties' https://untobaccocontrol.org/impldb/wp-content/uploads/reports/rwanda_2012_report.pdf (accessed 12 September 2021)
Republic of Rwanda 'Third national report to the secretariat of the conference of parties' https://untobaccocontrol.org/impldb/wp-content/uploads/Rwanda_2018_report.pdf (accessed 12 September 2021)
Rwanda Education Board 'S2: *Kinyarwanda*' https://elearning.reb.rw/course/view.php?id=273&section=8 (accessed 16 September 2021)
Tobacco Atlas 'Rwanda country profile factsheet' https://files.tobaccoatlas.org/wp-content/uploads/pdf/rwanda-country-facts-en.pdf (accessed 25 September 2021)
Umwanditsi, M 'Kunyara ku muhanda, imwe mu ngeso mbi nyinshi zacitse burundu mu Banyarwanda' *Kigali Today* 20 June 2008 https://www.kigalitoday.com/amakuru/amakuru-mu-rwanda/article/kunyara-ku-muhanda-imwe-mu-ngeso-mbi-nyinshi-zacitse-burundu-mu-banyarwanda (accessed 27 September 2021)
UN CESCR General Comment 14: The Right to the Highest Attainable Standard of Health (art 12) (2000) UN Doc E/C.12/2000/4 dated 11 August 2000 UN General Assembly, Convention on the Elimination of All Forms of Discrimination Against Women, 18 December 1979, United Nations, Treaty Series, vol 1249, p 13UN General Assembly, Convention on the Rights of the Child, 20 November 1989, United Nations, Treaty Series, vol 1577, p 3
UN General Assembly, Convention on the Rights of Persons with Disabilities: Resolution/Adopted by the General Assembly, 24 January 2007, A/RES/61/106
UN General Assembly, International Covenant on Civil and Political Rights, 16 December 1966, United Nations, Treaty Series, vol 999, p 171
UN General Assembly, International Covenant on Economic, Social and Cultural Rights, 16 December 1966, United Nations, Treaty Series, vol 993, p 3
WHO 'Biennial Report 2016–2017: The work of WHO Rwanda in the domestication of the SDGs, the transformation agenda, emergency preparedness and response' https://reliefweb.int/sites/reliefweb.int/files/resources/WHO%20Rwanda%20Biennial%20report%202016%202017_0.pdf (accessed 20 July 2020)
WHO Framework Convention on Tobacco Control, 2003
WHO 'Non-communicable diseases (NCDs): Country profiles' (2018) https://www.who.int/nmh/countries/rwa_en.pdf?ua=1 (accessed 15 September 2021)

9 The state of Zimbabwe's compliance with the WHO FCTC

Michelle Rufaro Maziwisa and Ebenezer Durojaye

9.1 Introduction

The high incidence of non-communicable diseases (NCDs) is alarming. Various factors such as air pollution, alcohol abuse, high blood pressure, high blood sugar, excess intake of sodium, lack of exercise, tobacco use (smoking, chewing and snuff) and obesity are risk factors for NCDs.[1] Additionally, access to clean and safe potable water and nutrition can influence the increase or decrease in NCDs.[2] In this chapter, the focus is placed on tobacco-related NCDs.

With an HIV prevalence of 24.6 per cent in the country (almost a quarter of the population),[3] this calls for special attention to the risk of NCDs among people living with HIV. There is a significantly higher risk of NCDs among people living with HIV, at 33 per cent compared to people living without HIV (14 per cent). The most prevalent NCDs in the country include cancer, hypertension, and depression, while asthma and diabetes are common. Mufunda and others note that in 2006, the prevalence of hypertension (measured as blood pressure greater than or equal to 140/90 mm Hg) stood at 35 per cent in women and 24 per cent in men, highlighting that women experience certain NCDs more than or differently from men.[4] These statistics highlight the risk posed to this particular demographic.

Tobacco-related NCDs are the most preventable in the world, yet tobacco takes approximately 8 million lives each year, which is more than the deaths caused

1 United Nations *Transforming our world: The 2030 agenda for sustainable development* (2015).

2 BK Twinomugisha 'Using the right to health framework to tackle non-communicable diseases in the era of neo-liberalism in Uganda' (2020) 20 *African Human Rights Law Journal* 149; C Lachat & others 'Diet and physical activity for the prevention of non-communicable diseases in low and middle-income countries: A systematic policy review' (2013) 10 *Public Library of Science and Medicine* 6.

3 WHO 'Country profile factsheet: Zimbabwe' https://www.who.int/hiv/HIVCP_ZWE.pdf (accessed 6 May 2021).

4 J Mufunda et al. 'Emerging non-communicable disease epidemic in Africa: Preventive measures from the WHO Regional Office for Africa' (2006) 16 *Ethnicity & Disease* 521.

DOI: 10.4324/9781003264248-11

by tuberculosis, HIV/AIDS and malaria put together.[5] Seven million die from illnesses caused by using tobacco, and 1.2 million are non-smokers exposed to second-hand smoke. Tobacco-related illnesses caused the deaths of over 100 million people in the 20th century, and the transnational tobacco industry aggressively promotes the use of tobacco products and the expansion of tobacco markets, including by lobbying governments in order to weaken state regulation.[6] This creates a tug of war between economic interests on the one hand, and health and life on the other hand.

9.1.1 *What do the numbers say nationally?*

Tobacco use among adults in Zimbabwe declined from 16.4 per cent in 2007 to 13 per cent in 2018[7] and is more prevalent among men (31.2 per cent), than women (2.1 per cent).[8] Minors (persons below 18 years of age) generally use less tobacco than adults.[9] In the capital city, Harare, as at 1999, 11.6 per cent of boys and 9.9 per cent of girls smoked cigarettes. A marked decline ensued between 1999 and 2008 for adolescents between 13 and 15 years of age, most likely due to the country's economic decline and hyperinflationary environment which put the price of cigarettes beyond reach, but use of other tobacco products did not decline.[10] In Bulawayo, the second-largest city, trends among adolescents are similar.[11] Cigarette smoking dropped significantly among boys, from 12.4 per cent in 2003 to 3.7 per cent in 2008, and among girls from 4.5 per cent in 2003 to 1.1 per cent in 2008. Currently, according to the Tobacco Atlas, about 0.7 per cent of boys and 0.03 per cent of girls use tobacco in Zimbabwe reflecting gender differences in the use of tobacco among boys and girls.[12]

While several authors have written on the subject of NCDs in Zimbabwe, most focus on NCDs among people living with HIV[13] and are not grounded in law

5 WHO 'Zimbabwe report card' (2017) https://www.afro.who.int/sites/default/files/2017-09/Zimbabwe_report_card_0.pdf (accessed 16 June 2020); WHO 'Tobacco factsheet' https://www.who.int/news-room/fact-sheets/detail/tobacco (accessed 6 May 2021).

6 EA Lown, PA McDaniel & RE Malone 'Tobacco is "our industry and we must support it": Exploring the potential implications of Zimbabwe's accession to the framework convention on tobacco control' (2016) 12 *Globalisation and Health* 1.

7 The World Bank 'Prevalence of current tobacco use (% of adults) in Zimbabwe' https://data.worldbank.org/indicator/SH.PRV.SMOK?locations=ZW (accessed 6 May 2021).

8 The Tobacco Atlas 'Zimbabwe' https://tobaccoatlas.org/country/zimbabwe/ (accessed 16 October 2021).

9 WHO (n 5) 5.

10 As above.

11 As above.

12 The Tobacco Atlas (n 8).

13 L Gonah, I Moodley & K Hlongwana 'Capacity of antiretroviral therapy sites for managing NCDs in people living with HIV in Zimbabwe' (2020) 21 *Southern African Journal of HIV Medicine* 1; I Magodoro, T Esterhuizen & T Chivese 'A cross-sectional, facility based study of comorbid non-communicable diseases among adults living with HIV infection in Zimbabwe' (2016) 9 *BMC Research Notes* 1; Mufunda & others 'Emerging non-communicable

or human rights. This chapter therefore addresses an important gap in literature. The chapter takes stock of how Zimbabwe has fared in relation to the World Health Organization (WHO) Framework Convention on Tobacco Control (FCTC) and evaluates opportunities and challenges in the implementation of the FCTC and the extent of compliance.

The chapter argues that while Zimbabwe has a robust legal framework, there may be gaps in the legislative text and in the implementation of tobacco control measures, which not only leaves Zimbabweans at risk of tobacco-related NCDs but may also amount to a violation of their human rights, more specifically, the right to health.

The chapter has discussed the rate of NCDs and provided tobacco-use statistics in Zimbabwe. The chapter will also discuss the legislative framework relevant to the right to health in Zimbabwe and draw the nexus between the right to health and NCDs, including the effects of tobacco use. Then the chapter will explore the link between the FCTC and the right to health in Zimbabwe and discuss the historical development of tobacco regulation and the domestication of the provisions of the FCTC in Zimbabwe. The chapter will also evaluate the relevant domestic legislative framework to review the implementation of the FCTC in Zimbabwe. The MPOWER framework of the WHO provides guidance in this regard. Then the chapter will provide an analysis of relevant case law to determine the stance of courts in the application of the domestic legislative framework. Finally, the chapter makes recommendations.

The following section examines NCDs within the context of the human rights framework, with a particular focus on the right to health, in order to highlight the linkages between the right to health and NCDs.

9.2 The intersections between the right to health and NCDs

This section examines the right to health in relation to NCDs and evaluates the uptake of international and regional human rights instruments within the domestic legislative framework of Zimbabwe.

The Constitution of Zimbabwe is the supreme law of the country, and any law, practice, custom or conduct inconsistent with it is invalid.[14] The Constitution is legally binding on all organs of state and on all natural and juristic persons. While Zimbabwe is a sovereign state, it has surrendered some of its sovereignty by committing to be bound by the provisions of international bodies by ratifying various treaties and conventions. However, Zimbabwe has a dualistic legal system in terms of which international treaties concluded or executed by or under the president's authority do not become legally binding until they have been

disease epidemic in Africa: Preventive measures from the WHO regional office for Africa' (2006) 16 *Ethnicity & Disease* 521.

14 Constitution of Zimbabwe (Amendment 20), 2013 (Constitution).

approved by Parliament, and they do not form part of domestic law unless they have been incorporated through an Act of Parliament.[15] Zimbabwe has ratified various international human rights instruments regulating the right to health, and these are considered below.

9.2.1 The right to health under international law

The term 'right to health' may not be seen verbatim in specific international instruments, but it has been described as shorthand for the more detailed language contained in international treaties and fundamental principles of human rights, such as non-discrimination and equality .[16]

The first enquiry is into what constitutes 'health'. The WHO defines health as 'a state of complete physical, mental and social well-being and not merely the absence of disease and infirmity'. This definition of health as a complete state has been criticised for incorrectly perceiving health as 'static' and thereby ignoring the changing patterns of morbidity.[17] Health incorporates various factors beyond mere biology or genetics and can be affected by various factors, which may include social and economic status, poverty, disability, mental health, gender and age, amongst others. It is important to frame health in the context of human rights as this confers on it a special status and trumps other claims.[18]

The international community recognises health as a fundamental right, as evidenced by the adoption of the WHO Constitution in 1946.[19] Van Boven has argued that the right to health must include three elements: 'the declaration of the right to health as a basic human right; the prescription of standards aimed at meeting the health needs of specific groups of persons; and the prescription of ways and means of implementing the right to health'.[20]

The commitments made by heads of state and governments in various instruments, such as the Global Action Plan for the Prevention and Control of Non-Communicable Diseases 2013–2020 (NCD-GAP), and acceptance of the UN

15 Sec 327(3) Constitution.

16 V Leary 'The right to health in international law' (1994) 1 (1) *Health and Human Rights* 24–53.

17 Twinomugisha (n 2) 152; M Jambroes & others 'Implications of health as "the ability to adapt and self-manage" for public health policy: A quantitative study' (2016) 26 *European Journal of Public Health* 412.

18 See generally, Ronald Dworkin *Taking rights seriously* (1997).

19 The Constitution was adopted by the International Health Conference held in New York from 19 June to 22 July 1946, signed on 22 July 1representatives of 61 States (Off Rec WHO 2, 100), and entered into force on 7 April 1948. Amendments adopted by the Twenty-sixth, Twenty-ninth, Thirty-ninth and Fifty-first World Health Assemblies (resolutions WHA26.37, WHA29.38, WHA39.6 and WHA51.23) came into force on 3 February 1977, 20 January 1984, 11 July 1994 and 15 September 2005, respectively, and are incorporated in the present text https://www.who.int/governance/eb/who_constitution_en.pdf (accessed 22 April 2021).

20 As cited in Leary (n 16) 29.

Sustainable Development Goals (SDGs) indicate a willingness to respect, protect and fulfil the right to health, especially in relation to NCDs.[21] SDG Goal 3, target 4, for example, envisages the reduction of premature mortality emanating from NCDs.

Although the Universal Declaration of Human Rights is not itself a treaty as such, most of its provisions are generally accepted as constituting customary international law.[22] Article 25 of the Universal Declaration guarantees everyone's right to a standard of living adequate for the health and well-being of an individual and their family.[23] This is reiterated in more detail in article 12 of the International Covenant on Economic, Social and Cultural Rights (ICESCR), which guarantees the right of everyone to the enjoyment of the 'highest attainable standard of physical and mental health'.[24] This is, of course, bearing in mind that different states have different means, and that different people have different morbidities, lifestyles and genetic dispositions. To achieve the full realisation of this right, member states are enjoined to ensure progressive realisation of the right to health, by taking steps to prevent, treat and control occupational and other diseases, among other things.

The Committee on Economic, Social and Cultural Rights (CESCR) has further elaborated on the right to health in its General Comment 14. Although states cannot make every person healthy, they do have a duty to ensure certain things are in place to facilitate the fulfilment of the right to health. Of particular interest is paragraph 12, which stipulates that health services must be available, accessible, acceptable and of good quality. 'Availability' means the state must provide adequately trained health workers who are paid competitively within the domestic market, and facilities and buildings such as hospitals and clinics, and a functioning public health system must be provided, for example. 'Accessibility' means that health facilities, goods and services must be accessible to all people without discrimination. Accessibility has four components: non-discrimination, physical accessibility, economic accessibility (meaning affordability) and information accessibility. 'Acceptability' means that health facilities, goods and services must be respectful of medical ethics, culture, ethnic minorities, gender, life-cycle requirements and confidentiality. 'Quality' requires scientifically and medically

21 UN General Assembly, Political Declaration of the third high-level meeting of the General Assembly on the prevention and control of NCDs 'Time to deliver: Accelerating our response to address non-communicable diseases for the health and well-being of present and future generations' A/RES/73/2 (17 October 2018) https://www.un.org/en/ga/search/view_doc.asp?symbol=A/RES/73/2 (accessed 2 May 2021).

22 Leary (n 16) 32.

23 UN General Assembly, Universal Declaration of Human Rights, 10 December 1948, 217 A (III) https://www.refworld.org/docid/3ae6b3712c.html (accessed 9 July 2020).

24 UN Committee on Economic, Social and Cultural Rights (CESCR) General Comment 14: The right to the highest attainable standard of health (art 12 of the Covenant) (2000) UN Doc E/C.12/2000/4 dated 11 August 2000 https://www.refworld.org/docid/4538838d0.html (accessed 30 April 2021); General Comment 14 gives insight and clarity on the right to the highest attainable standard of health.

appropriate treatment, trained health workers, approved and unexpired medication and equipment, potable water and adequate sanitation. These factors are not exhaustive, but they provide valuable insights into what to expect from states in terms of the realisation of the right Io health.

The Committee has also noted intersections of the right to health with other rights such as privacy, life, dignity and non-discrimination.[25] States must not only address threats to the enjoyment of the rights to health but must also take appropriate measures to combat disease and develop preventive healthcare.[26] In this regard, community participation approaches may be useful, provided the communities are supported through education, information and communication interventions.[27]

In addition, article 7(b) of ICESCR enjoins states to ensure that working conditions are safe and healthy. In this regard, special protection should be given to women who are pregnant and new mothers. Women are often at particular risk of NCDs due to the disproportionate exposure and vulnerability to NCD risk factors, such as passive tobacco smoking, domestic roles which may lead to women being more exposed to smoke, dust and soot when cooking, and also due to reproductive functions such as pregnancy which may lead to increased blood pressure. According to the WHO, NCDs have been the leading cause of death among women globally over the last three decades, and they currently account for two out of every three deaths among women annually.[28] With this in mind, article 12 of CEDAW requires state parties to take appropriate measures to eliminate discrimination against women in the field of healthcare to ensure equal access to health services.

The duties in relation to the right to health not only fall on the state but also on corporations. The current neoliberal agenda, which prioritises economic growth over human rights, adds to the challenges of the NCD epidemic. The structural reforms of the 1980s to 1990s initiated by the International Monetary Fund (IMF) and the World Bank were based on neoliberal principles, which sought to remove 'socialist' governance models and replace them with 'free market' models. This necessitated the shifting of certain public goods and services to the private sector and has in many ways shaped the current health system, which is dominated by expensive private healthcare and under-resourced public health facilities. Neoliberalism also meant the liberalisation of international trade by reducing tariff and non-tariff barriers, which enables transnational

25 As above.

26 Art 24 UN General Assembly, Convention on the Rights of the Child, 20 November 1989, United Nations, Treaty Series, vol. 1577, 3 https://www.refworld.org/docid/3ae6b38f0.html (accessed 10 July 2020).

27 Twinomugisha (n 2) 175.

28 WHO *Global coordination mechanism on the prevention and control of NCDs* (2020) https://www.who.int/global-coordination-mechanism/ncd-themes/NCD-and-women/en/#:~:text=NCDs%20have%20been%20the%20leading,Low%20and%20Middle%20income%20Countries (accessed 2 May 2021).

corporations to conduct their businesses abroad and to import and export various goods according to their own needs. The challenge is that private corporations operate for profit, and evidence shows that corporations are capable of violating human rights in the conduct of their business. Moreover, trade liberalisation has contributed to the increased importation of harmful and sometimes culturally inappropriate and low-grade goods such as tobacco, foreign seed and genetically modified foods (GMOs), which can negatively affect health, food security, food sovereignty and biodiversity, and in some instances have taken over rural women's role as custodians of seed.

To mitigate the risks of corporate conduct, the UN Guiding Principles on Business and Human Rights stipulate that businesses 'should avoid infringing on the human rights of others and should address adverse human rights impacts with which they are involved'.[29] It further states that businesses should have a policy on how they will comply with their human rights obligations, conduct due diligence to identify, prevent, mitigate and account for human rights impacts, and establish processes to enable the remediation of any adverse human rights impacts caused by them.[30] In most instances, corporations are not party to international human rights treaties, thus the duty falls on the state to ensure that corporations are in fact complying with national laws and not violating the international commitments made by the state, one of which is to respect the right to health in the conduct of their business. This is especially important in the tobacco industry, as there is evidence of the employment of women and children and the use of harmful chemicals in the agricultural production and processing of tobacco, and further, because of the health risk of tobacco use and tobacco exposure once it has been processed.

9.2.2 The right to health under regional law

At the regional level, the African Charter secures the right of every individual 'to enjoy the best attainable state of physical and mental health' and enjoins states to 'take the necessary measures to protect the health of their people and to ensure that they receive medical attention when they are sick'.[31] Legislative and budgetary measures could be especially useful in the fight against the NCD epidemic, as state regulation and enforcement can deter harmful conduct, and well-resourced state facilities and health workers are crucial for providing adequate medical attention to people when they are sick or seeking to cease harmful behaviour, such as quitting smoking.

29 UN 'Guiding principles on business and human rights' (2011) See https://www.ohchr.org/documents/publications/guidingprinciplesbusinesshr_en.pdf (accessed 10 July 2020).

30 As above.

31 Art 16, African Union, African Charter on Human and Peoples' Rights (Banjul Charter), 27 June 1981, CAB/LEG/67/3 rev 5, 21 ILM 58 (1982) https://www.refworld.org/docid/3ae6b3630.html (accessed 9 July 2020).

Article 18(3) of the African Charter obliges states to protect the rights of women and children. Children should be protected from work that is harmful to their health or life and work that can hamper their normal development. Article 24 of the UN Convention on the Rights of the Child (CRC) guarantees the right of children to the 'enjoyment of the highest attainable standard of health'. Article 14 of the African Children's Charter stipulates that 'every child shall have the right to enjoy the best attainable state of physical, mental and spiritual health'.[32] These provisions are especially important, as there is evidence of child labour in tobacco farming, and this compromises children's right to health. States therefore have a duty to address threats to children's health; this can be done through enacting and enforcing appropriate laws.

9.2.3 The right to health under national law

At the national level, section 29 of the Constitution incorporates aspects of the ICESCR by explicitly placing the obligation for the provision of health services on the state. Section 29(1) of the Constitution stipulates that the state must 'take all practical measures to ensure the provision of basic, accessible and adequate health services throughout Zimbabwe'.[33] One might cautiously assume that 'adequate' health services here encapsulate the important elements stipulated in General Comment 14, paragraph 12 to include available, accessible, acceptable and quality health goods, services and facilities. However, section 29(3) of the Constitution claws back by introducing the progressive realisation provision, as commonly appears in socio-economic rights provisions, and simply asks the state to take preventive measures 'within the limits of the resources available to it'.

The Constitution recognises the importance of education and public awareness of health and the right to health.[34] This is critical for the reduction of NCD prevalence, as education and information empower people. Every citizen and permanent resident of Zimbabwe has the right to have access to basic healthcare services, including every person living with a chronic illness (including those that may typically be associated with tobacco use or exposure), the key focus perhaps being 'basic' healthcare services.[35] However, this is limited to the available resources of the state.

There is a special focus on children in the legislative framework. Section 19(3) of the Constitution requires the state to take legislative and other measures to protect the health and well-being of children, including physical, mental, spiritual or moral health and social development. This is supported by section 11 of the Labour Act, which prohibits the employment of minors below the age of 15, except under specified conditions, and criminalises the employment of children

32 African Union, African Charter on the Rights and Welfare of the Child, 11 July 1990, CAB/LEG/24.9/49 (1990) https://www.refworld.org/docid/3ae6b38c18.html (accessed 10 July 2020).
33 Sec 29(1) of the Constitution.
34 Sec 29(3) of the Constitution.
35 Sec 76(2) of the Constitution.

under 18 years to 'perform any work which is likely to jeopardise [their] health, safety or morals'.[36] This provision is also important in relation to children's work in tobacco farms, which is typically harmful to their health. However, implementation remains problematic, especially in light of poverty which has pushed many children out of school and into the workforce for survival.

Section 84(1) of the Public Health Act (PHA) is also important, as it defines an NCD as a health condition or disease that is not an infectious disease, while section 31 PHA establishes core principles for public health management in terms of which every person has the duty to avoid harm to public health, to report suspected health risks and to actively promote compliance with the PHA.

In the following section we discuss the FCTC as a treaty to advance the realisation of the right to health.

9.3 The FCTC as a treaty to realise the right to health at the national level

This section evaluates the effectiveness of the FCTC within the national law. It is important to establish the context by stating some of the risks of tobacco use, reviewing the historical development of tobacco regulation in Zimbabwe and analysing the extent of alignment of national laws with the FCTC.

9.3.1 Risks associated with tobacco

Some of the risks associated with tobacco are discussed in this section.[37] Tobacco is often consumed smokeless (snuff or chewing), or by smoking cigarettes, which accounts for 65–85 per cent of global tobacco consumption. It is characterised by nicotine addiction, amongst others, and there is often a time lag between tobacco use and the onset of its effects. Smoking tobacco can cause various respiratory disorders such as chronic obstructive pulmonary disease (COPD) and emphysema, vascular spasm and atherosclerosis which may lead to myocardial events, cerebral and peripheral vascular diseases, and 12 types of cancers, including lung cancer. Non-smokers exposed to tobacco are at double the risk and may face other risks associated with respiratory tract infections and ischemic heart diseases. Pregnant women risk losing or complicating the pregnancy, and the foetus is at risk of growth retardation and perinatal morbidity and mortality.

9.3.2 Development of the tobacco industry and regulation in Zimbabwe

Tobacco farming in Zimbabwe (formerly Rhodesia) can be traced to the British South Africa Company (BSAC), which was permitted through the United

36 Labour Act, Zimbabwe, Chapter 28:01.

37 M Bartal 'Health effects of tobacco use and exposure' (2001) 56 *Monaldi Archives for Chest Disease* 545.

Kingdom Royal Charter to conduct commercial activities in Southern Africa in 1950.[38] The Pioneer Column (comprising British adventurers and potential settlers) settled in Zimbabwe with hopes of finding gold; however, no gold deposits were found at the time, and instead the BSAC gave them large tracts of farmland, much of which became dedicated to tobacco farming.[39] In 1903 and 1904, about 100 farms grew tobacco.[40] The creation of the Rhodesia Tobacco Association to represent the interests of tobacco growers in production and marketing in 1928 (while under the government of 'responsible self-rule') signified the growth of the tobacco industry. The Tobacco Levy Act was enacted in 1933, introducing a new tobacco levy and establishing the Tobacco Marketing Board. To expand production, the colonial government forcibly removed indigenous Zimbabweans from their land, making more land available to white tobacco farmers by 1940. By 1946, more than 1250 farmers were producing tobacco. In 1936, the Tobacco Marketing and Levy Act was enacted which introduced the requirement for all tobacco sales to be conducted through registered auction floors. By 1938, tobacco growers had established the Tobacco Hail Insurance Fund; new institutions such as the Tobacco Research Board and the Tobacco Trade Association were later established (1950) for research and development.[41]

Politically, the government under Ian Smith made a unilateral declaration of independence of Southern Rhodesia from the United Kingdom in 1965, which led to sanctions being imposed by the Crown against Southern Rhodesia, and this marked the start of economic dependence on tobacco.[42]

Zimbabwe had two major cigarette manufacturers, British American Tobacco (BAT) Zimbabwe and Rothmans of Pall Mall Zimbabwe; the two merged in the mid-1990s, creating a monopoly.[43] By the early 1990s, the yield of flue-cured tobacco had risen from 8.4 kg/ha (before 1950) to 73.3 kg/ha between 1990 and 1995.[44] By 1996, Zimbabwe had at the time 'the largest tobacco auction floor in the world'.[45] Further, with an increased policy focus on indigenisation, a local businessman, Roger Boka, made major inroads in the previously white-dominated terrain of tobacco auction floors by being the first black person in Zimbabwe to hold a tobacco merchant's licence; he later established the Boka Auction Floors.[46]

The Tobacco Industry and Marketing Act of 1997 (TIMA) replaced the 1936 Act and changed the name of the Tobacco Marketing Board to the Tobacco Industry Marketing Board, presumably to signal the growth of tobacco production to a fully

38 G Woelk, S Mtisi & P Vaughan 'Prospects for tobacco control in Zimbabwe' (2001) 57 *Health Policy* 179 at 181.

39 As above.

40 As above.

41 As above 182.

42 As above.

43 As above.

44 As above.

45 Staff Reporter 'Shadowy giant in Zim tobacco trade Roger Boka' *Mail & Guardian* 13 September 1996 https://mg.co.za/article/1996-09-13-shadowy-giant-in-zim-tobacco-trade-roger-boka-the/ (accessed 6 May 2021).

46 Woelk, Mtisi & Vaughan (n 38) 184.

fledged industry between 1936 and 1997. As at 2001 the Tobacco Trade Association had 35 members, many of whom were affiliated with transnational corporations, and the Ministry of Agriculture became a member of the Tobacco Research Board.[47]

In the early 1990s, the economic structural adjustment programme (ESAP) led by the IMF and the World Bank under the new government of independence of Robert Mugabe forced the country to shift from its erstwhile Marxist-Leninist economic agenda to a free market one advanced by the two international financial institutions. Manufacturing industries suffered significantly; the mining industry was depressed at the same time, and a combination of these factors led to renewed reliance on the tobacco industry for economic growth.[48]

Tobacco control has not gained momentum in Zimbabwe because of the heavy economic reliance on tobacco and the prioritisation of other health issues such as HIV, malaria and alcohol abuse.[49] In practice there were few health warnings about tobacco in the early 1990s, and in 1995 companies had the option to affix health warnings on cigarette packets and marketing material.[50] It was only in 1997 that a formal obligation was placed on corporations to affix health warnings on cigarette packets and marketing materials in terms of the Statutory Instrument on Public Health (Control of Smoking) Regulations of 1997. The 1997 Regulations were subsequently replaced by Statutory Instrument 264 of 2002 (Tobacco Regulations), which introduced new obligations on various demand-side issues such as public awareness, prevention of smoking in public places and health warning labels.

Tobacco farmers were largely spared from the expropriation that took place under the Land Redistribution Programme due to interventions by the Commercial Farmers Union, which also represents members of the Zimbabwe Tobacco Auctions.[51] Since then, new small-scale farmers were integrated into the tobacco industry by enabling contract farming through an amendment to TIMA in 2004,[52] and there has been increased state support.

Despite the disruptions in agricultural production pursuant to the Land Redistribution Programme in 2000–2001, Zimbabwe has continued to be one of the top tobacco-producing countries in Africa; in 2012 it was named the sixth-largest tobacco producer in the world.[53] About 98 per cent of tobacco produced in Zimbabwe is exported.[54] Apart from Malawi, Zimbabwe receives the highest revenue from tobacco than any other country in the world, which is partly due

47 As above.
48 As above 185.
49 As above.
50 As above 187.
51 As above 184.
52 Whereas auction selling is based on the tobacco grower investing his/her own resources as inputs, choosing an auction floor and bringing their produce for sale to the highest bidder, contract floors are based on the buyer providing inputs to the grower on condition that the buyer will buy all the produce at an agreed price (per grade) which price should be equal or higher than the prevailing price on the auction floors. See Tobacco Industry and Marketing Board of Zimbabwe (TIMB) 'History' https://www.timb.co.zw/about-us/history (accessed 7 July 2020).
53 Lown (n 6) 3.
54 As above.

to its taxation system which imposes levies on both growers and buyers, and is supported by tough customs control.[55]

The Ministry of Agriculture and the Ministry of Industry and Commerce regulate the tobacco industry primarily. The Tobacco Research Board and the Tobacco Industry and Marketing Board work closely with the tobacco industry, while the Zimbabwe Tobacco Association (ZTA), the Farmer's Development Trust (which came out of the ZTA) and the International Tobacco Growers Association (ITGA) advance the interests of tobacco growers and producers.[56]

9.3.3 Evaluating the alignment of national laws with the FCTC

The WHO adopted the FCTC in 2003 and it came into effect in 2005; later the WHO established the Protocol to Eliminate Illicit Trade in Tobacco Products (Tobacco Protocol).[57] The FCTC entered into force in 2005 with 40 founding states. Zimbabwe had already enacted the TIMA and Statutory Instrument 264 of 2002 (Tobacco Regulations) prior to the adoption of the FCTC. Zimbabwe signed the FCTC almost ten years later, in December 2014, and became a party in 2015, but it is not party to the Tobacco Protocol.

Due to Zimbabwe's economic reliance on the tobacco industry, it would have been counterintuitive to sign the FCTC. During his presidency, Robert Mugabe stated in relation to tobacco that 'if we sell it, we must grow it as well. It is our industry and we must support it'.[58] Additionally, prior to Zimbabwe's accession to the FCTC, the ZTA and ITGA (two of the main associations for the tobacco industry) described the FCTC as a 'thoroughly bad and damaging international attack' on Zimbabwe's sovereignty.[59] Consequently, some authors suggest that Zimbabwe only signed the treaty to bring its enemies closer. Lown and others argue that Zimbabwe's ratification was not an indication of Zimbabwe's intention to restrict the tobacco industry but rather its efforts to influence the international tobacco control processes from the inside, in order to protect the interests of Zimbabwe's tobacco industry.[60]

The transnational tobacco industry enjoys strong bargaining power due to its financial resources: 'The combined revenues of the world's six largest tobacco companies in 2016 was more than USD 346 Billion, 2231% larger than the gross national income of Zimbabwe'.[61] As tobacco use is decreasing in high-income countries, the transnational tobacco industry is more aggressively marketing tobacco products in low-income countries.[62] In countries such as Zimbabwe,

55 As above.
56 As above 3.
57 WHO, Seoul, 12 November 2012.
58 Lown (n 6) 3.
59 As above.
60 As above.
61 The Tobacco Atlas 'Zimbabwe fact sheet' https://tobaccoatlas.org/country/zimbabwe/ (accessed 12 July 2020).
62 Lown (n 6) 2.

there is high economic dependency on tobacco because of its foreign currency earnings, although tobacco use is relatively low. For example, in 2019, tobacco export earnings amounted to US$203.9 million, making it the second-highest foreign currency earner in Zimbabwe. This has given the tobacco industry leverage in influencing tobacco regulation in Zimbabwe.

The aims of the FCTC are to control both the supply and demand sides of tobacco. Table 9.1 illustrates selected provisions of the FCTC and the equivalent provisions under Zimbabwean national law.

Table 9.1 Level of Zimbabwe's compliance

FCTC Provision	*Equivalent Provision in Zimbabwe (Tobacco Industry and Marketing Act, Chapter 18:20 (TIMA))*	*Tobacco Regulations*	*Compliance (Full, Partial, Not Complied)*
Article 6 on price and tax measures to reduce the demand for tobacco.	Secs 53–58 TIMA – imposition of levy.	–	Full.
Article 8 on protection from exposure to tobacco smoke.	–	Sections 3 and 4 of the Tobacco Regulations prohibit smoking in public spaces and on public transport. Section 5 of the Tobacco Regulations requires 'No smoking' signs.	Full.
Article 9 on regulation of the contents of tobacco products.	–	–	None.
Article 10 on regulation of tobacco product disclosures.	–	Section 7(3) of the Tobacco Regulations requires labels to be affixed to tobacco packaging indicating the composition of the tobacco, particularly the percentage of tar and nicotine, but does not speak to notifying the states.	Partial.

(*Continued*)

Table 9.1 (Continued)

FCTC Provision	*Equivalent Provision in Zimbabwe (Tobacco Industry and Marketing Act, Chapter 18:20 (TIMA))*	*Tobacco Regulations*	*Compliance (Full, Partial, Not Complied)*
Article 11 on packaging and labelling of tobacco.	–	Section 7(3) of the Tobacco Regulations requires labels to be affixed to tobacco packaging indicating the composition of the tobacco, particularly the percentage of tar and nicotine, but does not speak to testing or measuring the contents.	Partial.
Article 12 on education, communication, training and public awareness.	–	Section 7(1) prohibits sales in the absence of the following health warnings: (a) 'SMOKING IS HARMFUL TO HEALTH' – for cigarettes, cigars and loose tobacco; or (b) 'SMOKING CAUSES CANCER' – for nasal and oral snuff; or (c) 'TOBACCO IS ADDICTIVE' – for snus. Section 7(3) requires product information, particularly the percentage of nicotine and tar and any other ingredients, to be clearly visible on the package or container and must comply with the detailed provisions of the Schedule to the Tobacco Regulations.	Partial.

FCTC Provision	*Equivalent Provision in Zimbabwe (Tobacco Industry and Marketing Act, Chapter 18:20 (TIMA))*	*Tobacco Regulations*	*Compliance (Full, Partial, Not Complied)*
		However, there is no mention of training for key groups such as health workers. No mention of inter-sectoral programming.	
Article 13 on tobacco advertising, promotion and sponsorship.	–	Section 7(2) sets strict rules for advertisements, and promotions. Must have the message in section 7(1) and: (a) for auditory advertisements – the warnings shall be clearly audible; or (b) the warning label should have the following font sizes: (i) 16 point if the container is less than 37 cm; (ii) 21 point if the container is greater than 37 cm and less than 85 cm; or (iii) 33 point if the container is greater than 85 cm. Section 8(7) prohibits the sale of unpackaged tobacco product, but this happens often in practice. Minors: Section 8(2): no minors are allowed at tobacco promotional events. Section 8(3): May not offer tobacco samples to minors	Partial.

(*Continued*)

Table 9.1 (Continued)

FCTC Provision	*Equivalent Provision in Zimbabwe (Tobacco Industry and Marketing Act, Chapter 18:20 (TIMA))*	*Tobacco Regulations*	*Compliance (Full, Partial, Not Complied)*
		Section 8(4): All promotional material must carry the stipulated health warning message and at the venue of the promotional activities. There is no blanket prohibition on all promotions, but Section 7(6) prohibits promotions at any educational establishment, health facility or religious facility. Schedules	
Article 14 on demand reduction measures concerning tobacco dependence and cessation.	–	–	None in the TIMA and Tobacco Regulations, but partial in the Public Health Act and Constitution.
Article 15 on illicit trade in tobacco products.	Section 24–25 TIMA – registration of tobacco growers. Section 36 TIMA – registration of tobacco buyers. Section 39 TIMA – registration of tobacco auction floors. Section 29 TIMA – all tobacco bales should be marked with the registered tobacco grower's number.	Section 9 requires all imported tobacco to carry an appropriate health message (warning) in English. No mention of origin.	Full.

FCTC Provision	*Equivalent Provision in Zimbabwe (Tobacco Industry and Marketing Act, Chapter 18:20 (TIMA))*	*Tobacco Regulations*	*Compliance (Full, Partial, Not Complied)*
	Section 44–46 TIMA – tobacco may only be sold at licensed auction floors. Section 75 and 66 TIMA – various rules on destruction of unsold tobacco, or tobacco of a variety that is not prescribed. Section 45 and 46 TIMA – different rules for local versus foreign grown tobacco. Zimbabwe is not a signatory to the FCTC Protocol. The TIMA does not have the exact provisions as the FCTC, but the domestic measures meet the objective, which is to reduce and prevent illicit trade in tobacco products. It can also be argued that the domestic provision is stronger in its effect than the FCTC provision.		

(*Continued*)

Table 9.1 (Continued)

FCTC Provision	*Equivalent Provision in Zimbabwe (Tobacco Industry and Marketing Act, Chapter 18:20 (TIMA))*	*Tobacco Regulations*	*Compliance (Full, Partial, Not Complied)*
Article 16 on sales to and by minors.	–	Section 6(1) prohibits tobacco sales, donations, prizes and promotions to minors. Section 6(2) requires every person selling tobacco or tobacco products by retail to prominently display, in the vicinity of the tobacco or tobacco products and at the cash sales point, a health warning and a sign that selling tobacco to minors is prohibited. Section 6(3): Minors are prohibited from selling or giving tobacco, or participating in any form of tobacco advertising or promotion.	Full.
Article 17 on provision of support for economically viable alternative activities.	–	–	Not compliant.
Article 18 on protection of the environment and the health of persons.	–	Sections 11–13 provide for a committee of various stakeholders, including health and environment ministries/officials, to inter alia advise the minister on the following:	

FCTC Provision	*Equivalent Provision in Zimbabwe (Tobacco Industry and Marketing Act, Chapter 18:20 (TIMA))*	*Tobacco Regulations*	*Compliance (Full, Partial, Not Complied)*
		policies to protect youths from smoking; to develop educational materials to protect the youth from smoking; general policy for tobacco control and management; and enforcement of tobacco control provisions, and education.	Partial (superficial provision that does not create specific obligations, therefore hard to hold someone accountable).
Article 19 on liability.	Throughout the Act, conduct of various stakeholders is criminalised including tobacco growers, graders, buyers and auctions.	Section 17 of the Tobacco Regulations creates criminal liability for failure to comply with sections 3–7 of the Tobacco Regulations.	Partial.

9.4 Effectiveness and implementation of the FCTC in Zimbabwe (MPOWER)

The WHO FCTC introduced the six MPOWER policies to help implement six best practice interventions in the FCTC, as follows: M – monitor tobacco use and prevention policies; P – protect people from tobacco smoke; O – offer help to quit tobacco use; W – warn about the dangers of tobacco; E – enforce bans on tobacco advertising, promotion and sponsorship; and R – raise taxes on tobacco.[63] This section evaluates the effectiveness and extent of implementation of FCTC provisions into Zimbabwean national law using the MPOWER framework.

63 WHO *MPOWER a policy package to reverse the tobacco epidemic* (2008) 41.

9.4.1 Monitor

The FCTC requires tobacco products to be tested to determine their contents and emissions.[64] In this regard, the national law provides somewhat less protection. Whereas samples of imported products are tested by Zimbabwe's Standards Association, it is not clear whether domestically produced goods undergo a similar assessment to determine the ingredients of tobacco products. Nonetheless, the producers have a duty to display the accurate tar and nicotine content and display the ingredients visibly on the package or container as per section 7(3) of the Tobacco Regulations.

The TIMA seems to dedicate itself to regulating the mechanics of institutions for tobacco control and not so much the actual control provisions, save for a sprinkling of provisions relating to licensing and registration of tobacco growers, buyers and auction floors, and financial matters pertaining to levies. Even so, the TIMA is silent on tobacco tax, and this is provided for in sections 95 and 96 of the Customs and Excise Act, Chapter 23:02, which levies a sin tax on tobacco products. The Tobacco Regulations are the main regulatory instrument for tobacco control.

9.4.2 Protect people from tobacco smoke

The MPOWER framework envisages the enactment and enforcement of 'completely smoke-free' environments in healthcare and educational facilities and in all indoor public places including workplaces, restaurants and bars. This reflects the earlier commitment in the FCTC for states to take measures to protect people from tobacco exposure in 'indoor workplaces, public transport, indoor public places and, as appropriate, other public places'.[65] In compliance with the FCTC, the Tobacco Regulations prohibit smoking on public transport[66] and in public spaces such as educational, healthcare and food facilities.[67] However, the Tobacco Regulations do not reflect the stricter stance of the MPOWER framework to have completely 'smoke-free public places', as restaurants are permitted to demarcate a smoking area within the premises, provided that such designated area does not exceed 20 per cent of the total floor area and does not contaminate the principal area.[68] Further, the manager, owner or person in charge of any public premises (including an aircraft, train or vehicle) must 'prominently display clearly legible visible signs indicating areas in which smoking is prohibited or permitted'.[69] The liability in this case is placed on the person in charge who can facilitate compliance and accountability. Moreover, as Zimbabweans generally perceive smoking

64 Arts 9–10 FCTC.
65 Arts 7 and 8 FCTC.
66 Sec 4.
67 Sec 3.
68 Sec 3 Public Health (Control of Tobacco) Regulations, Statutory Instrument 264 of 2002.
69 Sec 5, SI 264 of 2002.

as taboo and culturally inappropriate, especially for women, communities usually police smoking in public places; consequently, this provision is possibly implemented by individual members of a community and general community mores, more than it is implemented by the state.

One could argue that the MPOWER framework has gaps, in that it addresses smoking in public places and ignores smoking in private places where women and children tend to be at increased risk of passive smoking and its deleterious effects. The FCTC takes a rather gender-neutral approach to tobacco control by merely asking states to take into account the needs of vulnerable groups.[70] This gap can also be seen in the national framework. As smoking is generally perceived as taboo for women in Zimbabwe due to existing gender biases, women are at a higher risk of passive smoking and thereby are at an increased risk of cancer, COPD and asthma. This risk doubles for pregnant women, as it affects both the woman and the foetus.[71] In addition, women and children also tend to be financially dependent on smokers, and smoking contributes to increased 'household poverty when males take up smoking that may lead to compromised family nutrition'.[72] This is more complex because it requires the disestablishment of broader societal gender biases towards men and women, such as the capacity to earn and allocate household income.

The language of the FCTC MPOWER framework also seems to take a greater interest in the needs of the developed world as a net 'consumer' of tobacco products, and not tobacco producers. The shortcoming of the FCTC in this regard is that it only speaks to the protection of people from tobacco smoke, yet in developing countries such as Zimbabwe, there is an equally important risk of exposure to tobacco through tobacco growing. The situation is mirrored in the TIMA despite Zimbabwe's commitments under article 7(b) of the ICESCR to make provisions for the special protection of women who are pregnant, yet women in the tobacco supply chain are at high risk. Further, both instruments fail to mention and distinguish the risks of agricultural production of tobacco, especially for women and children, particularly the health risks associated with green tobacco and pesticides on the health of women and girls, thereby undermining article 12 of the ICESCR.

9.4.3 Offer help to quit tobacco use

The TIMA and Tobacco Regulations appear to be silent on offering help to quit tobacco use, and it is not clear whether there are any state-sponsored tobacco

70 Art 4(b) FCTC.

71 L Greaves & N Jategaonkar 'Tobacco policies and vulnerable girls and women: Toward a framework for gender sensitive policy development' (2006) 60 *Journal of Epidemiology and Community Health* 57.

72 As above.

addiction hotlines or other facilities to counsel those who desire to quit tobacco use, and the cost of private rehabilitation facilities puts them beyond reach, where over 70 per cent of the population lives in poverty. Zimbabwe is thus failing to meet its commitment in section 29(3) of the Constitution to take all preventive measures towards the realisation of the right to health. It is also falling short of the MPOWER framework by failing to adequately offer help to those who may wish to give up smoking.

9.4.4 *Warn about the dangers of tobacco*

States carry the duty to ensure that their citizens are informed of the health consequences, addictive nature and mortal threat posed by tobacco, to prevent initiation, support cessation, and decrease tobacco consumption, taking into account the needs of vulnerable groups.[73] The MPOWER framework envisages that states will ensure adequate warning about the dangers of tobacco through three interventions: effective package warning labels, implementing counter-tobacco advertising, and obtaining free media coverage of anti-tobacco activities.

While the FCTC requires member states to raise awareness on the health risks and addictive nature of tobacco,[74] prevent tobacco use, and facilitate recovery from tobacco use,[75] in practice such programming is highly dependent on financial and human resources. Zimbabwe has made efforts to advance education and public awareness about the health risks of tobacco and exposure to tobacco smoke through the annual 'No Tobacco Day'.[76] While this is a good start, dedicating one day a year to raise awareness on the health risks of tobacco is not enough. Zimbabwe has a duty to develop programmes for tobacco control and not merely events.

Article 11 of the FCTC requires health warnings 'be approved by the competent national authority' and must be 'rotating', 'large, clear, visible and legible', must constitute '50% or more of the principal display areas but shall be no less than 30% of the principal display areas', and 'may be in the form of or include pictures or pictograms'.[77] In addition, unit and bulk packaging of tobacco products should display information about the constituents and emissions of tobacco products in the state's principal language(s).[78] Nationally, section 7(2) of the Tobacco Regulations prohibits advertising tobacco without the relevant health warning.[79] Although the health warning can be in the form of a picture or pictogram, section 7(1) of the Tobacco Regulations goes a step further and requires

73 Art 4(b) FCTC.
74 Art 12 FCTC.
75 Art 14 FCTC.
76 WHO 'Zimbabwe commemorates world no tobacco day' (2019) https://www.afro.who.int/news/zimbabwe-commemorates-world-no-tobacco-day-0 (accessed 12 July 2020).
77 Art 11 FCTC.
78 As above.
79 Sec 7(2) SI 264 of 2002.

a specific written text to be on the face of tobacco products, depending on the nature of the product. For cigarettes, the package should carry the health label 'SMOKING IS HARMFUL TO HEALTH'; for nasal and oral snuff, 'SMOKING CAUSES CANCER'; and for snus, 'TOBACCO IS ADDICTIVE'.[80]

Although the legislative requirement is largely compliant with article 11 of the FCTC, the implementation is problematic. For example, cigarettes are not always sold in packages. With Zimbabwe's formal sector declining and the informal sector burgeoning, many people have less disposable income, which makes it more desirable to sell and buy individual cigarettes, which would be cheaper than whole packages and accessible from tuck shops and street vendors.[81] As cigarettes are not individually labelled with health warnings, this reduces the awareness impact, and may result in increased consumption and exposure to minors. Despite requiring 'prominent' labels, the Tobacco Regulations only require the health warning labels to cover 20 per cent of the packaging,[82] not the minimum 30 per cent suggested by the FCTC. Further, locally produced and imported tobacco products must have health warnings in English.[83] The immediate concern is that although English is the principal language in Zimbabwe, many tobacco consumers are conversant in other official languages such as Shona and Ndebele, and recognised dialects such as Kalanga and Xhosa minorities may be excluded if they do not understand the health warning. Further, ingredients' technical names may not be easily understood by lay persons even if they are listed on the label, and such information should be conveyed in simple language where possible.

The MPOWER encourages anti-tobacco advertising; however, the national laws do not necessarily encourage anti-tobacco advertising but rather prohibit tobacco advertising, promotion and sponsorship under specific circumstances. For example, article 13 of the FCTC encourages states to ban false, misleading or deceptive tobacco advertising, promotion and sponsorship.[84] Domestically, the Tobacco Regulations provide even greater protection for minors by prohibiting the sale, donation and giving of tobacco products as prizes or promotions to minors.[85] Going a step further than the FCTC, the Tobacco Regulations also prohibit minors from themselves selling, donating or advertising tobacco products.[86]

80 SI 264 of 2002.
81 CY Rusere 'Tobacco control in Zimbabwe and the WHO framework convention on tobacco control (WHO FCTC): State of affairs' Unpublished master of commerce thesis, University of Cape Town, 2019 at 48.
82 Annexure to the Tobacco Regulations SI 264 of 2002.
83 Sec 9 SI 264 of 2002.
84 Art 13 FCTC.
85 Sec 6(1), SI 264 of 2002.
86 Sec 6(3), SI 264 of 2002.

9.4.5 Enforce bans

The Tobacco Regulations establish criminal liability for non-compliance by stipulating that

> any person who contravenes sections 3, 4, 5, 6 or 7 shall be guilty of an offence and liable to a fine not exceeding five hundred dollars or imprisonment for a period not exceeding six months or to both such fine and such imprisonment.

Similarly, there is criminal liability for breaching the provisions of TIMA relating to the registration of tobacco growers;[87] licensing of graders, buyers and auction floors;[88] and non-payment of relevant tobacco levies.[89] In the event of violating licensing and registration requirements for the above, the criminal penalty is a level 5 fine, or 6 months' imprisonment. However, for flouting the payment of levies, section 57(1) of TIMA provides that once a person is convicted of not paying the levy, the court may proceed with the hastened civil proceedings for summary judgment for purposes of recovering the levy amount.

These provisions illustrate a strict stance on tobacco control in line with the aims of the MPOWER framework and the FCTC broadly. Section 5 in this chapter will analyse the implementation of these provisions in selected case law.

9.4.6 Raise taxes

The MPOWER framework target to raise taxes on tobacco products has two main interventions: to increase tax rates for tobacco products to keep tobacco too expensive for consumers to buy, and to strengthen tax administration to reduce illicit trade in tobacco products.

The FCTC encourages states to reduce demand for tobacco by levying taxes on tobacco products.[90] Licensing is an additional measure used to regulate the production and distribution of tobacco products.[91] In compliance with article 6 of the FCTC, the TIMA imposes a levy on tobacco sold or grown in Zimbabwe, however, this levy is arrived at in consultation with tobacco growers and buyers,[92] and sections 95 and 96 the of Customs and Excise Act regulate excise duties.[93] However, the strong lobby power of the tobacco industry impinges efforts towards reducing tobacco supply. For example, in 2016, BAT conceded that it would 'continue engaging with government for a sustainable excise rate'.

87 Sec 25(1a) TIMA.
88 Secs 33(3), 36(3) and 40(2) TIMA.
89 Secs 57(1) and 58 TIMA.
90 Art 6 FCTC.
91 Art 15 FCTC.
92 Sec 53 read with sec 1 TIMA.
93 Secs 95 and 96 Customs and Excise Act Chapter 23:02.

Nonetheless, Zimbabwe still has one of the highest rates of excise duty in Africa. In 2016, Zimbabwe's excise duties for cigarettes was 186 per cent.[94]

A discussion on selected tobacco-related cases follows.

9.5 Case law on tobacco control

In this section, a review of case law is conducted to illustrate the enforcement of tobacco control nationally. While in Zimbabwe there are several cases dealing with the enforcement of restrictions on tobacco sales and exports, one is hard-pressed to find case law on contestations to tobacco regulations, although news reports identify various lobby actions by tobacco companies. In light of this, the chapter draws from other countries within the region.

In 2016, the Kenyan government enacted tobacco regulations to bring Kenyan laws into alignment with the FCTC; however, this was met with contestations. BAT, for example, instituted legal action against the Kenyan government in *British American Tobacco v Ministry of Health* (Kenya).[95] In this case, BAT challenged the constitutionality of the Tobacco Control Regulations which give life to the Tobacco Control Act and align with the FCTC. The court a quo held that the legislative process had been conducted lawfully and that the regulations are within the parameters of the Tobacco Control Act and were designed to implement the FCTC. Interestingly, the court weighed the interests of the tobacco industry as a commercial enterprise, against the interests of the public, in terms of health and the public health system in Kenya. These regulations required, inter alia, annual contributions of 2 per cent from the tobacco industry, to be used to support research and education; a picture health warning; disclosure of ingredients and tobacco sales; and creating 'smoke-free' public spaces. BAT appealed this decision twice without success, in the Appeals Court in 2017[96] and in the Supreme Court of Appeal in 2019.[97] This is a good example of where the courts played an important role as gatekeepers for the enjoyment of the right to health and promoted the implementation of the FCTC from the bench.

Similarly, in what the Ugandan court recognised as bad faith and a global strategy by tobacco companies to fight tobacco control regulations, British American Tobacco Uganda (BATU) in *BAT Uganda Ltd v Attorney General & Center for Health, Human Rights and Development* challenged the constitutionality of various provisions of the Tobacco Control Act of 2015. The Act requires at least 65 per cent or larger picture health warnings. It places a ban on smoking in indoor

94 V Mtomba 'BAT to engage government on excise duty' *Newsday* 27 July 2016 https://www.newsday.co.zw/2016/07/bat-engage-govt-excise-duty/ (accessed 5 July 2020).

95 24 March 2016.

96 17 February 2017.

97 *British American Tobacco Kenya, PLC (Formerly British American Tobacco Kenya Limited) v Cabinet Secretary for the Ministry of Health; Kenya Tobacco Control Alliance (Interested Parties); Mastermind Tobacco Kenya Limited (The Affected Party)* [2019] eKLR (26 November 2019).

public spaces and workplaces, and some outdoor public spaces, and bans tobacco advertising, promotions, sponsorship and product display at points of sale. The Act also prohibits tobacco sales at health centres and schools, for example, as well as the use of vending machines for tobacco sales. The Act further prohibits the importation, manufacture, distribution and sale of electronic cigarettes and flavoured tobacco inter alia. While this Act is far-reaching, it is necessary for the protection of the right to health, and the Court's decision highlights the issue of health. The Court ordered against BATU, with costs. The Court dismissed the petition in its entirety and awarded costs to the government, holding that the petition was made in bad faith.[98] Again, in this case the Court prioritised health over corporate interests, and this is progressive. However, it is unlikely that if a similar matter appeared before the courts in Zimbabwe that the outcome would be the same, for two reasons. First, there has been speculation in the past about the absence of judicial impartiality in some matters. Second, the national government is capable of putting pressure on the judiciary, bearing in mind that the economy is heavily dependent on tobacco as mentioned above. Indeed, the fact that it is difficult to find any cases could suggest that most of contestations might be taking place in private lobbying outside the courtroom.

9.6 Conclusion and recommendations

The fight to stop tobacco-related NCDs is an ongoing one, and it must continue if Zimbabwe is to fulfil its human rights obligations, in particular, its obligation to respect, protect and fulfil the right to health. It is evident that tobacco has immeasurable deleterious effects on health and takes too many lives; however, the enormous economic dependence on the tobacco industry and the absence of economically viable alternatives makes it difficult for countries such as Zimbabwe to fulfil their international and regional commitments.

An evaluation of the extent of compliance and implementation of the FCTC through the MPOWER framework nationally reflects that the TIMA and the Tobacco Regulations are for the most part compliant with the FCTC. However, there remain some gaps, particularly the regulation, testing and measuring of the contents of tobacco products. There is also a gap on offering help to quit smoking. Additionally, it is evident from the aforementioned cases that lower courts require capacity building on rules of court procedure and investigation as to why sentencing in selected tobacco cases seems to result in lower penalties on appeal might be useful. Finally, as briefly suggested above, the FCTC and MPOWER framework seem to have drawn more attention on challenges that are of more concern for the developed world, such as exposure to tobacco smoke and tobacco advertising, and to have perhaps neglected challenges more relevant to

98 *British American Tobacco (Ltd) v The Attorney General and the Center for Health, Human Rights and Development* (2016) The Republic of Uganda in the Constitutional Court of Uganda at Kampala Constitutional Petition 46 of 2016.

Zimbabwe (and other developing countries), such as issues around agricultural production of tobacco and illicit trade.

Bibliography

African Union, African Charter on Human and Peoples' Rights (Banjul Charter), 27 June 1981, CAB/LEG/67/3 rev 5, 21 ILM 58 (1982) https://www.refworld.org/docid/3ae6b3630.html (accessed 9 July 2020)

African Union, African Charter on the Rights and Welfare of the Child, 11 July 1990, CAB/LEG/24.9/49 (1990) https://www.refworld.org/docid/3ae6b38c18.html (accessed 10 July 2020)

Bartal, M 'Health effects of tobacco use and exposure' (2001) 56 *Monaldi Archives for Chest Disease* 545

British American Tobacco Kenya, PLC (formerly British American Tobacco Kenya Limited) v Cabinet Secretary for the Ministry of Health; Kenya Tobacco Control Alliance & another (Interested Parties); Mastermind Tobacco Kenya Limited (The Affected Party) [2019] eKLR (26 November 2019)

British American Tobacco (Ltd) v the Attorney General and the Center for Health, Human Rights and Development (2016) The Republic of Uganda in the Constitutional Court of Uganda at Kampala Constitutional Petition 46 of 2016

Clark, M; Magati, P; Drope, J & Lecunca, R 'Understanding alternatives to tobacco production in Kenya: A qualitative analysis at the sub-national level' (2020) 17 *International Journal of Environmental Research and Public Health* 1

Constitution of the Republic of Zimbabwe (Amendment No 20) 2013

Customs and Excise Act Chapter 23:02

Drope, J; Makoka, D; Lecunca, R & Appau, A 'Farm-level economics of tobacco production in Malawi' Revised Report Centre for Agricultural Research and Development (CARD) Lilongwe University of Agriculture and Natural Resources (LUANAR) (April 2016) https://www.cancer.org/content/dam/cancer-org/research/economic-and-healthy-policy/farm-level-economics-of-tobacco-production-in-malawi-full-report.pdf (accessed 8 July 2020)

Dworkin, R *Taking rights seriously* (R Dworkin 1997)

Gonah, L; Moodley, I & Hlongwana, K 'Capacity of antiretroviral therapy sites for managing NCDs in people living with HIV in Zimbabwe' (2020) 21 *Southern African Journal of HIV Medicine* 1

Government of Zimbabwe Core Questionnaire of the Reporting Instrument of WHO FCTC (2016) Submitted to the FCTC by Dorcas Sithole on Behalf of the Ministry of Health and Child Care (2016 Report) https://untobaccocontrol.org/impldb/wp-content/uploads/final_zimbabwe_2016_report.pdf (accessed 8 July 2020)

Government of Zimbabwe Core Questionnaire of the Reporting Instrument of WHO FCTC (2018) Submitted to the FCTC by Dorcas Sithole on Behalf of the Ministry of Health and Child Care (2018 Report) https://untobaccocontrol.org/impldb/wp-content/uploads/Zimbabwe_2018_report.pdf (accessed 8 July 2020)

Greaves, L & Jategaonkar, N 'Tobacco policies and vulnerable girls and women: Toward a framework for gender sensitive policy development' (2006) 60 *Journal of Epidemiology and Community Health* 57

Ho, L; Schafferer, C, Lee, JM; Yeh, C-Y & Hsieh, C-J 'Raising cigarette excise tax to reduce consumption in low-and middle-income countries of the Asia-pacific region:

A simulation of the anticipated health and taxation revenues impacts' (2018) 18 *BMC Public Health* 1

Human Rights Watch *A bitter harvest: Child labour and human rights abuses on tobacco farms in Zimbabwe* (Human Rights Watch 2018)

Human Rights Watch 'Zimbabwe: Tobacco work harming children' https://www.hrw.org/news/2018/04/05/zimbabwe-tobacco-work-harming-children (accessed 12 July 2020)

Jambroes, M & others 'Implications of health as "the ability to adapt and self-manage" for public health policy: A quantitative study' (2016) 26 *European Journal of Public Health* 412

Labour Act Chapter 28:01

Leary, V 'The right to health in international human rights law' (1994) 1(1) *Health and Human Rights* 23–54

Lown, EA; McDaniel, PA & Malone, RE 'Tobacco is "our industry and we must support it": Exploring the potential implications of Zimbabwe's accession to the framework convention on tobacco control' (2016) 12 *Globalisation and Health* 1

Magodoro, I; Esterhuizen, T & Chivese, T 'A cross-sectional, facility based study of comorbid non-communicable diseases among adults living with HIV infection in Zimbabwe' (2016) 9 *BMC Research Notes* 1

Mahove, C '70% of Zimbabweans live in poverty' https://www.iol.co.za/news/africa/70-of-zimbabweans-live-in-poverty-2073058 (accessed 12 July 2020)

McKnight, R; Spiller, H & Abat, D 'Green tobacco sickness in children and adolescents' (2005) 120 *Public Health Reports* 120

Mtomba, V 'BAT to engage government on excise duty' *Newsday* 27 July 2016 https://www.newsday.co.zw/2016/07/bat-engage-govt-excise-duty/ (accessed 5 July 2020)

Muchinjo, E 'Zimbabwe tobacco farms: Child labour, abuse rife, HRW says' *Al Jazeera* 8 April 2018 https://www.aljazeera.com/news/2018/04/zimbabwe-tobacco-farms-child-labour-abuse-rife-hrw-180408072948552.html (accessed 12 July 2020)

Mufunda, J; Chatora, R; Ndambakuwa, Y; Nyarango, P; Kosia, A; Chifamba, J; Filipe, A; Usmana, A & Harvey Sparks, V 'Emerging non-communicable disease epidemic in Africa: Preventive measures from the WHO Regional Office for Africa' (2006) 16 *Ethnicity & Disease* 521

Otanez, M; Mamudu, HM & Glantz, SA 'Tobacco companies' use of developing countries' economic reliance on tobacco to lobby against global tobacco control: The case of Malawi' (2009) 99 *Health Policy and Ethics* 1759

Public Health Act Chapter 15:17

Public Health (Control of Tobacco) Regulations, Statutory Instrument 264 of 2002

Rusere, CY 'Tobacco control in Zimbabwe and the WHO framework convention on tobacco control (WHO FCTC): State of affairs' Unpublished Master of Commerce thesis, University of Cape Town, 2019

'Shadowy giant in Zim tobacco trade Roger Boka' *Mail & Guardian* 13 September 1996 https://mg.co.za/article/1996-09-13-shadowy-giant-in-zim-tobacco-trade-roger-boka-the/ (accessed 6 May 2021)

The Tobacco Atlas 'Zimbabwe fact sheet' https://tobaccoatlas.org/country/zimbabwe/ (accessed 12 July 2020)

Tobacco Industry and Marketing Act Chapter 18:20

Tobacco Industry and Marketing Board of Zimbabwe (TIMB) 'History' https://www.timb.co.zw/about-us/history (accessed 7 July 2020)

Tobacco Marketing and Levy Act (1936)

United Nations Committee on Economic, Social and Cultural Rights (CESCR), General Comment 14: The Right to the Highest Attainable Standard of Health (art 12 of the Covenant) (2000) UN Doc E/C.12/2000/4, dated 11 August 2000 https://www.refworld.org/docid/4538838d0.html (accessed 12 July 2020)

United Nations General Assembly, Convention on the Rights of the Child, 20 November 1989, United Nations, Treaty Series, vol 1577, p 3 https://www.refworld.org/docid/3ae6b38f0.html (accessed 10 July 2020)

United Nations General Assembly, International Covenant on Economic, Social and Cultural Rights (CESCR), 16 December 1966, United Nations, Treaty Series, vol 993, p 3 https://www.refworld.org/docid/3ae6b36c0.html (accessed 9 July 2020)

United Nations General Assembly, Universal Declaration of Human Rights, 10 December 1948, 217 A (III) https://www.refworld.org/docid/3ae6b3712c.html (accessed 9 July 2020)

United Nations Guiding Principles on Business and Human Rights https://www.ohchr.org/documents/publications/guidingprinciplesbusinesshr_en.pdf (accessed 10 July 2020)

WHO Framework Convention on Tobacco Control, Geneva, 21 May 2003

WHO Protocol to Eliminate Illicit Trade in Tobacco Products, Seoul, 12 November 2012

WHO *Tobacco industry interference with tobacco control* (WHO Press 2008)

WHO 'Zimbabwe commemorates "world no tobacco day"' (2019) https://www.afro.who.int/news/zimbabwe-commemorates-world-no-tobacco-day-0 (accessed 12 July 2020)

WHO 'Zimbabwe global youth tobacco survey' https://extranet.who.int/ncdsmicrodata/index.php/catalog/167 (accessed 18 June 2020)

WHO 'Zimbabwe report card' (2017) https://www.afro.who.int/sites/default/files/2017-09/Zimbabwe_report_card_0.pdf (accessed 16 June 2020)

Woelk, G; Mtisi, S & Vaughan, P 'Prospects for tobacco control in Zimbabwe' (2001) 57 *Health Policy* 179

10 Assessing the level of compliance of the domestic normative framework on tobacco products of Mauritius with the FCTC

Roopanand Mahadew

10.1 Introduction

The consumption of tobacco products in Mauritius has been on the rise in the last few decades. Indeed, a number of the non-communicable diseases (NCDs) in the country are the result of tobacco products consumption. While tobacco products had been considered as one of the main causes of death by various stakeholders, the normative framework on their control had been seriously lacking. In 2004, this situation would change with Mauritius ratifying the World Health Organization's (WHO) Framework Convention on Tobacco Control (FCTC). Indeed, this international framework convention has ameliorated the normative framework on tobacco control in Mauritius significantly. The domestic normative framework on the subject matter has been elevated to a standard that would be internationally acceptable especially by an institution such as the WHO.

Despite some remarkable progress, there are still certain gaps and challenges that need to be addressed and overcome to enhance the degree of implementation and compliance with the FCTC. To complicate matters, the number of deaths caused by tobacco products and the number of NCDs related to tobacco have been on the rise despite the ratification of the FCTC. It is therefore clear that the mere ratification of the FCTC and the partial implementation of it has not been sufficient, even though it has elevated the quality and effectiveness of the normative framework on tobacco control in Mauritius. This chapter therefore peruses and assesses the degree of compliance and implementation of the FCTC in Mauritius in view of highlighting the hurdles and barriers to full compliance.

In line with the above-mentioned focus, the chapter presents an overview of the key facts and figures related to NCDs and tobacco consumption in Mauritius in order to contextualise the subject matter. This is followed by a glimpse at the legal analysis of the history of tobacco law in the country pre- and post-FCTC. The right to health in the context of tobacco consumption is eventually presented to discuss tobacco control as a component of the right to health. The next section then assesses the legislation on tobacco control in Mauritius using the FCTC as the standard. Finally, hurdles and barriers to the full compliance of tobacco laws in Mauritius with the FCTC is discussed before the work is concluded.

DOI: 10.4324/9781003264248-12

Mauritius has undergone rapid industrialisation and economic growth since independence in 1968, which has also brought along a significant shift in the disease pattern.[1] Economic development has resulted in general improvements in the living standards of Mauritians which has resulted in a worrying impact on NCDs.[2] Various surveys have been regularly conducted by the Ministry of Health and Quality of Life (MHQL) in collaboration with partners such as the WHO and Baker IDI Heart and Diabetes Institute in 1987, 1992, 1998, 2004 and 2009, indicating that the prevalence of diabetes mellitus was increasingly very high throughout these years.[3] Deaths caused by diseases of the circulatory system and diabetes mellitus have drastically increased from 31 per cent of total deaths in 1975 to 59 per cent in 2007.[4] Since then, the death rate caused by the mentioned diseases has been oscillating between 56 per cent and 57 per cent of total deaths in the country.[5]

Research conducted by the MHQL under the leadership of Professor Zimmet from the Baker IDI Heart and Diabetes Institute since 1987 has clearly demonstrated that NCDs have emerged in parallel to the change of lifestyle of Mauritians.[6] Since then, there has been a significant rise in NCDs, which is considered a cause of great worry and concern to the whole Mauritian population. The survey dating back to 1987 showed that there was an overall crude prevalence of 14.3 per cent for type 2 diabetes mellitus and 19.3 per cent for impaired glucose tolerance, which is a risk indicator for cardiovascular diseases and type 2 diabetes mellitus.[7] Ischemic heart disease was also a commonality among people within the age range of 35 to 74, with 19 per cent of men and 31 per cent of women suffering from this disease.[8] The 1992 follow-up survey showed a moderate increase in the prevalence of diabetes mellitus and impaired glucose tolerance. The ensuing 2009 survey further showed that the risk factors for NCDs in Mauritius were very high with diseases such as diabetes, cardiovascular diseases and hypertension on a worrying rise.[9]

The most recent survey was conducted in 2015 providing for key statistics on NCDs and their risk factors such as diabetes mellitus, being overweight and

1 G Dowse & others 'High prevalence of NIDDM and impaired glucose tolerance in Indian, Creole and Chinese Mauritians' (1990) 39 *Diabetic Medicine* 390.

2 Republic of Mauritius 'Government spends Rs 9 billion yearly for prevention and treatment of non-communicable diseases, says Health Minister' http://www.govmu.org/English/News/Pages/Government-spends-Rs-9-billion-yearly-for-prevention-and-treatment-of-Non-Communicable-Diseases,-says-Health-Minister.aspx (accessed 20 September 2021).

3 S Söderberg & others 'Increasing prevalence of Type 2 diabetes mellitus in all ethnic groups in Mauritius' (2004) 22 *Diabetic Medicine* 61.

4 Ministry of Health and Quality of Life 'The trends in diabetes and cardiovascular disease risk in Mauritius – The Mauritius non communicable diseases survey 2015' (2015) 10.

5 As above.

6 Mauritius Non Communicable Diseases Survey 2015 (n 4).

7 As above.

8 As above.

9 As above 11.

obesity, hypertension, lipids, smoking, alcohol consumption, kidney disease, disability, depression and asthma. The prevalence of type 2 diabetes mellitus was 20.5 per cent (196 per cent of men; 21.3 per cent women).[10] There are 257,442 people with diabetes in Mauritius. The prevalence for obesity was 19.1 per cent (11.9 per cent of men; 25.6 per cent of women).[11] The number of overweight or obese Mauritians between the age of 25 to 74 was 398,417 people out of a total population of around 1.3 million. Hypertension was prevalent among 28.4 per cent (30.3 per cent of men; 27 per cent of women). Elevated total cholesterol was prevalent among 44.1 of Mauritians (47.1 per cent of men; 41.8 per cent of women).[12] Albuminuria, an index of kidney disease, was found in 6.8 per cent of the surveyed population, with 7.1 per cent of men and 6.6 per cent of women having micro albuminuria.[13]

Regarding consumption of tobacco and smoking behaviours, the age- and gender-standardised prevalence of smoking was 3.9–19.3 per cent in women and 38 per cent in men.[14] The prevalence of smoking was highest in the younger age groups, with over 50 per cent of men aged 19–24 years of age reporting smoking.[15] It has also been noted that smoking decreased with age in both men and women. It has been reported that more than 1,200 people are killed by tobacco-related diseases annually. In 2015, 1,000 children between the ages of 10 and 14 and 159,000 adults were regular consumers of tobacco.[16] In 2016, the value for smoking prevalence was 21.60 per cent with 3.20 per cent among women and 40.70 among men.[17]

10.2 Right to health and NCDs

According to the UN Committee on Economic, Social and Cultural Rights (CESCR),

> health is a fundamental human right indispensable for the exercise of other human rights and every human being is entitled to the enjoyment of the highest attainable standard of health conducive to living a life in dignity.[18]

10 As above 5.
11 As above 6.
12 As above.
13 As above 7.
14 As above 29.
15 As above.
16 The Tobacco Atlas 'Mauritius' https://tobaccoatlas.org/country/mauritius/ (accessed 20 September 2021).
17 Index Mundi 'Mauritius – Smoking prevalence' https://www.indexmundi.com/facts/mauritius/smoking-prevalence (accessed 20 September 2021).
18 UN CESCR General Comment 14: The Right to the Highest Attainable Standard of Health (Article 12 of the International Covenant on Economic, Social and Cultural Rights) (2000) UN Doc E/C.12/2000/4 Dated 11 August 2000) para 1.

The right to health is considered an inclusive right, extending not only to appropriate and timely healthcare, but more importantly to the underlying determinants of health such as access to safe and potable water and adequate sanitation, an adequate supply of safe food, nutrition and housing, healthy occupational and environmental conditions, and access to health-related education and information.[19] The right to health has essential elements inherent in it, such as availability, accessibility, acceptability, quality, participation and accountability.[20]

The above-mentioned determinants of the right to health are fundamental to preventing NCDs. Therefore, the link between the two is a rather direct and irrefutable one. The normative framework within which the right to health operate provides the possibility for states to combat the issue of NCDs, implying that health services which are readily available, easily accessible, widely acceptable and of decent quality, participatory in approach and which can be used to hold states accountable are imperative in combatting NCDs. The connection of the right to health and the FCTC is evident as from its Preamble, whereby the FCTC clearly recognises the serious consequences of tobacco products on health and recalls article 12 of the International Covenant on Economic, Social and Cultural Rights (ICESCR) on the right for everyone to the enjoyment of the highest attainable standard of physical and mental health. In addition, article 18 of the FCTC directly imposes an obligation on states to protect health of persons in respect of tobacco cultivation and manufacture. In addition, the FCTC adopts a framework which is closely reflective of the essential elements of the right to health, as stated above. There is therefore a direct nexus between the right to health and NCDs and the FCTC, which corroborates the efforts of the WHO to combat the ill effects of tobacco products on human health on the basis of the right to health.

10.2.1 The right under the current legal framework

The state of Mauritius has provided for health services to the population under the welfare state system since independence.[21] This is echoed in the vision statement of the MHQL which is 'a healthy nation with a constantly improving quality of life'.[22] In terms of the mission of the state of Mauritius through the MHQL in relation to health, it is to transform existing health services into a modern high-performing quality health system that is patient centred, accessible, equitable, efficient and innovative; improve quality of life and well-being of the population

19 As above, para 4.

20 As above, paras 11–13.

21 For a discussion on the welfare state system of Mauritius see in general R Mahadew 'The right to health in Mauritius: Is the state doing enough or is the constitutional protection of the right to health still required?' in E Durojaye (ed) *Litigating the right to health in Africa: Challenges and prospects* (2015) 167.

22 Republic of Mauritius Ministry of Health and Wellness 'Mission and vision' http://health.govmu.org/English/the-ministry/Pages/Mission-and-Vision.aspx (accessed 10 September 2021).

through the prevention of communicable and non-communicable diseases; promote healthy lifestyles and an environment conducive to health; harness the full potential of information and communication technology to empower people to live healthy lives; ensure that the available human, financial and physical resources lead to the achievement of better health outcomes; and facilitate the development of Mauritius into a medical and knowledge hub and support the advancement of health tourism.

In order to realise the vision and mission stated above, a number of acts of Parliament have been created or maintained from the time of colonisation, forming the legislative framework on health in Mauritius. Some of these acts of Parliament are the Allied Health Professionals Council Act 2017, the Pharmacy Act 2015, the Food Regulations 1999, the Human Tissue (Removal, Preservation and Transplant) Act, the Food Act 1998, Medical Council Act, the Public Health Act 1925, the Pharmaceutical Products (Fees) Regulations 2016, the Mental Health Care Act 1998 and the Dangerous Chemical Control Act 2004. As can be inferred from the title of the acts and regulations, each of them legally caters for specific issues related to health in Mauritius.

The public health system of Mauritius, which is completely free, is supported by regional hospitals, district hospitals, specialised hospitals, medi-clinics, community hospitals, area health centres, community health centres and family health clinics.[23] Together they represent over 100 health centres for a population of 1.3 million. In addition to that, there are 11 private clinics offering world-class medical and health services.[24] The annual budget of the country allocates a large proportion to healthcare and services, as illustrated by the 2020–2021 budget, which has allocated 12.4 billion Mauritian rupees (around US$355 million).[25] This has increased compared to the 2018–2019 budget, where the health sector was allocated a sum of 12.2 billion Mauritian rupees (US$349 million).[26]

While there can be little doubt that health and medical services to the population have always been a top priority of every government of the welfare state of Mauritius since independence, one may still be surprised by the fact that there is no right to health in the Constitution of Mauritius. Indeed, there seems to be a de facto right to health in Mauritius with the welfare system of healthcare without a de jure one. Even the acts of Parliament cited above do not explicitly provide

23 Republic of Mauritius Ministry of Health and Wellness 'Health centres' http://health.govmu.org/English/ServicesHealth/Health-Centres/Pages/Mauritius.aspx (accessed 10 September 2021).

24 See Ministry of Health and Wellness 'Hospitals and private clinics in Mauritius' http://health.govmu.org/English/ServicesHealth/Health-Centres/Pages/Mauritius.aspx (accessed 10 September 2021).

25 See KPMG 'Mauritius budget highlights 2020/2021' https://assets.kpmg/content/dam/kpmg/mu/pdf/2020/mu-Mauritius-Budget-Highlights-2020-2021.pdf (accessed 10 September 2021).

26 See Republic of Mauritius 'Budget 2018–2019: Rs 12.2 billion earmarked to uplift health care and quality of life' http://www.govmu.org/English/News/Pages/Budget-2018-2019-Rs-12.2-billion-earmarked-to-uplift-health-care-and-quality-of-life.aspx (accessed 10 September 2021).

for a fundamental right to health to every Mauritian. Referring specifically to the Constitution, it is noted that its Bill of Rights (Chapter 2) only provides for civil and political rights and there is no mention of socio-economic rights. It implies that there is no right to health provided by the Mauritian Constitution. The general absence of socio-economic rights from the Constitution has been underlined with concern by the CESCR, questioning Mauritius on whether it plans to enshrine second-generation rights in the Bill of Rights.[27] The response of Mauritius was as follows:

> Mauritius fully subscribes to the view that all human rights are indivisible, interdependent and interrelated. In this regard, side by side with the strengthening of the protection of civil and political rights, Mauritius has spared no efforts to advance the realisation of economic, social and cultural rights for its citizens through, inter alia, measures to combat poverty and enhance social enlistment. Mauritius is a welfare state offering free education, free health services, universal old age pensions, social security aids and benefits for widows, orphans and persons with disabilities, free public transport for students and old-aged persons and other financial assistance schemes to the needy.[28]

10.2.2 The effect of the current laws on tobacco use

It is therefore clear that there is a confident reliance by the State of Mauritius on the welfare state system to provide for health services and facilities. The overarching question therefore remains whether there is a substantive right to health which is enforceable and justiciable upon which tobacco legislations can be premised.

It is apposite here to consider whether there is a right to health available to Mauritians through international human rights conventions on the basis of which Mauritius has certain legal obligations. Mauritius is indeed a state party to the ICESCR, which enshrines the right to health in its article 12. It is also a state party to the African Charter on Human and Peoples' Rights, which provides for the right to health in its article 16. While the ratification of these international conventions no doubt imposes international obligations related to the right to health on Mauritius, it is still very much a grey area whether these provisions can be invoked and enforced directly by Mauritian courts and therefore whether there is a domestic right to health.

The Constitution does not provide for any indication whatsoever on the application of international law in domestic courts. However, the fact that it is clear that the dualist doctrine is followed in Mauritius, there is the need for

27 See Examination of the Second, Third and Fourth Periodic Reports on the Implementation by Mauritius of the International Covenant on Economic, Social and Cultural Rights, 44th Session of the CESCR, Palais Wilson, Geneva, 7 May 2010).

28 CESCR (n 27) introductory para.

international law to be incorporated in domestic laws by enabling acts of Parliament.[29] The case of *Permal v The Illois Trust Fund* sheds more light on this matter by stating that international law 'by itself does not have force of law . . . nevertheless specific provisions of an agreement, treaty or convention do have force of law . . . to the extent they are given effect to it in an act of parliament or other enactment'.[30] The Supreme Court has also stated:

> Whilst it is a well-established canon of interpretation that domestic legislations should, if possible, be construed so as to conform to international instruments to which the state is a party, it is the practice in Mauritius that a treaty or convention must as a rule be incorporated into domestic law before the courts will apply it. The provisions contained in international instruments can therefore hardly be of help to respondents when there is no evidence of their incorporation in our domestic laws.[31]

The absence of a substantive right to health constitutionally protected has an impact on legislation on tobacco use and products in Mauritius. Despite the relatively strong legislative framework on tobacco use, it is not premised on the right to health enforceable and justifiable by a court of law. In other words, tobacco legislation is enacted in Mauritius for the better health of the Mauritian population but not as an essential component for respecting, fulfilling and protecting the right to health of Mauritians, which is indeed absent. Tobacco legislation therefore is devoid of a rights-based approach. Indeed, even the 2008 Regulations on Tobacco do not make any mention of the right to health, and there is no explanatory memorandum which states that the said regulations are an attempt to implement the right to health of Mauritians.

10.3 The FCTC as a treaty to realise the right to health at the national level

The effectiveness of the FCTC as a Treaty has to be examined against the history of tobacco law in Mauritius. An analysis of tobacco legislation in Mauritius since independence is conducted next, followed by an assessment of the effectiveness of the FCTC under domestic laws.

29 See F Viljoen *International human rights law in Africa* (2007) 18.
30 *Permal v The Illois Trust Fund* (1984) SCJ 173 at 7.
31 *Pulluck v Ramphul* (2005) SCJ 196.

10.3.1 An analysis of the history of tobacco law in Mauritius

The FCTC was signed by Mauritius in June 2003 and ratified in May 2004.[32] It has to be noted that there was no comprehensive legal and normative framework on consumption of tobacco products and smoking in general in the country prior to the signature of the FCTC in 2003. The only existing legislation was the Public Health (Restrictions on Tobacco Products) Regulations of 1999. As per this law, health warning labels on cigarette packages in Mauritius had one text-based message reading 'smoking causes cancer, heart disease and bronchitis'.[33] The 1999 Regulations also provided that smoking was to be banned in institutions providing for healthcare, educational and sports premises and institutions, public transportation, office areas or workplaces open to the public, public places in general such as museums and transport stations, and for activities related to preparing, serving or selling food to the public.[34] This 1999 Regulation had also imposed a ban on tobacco advertising and promotion as well as the prohibition of sponsorship by tobacco companies.[35] It also banned the sale of tobacco to minors and smoking in public transportation facilities since 1999.[36]

With the ratification of the FCTC by Mauritius, higher standards were set in relation to tobacco use and smoking which required a significant review of the 1999 Regulations which was not integrally aligned with the provisions of the WHO Convention. In 2007, a National Action Plan on Tobacco Control 2008–2012 was developed by the Mauritian government in collaboration with the WHO.[37] The primary goal of this Action Plan was to decrease mortality and morbidity related to tobacco consumption by prohibiting the use of tobacco products, encouraging cessation of smoking and protecting people from passive smoking. The spirit and aim of the Action Plan were further consolidated by the coming into force of Public Health (Restrictions on Tobacco Products) Regulations 2008 (2008 Regulations), which by its nature was legally binding as compared to the Action Plan. It should be noted that the said regulation was issued by the Minister of Health through the power granted to it by the Public Health Act 1925, and it updated the 1999 policies on smoking.

In essence, the 2008 Regulations imposed a total ban on advertising, promotion of cigarette brands and sponsorship by tobacco companies. There was also a ban on product display at points of sale of tobacco. There was also the prohibition of the sale of tobacco products at a discounted price or their offering for free. The 2008

32 See FCTC 'Mauritius' https://www.who.int/fctc/reporting/mus/en/ (accessed 22 September 2021).

33 International Tobacco Control Policy Evaluation Project 'ITC Mauritius National Report' (2010) 6.

34 The Tobacco Atlas (n 16) 7.

35 Sec 6 of the Public Health (Restrictions on Tobacco Products) Regulations 2008.

36 Secs 5 and 3 of the Public Health (Restrictions on Tobacco Products) Regulations 2008.

37 The Tobacco Atlas (n 16) 6.

Regulations equally strengthened the smoke-free policy by including places such as public indoor and outdoor areas, venues related to hospitality, recreational venues and areas and privately registered vehicles carrying passengers.[38] It should, however, be noted that there are still designated smoking areas in workplaces. A ban was also imposed on tobacco vending machines, on the sale of tobacco products to and by minors under 18 years, and on sweets or toys in the form of cigarettes.[39]

Another important area covered by the 2008 Regulations are the product packaging and labelling requirements. Eight rotating graphic pictorial warning labels were imposed. The front of the package contains the pictorial warning in French occupying 60 per cent of the package; and the back is occupied by the same pictorial message in English on up to 70 per cent of the total area of the back of the package.[40] In addition, 65 per cent of the sides of the package are occupied by text messages in French and English.[41] Descriptions such as 'mild', 'light' or 'low tar' on packets were prohibited. The display of tar or nicotine content or the carbon monoxide yield were also outlawed similar to the sale of single or 'loose' cigarettes, which could now only be sold in packages of 20.[42]

These 2008 Regulations are supplemented by provisions in the Consumer Protection (Price and Supplies Control) Act 1998 (dealing with point-of-sale product displays) and the Occupational Safety and Health Act 2005 regulating smoke-free policies at the workplace. The 2008 Regulations were amended twice in 2009 by the Public Health (Restrictions on Tobacco Products) (Amendment) Regulations 2009 and then by the Public Health (Restrictions on Tobacco Products) (Amendment 2) Regulations 2009. These two amendments dealt with the duties imposed upon traders and business owners in relation to the enforcement of smoke-free policies, health signs and warnings, and emission yields on tobacco packages.

It has been argued that the 1999 Regulations were already strong and that the 2008 Regulations have come to further strengthen existing laws.[43] By doing so, Mauritius has emerged as a world leader by taking steps such as prohibiting corporate social responsibility activities by tobacco companies and by imposing large health warning signs and pictorial messages as explained above.[44] There has also been a clear and strong political commitment sourcing from the highest levels of the political hierarchy to discourage tobacco consumption despite

38 Sec 3 of the Public Health (Restrictions on Tobacco Products) Regulations 2008.

39 Sec 4 of the Public Health (Restrictions on Tobacco Products) Regulations 2008.

40 Third Schedule of the Public Health (Restrictions on Tobacco Products) Regulations 2008.

41 See Mauritius' Pictorial Health Warning Label images at the Tobacco Labeling Resource Centre website http://www.tobaccolabels.ca/currentl/mauritius (accessed 10 September 2021).

42 Sec 4 of the Public Health (Restrictions on Tobacco Products) Regulations 2008.

43 P Burhoo, D Mohee & L Moussa 'Mauritius' in J Drope (ed) *Tobacco control in Africa: People, politics and policies* (2011) 185.

44 As above.

discontentment from consumers.[45] This was reiterated by the following extract from the speech of the then prime minister in March 2009 during the Independence Day celebration:

> The Public Health (Restrictions on Tobacco Products) Regulations have recently been promulgated. Contrary to what some may think, this is not a measure to restrict liberty. It is meant to free you from a scourge that was becoming far too widespread and wrecking innocent lives. Smoking, far from being a liberating act of defiance, is the first step to an addiction that enslaves you and destroys your health. Smoking is neither cool nor smart. Be resolute in resisting the pressure of your peers who would lead you astray.[46]

It can arguably be said that the 2008 Regulations have been a major improvement on the 1999 Regulations concerning restrictions on tobacco products in Mauritius. This is hugely credited to the positive effects of the ratification by the country of the FCTC in 2004.[47] The domestication of the latter's provisions have been laudable and in some instances, the domestic law on tobacco has surpassed the recommendations of the FCTC. Having said this, there are still some imperfections in the law as will be discussed later in the chapter.

10.3.2 Compliance with the FCTC

This section of the chapter will assess the degree of compliance of tobacco laws and regulations with the FCTC after the latter was ratified by Mauritius. An article-wise approach will be adopted here to critically assess whether tobacco laws in Mauritius are in full, partial or non-compliance with the FCTC. By so doing, the degree of implementation as well as the gap in the local laws on tobacco will be highlighted using the FCTC as the standard.

Article 2(1) of the FCTC requires state parties to implement measures that are beyond those provided by the Convention itself and they are also encouraged to adopt stricter measures than those prescribed in the FCTC. It is noted that Mauritius has not adopted any measure which is beyond the scope of the Convention. It can be argued that while the FCTC sets the standard and provides for an overarching framework on tobacco control, state parties have the responsibility of adopting legislation that goes beyond what is provided by the FCTC since each country has its own specificities which is best dealt with in a contextualised and tailor-made manner. A comparative assessment of the implementation of the FCTC in Mauritius is highlighted in Table 10.1.

45 As above.
46 The Tobacco Atlas (n 16) 192.
47 As above.

Table 10.1 Level of Mauritius' compliance

FCTC Provision	*Equivalent Provision in Mauritian Legislations*	*Compliance (Full [F], Partial [P], Not Complied [NC])*
Article 6 on price and tax measures to reduce the demand for tobacco	Budgetary measures	P
Article 8 on protection from exposure to tobacco smoke	Section 3 and First Schedule of the 2008 Regulations	F
Article 9 on regulation of the contents of tobacco products	–	NC
Article 11 on packaging and labelling of tobacco	Third, Fourth and Fifth Schedules of the 2008 Regulations	F
Article 12 on education, communication, training and public awareness	No equivalent provisions in the law, but education, training and public awareness conducted as a matter of practice	F
Article 13 on tobacco advertising, promotion and sponsorship	Section 6 of the 2008 Regulations	F
Article 14 on demand reduction measures concerning tobacco dependence and cessation	National Action Plan for Tobacco Control (2008–2012)	P
Article 15 on illicit trade in tobacco products	National Action Plan for Tobacco Control (2008–2012)	P
Article 16 on sales to and by minors	Section 5 and the Sixth Schedule of the 2008 Regulations	F
Article 17 on provision of support for economically viable alternative activities	–	NC
Article 18 on protection of the environment and the health of persons	National Action Plan for Tobacco Control (2008–2012)	P
Article 19 on liability	Section 7 of the 2008 regulations	F

10.4 An assessment of the effectiveness of efforts to implement the FCTC

Such an assessment is informed by the application of the WHO MPOWER initiative. This method of engaging the FCTC is related to several aspects: monitoring tobacco and prevention policies; protecting people from tobacco smoke; offering help to quit tobacco use; warning about the dangers of tobacco use; enforcing bans on tobacco advertising, sponsorship and promotion; and raising taxes on tobacco.[48] The following section discusses these parameters and their application.

10.4.1 Guiding principles

With regard to the guiding principles as spelt out in article 4 of the FCTC, an important principle is the special contribution of nongovernmental organisations and members of the civil society ranging from health professional bodies to women's groups to academic institutions. Indeed, article 4(7) recognises that 'the participation of civil society is essential in achieving the objective of the Convention and its protocols'. It should be noted that there is no provision similar to that of article 4(7) in the 2008 Regulations.

Local organisations such as VISA Mauritius, the National Agency for the Treatment and Rehabilitation of Substance Abuse and Ligue Vie et Sante do collaborate with the Ministry of Health and Wellness of Mauritius. Their work is focuses mainly on advocacy and training programmes on tobacco and its uses and effects, implementation of research in support of policy development, running awareness programmes at the community level and technical assistance to the development of technical documents such as the National Tobacco Action Plan. It should be noted that while the government does provide for grants to financially contribute to their work, civil society organisations are compelled to find their own sources of funding. They are also known to operate on the basis of voluntary workers and supporters. In view of their important roles, it is critical that civil society organisations be properly structured and supported financially so that they can operate at the highest level.

Article 5(1) of the FCTC calls upon parties to develop, implement, periodically update and review comprehensive multi-sectorial national tobacco control strategies, plans and programmes in line with the provisions of the Convention. In line with this provision, a National Action Plan for Tobacco Control (2008–2012) was created and implemented.[49] The main aim of the National Action Plan on Tobacco Control was to reduce mortality and morbidity related to tobacco use by preventing the use of tobacco products, promoting cessation and protecting

48 WHO 'MPOWER: Six policies to reverse the tobacco epidemic' http://bit.ly/3eiGzN1 (accessed 10 September 2021).

49 Ministry of Health & Quality of Life 'National action plan on tobacco control: 2008–2012' (2008) https://untobaccocontrol.org/impldb/wp-content/uploads/reports/Annexfive-mauritius.pdf (accessed 10 September 2021).

from exposure to environmental tobacco smoke.[50] The Action Plan elaborated on the following guiding principles which aimed at guiding its implementation:

1 Every individual in society has the right to be adequately informed on tobacco, its use and consequences.
2 Every individual in society has the right to live in a tobacco smoke–free environment.
3 Partnership with all sectors will be promoted based on a clear definition of the roles and responsibilities of each partner.
4 Community involvement and community empowerment will be encouraged in all tobacco control activities.
5 Vulnerable groups like young people and women will receive particular attention in the tobacco control programme.
6 Collaboration with international and regional organisations will be consolidated to attract expertise and control illicit trade in tobacco.
7 Accessibility to tobacco products especially to minors will be reduced.
8 Cessation facilities will be made available to smokers who want to quit.
9 The influence of the tobacco industry will be considerably reduced by adopting the appropriate regulatory measures.
10 Monitoring and evaluation mechanism will be set up to assess the effectiveness of interventions.
11 Political support will be maintained by continued allocation of resources from the national budgets and donors and promoting the policy agenda on tobacco control.

It is important to note that at around 2013, the Ministry of Health of Mauritius was envisaging to develop a new National Action Plan for Tobacco Control 2013–2016 based on the experience and outcome of the previous one. The new Action Plan was supposed to provide a comprehensive four-year plan based on demand-reduction and supply-reduction measures. Its vision was to create a tobacco-free society through individual and community responsibility and political commitment. Its main goal was to reduce the health, economic and social impacts of tobacco use.[51] Unfortunately, seven years on, the new Action Plan has yet to see the day.

Another general obligation imposed by article 5(2) of the FCTC is to establish or reinforce and finance a national coordinating mechanism or focal points for tobacco control. The 2008 Regulations, as the main law on tobacco, did not establish any such mechanism or committee. On the contrary, the National Steering Committee for Tobacco Control was established by the Ministry of Health as part of its implementation of the National Action Plan for Tobacco Control

50 National Action Plan on Tobacco Control 2008–2012, iii.
51 FCTC Secretariat 'Needs assessment for implementation of the WHO framework convention on tobacco control in Mauritius' (2013) 10.

2008–2012. The main aim of this committee is to guide the government on tobacco control policies and to coordinate and monitor the implementation of the 2008–2012 Action Plan.[52] It should be noted that the composition of the Steering Committee does reflect the requirement of article 5(2) since it provides for participation from various sectors of government and is geared towards the review and update of tobacco control strategies and programmes.

However, the mandate and operation of the Committee are in need of further strengthening in view of enhancing its effectiveness. To illustrate this point, the mandate of the Committee does not include reviewing and advising on the implementation of the FCTC. In addition, the Committee lacks a formal legal basis, which does not allow it to be regular and sustainable in its operation and impacts on its capacity to convene meetings, develop agendas and prepare documentation on tobacco control.

Article 5(2)(b) calls on parties to adopt and implement effective legislative, executive, administrative and/or other measures, and cooperate, as appropriate, with other parties in developing appropriate policies, for preventing and reducing tobacco consumption, nicotine addiction and exposure to tobacco smoke. In relation to this obligation under the FCTC, the Public Health Act 1925, the Minister of Health and Quality of Life issued the Public Health (Restrictions on Tobacco Products) Regulations of 2008, as discussed in section 3 of this chapter. These are the main regulations governing tobacco control in the country. The provisions of the said regulations are comprehensive as they cover major and primary areas of the Convention. These include restrictions on smoking in public places;[53] restrictions on tobacco advertising,[54] promotion and sponsorship;[55] and tobacco product packaging and labelling requirements.[56] Two amendments were brought to these regulations in 2009: the Public Health (Restrictions on Tobacco Products) (Amendment) Regulations 2009 and the Public Health (Restrictions on Tobacco Products) (Amendment 2) Regulations 2009. They were mainly focused on duties imposed upon trade owners regarding enforcement of policies related to smoke-free areas, health warnings, and emission yields on product packaging.

However, certain gaps have to be highlighted regarding these regulations. For instance, the timing of enforcement actions is from sunrise to sunset, which acts as a barrier to enforcement efforts. In addition and importantly, there is no clear provision on rendering the tobacco industry liable for the public health and other tobacco control harms. There are no direct legal obligations imposed on them in that sense.[57] Point-of-sale and cross-border advertising and implementation of article 5(3) of the FCTC have not been comprehensively regulated in the existing laws/regulations.

52 FCTC Secretariat (n 51 above) iv.
53 Sec 3 of the 2008 Regulations.
54 Sec 6 of the 2008 Regulations.
55 As above.
56 Third, Fourth and Fifth Schedules of the 2008 Regulations.
57 The Tobacco Atlas (n 16).

With reference specifically to article 5(3), there is a crucial obligation imposed on state parties which provides that in setting 'public health policies with respect to tobacco control, Parties shall act to protect these policies from commercial and other vested interests of the tobacco industry'. Implementation guidelines for this article stipulate that all branches of government 'should not endorse, support, form partnerships with or participate in activities of the tobacco industry described as socially responsible'. A similar section exists in the 2008 Regulations, more precisely in section 2, where the term 'sponsorship' has been defined as 'any form of contribution to any event, activity or individual with the aim, effect or likely effect of promoting a tobacco product or tobacco use directly or indirectly'. It should be underlined that currently no tobacco manufacturing plant is operational in Mauritius, the last one having ceased its activities in 2008. In relation to article 5(3) of the Convention, the only relevant measure in the 2008 Regulations is the prohibition on the corporate social responsibility–related activities of the tobacco industry.

The implementation guidelines for article 5(3) recommend that state parties should not give preferential treatment to the tobacco industry by granting incentives, privileges or benefits to the industry to establish or run their businesses and not to invest in the tobacco industry and related ventures. There is no explicit provision that prohibits the tobacco industry and associates from impacting public health policy in any of the normative documents in effect. In addition, there is no provision that strictly regulates the interaction of public officials with the tobacco industry and its affiliates, such as a code of conduct.

10.4.2 Price and tax measures

State parties to the Convention recognise that 'price and tax measures are an effective and important means of reducing tobacco consumption by various segments of the population, in particular young persons'.[58] State parties also have the obligation to account for its national health objectives concerning tobacco control through the implementation of 'tax policies and, where appropriate, price policies, on tobacco products so as to contribute to the health objectives aimed at reducing tobacco consumption'.[59]

In Mauritius, there are three types of taxes levied on tobacco products; however, there is no uniformity in their application to all tobacco products. In the case of cigarettes, an average of 65 per cent of the retail price of the most popular brand goes to taxes.[60] The application of these types of taxes are based on import duty, specific excise duty and a 15 per cent value added tax (VAT) which is applied on top of all aforementioned taxes. Regarding cigars, cheroots and cigarillos, a

58 Art 6(1) of the FCTC.
59 As above.
60 J Valdois & C Walbeek 'A review of excise taxes on cigarettes in Mauritius' (2018) 14.

single excise rate applies, which is around 13,000 Mauritian Rupees per kilogram.[61] The taxation system applicable to tobacco products has witnessed vital changes in the past few years. From 2005 to 2008, tax rates were distinguished by quadruple categorisation of cigarettes, with the most expensive ones taxed at higher rates. Such differentiation came to an end in July 2008, and a constant specific excise tax rate of 2,200 Mauritian Rupees per 1,000 cigarettes was introduced. This rate changes on a yearly basis, with increases above the consumer price index, reaching 5,111 Mauritian Rupees in 2018.[62] By a regular implementation of such tax increases, Mauritius is in compliance with its obligations under article 6 of the FCTC. However, in spite of the regular tax increases which also increase the prices of cigarettes, the latter remain highly affordable in Mauritius.[63]

In addition, article 6(2) requires state parties to prohibit or limit the sales and importation by international travellers of tax and duty-free tobacco products. It should be noted that the 2008 Regulations do not contain any provisions in line with article 6(2). Such prohibition and limitation reshape the sales and importation of tobacco products by travellers and are catered for by the Mauritius Revenue Authority Regulations. Accordingly, sales of tobacco products which are duty-free are allowed in the airport and in tax-free shops. This applies to travellers who will take the purchase out of the country, thus exempting them from paying local taxes and duties. The purchased products are accessible only at the airport upon departure and therefore are not consumable on Mauritian territory. Returning passengers are limited to 250 grams of any tobacco products, which is equal to 200 cigarette sticks. This allowance can be brought into Mauritian territory by all passengers above the age of 18 years. It can thus be said that Mauritius is in compliance with article 6(2) of the FCTC by limiting the sales of duty-free tobacco products to duty-free shops and by imposing quantity restrictions on the purchase of such products by returning passengers.

10.4.3 Protection from exposure to tobacco smoke

Article 8(2) requires state parties to

> adopt and implement in areas of existing national jurisdiction as determined by national law and actively promote at other jurisdictional levels the adoption and implementation of effective legislative, executive, administrative and/or other measures, providing for protection from exposure to tobacco smoke in indoor workplaces, public transport, indoor public places and, as appropriate, other public places.

61 The Tobacco Atlas (n 16).

62 J Valdois & others 'Tobacco industry tactics in response to cigarette excise tax increases in Mauritius' (2020) 29 *Tobacco Control* e115.

63 N Fakun 'Quit smoking or die trying' (2016) https://defimedia.info/quit-smoking-or-die-trying-50-young-men-smoke (accessed 10 September 2021).

The article 8 guidelines accentuate the fact that 'there is no safe level of exposure to tobacco smoke' and call on all states to 'strive to provide universal protection within five years of the WHO Framework Convention's entry into force for that Party'.

In Mauritius, smoking in public is regulated by two laws: the Public Health (Restrictions on Tobacco Products) Regulations 2008 and the Occupational Health and Safety Act 2005. The 2008 Regulations prohibit smoking in public places, including but not limited to indoor public areas, public transport, bus stands and bus stations, private vehicles carrying passengers, recreational places (except public beaches), cafes, bars, restaurants and night clubs.[64] Smoking is banned in healthcare facilities, including hospitals, public areas and patient rooms of residential healthcare facilities and in non-residential healthcare facilities.[65] Smoking is also banned in all educational premises, including childcare facilities/ preschools, primary and secondary schools, and tertiary and vocational facilities.[66] Owners of public premises and facilities are required to display signs demonstrating that smoking and selling tobacco products to minors are not allowed. Owners or the responsible persons of public premises are also required to ask anyone smoking to stop or to leave, or eventually to call the police if they do not stop smoking or leave.[67]

The definition of public place in relation to workplace by the 2008 Regulations needs to be highlighted here. As per the 2008 Regulations, a public place means a workplace but excludes an area demarcated for smoking purpose.[68] This definition of the 2008 Regulations is in harmony with the Occupational Health and Safety Act of 2005. However, they are not in line with the definitions recommended by the guidelines for implementation of article 8 of the Convention. In addition, the Occupational Health and Safety Act of 2005 is not only in disharmony with the requirements of the FCTC and the relevant implementation guidelines but also with the spirit of the 2008 Regulations. The Occupational Health and Safety Act of 2005 (paragraph (e)) requires that 'every employee shall, while at work . . . not smoke at the place of work, except in an area demarcated for that purpose'.[69] Such a 'demarcated area' is to be designated by the workplace owners and managers but there is not prescribed and specific requirement in designating such an area.

64 First Schedule of the 2008 Regulations.
65 The Tobacco Atlas (n 16).
66 'Be mindful of where you are smoking' *Le Defimedia* 19 July 2017 https://defimedia.info/sabah-says-be-more-mindful-where-youre-smoking (accessed 10 September 2021).
67 T Durgahee 'A plea for smoking zones in restaurants' *Lexpress.mu* 24 March 2005 https://www.lexpress.mu/node/148095 (accessed 10 September 2021).
68 Sec 2 of the 2008 Regulations.
69 Sec 14.

10.4.4 Regulation of tobacco products and disclosures

There exists a legal obligation on state parties to 'adopt and implement effective legislative, executive and administrative or other measures' for the purposes of conducting tests and measurements of the contents and emissions of tobacco products.[70] With respect to the implementation of article 9 of the FCTC, no measures have been implemented so far by Mauritius. It should be noted that the 2008 Regulations provide for no regulations of contents and emissions of tobacco products. There is also no designation of a laboratory for the conduct of testing of emissions and contents of tobacco products.

The FCTC also requires state parties to 'adopt and implement effective legislative, executive, administrative or other measures requiring manufacturers and importers of tobacco products to disclose to governmental authorities information about the contents and emissions of tobacco products'. They are also required to 'adopt and implement effective measures for public disclosure of information about the toxic constituents of the tobacco products and the emissions that they may produce'.[71] There is no legal obligation in Mauritius for importers to submit to the relevant authority any information about the contents and emissions of tobacco products since there is no law or regulation that requires this. The situation is similar with regard to reporting on ingredients and components added to tobacco products and the level of carbon monoxide, nicotine and tar in tobacco smoke.[72] It was reported that the establishment of the National Agricultural Products Regulatory Office under the aegis of the Ministry of Agro-Industry was meant to cater for the obligations under articles 9 and 10.[73] However, control and regulation of tobacco contents and emissions were finally not included in the mandate of the Office as matters stand.

10.4.5 Packaging and labelling of tobacco products

Article 11 requires state parties to adopt effective measures on packaging and labelling of tobacco products 'within a period of three years after entry into force of the Convention'.[74] It has to be noted that Mauritius has taken consequential measures to fulfil this obligation resulting in the country having the strongest health warning signs policies in the world. The Mauritius tobacco-labelling requirements are outlined in the 2008 Regulations,[75] in force since 1 June 2009. This is in sharp contrast with what used to be the requirement under the

70 Art 9 of the FCTC.
71 Art 10 of the FCTC.
72 Tobacco Control Laws 'Legislation by country – Mauritius' (2019) https://www.tobaccocontrollaws.org/legislation/country/mauritius/summary (accessed 10 September 2021).
73 The Tobacco Atlas (n 16).
74 Art 11 of the FCTC.
75 Third, Fourth and Fifth Schedules of the 2008 Regulations.

Government Notice 1999 of the Public Health Act. Indeed, the latter only required a text-only warning for cigarettes with the law specifying the colour, location or size of the warning. In addition, this was required only for cigarettes and not for other tobacco products. Previous regulations only had text warnings appearing in small fonts on the side of the packaging. The draft National Tobacco Control Action Plan (2013–2016), to be finalised and approved by the government soon, promotes the introduction of plain packaging in Mauritius. The members of the mission also learnt about the efforts of the Ministry of Health and Quality of Life to strengthen its packaging and labelling policies further, by moving towards the introduction of plain packaging. The 2008 Regulations require the sizes of the warning to be 60 per cent of the front and 70 per cent of the back.[76]

In 2009, Mauritius became the first African state to require pictorial warnings. A series of eight picture-based bilingual health warnings must cover 60 per cent of the front (with French text) and 70 per cent of the back (with English text); and on 65 per cent of each of the left and right sides of cigarette packages, the text message 'Smoking kills' appears in French on one side and in English on the other.[77] The cigarette health warning requirements also find their application to cigarette cartons. There is therefore a picture warning on 60 per cent in French of the front principal display area, and 70 per cent in English of the back principal display area. The text message which reads as 'Smoking kills' appears on 65 per cent of two other carton sides, with one side in English and the other in French.

Contrary to cigarette packaging, warnings on other tobacco product packages are only textual in nature. For cigars and pipe tobacco, there is only a single text warning in French and English which reads as follows: 'Smoking causes cancer, heart disease, bronchitis and early death'. The warning can be located anywhere on the package, with the side of the packaging being mostly preferred by manufacturers. Generally, the warning size does not cover even up to 30 per cent of the principal display surfaces as required by the FCTC.[78] In addition, there is only a single warning without any rotation of any kind. Mauritius has no warning requirements whatsoever for tobacco products except for cigarettes, cigars and pipe tobacco. Health warnings are not mandatory on packages of other products such as bidis, chewing tobacco, snuff, water pipes and roll-your-own tobacco. It is important to note that cigarette papers are banned and water pipe tobacco is banned in Mauritius. [79] Chewing tobacco and snuff are also very rare in Mauritius.

It has to be highlighted that despite some gaps in the law, Mauritius has indeed achieved a significantly high level of compliance with the FCTC regarding warning requirements for cigarettes. More and more smokers have pondered the

76 See section 3 of this chapter.

77 The Tobacco Atlas (n 16).

78 Fifth Schedule of the 2008 Regulations.

79 Sec 13 of the Consumer Protection (Control of Imports) Regulations 1999, Government Notice 135 of 1999, Second Schedule.

health risks of cigarettes and contemplate quitting due to the effects of these warnings.[80] Mauritius has already allowed for its warning pictures to be included in the FCTC database. It has also granted permission to countries such as Iran, Russia, Seychelles and Togo to use those images.[81]

10.4.6 Education, communication, training and public awareness

The FCTC imposes on state parties the obligation to

> adopt and implement effective legislative, executive, administrative or other measures to promote education, communication and public awareness about the health, economic and environmental consequences of tobacco consumption and exposure to tobacco smoke, the benefits of tobacco cessation and tobacco-free lifestyles, as well as training for all concerned persons and public access to information on the tobacco industry.[82]

In 2010, the Conference of Parties adopted guidelines for implementation of article 12. These guidelines provide in-depth advice on running effective education, communication and training programmes on the same wavelength with the requirements of the FCTC.

Recently, Mauritius has implemented a number of awareness-raising and information programmes in line with the 2008–2012 National Tobacco Control Action Plan under the coordination of the Ministry of Health and Quality of Life. Such programmes consisted of a campaign to raise awareness of the new Regulations of 2008 through mass media and social network with specific sessions organised with different target groups, creation and distribution of materials on health education with messages such as 'say no to cigarettes', media campaigns on the ill effects of cigarettes with advertisements in newspapers, the organisation of World No Tobacco Day[83] and advocacy workshops providing for information on the effects of smoking and the implementation of a smoke-free policy to stakeholders. The Ministry of Health has also taken initiatives such as smoking cessation programmes to help people quit smoking.[84]

80 The Tobacco Atlas (n 16) 3.

81 See WHO FCTC 'Health warnings database' http://www.who.int/tobacco/healthwarningsdatabase/en/index.html (accessed 10 September 2021).

82 Art 12 of the FCTC.

83 YUVA 'World No Tobacco Day 2019: How tobacco endangers the lung health of people worldwide' (2019) https://yuvamauritius.com/2019/05/24/world-no-tobacco-day-2019-how-tobacco-endangers-the-lung-health-of-people-worldwide/ (accessed 10 September 2021).

84 WHO 'Smoking cessation programmes in Mauritius help tobacco users kick the habit' (2015) https://www.afro.who.int/news/smoking-cessation-programmes-mauritius-help-tobacco-users-kick-habit (accessed 10 September 2021).

10.5 Barriers against the effective implementation of the provisions of the FCTC in Mauritius

From the preceding discussion, it is arguably fair to state that Mauritius has demonstrated the right political will and intention to implement the provisions of the FCTC. However, at this stage, it cannot be said that Mauritius is fully compliant with the Convention. The previous section elaborated on the gaps in the 2008 Regulations, which clearly demonstrate that there is still scope for improving the legislative and normative framework on tobacco products control. To achieve this specific purpose, it is important to consider some potential barriers that must be overcome before Mauritius can become a fully compliant country with the FCTC.

The effects of tobacco products and their consumption can be social, economic and health-related. While the previous two are important effects that no doubt need attention, the health aspect of smoking is more known to the general public and more serious in relative terms. In simple terms, smoking is a serious health hazard. It is therefore fundamental that for the state to adopt a human rights-based approach towards the combat against tobacco, the right to health must first be enshrined in Mauritian law. As explained earlier, there are no socio-economic rights provisions, and more precisely the right to health, in the Mauritian Constitution, and there is an over-reliance on the concept of welfare state in Mauritius.[85] The absence of the right to health is therefore a serious barrier in the combat against tobacco consumption.

The legal status of the ICESCR and its article 12, which provides for the right to health, is also ineffective domestically since there is no possibility of invoking this right in domestic courts due to lack of domestication. In addition, health-related laws, regulations and rules including the 2008 Regulations or the general Public Health Act 1925 also are not geared towards the right to health, even indirectly or non-explicitly. Thus while everyone agrees that smoking is a serious health hazard, it is not yet possible to state that smoking is an infringement of one's own or another person's right to health. In the same vein, one cannot contend that the Mauritian government has a positive obligation to respect, protect, fulfil and respect the need to ban or at least strictly regulate smoking and consumption of tobacco products, as is the case for the right to health.

Regarding the FCTC itself, as an international convention, it faces the dilemma of Mauritius being a dualist country which requires domestication. As stated above, Mauritius is no doubt endeavouring to implement the FCTC. However, the effectiveness of such an implementation effort is thwarted by the fact that it has not yet been domesticated. The nature of the FCTC and its provisions is such that a state can hardly place any reservation on them or argue contrary to what they provide for. In this respect, it is difficult to understand what prevents the government of Mauritius to domesticate the whole Convention, giving effect

85 See section 2.2 of this chapter.

to all its provisions. After this essential step, the government can gear its effort towards the full implementation and compliance of each and every article of the FCTC. In addition, a lack of domestication also prevents the provisions from being invoked before a court of law in any case, directly or indirectly related to tobacco consumption.

Referring specifically to the court cases on tobacco consumption, it has to be highlighted that there are no cases taken to court from a human rights-based approach towards the combat against tobacco consumption and smoking. The only nature of judicial decisions rendered by local courts are in relation to contraventions regarding smoking in public places or other infringements provided by the 2008 Regulations and other laws. There is therefore no litigation on the right to health which could have been a basis for more effective action against tobacco. It should also be added that with the nature of the Supreme Court of Mauritius, which is conservative and not known at all to apply judicial activism, the prospect of indirect litigation against tobacco consumption can hardly be envisaged. In addition, the *locus standi* before Mauritian courts is very high, and legal proceedings such as public interest litigation or *actio popularis* are not possible.

The economic impact and effect of the tobacco industry is perhaps one of the most crucial hurdles towards the effective implementation of the FCTC. While there are no tobacco manufacturing plants in Mauritius and it cannot be said that this is an economic sector that employs many people, it cannot be denied that the sales of tobacco are a major source of revenue in Mauritius. With all the different types of taxes levied on tobacco products as discussed earlier, it is very difficult for the government to close down this industry or to adopt more draconian laws. For instance, for a long time there was enormous hesitation for cigarettes to be sold as loose draw. Sellers were extremely cautious to do so, fearing enforcement of the law against them. However, after some time, this situation has evolved regressively. Loose draws are sold rather openly, and there is no enforcement against this non-respect of the law. It has almost become an accepted practice since the authority perhaps is unofficially aware that such sales are important for the sellers themselves and, on a larger scale, the economy in general. This is no doubt a complex area which is often characterised by the question: why does the government not ban smoking and the sale of tobacco products knowing that they are serious killers?

10.6 Conclusion and recommendations

Smoking is a major scourge in Mauritian society, and its impacts are being felt in the most serious manner. The law is one of the ways to combat this social ill, and this is spearheaded by the ratification of the FCTC by Mauritius. Considerable efforts have been made by Mauritius to render effective the implementation and compliance level of domestic laws of the FCTC. There are still certain gaps that need to be addressed.

First, a right-based approach must crucially be adopted, and for that matter, the enshrinement of the right to health in the Constitution is mandatory. Second, institutions created under the 2008 Regulations as discussed previously must be strengthened with a more robust legal mandate. Third, there is the need to demonstrate more seriousness with regard to meetings, documentation and policy-drafting exercises, which is not the case currently. Fourth, the enforcement of existing provisions such as smoke-free policy, sales of loose draw, sales of tobacco products to persons under the age of 18 and illegal importation of tobacco products should be treated more strictly. There is a noted sense of complacency on behalf of enforcement authorities regarding the said activities. Taxation measures must also be more effective and much higher to discourage people from smoking, as for now, tobacco products remain highly affordable to all classes of the Mauritian society.

There is finally a pressing need for stakeholders such as civil society organisations and even the judiciary to play a crucial role in the fight against tobacco products and smoking. In addition, the family and parental attention are crucial in the education and sensitisation of people, especially those of younger ages, about the ill effects of tobacco products. In the end, arguably the biggest responsibility remains with the person himself who wishes to indulge in smoking or tobacco products consumption. A high degree of discipline and self-restriction are essential to never start or to quit smoking and tobacco products consumption.

Bibliography

Burhoo, P; Mohee, D & Moussa, L 'Mauritius' in Drope, J (ed) *Tobacco control in Africa: People, politics and policies* (Cambridge University Press 2012)

Consumer Protection (Control of Imports) Regulations 1999

Dowse, G; Gareeboo, H; Zimmet, PZ; Alberti, KG; Tuomilehto, J; Fareed, D; Brissonnette, LG & Finch, CF 'High prevalence of NIDDM and impaired glucose tolerance in Indian, Creole and Chinese Mauritians' (1990) 39 *Diabetic Medicine* 390

Durgahee, T 'A plea for smoking zones in restaurants' https://www.lexpress.mu/node/148095 (accessed 10 September 2021)

Fakun, N 'Quit smoking or die trying' (2016) https://defimedia.info/quit-smoking-or-die-trying-50-young-men-smoke (accessed 10 September 2021)

Hospitals and Private Clinics in Mauritius http://health.govmu.org/English/Services Health/Health-Centres/Pages/Mauritius.aspx (accessed 10 September 2021)

Index Mundi 'Mauritius – smoking prevalence' https://www.indexmundi.com/facts/mauritius/smoking-prevalence' (accessed 20 September 2021)

International Tobacco Control Policy Evaluation Project 'ITC Mauritius National Report' (2010)

KPMG 'Mauritius budget highlights 2020/2021' https://assets.kpmg/content/dam/kpmg/mu/pdf/2020/mu-Mauritius-Budget-Highlights-2020-2021.pdf (accessed 10 September 2021)

Le Defimedia 'Be mindful of where you are smoking' https://defimedia.info/sabah-says-be-more-mindful-where-youre-smoking (accessed 10 September 2021)

Mahadew, R 'The right to health in Mauritius: Is the state doing enough or is the constitutional protection of the right to health still required?' in Durojaye, E (ed) *Litigating the right to health in Africa: Challenges and prospects* (Nomos 2015)

Ministry of Health & Quality of Life 'National action plan on tobacco control: 2008–2012' (2008) https://untobaccocontrol.org/impldb/wp-content/uploads/reports/Annexfivemauritius.pdf (accessed 10 September 2021)

Ministry of Health & Quality of Life 'The trends in diabetes and cardiovascular disease risk in Mauritius – The Mauritius non communicable diseases survey 2015' (2015) 10

MPOWER: Six policies to reverse the tobacco epidemic http://bit.ly/3eiGzN1 (accessed 10 September 2021)

Permal v The Illois Trust Fund (1984) SCJ 173

Public Health (Restrictions on Tobacco Products) Regulations 2008

Pulluck v Ramphul (2005) SCJ 196

Republic of Mauritius 'Budget 2018–2019: Rs 12.2 billion earmarked to uplift health care and quality of life' http://www.govmu.org/English/News/Pages/Budget-2018-2019-Rs-12.2-billion-earmarked-to-uplift-health-care-and-quality-of-life.aspx (accessed 10 September 2021)

Republic of Mauritius 'Government spends Rs 9 billion yearly for prevention and treatment of Non-Communicable Diseases, says Health Minister' http://www.govmu.org/English/News/Pages/Government-spends-Rs-9-billion-yearly-for-prevention-and-treatment-of-Non-Communicable-Diseases,-says-Health-Minister.aspx (accessed 20 September 2021)

Republic of Mauritius Ministry of Health and Wellness 'Health centres' http://health.govmu.org/English/ServicesHealth/Health-Centres/Pages/Mauritius.aspx (accessed 10 September 2021)

Republic of Mauritius Ministry of Health and Wellness 'Mission and vision' http://health.govmu.org/English/the-ministry/Pages/Mission-and-Vision.aspx (accessed 10 September 2021)

Söderberg, S; Zimmet, P; Tuomilehto, J; De Courten, M; Dowse, GK; Chitson, P; Gareeboo, H; Alberti, KGMM & Shaw, JE 'Increasing prevalence of Type 2 diabetes mellitus in all ethnic groups in Mauritius' (2004) 22 *Diabetic Medicine* 61

Third Schedule of the Public Health (Restrictions on Tobacco Products) Regulations 2008

The Tobacco Atlas 'Mauritius' https://tobaccoatlas.org/country/mauritius/ (accessed 20 September 2021)

Tobacco Control Laws 'Legislation by country – Mauritius' (2019) https://www.tobaccocontrollaws.org/legislation/country/mauritius/summary (accessed 10 September 2021)

Tobacco Labelling Resource Centre 'Mauritius' http://www.tobaccolabels.ca/currentl/mauritius (accessed 10 September 2021)

UN CESCR Examination of the Second, Third and Fourth Periodic Reports on the Implementation by Mauritius of the International Covenant on Economic, Social and Cultural Rights (7 May 2010)

UN CESCR General Comment 14: The Right to the Highest Attainable Standard of Health (Article 12 of the International Covenant on Economic, Social and Cultural Rights) (2000) UN Doc E/C.12/2000/4 dated 11 August 2000

Valdois, JB; Van Walbeek, C; Hana Ross, H; Soondram, H; Jugurnath, B; Chan Sun, M & Mohee, D 'Tobacco industry tactics in response to cigarette excise tax increases in Mauritius' (2020) 29 *Tobacco Control* e115

Valdois, JB & Walbeek, C 'A review of excise taxes on cigarettes in Mauritius' (2018) *Ministry of Finance*

Viljoen, F *International human rights law in Africa* (Oxford University Press 2012)
WHO FCTC 'Mauritius' https://www.who.int/fctc/reporting/mus/en/ (accessed 22 September 2021)
WHO FCTC Secretariat 'Needs assessment for implementation of the WHO framework convention on tobacco control in Mauritius' (2013)
WHO 'Smoking cessation programmes in Mauritius help tobacco users kick the habit' (2015) https://www.afro.who.int/news/smoking-cessation-programmes-mauritius-help-tobacco-users-kick-habit (accessed 10 September 2021)
YUVA 'World no tobacco day 2019: How tobacco endangers the lung health of people worldwide' (2019) https://yuvamauritius.com/2019/05/24/world-no-tobacco-day-2019-how-tobacco-endangers-the-lung-health-of-people-world-wide/ (accessed 10 September 2021)

Part III

Lessons from other jurisdictions

11 The David and Goliath tale of Uruguay's tobacco control measures

Lessons for the region and beyond

Lucía Berro Pizzarossa, Andrés Constantin and Lucía Giudice

11.1 Introduction

Tobacco smoking is the single most preventable cause of premature mortality in the world. In Latin America and the Caribbean, tobacco use and exposure to tobacco smoke are responsible for 80 per cent of all deaths and 77 per cent of premature deaths.[1] Tobacco consumption accounts for a substantial proportion of health expenditure in the region, with tobacco-related health problems representing a direct cost to health systems, a cost that in Latin America rises to US$87 billion.[2] For decades, Latin America and the Caribbean have led tobacco control efforts globally.[3]

With a stable democracy and a long-standing tradition of respect for human rights, Uruguay is a pioneer in tobacco control efforts globally.[4] Uruguay became a democratic republic in 1984, following a period of civil-military rule. With a population of 3.44 million people, Uruguayans have a longer average life expectancy and a lower rate of under-five child mortality than any other country in the Latin American and Caribbean region.[5] Uruguay has been a high-income country since 2012, with a gross national income of US$15,230 per capita per year

1 PAHO *Report on Tobacco Control for the Region of the Americas – WHO Framework Convention on Tobacco Control: 10 Years Later* (2016).

2 A Pichon-Riviera & others 'Economic impact of smoking on health systems in Latin America: A study of seven countries and its extrapolation to the regional level' (2016) 40 *Pan American Journal of Public Health* 213 https://pdfs.semanticscholar.org/8416/fcbd-1327949649ecd9e7375fb37df0ed6d8d.pdf (accessed 15 September 2021).

3 E Bianco, B Champagne & J Barnoya 'The tobacco epidemic in Latin America and the Caribbean: A snapshot' (2005) 1 *Prevention and Control* 311; BM Champagne, E Sebrié & V Schoj 'The role of organized civil society in tobacco control in Latin America and the Caribbean' (2010) 52 *Salud publica de Mexico* 330.

4 S Kalkhoran & others 'Effect of Uruguay's national 100% smokefree law on emergency visits for bronchospasm' (2015) 49 *American Journal of Preventive Medicine* 85.

5 World Bank 'Uruguay' (2015) https://data.worldbank.org/country/uruguay (accessed 7 September 2021).

DOI: 10.4324/9781003264248-14

in 2016 (compared to the regional average of US$8,252 per capita). Uruguay's Human Development Index score increased from 0.692 in 1990 to 0.795 in 2015 (out of 1.0), reflecting improvements to health and life expectancy, access to education and knowledge, and the overall standard of living.[6]

The country was the first Latin American country to adopt a comprehensive smoke-free national law as part of a nationwide tobacco control campaign.[7] This chapter begins with a brief discussion of the role of law and, in particular, human rights, in the prevention of non-communicable diseases (NCDs). It then turns to an analysis of Uruguay's context and situation within the Latin American region. After such analysis, it proceeds to describe Uruguay's strategy to address smoking and the country's different measures to tackle this challenge. Using Uruguay's case as an example, the chapter showcases a broader reflection on the corporate practices and the challenges they pose to countries adopting tobacco control policies. It describes the tobacco industry's opposition to Uruguay's measures, which motivated Philip Morris to initiate an arbitration procedure against the country before the International Centre for Settlement of Investment Disputes (ICSID). Next, it explains and discusses the impact of Uruguay's policies. Reflecting on these challenges, the chapter concludes with a suggestion of what steps should be taken to promote effective tobacco control measures and counter the tobacco industry's pervasive opposition.

11.2 Right to health and NCDs

11.2.1 Human rights, NCDs and tobacco control

The prevention of NCDs and, in particular, the adoption of tobacco control measures is a cross-cutting issue that relates to economic, social, cultural, civil and political rights, as well as human rights aimed at protecting population groups (e.g. women and children).[8]

Human rights law can be an adequate legal framework to influence policy debates when applied to political discourse, both at the national and international level. Legal scholars have considered human rights and tobacco control to be mutually reinforcing frameworks, as human rights norms can be powerful to advance tobacco control while protecting people's human rights.[9]

6 UN Development Programme 'Briefing note for countries on the 2016 Human Development Report' (2016) http://hdr.undp.org/sites/all/themes/hdr_theme/country-notes/URY.pdf (accessed 17 September 2021).

7 W Abascal & others 'Tobacco control campaign in Uruguay: A population-based trend analysis' (2012) 380 *The Lancet* 1575.

8 See ME Gispen & B Toebes 'The human rights of children in tobacco control' (2019) 41 *Human Rights Quarterly* 340 for the protection of children; See R Appleberry 'Breaking the camel's back: Bringing women's human rights to bear on tobacco control' (2001) 13 *Yale Journal of Law and Feminism* 71 for the protection of women. Regarding persons with disabilities, see, for example, Y van der Eijk 'The convention on the rights of persons with disabilities as a tobacco control tool in the mental health setting' (2018) 27 *Tobacco Control* 637.

9 OA Cabrera & LO Gostin 'Human rights and the framework convention on tobacco control: Mutually reinforcing systems' (2011) 7 *International Journal of Law in Context* 285.

Not only do the right to health and other health-related rights provide the normative basis for the protection of people from the hazards derived from tobacco products, but they also contribute to shaping and clarifying the foundations for governmental action and regulation. They mandate states to adopt legislative and administrative measures and give people the ability to claim the enforcement and protection of their rights through judicial recourse.[10]

At the same time, international human rights mechanisms provide promising avenues for monitoring the implementation of human rights obligations related to tobacco control, contributing to the development of standards that facilitate the interpretation of tobacco control norms.[11] In the last couple of years, States parties' to the World Health Organization (WHO) Framework Convention on Tobacco Control (FCTC) recognised this link between human rights and tobacco control in the context of the 2016 Conference of the Parties (COP7) held in India and by including it as an agenda item for the 2018 COP8 in Geneva.[12]

At least 115 constitutional frameworks and multiple international and regional human rights instruments recognise the right to the enjoyment of the highest attainable standard of physical and mental health.[13] The right was first elucidated in the WHO Constitution in 1948. The Constitution declares that 'the enjoyment of the highest attainable standard of health' is a fundamental right belonging to every human being.[14] That same year, the UN General Assembly adopted the Universal Declaration of Human Rights, which also recognised the right to health as a fundamental human right.[15] The right to health was codified seminally in the International Covenant on Economic, Social and Cultural Rights (ICESCR), which provided for the 'right of everyone to the enjoyment of the highest attainable standard of physical and mental health'.[16] The UN Committee on Economic, Social and Cultural Rights (CESCR) clarified the substance and scope of the right to health in General Comment 14. It noted that the right to health encompasses healthcare, preventative programmes and the underlying socio-economic determinants of health, including 'an adequate supply of safe food' and nutrition.[17]

10 C Dresler & S Marks 'The emerging human right to tobacco control' (2006) 28 *Human Rights Quarterly* 599.
11 C Dresler & others 'Human rights-based approach to tobacco control' (2012) 21 *Tobacco Control* 208.
12 WHO FCTC 'COP8 is coming up, with important progress to report' (2018) http://www.who.int/fctc/mediacentre/news/2018/cop8-coming-up/en/ (accessed 1 October 2021).
13 UN OHCHR & WHO *Fact Sheet 31: The right to health* (2008) 10.
14 Constitution of the World Health Organization, 1950, Preamble.
15 UN General Assembly, Universal Declaration of Human Rights, 10 December 1948, 217 A (III) (1948).
16 Constitution of the World Health Organization, 1948.
17 See UN Committee on Economic, Social and Cultural Rights (CESCR), General Comment 14: The right to the highest attainable standard of health (art 12 of the Covenant) (2000) UN Doc E/C.12/2000/4, dated 11 August 2000.

The right to health provides a relevant legal framework for tobacco control policies. The obligation to respect, protect and fulfil the right to health compels states to refrain from spreading the tobacco epidemic. From this perspective, for instance, states should avoid holding ownership of tobacco companies.[18] Moreover, a state's obligation to protect people's right to health from the threat of tobacco also calls for regulation of private activities that constitute a breach of human rights,[19] for instance, adopting smoking bans in public places, bans on advertising, promotion, sponsorship of tobacco products, and taxation of tobacco products.[20] A state's international commitment to the right to health also requires adequate implementation of all relevant domestic legislation and budgetary allocation to contribute to effective tobacco control regulation, including the provision of health services for the treatment of diseases stemming from tobacco use, facilitating smokers' access to cessation programmes and prevention campaigns that inform the population about the dangers associated with tobacco use.[21]

Thus, tobacco control should be framed not only as a public health matter but also as a human rights and social justice issue.[22]

11.2.2 The regional context: tobacco control in Latin America and the Caribbean

There are an estimated 69 million smokers in Latin America and the Caribbean, representing 6 per cent of all smokers worldwide. About 68 per cent (47 million) smokers are men and 32 per cent (22 million) are women. The Americas are second only to Europe among WHO regions regarding the relative prevalence of women who smoke.[23]

18 For further discussion, see SL Hogg, SE Hill & J Collin 'State-ownership of tobacco industry: A "fundamental conflict of interest" or a "tremendous opportunity" for tobacco control?' (2016) 25 *Tobacco Control* 367.

19 See UN Committee on Economic, Social and Cultural Rights (CESCR), General Comment 24 on State obligations under the International Covenant on Economic, Social and Cultural Rights in the context of business activities (10 August 2017) UN Doc E/C.12/GC/24 (2017).

20 OA Cabrera & A Madrazo 'Human rights as a tool for tobacco control in Latin America' (2010) 52 *Salud Publica de Mexico* S288.

21 As above.

22 O Cabrera & A Constantin 'Tobacco control in international human rights law' in ME Gispen & B Toebes (eds) *Human rights and tobacco control* (2020) 45.

23 PAHO 'WHO report finds dramatic increase in life-saving tobacco control policies in last decade' https://www.paho.org/hq/index.php?option=com_content&view=article&id=13496:who-report-finds-dramatic-increase-in-life-saving-tobacco-control-policies-in-last-decade&Itemid=135&lang=pt (accessed 7 September 2021).

Undoubtedly, tobacco use is a human rights concern and is a pervasive global health challenge. As Toebes explains:

> The harmful effects of production, sale and exposure to tobacco are not only a public health concern but also a matter of social justice in the way tobacco negatively impacts on the lives and wellbeing of individuals – smokers and non-smokers alike.[24]

The tobacco industry's attempts to conceal the harmful effects of tobacco smoking, the deliberate manipulation of nicotine content, and tobacco products' toxicity were made public at the end of the 20th century. In response, countries in North America and Europe have ramped up their regulation.[25]

Although tobacco consumption still poses a major public health threat in these regions, in the face of stricter regulation, the tobacco industry shifted its focus to poorer regions in the world, including untapped markets in Africa, Asia, Eastern Europe and Latin America, with devastating effects.[26] From a socio-economic standpoint, the tobacco epidemic burden is not fairly distributed: tobacco consumption rates are much higher among poor communities.[27] According to the WHO, 'it is the poorer and the poorest who tend to smoke the most. Globally, 84% of smokers live in developing and transitional economy countries'.[28] The literature confirms the strong association between a higher prevalence of current smoking and lower income levels in the region. In Latin America and the Caribbean, being in the low-income category entails nearly twice the probability of being a current smoker, compared to a high-income category.[29]

From a gender lens, female smoking is predicted to double by 2025.[30] The growing 'feminization' of tobacco use in the region is a major concern considering the several negative effects of tobacco consumption on women's health.[31] As a matter of fact, since 1980 one in three women has died from cardiovascular

24 B Toebes 'The value of a human rights-based approach to tobacco control' (2018) 4 *Tobacco Prevention & Cessation* A66 https://doi.org/10.18332/tpc/91957 (accessed 10 September 2021).

25 OA Cabrera & LO Gostin 'Human rights and the framework convention on tobacco control: Mutually reinforcing systems' (2011) 7 *International Journal of Law in Context* 285.

26 TJ Bollyky & LO Gostin 'The United States' engagement in global tobacco control: Proposals for comprehensive funding and strategies' (2010) 304 *JAMA* 2637.

27 Cabrera & Gostin (n 25).

28 WHO 'Tobacco and poverty: A vicious circle' (2004) https://apps.who.int/iris/handle/10665/116428 (accessed 14 September 2021).

29 A Bardach & others 'Niveles de ingreso y prevalencia de tabaquismo en América Latina: Revisión sistemática y metaanálisis' (2016) 40 *Rev Panam Salud Publica* 263.

30 A Amos & others 'Women and tobacco: A call for including gender in tobacco control research, policy and practice' (2012) 21 *Tobacco Control* 236. See also, J Samet & others 'Women and the tobacco epidemic: Challenges for the 21st century' (2011) http://www.who.int/iris/handle/10665/66799 (accessed 15 September 2021).

31 See generally WHO 'Gender, health and ageing' https://apps.who.int/iris/handle/10665/68893 (accessed 14 September 2021). See also WHO 'WHO Report on the

diseases,[32] and lung cancer has increased among women at an annual rate of 1.7 per cent due to tobacco consumption.[33] This is partly the result of the tobacco industry's marketing campaigns that since the 1920s have particularly targeted women.[34] Philip Morris International and British American Tobacco's campaign for International Women's Day is just the latest example of how tobacco industry marketing has sought to use emerging cultural contexts[35] and reference points to build positive associations with smoking as a feminist act.[36]

Women, young people[37] and marginalised communities in many countries have become a prime target for the tobacco industry. While the tobacco industry continues to target women as a group, efforts to adopt what the FCTC calls gender-specific tobacco control strategies are lagging.[38]

11.2.2.1 Panorama of measures adopted in different countries

The tobacco epidemic is well established in Latin America and the Caribbean. Still, countries are navigating through its various stages at different speeds, and health and mortality effects are heterogeneous. Most of the countries in the region have ratified the FCTC, which imposes binding obligations on states and has essential implications for human rights discourse.[39] State parties to the FCTC recognise the tobacco epidemic as a major threat to public health, and they acknowledge 'that scientific evidence has unequivocally established that tobacco consumption and exposure to tobacco smoke cause death, disease and disability'.[40] The FCTC introduced a package of evidence-based tobacco control measures.

Countries in Latin America and the Caribbean have achieved great progress in adopting effective tobacco control after the international momentum generated by the FCTC. It is relevant to note that organised civil society has been the engine for many of the accomplishments seen in tobacco control in the region.[41]

---

global tobacco epidemic: Raising tobacco taxes' https://www.who.int/teams/health-promotion/tobacco-control/global-tobacco-report-2021 (14 September 2021).

32 See e.g. M Sosa Liprandi 'Causes of death in women and the trend over the last 23 years in Argentina' (2006) 74 *Argentine Journal of Cardiology* 297.

33 H Schargrodsky & others 'CARMELA: Assessment of cardiovascular risk in seven Latin American cities' (2008) 121 *American Journal of Medicine* 58.

34 A Amos 'How women are targeted by the tobacco industry' (1990) 11 *World Health Forum* 416.

35 D Hunt, M Hefler & B Freeman 'Tobacco industry exploiting international women's day on social media' (2020) 29 *Tobacco Control* e157.

36 A Amos & M Haglund 'From social taboo to "torch of freedom": The marketing of cigarettes to women' (2000) 9 *Tobacco Control* 3.

37 M Urrutia-Pereira & others 'Youth tobacco use in Latin America: What is the real extent of the problem?' (2019) 47 *Allergologia et Immunopathologia* 328.

38 Appleberry (n 8).

39 World Health Organization *Framework Convention on Tobacco Control* 230 UNTS 166.

40 Preamble, FCTC.

41 Champagne & others (n 3).

The WHO reports that 21 of the 35 countries in the Americas have implemented at least one comprehensive tobacco control measure. At least 15 countries have implemented two or more of these measures. As a result, smoking prevalence in the region has decreased in the last few decades. The Pan-American Health Organisation estimates that 'between 2007 and 2015, the prevalence of tobacco smoking dropped from 22.1% to 17.4%, a greater drop than that recorded globally'.[42] This trend is expected to continue, and the region has been singled out as the 'only WHO region expected to achieve a 30% relative reduction in the prevalence of current tobacco use by 2025'.[43]

Benefiting almost 500 million people in 18 countries (48.7 per cent of the population), smoke-free environment policies have been the region's most widely adopted measure. The second-most widespread measure in the region has been to include graphic health warnings on tobacco packaging, which have been implemented in 16 countries, covering 55 per cent of the population of the Americas.

11.3 The FCTC as a treaty to realise the right to health at the national level

11.3.1 Introduction to Uruguay

Against the regional landscape described in the preceding section, Uruguay stands out as a leader. An early supporter of the FCTC, Uruguay was among the original 40 countries to ratify it in September 2004 and bring it into force in early 2005. Uruguay is one of the seven countries of the region (Brazil, Chile, Costa Rica, Ecuador, Panama, Peru, and Uruguay) that are implementing FCTC main policies, known as MPOWER. This acronym stands for a package of six evidence-based tobacco control strategies: monitor tobacco use and prevention policies; protect people from tobacco smoke; offer help to quit tobacco use; warn about the dangers of tobacco; enforce bans on tobacco advertising, promotion and sponsorship; and raise taxes on tobacco.

Uruguay is one of only four countries (in addition to Brazil, Colombia and Panama) that are implementing and complying with article 13 on tobacco advertising, promotion, and sponsorship, implementing and complying with a 75 per cent or higher tax to tobacco products (Argentina, Brazil, Chile and Colombia) and implementing recommendations by WHO in MPOWER on enforcing bans

42 WHO 'WHO global report on trends in prevalence of tobacco use 2000–2025' (2019) https://www.who.int/publications/i/item/who-global-report-on-trends-in-prevalence-of-tobacco-use-2000–2025-third-edition (accessed 3 October 2021).

43 The Tobacco Atlas 'Nearly 70 million smokers in Latin America are at risk of tobacco-related death and disease' (2018) https://web.archive.org/web/20200228135136/https:/tobaccoatlas.org/2018/11/13/nearly-70-million-smokers-in-latin-america-are-at-risk-of-tobacco-related-death-and-disease/ (accessed 3 October 2021).

on tobacco advertising, promotion and sponsorship (Brazil, Colombia, Panama and Uruguay).[44]

Two of the multinationals that have operated in Uruguay are Philip Morris (represented by Abal Hnos SA) and British American Tobacco. Philip Morris first entered the country in 1979, having acquired the Uruguayan company Abal Hnos. Philip Morris closed its production plant in 2011, although it continued marketing its products in the Uruguayan market.[45]

11.3.2 Measures taken by the country in the period 2004–2020

Tobacco control measures in Uruguay have been firmly established as a national state policy. The scientific evidence about the health harms associated with smoking, along with the health, economic and environmental costs generated by tobacco use and exposure, seem to have converged into a broad consensus regarding the consideration of tobacco use as a public health problem. Within this framework, and unlike what happens with other public health policies, all measures linked to tobacco control in the country have been adopted and supported across all political parties and stakeholders. This is markedly different from other health policies, such as zero tolerance of alcohol consumption for drivers.

The tobacco control measures adopted by the country fit into a broader approach that recognises NCDs as a demo-epidemiological problem that requires multi-sectoral approaches, including the adoption of other measures such as national policies that limit saturated fatty acids and banning industrially produced trans fats or the implementation of the national awareness and public motivation programme about physical activity.[46] Examples include Law 19307 on audio-visual media (2014), which refers to health, and via article 33 it establishes the regulation of food advertising in accordance with the WHO standards; approval of Decree 114/018 of progressive and mandatory reduction of trans fats of industrial production (which has already been incorporated in the National Bromatological Regulation); Decree 272/18 of labelling the front of products with excessive content of fats, saturated fats, sugar and sodium, a fundamental measure for the prevention of NCDs; and Law 18213 (2009), which set

44 A Blanco 'La situación del control del tabaco en America Latina' Paper presented at 3er Congreso Uruguayo Tabaco o Salud, 16 August 2019, Piriapolis, Uruguay https://web.archive.org/web/20200226131311/https:/www.tabacoosalud.com.uy/images/Presentaciones/Track-POLITICAS/p1-control-de-tabaco-en-uruguay-y-latinoamerica-presente-y-futuro/3-Adriana-Blanco.pdf (accessed 15 September 2021).

45 A Sica & others 'Políticas de control del tabaquismo en Uruguay' (2013) *Banco Mundial, Prevención de factores de riesgo de la salud en América Latina y el Caribe: gobernanza de cinco esfuerzos multisectoriales.*

46 Ministry of Public Health 'Interpellations and responses to non-communicable diseases in Uruguay: Update document on the situation of NCDs in Uruguay' (December 2018) 64 https://www.paho.org/uru/index.php?option=com_docman&view=download&slug=interpellations-and-responses-to-non-communicable-diseases-in-uruguay&Itemid=307 (accessed 15 September 2021).

up physical education as a mandatory component in the curricula in all primary schools.

While action against tobacco consumption in Uruguay can be traced back at least to the 1950s,[47] it was at the beginning of the 21st century that measures to control smoking became specifically strong. This is closely connected to Uruguay's ratification of the FCTC in September 2004, which entered into force in February 2005. This ratification was the result of an important process of activism, awareness raising and negotiation between various actors at multiple levels. It should be noted that the context for the design and implementation of tobacco control public policy measures was marked by the parliamentary support of all the political parties for the ratification of the Convention, as well as the strong commitment announced by the first Frente Amplio government to implement the measures set out in the Convention and the figure of the president of the Republic, Dr Tabaré Vázquez, an oncologist by profession.[48]

The adopted regulations that form part of the anti-smoking policy were based on article 44 of the Constitution of Uruguay. This provision, in its first paragraph, declares that 'the State shall legislate in all matters relating to public health and hygiene, seeking the physical, moral and social improvement of all inhabitants'. Thus, in the understanding that the Constitution imposes on the State the obligation to ensure the health of its inhabitants and to legislate – in a broad sense – in this area, from September 2005 to the end of 2019, a number of resolutions, decrees and laws were adopted which constitute the policy under analysis. The explicit justification of the policy in section 44 of the Constitution is not a minor fact if one takes into account that, precisely when in 2010 Philip Morris sued Uruguay before the ICSID, the argument of health protection would be one of the main arguments invoked by the state's defence.

Although the Uruguayan Constitution does not expressly refer to the 'right to health', it is generally accepted by the doctrine and jurisprudence that this right arises from constitutional systematic reading and further developments of the concept of 'health' or the 'right to health'.[49] Furthermore, international standards have constitutional rank through the provision of section 72 of the national Constitution. Among these norms is article 12 of the ICESCR, which requires the States parties' to provide for (1) the reduction of stillbirth and infant mortality, and the healthy development of children; (2) the improvement in all aspects of the hygiene of work and the environment; (3) prevention and treatment of epidemic, endemic, occupational and other diseases, and the fight against them; and (4) the creation of conditions that assure everyone medical assistance

47 Sica & others (n 45).

48 F González Mora & M Barbero Portela 'El control del tabaco en Uruguay en perspectiva histórica' (2020) http://cardiosalud.org/wp-content/uploads/2020/02/El_control_del_tabaco_en_Uruguay_web_final.pdf (accessed 6 September 2021).

49 HL Fuenzalida-Puelma & SS Connor 'El derecho a la salud en las Américas: Estudio constitucional comparado' (1989) 509 *OPS Publicación Científica*.

and medical services in case of illness.[50] On the other hand, Law 9.202 of 12 January 1934 commits the Ministry of Public Health to the adoption of all the necessary measures to maintain collective health, and their execution by the personnel under their command, issuing all the regulations and provisions necessary for that primary purpose, to tend by all means to health education of the people and control drugs, among other functions.

The foundational regulatory act of Uruguayan domestic policy on tobacco smoking and exposure was Executive Decree 268/2005 of 5 September 2005. In this Decree, the government materialised some of the commitments adopted with the ratification of the FCTC. The decree stipulated that 'all enclosed public premises and all work areas, whether in the public or private sphere intended for the common use of persons, must be 100% smoke-free environments'. Since the entry into force of this standard, on 1 March 2006, Uruguay had become the first tobacco smoke–free state in the Americas and the seventh in the world.[51]

This was followed on 6 March 2008 by the 'Protección del derecho al medio ambiente libre de humo de tabaco y su consumo' (Protection of the Right to a Smoke-Free Environment and Tobacco Consumption) Law 18,256, which banned all forms of advertising, promotion, sponsorship and display of tobacco products, except at strictly determined points of sale. This law was later modified by Law 19,244 – 'Advertising, Promotion and Sponsorship of Tobacco Products' – of 2 September 2014, extending the total ban on tobacco product advertising also to points of sale.

Law 18,256 has a leading role in the tobacco control policy. Regulating article 44 of the Constitution, it enshrined in Uruguay's legislation the right of all persons

> to the enjoyment of the highest possible level of health, to improvement in all aspects of occupational and environmental hygiene, and to the prevention, treatment and rehabilitation of diseases, in accordance with the provisions of various international conventions, covenants, declarations, protocols and agreements ratified by law.

Likewise, in section 2 it established that the regulation contained in the law is of public order, which legally implies that it cannot be modified by agreement between private parties. On the other hand, the law explains that its purpose is 'to protect the country's inhabitants from the devastating health, social, environmental and economic consequences of tobacco consumption and exposure to tobacco smoke', seeking through the regulation of tobacco consumption 'to

50 M Risso 'Derecho Constitucional' Montevideo: FCU (2006) 741.

51 T Vázquez 'Discurso ante la 64° Asamblea General de la Organización de Naciones Unidas, 23 de setiembre de 2009' http://uruguayescribe.com/2009/09/23/discurso-del-presidente-dr-tabare-vazquez-En-la-onu-el-23-setiembre-2009/ (accessed 7 September 2021).

continuously and substantially reduce the prevalence of tobacco consumption and exposure to tobacco smoke, in accordance with the provisions of the World Health Organization's Framework Convention on Tobacco Control'.

In line with the bans on smoking in enclosed spaces, the Ministry of Health (MoH) adopted a series of guidelines for tackling smoking in healthcare services (produced in 2010) and campaigns aimed at the population seeking to reduce the percentage of people exposed to tobacco smoke in their own homes.[52]

In addition, manufacturers and importers of tobacco products were required by the law to provide the Ministry of Public Health, under the conditions laid down in the regulations, with any information deemed necessary concerning the content and emissions of tobacco products. In this regard, it was provided that manufacturers and importers of tobacco products sold in the country are obliged to disseminate information on the toxic components of tobacco products and the emissions that they may produce, every three months, in the main media, in accordance with the regulations.

The measures of the law were reinforced by the sanctioning of two ordinances and a decree of the Ministry of Public Health. First, the Ordinance of the Ministry of Public Health 514/008 of 18 August 2008 required the use of pictograms consisting of five images combined with five statements to be imposed on 50 per cent of the relevant areas (lower half) of all cigarette and tobacco product packs. Section 3 of the ordinance required each brand of tobacco products to have a unique presentation (eliminating misleading brand descriptors such as 'light', 'ultra-light', 'mild' or 'low tar'), thus prohibiting the use of multiple presentations of any brand of cigarettes. Tobacco companies could only market one variant for each family of brands.

Decree 287/009 of 15 June 2009 and Ordinance 466/009 of 1 September 2009 established the so-called 'Rule 80/80'. It imposed the mandatory use of health warnings in the form of pictograms on 80 per cent of the front and back of the box that clearly illustrate the harmful effects of tobacco consumption. Both measures implemented article 11 of the FCTC.

In 2019, through Decree 120/2019, the Executive Branch regulated article 8 of Law 18,256 with respect to neutral or generic packaging and labelling of all tobacco products and cigarettes. This reinforced existing regulations by introducing exhaustive information on the specifications of product packaging, including the inside of the product and the colour of the cigarette wrapper. In this regard, it was provided that 'the color of all tobacco product packaging shall be unique, uniform and correspond to Pantone 448C with a matte finish (equivalent to RGB 74 65 42)'. The decree also provided that

> each trade mark on neutral or generic packaging must correspond to a single presentation of tobacco products, and the use of terms, descriptive elements, figurative signs, logos or other distinctive signs, such as combinations

52 González Mora & Barbero Portela (n 48).

of numbers or letters which have the direct or indirect effect of creating the false impression that a particular product is less harmful than others, is prohibited.

Finally, it should be noted that, in addition to actions linked to advertising and packaging restrictions, as well as the banning of smoking in certain spaces, the Uruguayan State increased indirect taxes on tobacco products on several occasions. In 2007, value added tax was applied to tobacco products, and in 2009 and 2010, the specific internal tax (IMESI) was raised. Interestingly, however, tobacco companies moderated their prices during this period. Indeed, in response to the measures adopted by the country and in an effort to maintain the price for the consumer, tobacco companies decreased their earning margin. Therefore, since 2010 the real price has fallen as a result of a policy that kept the IMESI rate and an annual inflation of approximately 8 per cent.[53]

In October 2017, President Vázquez announced that his government would introduce plain packaging legislation, becoming the seventh country to do so, following Australia, UK, Ireland, France, Norway and Hungary.[54] In 2017, the Vázquez administration extended the indoor ban on smoking to e-cigarettes and similar products.

The tobacco control measures implemented in Uruguay quickly made the country an example to follow in the fight against the tobacco epidemic.[55] The country has been recognised by a wide range of actors, personalities from the political, academic and trade union spheres. In this sense, according to the opinion of the expert regional advisor of the Pan American Health Organization/WHO on tobacco control, the difference of the Uruguayan process with respect to other experiences can be found in the rapidity of the advances in relation to tobacco control.[56] Table 11.1 is a summary of the MPOWER policy package and the corresponding policies adopted at the national level.

53 P Triunfo, J Harris & A Balsa 'Evaluación de la campaña antitabaco en Uruguay: balance de diez años y desafíos' (2016) 40 *Rev Panam Salud Pública* 256.

54 Tobacco Free Union 'Uruguay becomes the first country to require plain packaging of tobacco products in Latin America' (9 August 2018) https://www.tobaccofreeunion.org/index.php/news-2/468-uruguay-becomes-the-first-country-to-require-plain-packaging-of-tobacco-products-in-latin-america (accessed 10 September 2021). Campaign for Tobacco Free Kids 'Uruguay becomes first country in Latin America to adopt plain packaging' (16 January 2019) https://www.tobaccofreekids.org/press-releases/2019_01_16_uruguay (accessed 3 October 2021).

55 G Heydari 'Which countries are the best in tobacco control? A quantitative analysis of the MPOWER 2017' (2019) 3 *Journal of Global Health Reports* e2019039.

56 González Mora & Barbero Portela (n 48).

Table 11.1 Summary of the MPOWER policy package and corresponding national policy

MPOWER Policy	*Uruguay's National Policies*
Monitoring tobacco use and prevention policies	Uruguay has a strong infrastructure for conducting ongoing monitoring of tobacco use (Law 18,256 and Law 19,244). The Global Adult Tobacco Survey was implemented in 2009 and 2017, and the Global Youth Tobacco Survey was implemented in 2000, 2007 and 2014.
Protecting people from tobacco smoke	100% smoke-free national policy (Executive Decree 268/2005). Sales to minors (under 18) are prohibited (Law 18,256 and Law 19,244).
Offering help to quit tobacco use	The MoH adopted a series of guidelines for tackling smoking in healthcare services (produced in 2010) and campaigns aimed at the population seeking to reduce the percentage of people exposed to tobacco smoke in their own homes (Law 18,256 and Law 19,244). National toll-free quit-line available. Cessation services are generally available and covered by general insurance/ public services (Law 18,256 and Law 19,244).
Warning about the dangers of tobacco	One of the authorised pictures and accompanying text warnings must be displayed on 80 per cent of the two principal display areas of each tobacco product package. Warnings must be distributed evenly across each brand, and new warnings are to be issued every 12 months. Six new graphic images appeared on packs in February 2010, covering the lower 80 per cent of both principal display areas of all tobacco packages. Misleading packaging and labelling, including terms such as 'light' and 'low tar' and other signs, is prohibited (Law 18,256 and Law 19,244, Ordinance of the Ministry of Public Health No. 514/008 of 18 August 2008, Decree 287/009 of 15 June 2009, Ordinance 466/009 of 01 September 2009). Total ban on tobacco promotion and sponsorship and outlawed most tobacco advertising except at the point of sale, with a requirement that health warnings of equivalent size and visibility appear alongside in-store tobacco displays. The colour of all cigarette packages will be uniform (Law 18,256 and Law 19,244]).
Enforcing bans on tobacco advertising, promotion and sponsorship	Uruguay's law bans all forms of tobacco advertising, promotion, and sponsorship, except for advertising and displays of tobacco products in stores (Law 18,256 and Law 19,244).
Raising taxes on tobacco products	Taxes were raised in several occasions since 2005 (Executive Decree 268/2005 and updates). However, other countries in the Americas have much higher taxes (Chile, Cuba and Venezuela).

Furthermore, the ICSID decision in the framework of the *Philip Morris v Uruguay* case in 2016, which will be analysed below, together with the impact of the policy on smoking reduction from its implementation to date, consolidated the success of what is currently considered a true state commitment to the fight against tobacco.

11.3.3 Uruguay as an experiment for international arbitration

In 2010, one of the largest transnational tobacco companies, Philip Morris Brand Sàrl (Suiza), Philip Morris Products SA (Suiza) y Abal Hnos SA (Uruguay), launched an arbitration under the Bilateral Investment Treaty (BIT) against Uruguay's tobacco control measures: (1) increasing the size of health warnings to 80 per cent of each package and (2) requiring a 'single presentation' – one variant per brand family. The claim consisted in the annulment of the provisions of domestic law governing the measures attacked, and the sum of $22.267 million was claimed as compensation, plus compound interest to be accrued from the date of the violation to the date of payment.

However, the arbitration was preceded by various proceedings in the Uruguayan domestic jurisdiction.

11.3.3.1 Domestic proceedings

First, on 11 September 2009, Abal filed an appeal of unconstitutionality before the Supreme Court of Justice (SCJ), which questioned the constitutionality of sections 9 and 24 of Law 18,256. The basis of Abal's action lay in the consideration that through those provisions, the Law gave the Executive Branch the power to require tobacco product manufacturers to place health warnings, occupying 'at least 50%' of the total main exposed surfaces of tobacco packages. To the extent that such powers were granted in an unlimited manner, constitutionally protected individual rights were violated, since such power is constitutionally reserved to the Law exclusively and cannot be delegated to the Executive Branch. According to Abal, the law delegated to the Executive Branch the unlimited power to reduce, distort and even eliminate the possibility of Abal SA to use its trademarks on its packages, when it simply allowed to require that the warnings occupy 80, 90 or 100 per cent of the packages. It claimed that such provisions deprived it of its right to use the surfaces of its packages, thus affecting the right of ownership and expropriating the use of the brand without fair compensation.

Second, and in conjunction with the proceeding of unconstitutionality before the SCJ, in March 2010 Abal filed a nullity action before the Contentious Administrative Court (TCA), requesting the annulment of requirement 80/80 contemplated in Ordinance 466 and Decree 287/00922. The basis of the appeal was that the scope of the above-mentioned regulations exceeded the scope established by Law 18,256. The TCA decided to suspend the proceedings until the

Supreme Court had ruled on the constitutional challenge, on the understanding that this decision included a 'prior issue'.[57]

On 10 November 2010, the SCJ issued Ruling 1713/2010 from which it unanimously decided to dismiss the action of unconstitutionality promoted, since it did not find that the contested provision granted unlimited powers to the Executive Branch to restrict individual rights in contravention of constitutional provisions. In this ruling, the SCJ clarified that the approval of

> Law No. 18.256 has its raison d'être in the development of a health policy carried out by the State, deepening the campaign against smoking and recognizes its immediate legal precedent in the sanctioning of Law No. 17.793 approving the World Health Organization Framework Convention on Tobacco Control (FCTC), adopted by the 56th World Health Assembly on 21 May 2003, which instructed on effective measures to ensure that all packages bear the legend of health warnings describing the harmful effect of tobacco consumption. Article 11 of the said Convention gives the main features set out by the legislator in the rules in question.

The SCJ added that

> public health is an essential task inherent in the State, and in cases such as this one, the legislation on smoking is a superior legal asset that participates in the notion of public order (article 44 of the Constitution), and it is therefore only natural that the Ministry of Public Health should be required to adopt such regulations, since under the Public Health Organization Act No. 9,202 it is incumbent on the Ministry to take all the measures it deems necessary to maintain collective health, issuing all the regulations and provisions required for this primary purpose (article 2).[58]

Specifically, with regard to the object of Abal's complaint, the SCJ expressed that a simple reading of the contested provisions shows that Parliament did not delegate competence, but on the contrary, following the anti-tobacco legislation assumed internationally by the country, it focused on the dictation of the relevant norms in the national sphere. It does not delegate to the Executive Branch a discretionary power to impose restrictions above this minimum, but imposes on the tobacco industry the obligation that the external labelling of packages should contain a warning occupying 'at least 50%' of the total main areas exposed and clarifies that the text of the rule 'at least' should be understood in the sense that the health warning could take up more space – if the tobacco industry so wished – but never less than the minimum set at 50 per cent. According to the Court,

57 Uruguay, Tribunal de lo Contencioso Administrativo (TCA), Res No 132/2010, 3 May 2010.

58 Uruguay, Suprema Corte de Justicia (SCJ), Sent No 1713/2010, 10 Nov 2010.

the only thing that the norm leaves to the Executive Branch (*Ministerio de Salud Pública* or MoH) is to control that the warnings and messages are clear, visible, legible and occupy at least 50 per cent of the total main surfaces exposed, as well as the periodic modification of the warnings referred to, an aspect that clearly refers to the message and not to the size of them.

Once the decision of the SCJ was issued, the suspension of the nullity process presented by Abal before the TCA was lifted and the court issued the ruling. The TCA rejected the challenge presented, stating:

> The WHO Framework Convention on Tobacco Control consists of a preamble and 38 articles. The first article explicitly states that smoking is an epidemic with serious global health consequences, while '. . . cigarettes and some other products containing tobacco are designed in a very sophisticated way to create and maintain dependence . . .', in that respect the provisions of the Convention seek to regulate the warnings on cigarette boxes so that the population has access to accurate information about the chemicals they are ingesting and consuming. For this reason, Law 18.256 is directly and frankly in line with international provisions, legislating and regulating the provisions of the Convention, in compliance with the obligations to humanity and the international community that the Republic of Uruguay has adopted. Thus, Law 18.256 clearly marks the legal minimum of the warning and entrusts the regulation with its extension and/or change, whose evident purpose is that the consumer does not become familiar with and live with it without perceiving the pernicious consequences attributable to tobacco products.[59]

It follows from the two decisions that the TCA's interpretation of section 9 of Law 18,256 appears to be contrary to the SCJ's previous interpretation that the provision did not authorise the requirement of graphic warnings covering more than 50 per cent of the surface of the packages of tobacco products. On the contrary, the TCA understood that this provision authorised precisely this result, providing the authorisation to configure the 80 per cent requirement contemplated in Decree 287/009 and Ordinance 466.

In this sense, despite the fact that the two courts rejected the actions brought by Abal, there was a clear contradiction between the interpretation that each one made of article 9 of Law 18,256. Thus, while the SCJ understood that the legislative provision simply established the minimum space that the warnings should occupy, with the rest of the administrative decision being subject to challenge before the TCA, the latter interpreted that it is precisely the legal provision that allows the 80 per cent requirement to be reached. This contradiction was one of the issues that later, in the arbitration, Philip Morris alleged as 'denial of justice', which was in fact rejected by ICSID.

59 Uruguay, Tribunal de lo Contencioso Administrativo, Sent. No 512/2012, 28 de agosto de 2012.

As Bas Vilizzio and Michelini point out, the Court noted that 'international investment tribunals cannot operate as an appeal court for the judgments of national courts or tribunals'. It also considered that the trato justo y equitativo-equal and fair treatment can be violated when there is a denial of justice; however, to make a complaint of denial of justice, one must first go through all the measures established by the country's judiciary, and 'there must be clear evidence of . . . an outrageous failure of the judicial system' or a demonstration of 'systemic injustice' or that the 'contested judgment was clearly wrong and open to criticism', which should have been proven by the petitioners. On the judgments of the SCJ and the TCA, the Court refers to the same judgments where it is stated that they are not obliged to have the same criteria, and that each of them circumvents its jurisdiction independently. In a way, the Court recognised that this institutional design, which allows for different rulings in the Uruguayan system, is unusual but in line with the tradition of Continental Law. On this point, the Court understood that there is no denial of justice given that the applicants enjoyed the opportunities to be heard by a court, and there was a judicial body available that was competent to examine the challenge to the 80/80 requirement and that issued a well-founded decision. And it noted that the fact that there is no other remedy against the TCA ruling, which did not follow the reasoning of the SCJ, seems to be a peculiarity of the Uruguayan judicial system. In sum, the majority of the court held that 'there was no denial of justice with respect to the processes of the Regulation of 80/80'.[60]

After this ruling, to date there have not been other constitutional processes against Article 9 of Law 18,256. Three years after ruling 1713/2010, Monte Paz SA (a local tobacco company) filed an appeal of unconstitutionality against article 18 of Law 18,256 (which determines the subjects responsible for the infractions determined by law in relation to the advertising of tobacco products). In ruling 696/2014, the SCJ dismissed the appeal by majority using the same reasons as in ruling 1713/2010, and referred to its reasoning there.

11.3.3.2 Philip Morris v Uruguay (ICSID)

This case had a great impact at the regional level and caught the attention of the entire tobacco control community worldwide. This was especially because Uruguay did not represent a big market for Phillip Morris, so the purpose of the claim was only to intimidate and push the government to refrain from adopting more restrictive tobacco control measures.

On 8 July 2016, the ICSID released its decision. On the merits, the Tribunal ruled in favour of Uruguay with respect to all claims, and the decision became ground-breaking as it protected public health policies over commercial interests. The award issued by the Tribunal included some relevant arguments that are

60 M Bas Vilizzio & F Michelini *Arbitraje de inversiones y derechos humanos: Un análisis particular del caso Philip Morris contra Uruguay* (2017) 103.

worth highlighting, especially when discussing trade arguments versus tobacco control regulations.

Philip Morris argued that the measures adopted by Uruguay constituted a violation to its trademark rights as they restricted their right to use granted trademarks. In that regard, the Tribunal stated that ownership of a trademark does, in certain circumstances, grant a right to use it. However, it is a right of use that exists vis-à-vis other persons – an exclusive right, but a relative one. The arbitrators recognised that a trademark right is not an absolute right to use that can be asserted against the state qua regulator.

> 271. The Tribunal concludes that under Uruguayan law or international conventions to which Uruguay is a party the trademark holder does not enjoy an absolute right of use, free of regulation, but only an exclusive right to exclude third parties from the market so that only the trademark holder has the possibility to use the trademark in commerce, subject to the State's regulatory power.

In addition, Philip Morris claimed that Uruguay had expropriated its investments in the country. The claimants affirmed that their business would have been more profitable if Uruguay had not adopted the challenged measures.

> 286. In the Tribunal's view, in respect of a claim based on indirect expropriation, as long as sufficient value remains after the Challenged Measures are implemented, there is no expropriation. As confirmed by investment treaty decisions, a partial loss of the profits that the investment would have yielded absent the measure does not confer an expropriatory character on the measure.

The tribunal recognised that regulatory authorities enjoy a 'margin of appreciation' when making public policy determinations in contexts involving health rights and the public's health.

> 399. The Tribunal agrees with the Respondent that the 'margin of appreciation' . . . 'applies equally to claims arising under BITs', at least in contexts such as public health. The responsibility for public health measures rests with the government and investment tribunals should pay great deference to governmental judgments of national needs in matters such as the protection of public health. In such cases respect is due to the 'discretionary exercise of sovereign power, not made irrationally and not exercised in bad faith . . . involving many complex factors'.

Furthermore, the Tribunal concluded that the Challenged Measures were a valid exercise by Uruguay of its police powers for the protection of public health. Protecting public health has long since been recognised as an essential manifestation of the state's police power. The principle that the state's reasonable bona fide exercise of police powers in such matters as the maintenance of public order, health or morality, excludes compensation even when it causes economic damage to an investor and that the measures taken for that purpose should not be considered as expropriatory.

The Challenged Measures were both adopted in good faith and were non-discriminatory. They were proportionate to the objective they meant to achieve, quite apart from their limited adverse impact on Philip Morris' business. The Challenged Measures were not 'arbitrary and unnecessary' but rather were potentially 'effective means to protecting public health'.

In addition to the points highlighted above, the discussion carried out by the Tribunal on the scientific evidence on which Uruguay based the adoption of its measures and their effectiveness is extremely relevant. In this regard, the claimants stated that there was no record of measures similar to those adopted by Uruguay in other countries. They also stated that these measures were not based on the FCTC recommendations.

The Tribunal disregarded the need to assess whether the measures actually had the effects sought by the state or whether or not they were effective in addressing public perceptions about tobacco safety. According to the arbitrators, it is sufficient in light of the applicable standard to hold that the policies adopted by Uruguay 'were an attempt to address a real public health concern, that the measure taken was not disproportionate to that concern and that it was adopted in good faith' (para 409).

> 418. In the Tribunal's view, the present case concerns a legislative policy decision taken against the background of a strong scientific consensus as to the lethal effects of tobacco. Substantial deference is due in that regard to national authorities' decisions as to the measures which should be taken to address an acknowledged and major public health problem.
>
> 419. . . . How a government requires the acknowledged health risks of products, such as tobacco, to be communicated to the persons at risk, is a matter of public policy, to be left to the appreciation of the regulatory authority.

Finally, it is important to highlight how the Tribunal assessed the plaintiffs' claim regarding legal uncertainty. The Claimants considered that the decisions adopted by Uruguay affected their legitimate expectations and modified the regulatory conditions that existed at the time of the investment. On this regard, the Tribunal recognised:

> 429. . . . [T]he present case concerns the formulation of general regulations for the protection of public health. There is no question of any specific commitment of the State or of any legitimate expectation of the Claimants vis-à-vis Uruguayan tobacco control regulations. Manufacturers and distributors of harmful products such as cigarettes can have no expectation that new and more onerous regulations will not be imposed, and certainly no

> commitments of any kind were given by Uruguay to the Claimants or (as far as the record shows) to anyone else.
>
> 430. On the contrary, in light of widely accepted articulations of international concern for the harmful effect of tobacco, the expectation could only have been of progressively more stringent regulation of the sale and use of tobacco products. Nor is it a valid objection to a regulation that it breaks new ground. Provisions such as Article 3(2) of the BIT do not preclude governments from enacting novel rules, even if these are in advance of international practice, provided these have some rational basis and are not discriminatory. Article 3(2) does not guarantee that nothing should be done by the host State for the first time.

In conclusion, the case represented a fundamental move towards the protection of public health at the country level. The decision set a positive precedent for those states with the political will to move forward with more restrictive tobacco control measures.

Tobacco companies have used bilateral investment agreements and international trade agreements as a mechanism to hinder the advancement of tobacco control policies. For these reasons, the way in which the Tribunal addressed those issues provide an accurate legal analysis that confirms that tobacco control policies, per se, do not violate commercial agreements.

11.3.3.3 Corporate practices and the challenges posed to the tobacco control policies

The above-mentioned case fits into a larger pattern on corporate practices that demand a closer look and a vigilant stance when it comes to tobacco companies. Corporations and other non-state actors are not traditionally understood to be legally bound by international human rights obligations. However, in recent decades, globalisation and liberalisation of commerce have enabled corporations to influence international and domestic law-making while causing detrimental human rights impacts. Despite a few successful cases, for many years, the tobacco industry 'co-opted' the human rights discourse. In fact, most proactive human rights–based litigation has been initiated by the industry; the public health community has generally been less successful in invoking human rights in court.

Commercial actors, particularly tobacco companies, have a long history of deploying a broad range of tactics to block, delay or challenge government regulatory interventions. One of their most common tactics is to threaten legal action under international trade law (under the World Trade Organization Technical Barriers to Trade Agreement, but also under other regional, multilateral or bilateral trade agreements, such as the Trans-Pacific Partnership Agreement or the US-Mexico-Canada Agreement [formerly known as NAFTA]), international investment law or domestic law. Industry operators, taking advantage of their economic power and resources, have resorted to litigation or threatened litigation, which is likely to be lengthy and expensive, often arguing that the government's public health regulatory measures unjustifiably infringe on commercial and consumer rights. In *Philip Morris v Uruguay*, the legal costs ($27.2 million) exceeded the plaintiff's compensation claim.[61] Industry-led litigation, or a threat thereof, can exert a 'chilling effect' on governments seeking to adopt and implement laws to reduce NCDs risk factors. This behaviour, of course, is not confined only to the tobacco industry, but rather is part of a systematic playbook that corporations follow, including but not limited to those in the food and beverages, alcohol, fossil fuels, firearms and pharmaceuticals industries.[62]

To overcome challenges associated with industry litigation, governments need to anticipate, prepare and, ultimately, mitigate the risk of legal challenges. To that end, governments should ensure that there is a strong, legitimate public health objective for the measures adopted; ensure that evidence is robust and understand how the chosen regulatory measure will achieve the policy objectives identified; and engage legal, trade, human rights, investment and marketing government officials early on in the design and development of the measure to be able to understand the broader legal implications and ensure that due diligence is followed. As such, governments should counter industry interference and influence in public health decision-making processes and safeguard against conflicts of interest.

Robust policy design is key to ensure governments are well suited to mitigate industry's opposition. When the adoption of a regulatory measure results from such a process, industry litigation may actually yield results that reinforce the legality of the challenged measure and of public health interventions more broadly.[63]

It is important, especially in courts, to reclaim and clarify that there is no inherent conflict between tobacco control and human rights law. Furthermore, as mentioned, human rights law has historically had a prominent role in shaping political and policy discourses to the extent that once a relevant societal issue acquires the status of a human right, it has special consideration in public policy.

11.3.4 Evaluation of Uruguay's policies

There is a high degree of consensus that Uruguay's anti-smoking campaign significantly reduced the prevalence of smoking in the general population, as well as smoking among two key groups: young people and pregnant women. It has also managed to improve the health of the population, as evidenced by the increase

61 *Philip Morris Brands Sàrl v Oriental Republic of Uruguay* http://www.italaw.com/sites/default/files/case-documents/italaw7417.pdf (accessed 30 September 2021).

62 N Freudenberg 'Lethal but legal: Corporations, consumption, and protecting public health' (2014) 131.

63 O Cabrera & J Carballo 'Tobacco control litigation: Broader impacts on health rights adjudication' (2013) 41 *Journal of Law, Medicine & Ethics* 147.

in birth weight in children of smoking mothers who stopped smoking during pregnancy.[64]

According to the latest National Survey on Drug Use in the General Population (Encuesta Nacional sobre Consumo de Drogas en Población General) conducted in Uruguay, there is a clear downward trend in the prevalence of tobacco use in the last 12 months and in the last 30 days since 2006 (when considering the two indicators that most accurately account for current and habitual consumption of tobacco since they do not include former users, as in the case of life prevalence). The data available shows a slowdown from 2011, but the trend remains the same.[65]

Empirical data shows that the decrease is practically sustained by the younger population, which has shown a constant and significant decrease in consumption since 2006.[66] On the other hand, the older segment (36 to 65), after a decrease experienced between 2006 and 2011, reverts the trend and slightly increases the percentage of consumers. This last behaviour could be explained by the return to consumption of ex-smokers or the incorporation of the cohort of smokers from the previous age range and not so much by the incorporation of new smokers, since the average age of initiation is significantly lower. What is clear from this distribution is the greater difficulty in stopping smoking at ages close to young adults.

With regard to the behaviour of consumers disaggregated by sex, the National Survey on Drug Use reveals that the decrease is greater in men compared to women in the period 2006–2018.[67]

Regarding the impact of the policy on tobacco use during pregnancy, Triunfo et al. point out that before 2007, smoking habits of pregnant women were recorded at the beginning of prenatal care, which prevented the observation of changes in behaviour during pregnancy. Under a new system implemented from 2007, a woman's smoking habit begins to be recorded in each trimester of pregnancy. Under this new system, data were obtained for more than 250,000 births between 2007 and 2013, with approximately 30,000 women smokers. Between 2007 and 2013, the proportion of pregnant women who stopped smoking by the

64 P Triunfo & others (n 53); W Abascal & others 'Impact of the tobacco control policies. 2006–2009 National Program for Tobacco Control' (2011) http://www.scielo.edu.uy/scielo.php?script=sci_arttext&pid=S1688-423X2013000400001 (accessed 8 September 2021); La Diaria (Montevideo) 'En los últimos 13 años el consumo de tabaco en Uruguay ha tenido un descenso sostenido, pero todavía hay 500.000 personas con esta adicción' (2019) https://ladiaria.com.uy/salud/articulo/2019/5/en-los-ultimos-13-anos-el-consumo-de-tabaco-en-uruguay-ha-tenido-un-descenso-sostenido-pero-todavia-hay-500000-personas-con-esta-adiccion/ (accessed 7 September 2021).

65 Junta Nacional de Drogas 'VII Encuesta nacional sobre consumo de drogas en población general – 2018' (2020) https://www.gub.uy/junta-nacional-drogas/comunicacion/publicaciones/vii-encuesta-nacional-sobre-consumo-drogas-poblacion-general-2018 (accessed 3 September 2021).

66 As above.

67 As above.

third trimester increased markedly from 15.4 per cent to 42.7 per cent. Research reveals two aspects of Uruguay's comprehensive tobacco control policy. First, the measures show an overall decline from 2005 to 2018 with small variations in the period. Second, policies were implemented to improve the treatment of nicotine dependence in different health centres providing antenatal care. It was observed that, among women who had quit smoking in a previous pregnancy, 51.2 per cent remained non-smokers, while 48.8 per cent relapsed in the subsequent pregnancy. However, within the relapse group, the probability of quitting again was 41 per cent. Finally, the impact of quitting smoking during pregnancy on perinatal health, as measured by birth weight, was analysed and it was found that quitting smoking in the third trimester was associated with an increase of 188 grams in birth weight. Tobacco control measures had no effect on the birth weight of babies born to non-smoking women.

Moreover, another interesting indicator that shows the impact of the policy is the evolution of people's perception of the risks involved in tobacco consumption. According to the VII National Survey on Drug Use, the perception of risk associated with frequent tobacco consumption had a constant growth between 2006 and 2014. The survey shows a decrease in perception after 2014, which requires a vigilant attitude. In terms of the gender breakdown of these statistics, there is a much higher percentage of perception of risk among women than among men.[68]

There are also changes in the evolution of people exposed to second-hand smoke in the home. Research in the field of medicine has shown a relationship between passive smoking or second-hand smoke and coronary heart disease.[69] It is claimed that tobacco use has direct effects on smokers and their environments and that second-hand smoke mainly affects populations considered to be more vulnerable from a health point of view.[70]

There has been a significant decrease in the number of people exposed to second-hand tobacco smoke in the home since 2006, and especially since 2009.[71] In 2006, more than one-third of 14- to 64-year-olds resided in households where smoke exposure occurred at least once a week; by 2018, only 8 per 100 people were in this situation. The percentage of households with children and with smokers shows a declining trend if we take 2006 as a starting point. There are fewer (in relative terms) households with children under 10 years of age with a member who smokes, and fewer households in which people smoke inside. In this case, the ratio is also approximately 3 to 1, now between households with children who smoke and households with children who smoke inside. While it is not possible to pinpoint a single explanation for this decline, one might think

68 As above.

69 M Bas Vilizzio 'El caso Aratirí y las lecciones del arbitraje inversor-Estado' (2020) https://ladiaria.com.uy/opinion/articulo/2020/8/el-caso-aratiri-y-las-lecciones-del-arbitraje-inversor-estado/ (accessed 4 October 2021).

70 González Mora & Barbero Portela (n 48).

71 As above.

that this corresponds to the fact that smoking is no longer a socially accepted and naturalised practice. Adult smokers are encouraged not to smoke in the home and even to quit more frequently than a decade ago. These developments over the period suggest the importance of tobacco control policy in the domestic and private sphere.[72]

11.4 Final considerations

Uruguay's case shows both the great impact and the challenges faced by those taking bold steps towards tobacco control.

On the one hand, the impact of these public health measures on the general population health is undeniable. After only a decade of tobacco control policies, there have been significant positive changes on the health of the country both associated with tobacco use and exposure. Indeed, the policies adopted show a clear decrease in the number of people who begin to consume tobacco products and an increase in the number of smokers who quit smoking. The holistic approach that Uruguay took (pricing, taxation, ban on indoor smoke, among other measures) impacted the perception of the risk of use and exposure. For example, the perception of smokers about the risks of stroke and impotence increased after the introduction of graphic health warnings on cigarette packages.[73]

Uruguay has historically been one of the countries in Latin America with the highest prevalence of smoking, and in the last decade the policies adopted have had very positive outcomes. There is a point to be made here about the importance of evidence and human rights–based policies to tackle global health challenges[74] and how reducing the burden of tobacco smoking is possible using MPOWER evidence-based policies. It is crucial for the country, the region and more generally the world to take stock of the measures that are effective in addressing tobacco consumption, to ultimately reduce the burden of NCDs.

On the other hand, the country faced serious backlash for adopting tobacco control measures. Phillip Morris' complaint against Uruguay had a chilling effect in the entire region, which might have been the ultimate goal pursued by the company. Just to show the power dynamics present in this case, as a note about the power dynamics in this case, Philip Morris had gross revenues (US$64 billion) double that of Uruguay's GDP (US$32 billion) in 2010.[75] It is safe to say that the objective of the company was to intimidate the country for being a pioneer in the adoption of tobacco control policies but also to prevent other countries from following Uruguay's lead. And the strategy was successful from 2010, when

72 As above.

73 Blanco (n 44).

74 LO Gostin & others 'The legal determinants of health: Harnessing the power of law for global health and sustainable development' (2019) 393 *The Lancet* 1857.

75 The Center for Public Integrity 'PART III: Uruguay vs Philip Morris' (2014) https://publicintegrity.org/2010/11/15/4036/part-iii-uruguay-vs-philip-morris (accessed 7 September 2021).

the claim was filed, to 2016, when the Tribunal issued its decision. During that period, only a few countries in the region moved towards the adoption of tobacco control measures, probably out of fear of being sued by the tobacco industry.

It is increasingly clear that governments must take bold action to prevent and tackle NCDs. By adopting strong tobacco control measures and resisting the tobacco companies' efforts to dismantle them, Uruguay paved the way for other countries to follow suit.

Bibliography

Abascal, W; Esteves, E; Goja, B; González Mora, F; Lorenzo, A; Sica, A; Triunfo, P & Harris, JE 'Impact of the tobacco control policies. 2006–2009 national program for tobacco control' (2011) http://www.scielo.edu.uy/scielo.php?script=sci_arttext&pid=S1688-423X2013000400001 (accessed 8 September 2021)

Amos, A 'How women are targeted by the tobacco industry' (1990) 11 *World Health Forum* 416

Amos, A; Greaves, L; Nichter, M & Bloch, M 'Women and tobacco: A call for including gender in tobacco control research, policy and practice' (2012) 21 *Tobacco Control* 236

Amos, A & Haglund, M 'From social taboo to "torch of freedom": The marketing of cigarettes to women' (2000) 9 *Tobacco Control* 3

Bardach, A; Perdomo, HAG; Gándara, RAR & Ciapponi, A 'Niveles de ingreso y prevalencia de tabaquismo en América Latina: revisión sistemática y metaanálisis' (2016) 40 *Rev Panam Salud Publica* 263

Bas Vilizzio, M 'El caso Aratirí y las lecciones del arbitraje inversor-Estado' (2020) https://ladiaria.com.uy/opinion/articulo/2020/8/el-caso-aratiri-y-las-lecciones-del-arbitraje-inversor-estado/ (accessed 4 October 2021)

Bas Vilizzio, M & Michelini, F *Arbitraje de inversiones y derechos humanos: Un análisis particular del caso Philip Morris contra Uruguay* (CSIC UDELAR 2017)

Bianco, E; Champagne, B & Barnoya, J 'The tobacco epidemic in Latin America and the Caribbean: A snapshot' (2005) 1 *Prevention and Control* 311

Bollyky, TJ & Gostin, LO 'The United States' engagement in global tobacco control: Proposals for comprehensive funding and strategies' (2010) 304 *JAMA* 2637

Cabrera, O & Carballo, J 'Tobacco control litigation: Broader impacts on health rights adjudication' (2013) 41 *Journal of Law, Medicine & Ethics* 147

Cassinelli Muñoz, H *'Uruguay' en El derecho a la salud en las Américas estudio constitucional comparado* (OPS 1989)

Champagne, BM; Sebrié, E & Schoj, V 'The role of organized civil society in tobacco control in Latin America and the Caribbean' (2010) 52 *Salud publica de Mexico* 330

Dresler, C; Lando, H; Schneider, N & Sehgal, H 'Human rights-based approach to tobacco control' (2012) 21 *Tobacco Control* 208

Dresler, C & Marks, S 'The emerging human right to tobacco control' (2006) 28 *Human Rights Quarterly* 599

González Mora, F & Barbero Portela, M 'El control del tabaco en Uruguay en perspectiva histórica' (2020) *Montevideo Comisión Honoraria para la Salud Cardiovascular/Ministerio de Salud* http://cardiosalud.org/wp-content/uploads/2020/02/El_control_del_tabaco_en_Uruguay_web_final.pdf (accessed 6 September 2021)

Gostin, LO; Monahan, JT; Kaldor, J; DeBartolo, M; Friedman, EA; Gottschalk, K; Kim, SC; Alwan, A; Binagwaho, A; Burci, GL; Cabal, L; DeLand, K; Evans, TG; Goosby, E; Hossain, S; Koh, H; Ooms, G; Periago, MR; Uprimny, R & Yamin, AE 'The legal determinants of health: Harnessing the power of law for global health and sustainable development' (2019) 393 *The Lancet* 1857

Heydari, G 'Which countries are the best in tobacco control? A quantitative analysis of the MPOWER 2017' (2019) 3 *Journal of Global Health Reports*

Junta Nacional de Drogas 'VII Encuesta nacional sobre consumo de drogas en población general – 2018' (2020) https://www.gub.uy/junta-nacional-drogas/comunicacion/publicaciones/vii-encuesta-nacional-sobre-consumo-drogas-poblacion-general-2018 (accessed 3 September 2021)

Kalkhoran, S; Sebrié, EM; Sandoya, E & Glantz, SA 'Effect of Uruguay's national 100% smokefree law on emergency visits for bronchospasm' (2015) 49 *American Journal of Preventive Medicine* 85

La Diaria Salud 'En los últimos 13 años el consumo de tabaco en Uruguay ha tenido un descenso sostenido, pero todavía hay 500.000 personas con esta adicción' (2019) https://ladiaria.com.uy/salud/articulo/2019/5/en-los-ultimos-13-anos-el-consumo-de-tabaco-en-uruguay-ha-tenido-un-descenso-sostenido-pero-todavia-hay-500000-personas-con-esta-adiccion/ (accessed 7 September 2021)

Ministry of Public Health 'Interpellations and responses to non-communicable diseases in Uruguay: Update document on the situation of NCDs in Uruguay' (December 2018) https://www.paho.org/uru/index.php?option=com_docman&view=download&slug=interpellations-and-responses-to-non-communicable-diseases-in-uruguay&Itemid=307 (accessed 15 September 2021)

Orginaización Panamericana de la Salud 'Uruguay demuestra nivel de cumplimiento de Convenio Marco con oms' https://www.paho.org/uru/index.php?option=com_content&view=article&id=366:uruguay-demuestra-nivel-cumplimiento-convenio-marco-oms&Itemid=238 (accessed 13 September 2021)

Pan American Health Organisation *Report on tobacco control for the region of the America. WHO framework convention on tobacco control: 10 years later* (2016)

Pan American Health Organisation 'WHO report finds dramatic increase in life-saving tobacco control policies in last decade' (2017) https://www.paho.org/hq/index.php?option=com_content&view=article&id=13496:who-report-finds-dramatic-increase-in-life-saving-tobacco-control-policies-in-last-decade&Itemid=135&lang=pt (accessed 7 September 2021)

Philip Morris Brands Sàrl et al. v Oriental Republic of Uruguay ICSID Case No ARB/10/7 https://www.italaw.com/cases/460 (accessed 4 October 2021)

Pichon-Riviere, A; Bardach, A; Augustovski, F; Alcaraz, A; Reynales-Shigematsu, LM; Pinto, MT; Castillo, M; Riquelme, M; Torres, EP; Osorio, DI; Hauyanay, L; Munarriz, CL; Sáenz de Miera-Juárez, B; Gallegos-Rivero, V; De la Puente, C; Navia-Bueno, MDP & Caporale, J 'Economic impact of smoking on health systems in Latin America: A study of seven countries and its extrapolation to the regional level' (2016) 40 *Pan American Journal of Public Health* 213

Risso, M *Derecho Constitucional* (FCU 2006)

Samet, JM; Yoon, SY & WHO Tobacco Free Initiative *Women and the Tobacco Epidemic: Challenges for the 21st Century* (WHO 2011)

Schargrodsky, H; Hernández-Hernández, R; Champagne et al. 'CARMELA: Assessment of cardiovascular risk in seven Latin American cities' (2008) 121 *American Journal of Medicine* 58

Sica, A; Mora, FG & Abascal, W 'Políticas de control del tabaquismo en Uruguay' in *Prevención de factores de riesgo de la salud en América Latina y el Caribe: gobernanza de cinco esfuerzos multisectoriales* (World Bank 2005) https://documents1.worldbank.org/curated/es/901881468279333864/pdf/878210WP0SPANI0o0de0la0salud0en0LAC.pdf (accessed 4 October 2021)

Sosa Liprandi, M 'Causes of death in women and the trend over the last 23 years in Argentina' (2006) 74 *Argentine Journal of Cardiology* 297

The Tobacco Atlas 'Nearly 70 million smokers in Latin America are at risk of tobacco-related death and disease' (2018) https://web.archive.org/web/20200228135136/https:/tobaccoatlas.org/2018/11/13/nearly-70-million-smokers-in-latin-america-are-at-risk-of-tobacco-related-death-and-disease/ (accessed 3 October 2021)

Toebes, B 'The value of a human rights-based approach to tobacco control' (2018) 4 *Tobacco Prevention & Cessation* A66

Triunfo, P; Harris, J & Balsa, A 'Evaluation of Uruguay's antismoking campaign: Progress and challenges at ten years' (2016) 40 *Revista Panamericana de Salud Publica* 256

UN Development Programme *Briefing note for countries on the 2016 Human Development Report* (2016)

Urrutia-Pereira, M; Solé, D; Chong Neto, HJ; Badellino, H; Acosta, V; Castro-Almarales, RL; León, MG; Avalos, MM; Fernández, CC; Sisul-Alvariza, JC; Oliano, VJ & Rinelli, PN 'Youth tobacco use in Latin America: What is the real extent of the problem?' (2019) 47 *Allergologia et immunopathologia* 328

Vázquez, T 'Discurso ante la 64° Asamblea General de la Organización de Naciones Unidas, 23 de setiembre de 2009'

WHO *Framework Convention on Tobacco Control* (WHO 2005)

WHO 'Tobacco and poverty: A vicious circle' (2004) https://apps.who.int/iris/handle/10665/116428 (accessed 14 September 2021)

12 Tobacco, health and regulations in India

A national overview

Upendra Bhojani, Riddhi Dsouza, Pragati Hebbar, Adhip Amin and Amiti Varma

12.1 Introduction

This chapter provides an analysis of legal developments concerning tobacco control in India. We write this chapter as people concerned about the public health implications of tobacco, bringing together expertise in public health, law and implementation science. We start by highlighting epidemiological transition in India with a high burden of non-communicable diseases (NCDs) that are the leading cause of deaths and disabilities in India. We implicate tobacco use as a significant driver of this burden and situate tobacco within India's public health and economic scene. We then describe historically and chronologically the legal developments concerning tobacco control, primarily at the national level but also flagging significant measures at the sub-national level, from the 1970s to 2020. We highlight the context in which these legal measures evolved and shaped the legal trajectory. India was among the earlier countries to sign and fully ratify the World Health Organization (WHO) Framework Convention on Tobacco Control (FCTC) in 2004. We compare the Indian law with key regulatory provisions of the Convention, highlighting some of the best practices from India, as well as areas that need further regulatory and administrative actions. We frame tobacco control in a broader discourse around health and human rights and examine the implications of India's international commitments for the prevailing tobacco control regulations. We then focus on the implementation of these legal measures. We use data from large-scale surveys as well as country reports to the FCTC Secretariat to analyse compliance with the prevailing regulations while identifying the gaps. Finally, we discuss select case law to understand the role of litigations in shaping tobacco control regulations and their implementation in India. We make concluding remarks summarising the key observations from various sections of this chapter and providing the way forward.

12.2 Disease and economic burden

In this section, we highlight the epidemiologic transition in India, outlining the disease and economic burden from NCDs and from tobacco use.

DOI: 10.4324/9781003264248-15

12.2.1 The burden of NCDs

NCDs are a leading cause of illness and death globally, accounting for 71 per cent or 40.5 million of all deaths in 2016.[1] In India, NCDs accounted for 63 per cent or over 5.9 million of all deaths in 2016. About 23 per cent of the population aged 30–70 years is at risk of premature death.[2] A majority of NCDs are chronic conditions requiring long-term management. Nearly 80 per cent of all the deaths from chronic conditions worldwide occur in low- and middle-income countries.[3]

In India, while the overall burden of communicable diseases has comparatively reduced over time, some of these diseases still exert a high burden leading to a dual burden of diseases in India. The study of the burden of diseases in India reveals a clear epidemiological transition over time. The proportion of all the deaths due to NCDs rose from 37.9 per cent in 1990 to 61.8 per cent in 2016.[4] Similarly, the proportion of overall disability-adjusted life years (a measure combining health loss due to premature death as well as disability suffered from the disease) due to NCDs rose from 30.5 per cent in 1990 to 55.4 per cent in 2016.[5] Within NCDs, the leading contributors of the overall DALYs include cardiovascular diseases (14.1 per cent), chronic respiratory diseases (6.4 per cent), mental health and substance use disorders (5.6 per cent), diabetes, blood and endocrine diseases (5.6 per cent) and cancers (5 per cent).[6] Among the overall deaths due to NCDs in India, the leading contributors include cardiovascular diseases (28.1 per cent), chronic respiratory diseases (10.9 per cent), cancers (8.3 per cent) and diabetes, blood and endocrine diseases (6.5 per cent).[7] NCDs are estimated to pose a huge economic burden. It has been estimated that the major NCDs including cardiovascular diseases, chronic respiratory diseases, cancers, diabetes and mental health conditions would cost India about US$2.3 trillion from 2011 through 2030, which would be nearly 35 times the total annual health spending in the country.[8]

12.2.2 The burden of tobacco use

Major NCDs have some behavioural risk factors in common including tobacco use, harmful use of alcohol, unhealthy diet and lack of adequate physical activity.

1 WHO 'NCD mortality and morbidity' https://www.who.int/gho/ncd/mortality_morbidity/en/ (accessed 30 August 2020).
2 WHO 'Noncommunicable diseases (NCD) country profiles – India (2018)' https://www.who.int/nmh/countries/2018/ind_en.pdf?ua (accessed 10 August 2020).
3 K Strong & others 'Preventing chronic diseases: How many lives can we save?' (2005) 366 *Lancet* 1578.
4 Indian Council of Medical Research, Public health foundation of India & institute for health matrics and evaluation India 'Health of the nation's states – the India state-level disease burden initiative New Delhi' India (2017) 34.
5 ICMR, PHFI & IHME (n 4) 46.
6 As above 28.
7 As above 46.
8 Non-communicable diseases threaten health of India's population *HSPH in the News* (Boston) 2012 https://www.hsph.harvard.edu/news/hsph-in-the-news/david-bloom-ncds-india/ (accessed 10 August 2020).

We focus on tobacco use, which is associated with all the leading NCDs mentioned earlier and others contributing to deaths and disabilities. Tobacco use has been long identified as the single largest source of preventable deaths. In 2016 alone, the use of tobacco led to over 7.1 million deaths worldwide.[9] India is the world's second-largest consumer of tobacco after China. In 2016, 28.6 per cent of adults (266.8 million) reported being current users of tobacco, and 24.9 per cent of these (232.4 million) were daily users.[10] About 42.4 per cent of men and 14.2 per cent of women use tobacco. Tobacco is used in a myriad of ways in India. The high use of smokeless tobacco products is unique to South Asia and India. In 2016, 21.5 per cent (199.4 million adults), including 29.6 per cent men and 12.8 per cent women, reported using smokeless tobacco, while 10.7 per cent (99.5 million adults), including 19.0 per cent men and 2.0 per cent women, reported smoking tobacco.[11] The average age of initiation of tobacco use was 18.8 years, indicating a large population was at potential risk of tobacco-related harms.[12] Within India, the prevalence of tobacco varies widely across states, ranging from 64.5 per cent in Tripura to 9.7 per cent in Goa.[13] In 2019, 8.5 per cent of students aged 13 to 15 years, including 9.6 per cent of boys and 7.4 per cent of girls, reported using tobacco in the 30 days preceding a nationwide survey.[14]

Tobacco use imposes a high health burden in India. Studies estimated that in the year 2010, tobacco smoking would have caused about 930,000 adult deaths, while smokeless tobacco would have accounted for 368,127 adult deaths.[15;16] India has the highest incidence of oral cancers worldwide that are largely attributed to smokeless tobacco use.[17] Furthermore, India also accounts for the highest-burden of tuberculosis globally, and it is well documented that tobacco smoking increases the risk of contracting tuberculosis by 2.5 times.[18] In fact, tobacco use is associated with a greater risk for a range of diseases.

Tobacco use puts a huge economic burden on families and health systems. The consumption expenditure on tobacco at the household level has been shown to crowd out spending on essential commodities/services such as milk,

9 J Drope & others *The Tobacco Atlas* (2018) 28.
10 WHO, *Tobacco free initiative global adult tobacco survey (GATS) India report 2016–17* (2017) 28.
11 WHO *GATS India Report 2016–17* (n 10) 60.
12 As above 69.
13 As above 78.
14 Government of India, International Institute for Population Sciences *GYTS-4 Global Youth Tobacco Survey Factsheet India 2019* https://main.mohfw.gov.in/newshighlights-57 (accessed 10 October 2021).
15 P Jha & others 'A nationally representative case-control study of smoking and death in India' (2008) 358 *New England Journal of Medicine* 1137.
16 DN Sinha & others 'Smokeless tobacco use: A meta-analysis of risk and attributable mortality estimates for India' (2014) 51 *Indian Journal of Cancer* 75.
17 PC Gupta 'Mouth cancer in India: A new epidemic?' (1999) 97 *Journal of the Indian Medical Association* 373.
18 WHO 'Fact sheet on tuberculosis and tobacco' (2009) https://www.who.int/tobacco/publications/health_effects/factsheet_tub_tob.pdf?ua=1 (accessed 10 August 2020).

education and clean fuels, specifically impacting women and children.[19] In 2011, the total economic cost of all diseases attributable to tobacco was estimated to be US$22.4 billion.[20] This amounted to 1.16 per cent of the GDP of India, whereas the public spending on healthcare constituted only 1.04 per cent of the GDP. It far exceeded the government expenditure on health as well as the total revenue generated from tobacco in that year. As over 69 per cent of India's healthcare is financed through household out-of-pocket payments, much of this burden falls on individuals and households, leading to impoverishment.[21]

In order to address the high burden of NCDs and tobacco use, India is one of the first countries to develop a national action plan and monitoring framework for the prevention and control of NCDs in 2013.[22] India has set targets and identified action strategies to reduce NCD risk factors and enhance NCD care services. As part of this, India aspires to reduce the prevalence of current tobacco use of 15 per cent by 2020 and 30 per cent by 2025. Available data shows that the prevalence of current tobacco use in India reduced from 34.6 per cent in 2010 to 28.6 per cent in 2017, showing an absolute reduction of 6 per cent and a relative reduction of 17 per cent during this period.[23]

12.3 Overview of tobacco regulations in India

While the right to health and healthcare is not expressed (directly) as a fundamental right in the Indian Constitution, it does, under the directive principles of state policy and fundamental duties, outline several areas related to the promotion and protection of health, including the provision of healthcare.[24] The courts in India have routinely interpreted that the right to health is integral to the expressed right to life (with dignity) enshrined in article 21 of the Indian Constitution. Several litigants acting in the public interest and demanding the provision of healthcare services (including for NCDs) have used this article of the Constitution. Furthermore, certain directive principles of state policy are very relevant to the prevention of NCDs including the prohibition of consumption of intoxicating drinks/drugs that are injurious to the health and protection of the environment.

19 R John 'Crowding out effect of tobacco expenditure and its implications on household resource allocation in India' (2008) 66 *Social Science & Medicine* 1363.

20 RM John & others *Economic burden of tobacco related diseases in India* (2014) 2.

21 National Health Systems Resource Centre *National health accounts: Estimates for India 2013–14* (2016) 15.

22 'India: First to adapt the global monitoring framework on noncommunicable diseases (NCDs)' *WHO Features* (2015) https://www.who.int/features/2015/ncd-india/en/ (accessed 10 August 2020).

23 WHO *GATS India Report 2016–17* (n 10) 72.

24 KR Rao & PR Panchamukhi 'Health and the Indian Constitution' CMDR Monograph Series No 7 http://cmdr.ac.in/editor_v51/assets/Mono-7.pdf (accessed 10 October 2021).

We will now highlight the major legal developments concerning tobacco in India. We do so in a chronological fashion, as these legal measures appeared mainly from a national perspective while taking note of the significant and widespread initiatives by states (federal units) in India.

12.3.1 Focus on cigarettes: health and trade-related enactments

In 1975, India enacted the Cigarettes (Regulations of Production, Supply and Distribution) Act,[25] bringing the cigarette industry under some amount of control. At this point, empirical evidence on negative health implications of smoking was widespread, and tobacco was beginning to be framed as a public health issue. The Cigarette Act mandated textual health warnings on cigarette packs and put restrictions on ways cigarettes could be advertised, but still allowing advertisements when specific warnings are displayed. Despite the widespread use of non-cigarette tobacco products like bidis, other smoking products and myriad other forms of smokeless tobacco products in India by then, the law prioritised only cigarettes.

In what may appear as a conflict with the spirit of the Cigarette Act, which aimed at controlling cigarettes through labelling, health warnings and restrictions on advertisements, the national government also enacted two tobacco laws the very same year: the Tobacco Board Act[26] and the Tobacco Cess Act.[27] The Tobacco Board Act aimed at bringing the tobacco industry, especially the flue-cured Virginia (FCV) tobacco – an economically lucrative form of tobacco crop used in making cigarettes – under control of the national government. Through this legislation, the Tobacco Board was set up in 1976 and entrusted with the integration of various aspects of FCV tobacco (e.g. research, market watch, promotion of production and export, auctioning) and promote the development of the tobacco industry dealing in FCV tobacco.[28] The focus on FCV tobacco was for the economic significance of this crop that constituted the majority of tobacco exports from India. The constitution of such a Board was an attempt to consolidate several individual agencies/initiatives, which were earlier promoting this segment of tobacco in India. On the other hand, the Tobacco Cess Act endowed the Tobacco Board with working funds by levying on its behalf the excise duty on the FCV tobacco grown and sold in India, as well as customs duty on all tobacco exported from India.

These 1975 enactments, while being limited in their focus on cigarettes, also represent somewhat diverse interests of governments: on one hand trying to raise awareness on health hazards of cigarettes, while on the other hand

25 Cigarette Act, 1975.
26 Tobacco Board Act, 1975.
27 Tobacco Cess Act, 1975.
28 Tobacco Board 'Main activities' https://tobaccoboard.com/bactivities.php (accessed 30 August 2020).

institutionalising mechanisms to promote economic interests of the tobacco industry through FCV tobacco marketing and production in India. The Tobacco Board remains functional to date providing various measures to promote the tobacco industry; for example, registration of FCV tobacco growers, provision of minimum support prices and other inputs to growers, market watch and crop regulations, facilitating auctions of tobacco, export promotion and providing credit. However, lately, referring to India's obligations under the FCTC, the Board has adopted a policy of restricting the horizontal expansion of tobacco growing areas by not granting new registrations to farmers or new licenses to create facilities for tobacco curing.[29]

Even before these national initiatives, Indian states rolled out a slew of tobacco control laws. For example, several states went on to enact their own laws prohibiting smoking (and even spitting) in publicly consumed spaces[30;31;32;33] and prohibiting the sale of tobacco to children.[34;35;36]

12.3.2 *Focus on chewing tobacco: national and sub-national regulations using a food law*

Smokeless tobacco has remained a dominant form of tobacco use in India. In 1990, India made it mandatory for chewing tobacco products to have textual health warnings through the then prevailing Prevention of Food Adulteration Act 1955.[37;38] Concerned by the harms of the easy availability of cheap chewing tobacco products and its potential for addiction and harm among children and youth, at least five Indian states banned gutka – commonly used mass-manufactured chewing tobacco product – and pan masala containing tobacco between 2001 and 2003 in their jurisdictions by operationalising provisions of the Prevention of Food Adulteration Act 1954.[39] While these were state-level regulations and limited to select chewing tobacco products, they marked a departure from earlier norms and paved the way for stricter regulations of chewing tobacco products. However, in 2004 these bans were struck down when a group of stakeholders with a commercial interest in the tobacco trade moved the Supreme Court challenging the validity of the bans enacted by state governments under this law.

29 Tobacco Board 'Production regulation' https://tobaccoboard.com/propolicy.php (accessed 30 August 2020).
30 Bombay Smoke Nuisances Act, 1912.
31 Rajasthan Prevention of Smoking Act, 1950.
32 Orissa Prohibition of Smoking (In Show Houses) Act 1961.
33 Bombay Smoke Nuisances (Provision for Extension and Amendment) Act, 1961.
34 Assam Students and Juvenile Smoking Act, 1923.
35 Himachal Pradesh Juvenile (Prevention of Smoking) Act, 1952.
36 Uttar Pradesh Prohibition of Smoking (Cinema Houses) Act, 1952.
37 Prevention of Food Adulteration Act, 1954.
38 R Mehrotra, V Mehrotra & T Jandoo 'Tobacco control legislation in India: Past and present' (2010) *Indian Journal of Cancer* 806.
39 KS Reddy & PC Gupta 'Report on tobacco control in India' (2004) 159.

12.3.3 National legislation specific to and covering all tobacco products

Following a decade-long process initiated in 1993, when the then government expressed intention to bring in comprehensive legislation regulating all the tobacco products, India enacted the Cigarettes and Other Tobacco Products (Prohibition of Advertisement and Regulation of Trade and Commerce, Production, Supply and Distribution) Act, 2003 (COTPA).[40,41] This enactment in a way marked a paradigm shift: It replaced the archaic Cigarettes Act 1975 and encompassed all the tobacco products under its regulatory gaze. It provided for several tobacco control measures including the prohibition on smoking in public places, prohibition on advertisements of tobacco in print and electronic media, prohibition of sale of tobacco to and by minors as well as around educational institutions, and mandatory pictorial health warnings on tobacco product packs. However, this legislation through the Health Ministry did not necessarily build on or consider all the earlier and parallel regulatory efforts for tobacco; for example, regulations like the Tobacco Board Act promoting tobacco industry development or earlier state-level regulations of smokeless tobacco through food laws. This dissonance in the regulatory framework engendered a series of conflicts between COTPA and other laws regulating tobacco, which courts were left to reconcile.

Before COTPA was enacted at the national level, a few Indian states enacted similar laws; however, they adopted COTPA once it was in place.[42] Also, the national government had amended or used a few other prevailing laws to restrict the promotion and advertisements of tobacco. For example, the Cinematograph Act, 1952[43] had been amended to prevent promotion or glorification of tobacco in films, and amendments in the year 2000 to the Cable Television Networks (Regulation) Act, 1994[44] prevented trade and advertisements of tobacco through cable television.[45] In 1992, amendments to the Drugs and Cosmetics Act, 1940[46] prohibited the manufacture and sale of cosmetics or drugs licensed as toothpaste/tooth powder if that contained tobacco.[47]

12.3.4 A global treaty on tobacco control and refinements to the national law

India was an active participant in negotiating the first-ever global health treaty, the WHO FCTC.[48] India signed and fully ratified the Convention in 2004. The

40 Cigarette & other Tobacco Products Act, 2003.
41 Mehrotra, Mehrotra & Jandoo (n 38) 806.
42 Reddy & Gupta (n 39) 158.
43 The Cinematograph Act, 1952.
44 The Cable Television Act, 1955.
45 Mehrotra, Mehrotra & Jandoo (n 38) 806.
46 The Drugs and Cosmetics Act, 1940.
47 Mehrotra, Mehrotra & Jandoo (n 38) 806.
48 WHO *Framework convention on tobacco control* (2003).

tobacco regulations in the post-FCTC period included detailing of existing laws and enactment of new laws. From 2004 onwards, rules for various provisions of COTPA were publicised as well as amendments made to some of the provisions to define certain terms or clarify the role of stakeholders.[49;50] The intent was to reduce the ambiguity in policy interpretation faced by law enforcers. Some of the major notifications under the COTPA include the 2008 prohibition of smoking in public places rules;[51] the multiple notifications for package warning specifying text, images and rotation;[52] the 2015 pack warning rules that required 85 per cent of pack area to be covered by specified warnings;[53] and 2018 inclusion of a quit-line number on tobacco packs.[54] Many of these notifications were met with legal hurdles in terms of challenges from the tobacco industry often leading to implementation delays and at times dilution of the provisions. This was evident in the case of the health warnings on tobacco products packs until the current large-size warnings were notified.[55;56] In 2007, India launched the National Tobacco Control Programme to ensure effective implementation of COTPA while raising awareness on tobacco harms and offering cessation services.[57] The programme provided institutional structure and resources for tobacco control efforts in the country.

12.3.5 *Revisiting the ban on smokeless tobacco through the new food law*

After an initial setback faced by a few Indian states in using the earlier food law to ban smokeless tobacco, the new food law (the Food Safety and Standards Act, 2006)

49 Ministry of Health and Family Welfare 'MOHFW GSR 561(E) 1 September 2004' https://www.tobaccocontrollaws.org/files/live/India/India%20-%20G.S.R.%20561%28E%29%20.pdf (accessed 30 August 2020).

50 Ministry of Health and Family Welfare 'MOHFW GSR 345(E) 31 May 2005' https://www.tobaccocontrollaws.org/files/live/India/India%20-%20G.S.R.%20345%28E%29.pdf (accessed 30 August 2020).

51 Ministry of Health and Family Welfare 'MOHFW GSR 417(E) 30 May 2008' https://www.tobaccocontrollaws.org/files/live/India/India%20-%20G.S.R.%20417%28E%29.pdf (accessed 30 August 2020).

52 Ministry of Health and Family Welfare 'MOHFW GSR 182(E) 15 March 2008' https://www.tobaccocontrollaws.org/files/live/India/India%20-%20G.S.R.%20182%28E%29.pdf (accessed 30 August 2020).

53 Ministry of Health and Family Welfare 'MOHFW GSR 739(E) 24 September 2015' https://www.tobaccocontrollaws.org/files/live/India/India%20-%20G.S.R.%20727%28E%29.pdf (accessed 30 August 2020).

54 Ministry of Health and Family Welfare 'MOHFW GSR 331(E) 3 April 2018' https://www.tobaccocontrollaws.org/files/live/India/India%20-%20G.S.R.%20331%28E%29.pdf (accessed 30 August 2020).

55 M Arora & A Yadav 'Pictorial health warnings on tobacco products in India: Socio-political and legal developments' (2010) 23 *National Medical Journal of India* 357.

56 M Arora & others 'Ineffective pictorial health warnings on tobacco products: Lessons learnt from India' (2012) 56 *Indian Journal of Public Health* 61.

57 Ministry of Health and Family Welfare 'National Tobacco Control Programme (NTCP)' https://nhm.gov.in/index1.php?lang=1&level=2&sublinkid=1052&lid=607 (accessed 30 August 2020).

provided Indian states with a renewed opportunity to regulate smokeless tobacco.[58] Section 2.3.4 of the Food Safety and Standards (Prohibition and Restrictions on Sales) Regulations 2011[59] prohibited the use of tobacco and nicotine as ingredients in food products. In a short duration of a few years, all the states and union territories prohibited one or more forms of smokeless, especially chewing, tobacco using this provision. While enacted by states using a national law, these measures indicated states' regulatory intentions to go beyond mere restrictions on sales to a complete ban on manufacture and sales of select forms of tobacco in India.[60] However, a majority of states banned only limited forms of chewing tobacco – gutka and pan masala containing tobacco – and the tobacco industry routinely flaunts the ban through a twin packaging that separates raw tobacco from other ingredients.[61] Parallel to these developments, India enacted the Juvenile Justice (Care and Protection of Children) Act, 2015 making the sale of tobacco products to minors a punishable offence, with the penalties (a fine of up to INR 100,000 and a jail term for seven years) being significantly higher than specified in COTPA.[62]

12.3.6 Preventing tobacco industry interference: sub-national enactments

Although the FCTC article 5.3 requires member governments to enact policy measures that protect their public health policies from the vested and commercial interests of the tobacco industry, the progress on this front in India has been rather slow. In 2015, the Indian state of Punjab adopted a protocol prescribing a code of conduct for public officials in dealing with the tobacco industry in line with the FCTC article 5.3 to prevent industry interference in tobacco control.[63] In the following years, at least 13 other Indian states adopted a similar policy.[64] These state-level enactments restricted interactions between public officials and the tobacco industry and prevented collaborations or joint programmes between the government agencies and the tobacco industry. In 2010, as part of public interest litigation (PIL), the national government indicated adopting such code for public officers.[65] While that did not happen, more recently in July 2020 the Ministry of Health and Family Welfare (Government of India) adopted such a code of conduct for officers in the ministry as well as in the institutions governed by this ministry to prevent tobacco industry interference.[66]

58 Food Safety and Standards Act, 2006.

59 Food Safety and Standards (Prohibition and Restrictions on sales) Regulations 2011.

60 R Dsouza & U Bhojani 'Strategic and contested use of food laws to ban smokeless tobacco products in India: A qualitative analysis of litigation' (2021) *Tobacco Control*.

61 G Kumar & P Kumar 'Ban on Gutka in India: Symbolic victory or actual end-game for smokeless tobacco. Large-scale household survey in Delhi finds out!' (2018) 16 *Tobacco Induced Diseases* A36.

62 Juvenile Justice (Care and Protection of Children) Act, 2015 (Act 2 of 2016).

63 U Bhojani 'Prevent tobacco lobby interference' *Deccan Herald* (Bengaluru) 12 August 2020.

64 As above.

65 WP No 27692/2010 High Court of Karnataka (2011).

66 'The Union congratulates India for measure to prevent tobacco industry interference in health policy' *The Union* 21 July 2020 https://www.theunion.org/news-centre/news/

12.3.7 Tax reforms with implications for tobacco control

In 2017, India overhauled the taxation system with the introduction of the goods and services tax (GST).[67] Before GST, a decentralised value added tax (VAT) system[68] existed wherein the tax rates on tobacco products were fixed by state governments and varied from one state to another and across types of tobacco products. The GST system made a single tax rate applicable across the entire nation. All the major tobacco products have been included in the highest tax slab of 28 per cent.[69] So, while GST attempted to harmonise taxes across products, reducing a huge disparity in taxing different tobacco products that existed in many states during the VAT regime, the prescribed GST rate is lower than the VAT rates levied by some of the states. This national policy change impacted tobacco control efforts by bringing the focus and discussion on tobacco taxation, albeit thwarting some state precedents of 75 per cent VAT and taking away the decision-making capacity of the states. Additionally owing to the appeals from the tobacco lobby imposition of cess on bidis was postponed in 2017.[70]

12.3.8 Prohibition on electronic nicotine delivery systems

As the scientific evidence over the addictive and harmful nature of electronic cigarettes grew, the Ministry of Health and Family Welfare (MOHFW) at the national level issued an advisory to all the principal secretaries of Indian states and union territories on electronic nicotine delivery systems in 2018.[71] This was followed by an advisory by the Ministry of Finance to the customs officials alerting them about the MOHFW advisory. The national government brought an ordinance in 2019, which culminated in the Prohibition of Electronic Cigarettes (Production, Manufacture, Import, Export, Transport, Sale, Distribution, Storage and Advertisement) Act 2019.[72]

Some of the other laws that have been under discussion and implemented in a few sub-national jurisdictions are a vendor licensing system to regulate the sale of tobacco products and prohibition of the sale of loose cigarettes (single sticks).

12.4 The FCTC and the Indian tobacco control law

Earlier, we provided an overview of the legal developments concerning tobacco in India. We now compare the prevailing tobacco control law in India with the

---

the-union-congratulates-indias-ministry-of-health-and-family-welfare-for-adopting-measure-to-prevent-tobacco-industry-interference-in-health-policy (accessed 30 August 2020).

67 Central Board of Indirect Taxes & Customs 'GST – Goods and services tax' https://www.cbic.gov.in/htdocs-cbec/gst/index-english (accessed 30 August 2020).

68 National Portal of India 'Value added tax act, 2005' https://www.india.gov.in/value-added-tax-act-2005-0 (accessed 30 August 2020).

69 R Prasad 'GST has made tobacco products only marginally costlier' (26 August 2019).

70 M Assunta 'Global tobacco industry interference index 2019' Global Center for Good Governance in Tobacco Control, Thailand (2019) 12.

71 Ministry of Health and Family Welfare 'MOHFW advisory on electronic nicotine delivery systems (ENDS)' (28 August 2018) https://www.tobaccocontrollaws.org/files/live/India/India%20%20MOHFW%20Advisory%20on%20ENDS.pdf (accessed 30 August 2020).

72 The Prohibition of Electronic Cigarettes (Production, manufacture, import, export, transport, sale, distribution, storage and advertisement) Act, 2019 (42 of 2019).

major provisions of the FCTC (see Table 12.1). The FCTC became one of the most widely ratified treaties that prescribe the minimum regulations that the parties to the Convention should implement in their pursuit to protect the health of their populations from tobacco-related harms. Article 2 of the Treaty clarifies that nothing in the treaty shall prevent the parties from imposing stricter regulations beyond the FCTC that are consistent with the provisions of the Treaty. We limit the comparison to only those FCTC articles that require regulatory or administrative measures impacting the supply and/or demand of tobacco.

Table 12.1 WHO FCTC and the Indian law regulating tobacco

WHO FCTC	*Indian Law*	*Comments*
Health Warnings **Article 11: Packaging and labelling of tobacco products** This article requires that the packaging and labelling do not promote a tobacco product by any means that are false, misleading, or deceptive. It shall not give an impression that certain forms of tobacco are safer than others. It also requires the health warning on tobacco product packs to be clear and legible. The warnings shall cover 50 per cent or more of the principal display areas of the packs, and the warning and messages must be rotating.	**COTPA** **Section 7: Restrictions on trade and commerce of tobacco products** No person shall, directly or indirectly, produce, supply or distribute tobacco products: (7.1) without including the specified warning, including a pictorial warning, on the label and package. **Section 8: Details of health warnings on tobacco products** (1) The specified warning on a package of tobacco products shall be: (a) legible and prominent; (b) conspicuous as to size and colour; (c) in such style or type of lettering as to be boldly and clearly presented in distinct contrast to the rest of packaging. **Section 9: Language of warning on tobacco products** (2) No package of cigarettes or any other tobacco products or its label shall contain any matter or statement, which is inconsistent with, or detracts from, the specified warning. The amended rules under these sections that came into force in 2016 require health warnings to cover 85 per cent of principal display areas of tobacco packs. Rotations in and new warnings are periodically notified.	Indian regulations are fully compliant with the FCTC and require stricter regulations. Globally, India was ranked fifth in terms of countries with larger pictorial warnings on tobacco packs in 2018.[73]

73 Canadian Cancer Society *Cigarette package health warnings international status report* (6th ed 2018) 4.

WHO FCTC	*Indian Law*	*Comments*
Content (Tobacco Products) Regulations		
Article 9: Regulation of the contents of tobacco products This article deals with the testing and measuring the contents and emissions of tobacco products. It requires that a national regulatory authority ensure the implementation of laws and regulations that deal with the content and emission of, and due to, tobacco products.	**COTPA** **Section 11: Testing nicotine and tar content in tobacco products** This section indicates the government will grant recognition to laboratories for testing nicotine and tar contents of tobacco products. This section came into effect from September 2019.	India notified the relevant section of COTPA in 2019 and commissioned three laboratories for testing of the nicotine while also formulating the operational guidelines for national tobacco testing laboratories.[74;75] Rules are yet to be notified for disclosures of contents on tobacco packs.
Article 10: Regulation of tobacco product disclosures This article requires tobacco companies to disclose the contents and emissions of tobacco products, including the toxicity, to the governmental authority and the public. Furthermore, the government should have administrative and legal mechanisms in place to implement this article.	**COTPA** **Section 7: Restrictions on trade and commerce of tobacco products** Section 7(5) requires that cigarettes or any other tobacco products have a label mentioning the nicotine and tar contents along with the maximum permissible limits thereof. **Section 10: Size of letters and figures** This section provides for specifying rules for the height of each letter and a figure of the warning or indication of nicotine and tar content.	

(*Continued*)

74 Ministry of Health and Family Welfare 'Operational guidelines for national tobacco testing laboratories' (2019).

75 K Ray 'Govt sets up three tobacco testing labs' *Deccan Herald* (New Delhi) 15 September 2019.

Table 12.1 (Continued)

WHO FCTC	*Indian Law*	*Comments*
Tobacco Taxes		
Article 6: Price and tax measures to reduce the demand for tobacco This article concerns taxation and price regulations to reduce tobacco consumption.	Since 2017, with the imposition of the **Goods and Service Tax**, tobacco products have been put in the highest tax bracket of 28 per cent. In addition to GST, National Calamity Contingent Duty, Compensation Cess and Excise Duty apply to tobacco products. These later forms of taxes vary across tobacco products. There is an exemption to Compensation Cess for bidis and exemption from GST for smaller manufacturers (having less than INR 4 million annual turnovers; registered manufacturing companies with fewer than 20 workers).	Overall taxes on tobacco products remains well below the recommended rate by the WHO, with taxes constituting about 75 per cent of retail prices of products. In that sense, the tax burden on cigarettes, smokeless tobacco and bidis remain 63, 60 and 22 per cent respectively. Tobacco products have become more affordable in the last few years.[76]
Protection from Exposure to Second-Hand Smoke		
Article 8: Protection from exposure to tobacco smoke To provide for legislation, administration and implementation of the 'protection from exposure to tobacco smoke in indoor workplaces, public transport, indoor public places and, as appropriate, other public places'.	**COTPA** **Section 4: Prohibition of smoking in public places** This article rules that smoking is prohibited in public places which include 'any place to which the public have access', such as 'auditorium, hospital buildings, railway waiting room, amusement centres, restaurants, public offices, court buildings, educational institutions, libraries, public conveyances . . . but does not include any open space'. The law provides for signages and penalties. Exceptions include hotels with more than 30 rooms, restaurants with more than 30 seating capacity and airports that may have designated smoking areas.	Indian regulations are compliant with the FCTC requirements, covering all kinds of smoke products. In 2019, India banned e-cigarettes.

76 Prasad (n 69).

WHO FCTC	*Indian Law*	*Comments*
Tobacco Advertisement, Promotion and Sponsorship		
Article 13: Tobacco advertising, promotion and sponsorship This article requires a prohibition on tobacco advertising, promotion and sponsorship. And if no such ban is in place, that tobacco companies must disclose to the government the expenditure that it spends on tobacco advertising and promotional activities.	COTPA **Section 5: Prohibition of direct or indirect advertisement, promotion and sponsorship of tobacco products** No person engaged in the production, supply or distribution of tobacco products should advertise or sell materials in any form that advertise tobacco products. No person shall, under a contract or otherwise, promote the consumption of any tobacco products or any trademark or brand name of any tobacco product in exchange for monetary or other benefits. Restrictions on tobacco advertising were further strengthened by the **Film and Television Programmes Rules, 27 October 2011**, which mandate justification of tobacco portrayal, display of 30 seconds anti-tobacco messaging, and disclaimers during smoking scenes while prohibiting the promotion of tobacco products and associated brands. The **Cable Television Networks (Regulation) Act, 1994** prevented trade and advertisements of tobacco through cable television.	While the prohibition on tobacco promotion and advertisement covers a wide range of media, there are no explicit regulations on cross-border advertisements as well as advertisements and promotion on the internet and on-demand streaming media platforms. Also, the promotion of tobacco brands/companies through sponsorship and corporate social responsibility remains commonplace.
Prevention of Youth Access to Tobacco		
Article 16: Sales to and by minors This Article requires parties to prohibit the sales of tobacco products to persons under the age set by domestic law, national law or 18. These measures may include: '(a) requiring that all sellers of tobacco products place a clear and prominent indicator inside their point of sale about the	COTPA **Section 6** No person shall sell, offer for sale, or permit the sale of, any tobacco product – (a) to any person who is under eighteen years of age, and (b) in an area within a radius of one hundred yards of any educational institution. The amended rules notified under this section prevent tobacco sales by minors, require warning/signage at the point of sale, prevent sales through vending machines, put the responsibility of ascertaining age proof on the seller, and prevent the display of products in a way that provides easy access to youth.	Indian law is compliant with the FCTC requirements but also provides for additional measures such as the ban on tobacco sales around educational institutions. Furthermore, all the states and union territories in India have banned one or more forms of smokeless

(*Continued*)

Table 12.1 (Continued)

WHO FCTC	*Indian Law*	*Comments*
prohibition of tobacco sales to minors and, in case of doubt, request that each tobacco purchaser provide appropriate evidence of having reached full legal age; (b) banning the sale of tobacco products in any manner by which they are directly accessible, such as store shelves; (c) prohibiting the manufacture and sale of sweets, snacks, toys or any other objects in the form of tobacco products which appeal to minors'.	These restrictions were further strengthened through the **Juvenile Justice (Care and Protection of Children) Act, 2015**. Section 77 provides for heavy penalties and imprisonment for giving tobacco products, liquor, drugs or psychotropic substances to a child.	tobacco that are often considered as starter products for children/youth. In 2019, India also banned e-cigarettes. However, the sale of tobacco in the form of single/ loose sticks of cigarettes remains commonplace, making it affordable. Some states in India have banned such sales.
Cessation Support		
Article 14: Demand reduction measures concerning tobacco dependence and cessation This article requires parties to promote tobacco cessation, to design and implement programmes aimed at cessation (including counselling, psychological support, nicotine replacement, and education) and to provide infrastructure to do so. They are also required to develop and disseminate national guidelines on tobacco cessation.	An important component of India's National Tobacco Control Programme (NTCP) is concerned with setting up and maintaining tobacco cessation centres at state and district levels. These centres are to be provided with staff, equipment, training and outreach activities. Further, since 2016, the NTCP also maintains a toll-free tobacco quit-line support service as well as a mobile-cessation service at the national level. Further, it is mandated that details of the quit-line be printed on all tobacco product packages.	India has undertaken several measures to reduce tobacco dependence and promote tobacco cessation. While these are not strictly regulatory measures, they form a crucial component of national health programmes. However, there is scope to strengthen these initiatives.

WHO FCTC	*Indian Law*	*Comments*
Protection of the Environment		
Article 18: Protection of the environment and the health of persons This article requires parties to protect the environment and the health of persons in relation to the environment, in view of tobacco cultivation and manufacture.	There are no specific regulations for the tobacco industry regarding environmental protection. However, in 2016, the Government of India banned the use of plastic material in any form in packaging for all smokeless types of tobacco through the Plastic Waste Management Rules (2016).[77]	A parliamentary report dated 2016 shows that India has not adequately complied with article 18 of the FCTC, and the government should prioritise environmental protection with regard to the tobacco industry.[78]
Protection from the Tobacco Industry		
Article 5.3 This article requires: 'In setting and implementing their public health policies with respect to tobacco control, Parties shall act to protect these policies from commercial and other vested interests of the tobacco industry in accordance with national law'.	For a long time, India did not have a national policy that laid down the guidelines or the framework which would regulate the government's dealing with the tobacco industry in terms of (a) under what context interaction between the government and the tobacco industry was to be allowed, (b) what would be the content of these meetings, and (c) the dissemination of the minutes or the facts of the meetings or the discussions between the tobacco industry – essentially, a code of conduct which would require both the government and the tobacco industry to adhere to, including the disclosure of instances of interaction between the government's officials and the tobacco industry. However, as of 2020, 14 Indian states have such a code of conduct.[79] More recently, in July 2020, the Ministry of Health	At best, there is a partial fulfilment of the FCTC requirements in the form of codes of conduct for public officials in some of the Indian states and the health ministry at the national level. There is no policy preventing the so-called corporate social responsibility activities of the tobacco industry. The industry is known to use

(*Continued*)

77 'Directions under section 5 of the environment (protection) act, 1986 regarding implementation of the plastic waste management rules, 2016 by the manufacturers of Gutkha, Tobacco and Pan Masala' http://www.indiaenvironmentportal.org.in/files/file/Direction%20PWMR%20Rules%202016.PDF (accessed 23 August 2020).

78 Parliamentary Standing Committee on Science & Technology, Environment & Forests 'Effects of Tobacco Curing on Environment and Health' Parliament of India, Rajya Sabha 285th Report (2016) 12.

79 Bhojani (n 63).

Table 12.1 (Continued)

WHO FCTC	*Indian Law*	*Comments*
	and Family Welfare at the national level adopted a code of conduct, which would regulate how, and on what terms, its officials could interact with the tobacco industry.[80] This code of conduct is limited to the health ministry and institutions governed by the health ministry. It does not apply to the 'whole of the government', a principle which ought to drive tobacco control efforts.	these activities to build a public image, partnerships with and access to public agencies and decision makers. In fact, the prevailing law mandates spending on corporate social responsibility by large companies.[81] There remains a lack of policy coherence on tobacco at the national level. While there are tobacco control regulations, there also exist statutory bodies and mandates to promote the tobacco industry (e.g. Tobacco Board, Central Tobacco Research Institute).[82;83]

80 The Union (n 66).

81 A Chugh & others 'Tobacco industry interference index: Implementation of the world health organization's framework convention on tobacco control article 5.3 in India' (2020) 32 *Asia Pacific Journal of Public Health* 172.

82 U Bhojani, V Venkataraman & B Manganawar 'Public policies and the tobacco industry' *Economic and Political Weekly* (2011) 27.

83 N Rao & others 'Conflicts of interest in tobacco control in India: An exploratory study' (2016) 25 *Tobacco Control* 715.

WHO FCTC	*Indian Law*	*Comments*
		There is also no explicit policy preventing public investment in tobacco companies and political funding by the tobacco industry. Both are commonplace in India, with consequent industry interference in public health policies.[84;85]

12.5 Health rights and implications on tobacco regulations

We looked at legal frameworks that, in part or entirety, dealt with regulating tobacco. Our interest in tobacco control stems from the enormous negative impact it has on population health in the form of diseases, disabilities and deaths, as well as through its environmental and economic impacts. Hence, it is worth looking beyond tobacco-specific frameworks to see how India's national and international commitments for realising the right to health inform and relate to the existing tobacco-related regulations.

12.5.1 Tobacco and human rights

India has signed and ratified the Universal Declaration of Human Rights, the International Covenant on Civil and Political Rights, the Convention on the Elimination of Discrimination against Women, and the Convention on the Rights of the Child (CRC), each of which casts a set of obligations on parties that directly and tangentially encompass the right to health and well-being. Hence, they are of relevance to tobacco control. For some time now, human rights frameworks have been carefully explored and strategically deployed to advance tobacco control, the world over. Cabrera and Gostin,[86] for example, demonstrate how human

84 Bhojani, Venkataraman & Manganawar (n 82).

85 Rao & others (n 83).

86 OA Cabrera & LO Gostin 'Human rights and the framework convention on tobacco control: Mutually reinforcing systems' (2011) 7 *International Journal of Law in Context* 285.

rights and tobacco control – especially with reference to the FCTC – are 'mutually reinforcing' and go on to argue that the pronouncements and structures related to international human rights could, in fact, facilitate enforcement of the FCTC, which appears to suffer from poor enforceability.

In article 12 of the International Covenant on Economic, Social and Cultural Rights (ICESCR), parties including India recognised the 'the right of everyone to the enjoyment of the highest attainable standard of physical and mental health'.[87] The steps that parties agreed to realise this included

> (b) The improvement of all aspects of environmental and industrial hygiene;
> (c) The prevention, treatment and control of epidemic, endemic, occupational and other diseases; (d) The creation of conditions which would assure to all medical service and medical attention in the event of sickness.[88]

The Committee on Economic, Social and Cultural Rights (CESCR) in its General Comment 14 on article 12 makes direct references to tobacco:

> Article 12.2(b) [that is, The right to a healthy natural workplace environment] also embraces adequate housing and safe and hygienic working conditions, an adequate supply of food and proper nutrition, and discourages the abuse of alcohol, and the use of tobacco, drugs and other harmful substances.[89]

While expanding on the violations of obligations to protect these rights, the Committee states:

> This category includes such omissions as the failure to regulate the activities of individuals, groups or corporations so as to prevent them from violating the right to health of others; the failure to protect consumers and workers from practices detrimental to health, e.g. by employers and manufacturers of medicines or food; the failure to discourage production, marketing and consumption of tobacco, narcotics and other harmful substances.[90]

So, article 12 of the ICESCR including the outlined steps and comments provides for several tobacco control measures. The Indian law addresses many of these already, for example, large pictorial health warnings and a tobacco quit-line number on tobacco packs for consumer information and support; prohibition on

87 UN General Assembly, International Covenant on Economic, Social and Cultural Rights, 16 December 1966, United Nations, Treaty Series, vol. 993, 3 https://www.ohchr.org/en/professionalinterest/pages/cescr.aspx (accessed 30 August 2020).

88 As above.

89 CESCR General Comment 14: The right to the highest attainable standard of health (art 12) (2000) UN Doc E/C.12/2000/4 dated 11 August 2000 para 15https://www.refworld.org/pdfid/4538838d0.pdf (accessed 30 August 2020).

90 Para 51 of General Comment 14.

smoking in public places including workplaces; and limited restrictions on the tobacco industry (in terms of a ban on advertisements, ban on select products, restrictions on sale to minors, and a policy to stop the horizontal expansion of tobacco crop). However, this article and its interpretation provide further scope to actively discourage the tobacco industry and address the current lack of coherence in public policy related to tobacco in India.

12.5.2 Tobacco and child rights

Children and youth remain a particularly vulnerable population group and are often the 'target' of tobacco industry marketing. Toebes and others[91] make a stronger case to adopt a child rights approach to tobacco control, particularly as the tobacco industry considers youth to be potential users of tobacco, and that most adults who have taken to smoking or other forms of tobacco consumption begin as adolescents, and therefore the tobacco industry have devised marketing strategies aimed at youth. They argue that the CRC 'obliges governments and third parties to protect and promote a range of rights relevant to tobacco control', especially with regard to 'children's right to health (Article 24 CRC)', and that 'children's best interests shall be a primary consideration in the application and implementation of the Convention (Article 3 CRC)'.[92] Gispen and Toebes[93] argue that tobacco disproportionately affects youth in low- and middle-income countries and populations, especially with respect to being linked to the tobacco supply chain, in particular tobacco farming.

In light of this, article 32(1) of the CRC states that children need to be protected from 'performing any work that is likely to be hazardous or to interfere with the child's education, or to be harmful to the child's health or physical, mental, spiritual, moral or social development'.[94] More directly, in its General Comment concerning adolescent health and development, the CRC expresses its concern about the influence of marketing of unhealthy commodities on adolescent health and asks parties 'to regulate or prohibit information on and marketing of substances such as alcohol and tobacco, particularly when it targets children and adolescents'.[95] The CRC also stresses that parties shall ensure that adolescents have access to 'accurate and appropriate information on how to protect their

91 B Toebes & others 'A missing voice: The human rights of children to a tobacco-free environment' (2018) 27 *Tobacco Control* 3.

92 As above.

93 MEC Gispen & BC Toebes 'The human rights of children in tobacco control' (2019) 41 *Human Rights Quarterly* 340.

94 UN General Assembly, Convention on the Rights of the Child, 20 November 1989, United Nations, Treaty Series, vol 1577, 3 (accessed 30 August 2020).

95 UN Committee on the Rights of the Child (CRC), General Comment 4 (2003): Adolescent health and development in the context of the Convention on the Rights of the Child (1 July 2003) UN Doc CRC/GC/2003/4 (2003) https://www.refworld.org/docid/4538834f0.html (accessed 30 August 2020).

health and development and practise healthy behaviour', mentioning awareness on tobacco use as an example.[96] Therefore, there is much potential in the CRC to safeguard the rights of children in tobacco control.

The Indian law on tobacco control does address the implications of realising these rights of children. The COTPA prohibits sale of tobacco to minors and also within 100 yards of educational institutions, including the need for relevant signage at schools and the point of sales. Protecting youth from addiction and harm has been the core concern that led to a ban on certain forms of smokeless tobacco products and more recently e-cigarettes. School-based awareness initiatives have been one of the main areas of the National Tobacco Control Programme.[97] The Ministry of Health and Family Welfare has developed 'Guidelines for Tobacco Free Educational Institutions in India' that provide steps towards making educational institutions tobacco-free, including the role of national and sub-national governments and civil society organisations in such initiatives.[98]

However, there are a few areas where there is scope for further regulatory actions to protect children from tobacco. In India, tobacco products, often cigarettes, are routinely sold by vendors loose or as single sticks. Such practice defeats the prevailing regulations that require health warnings on tobacco packs and also makes it affordable for youth to buy tobacco products. Some Indian states have prohibited such sales, but there is a need to have strict nationwide measures that discourage such practice. Furthermore, despite the regulations in place, studies highlight implementation gaps as children continue to remain 'targets' by the tobacco industry with tobacco advertising and displays targeting youth; and vendors selling tobacco products around schools including offering free tobacco samples to youth.[99] The other area that needs attention is the presence of child labour in the tobacco sector. Despite the prohibition on child labour in hazardous industries, the 2001 census suggested that the tobacco sector (paan, bidis and cigarettes) accounted for the maximum share (21 per cent or over 2.5 million children) of child labour in hazardous industries.[100] The unofficial estimates indicate that child labour could be anywhere between 25 and 40 per cent of the workforce in the bidi industry, which is largely informal home-based work of bidi rolling.[101]

96 As above.

97 Ministry of Health and Family Welfare, Government of India 'Guidelines for tobacco free educational institutions (revised)' https://ntcp.nhp.gov.in/assets/document/TEFI-Guidelines.pdf (accessed 30 August 2020).

98 As above.

99 India Tiny Targets Report 'Tobacco advertisement, sales, product displays, and purchase incentives around primary and secondary schools' (2018) https://www.takeapart.org/wp-content/uploads/2019/02/India-Tiny-Targets-Report.pdf (accessed 30 August 2020).

100 Y Dube & G Mohandoss 'A study on child labor in Indian bidi industry' National Commission for Protection of Child Rights (2013) http://www.nipccd-earchive.wcd.nic.in/sites/default/files/PDF/A%20study%20on%20Child%20Labour%20in%20Indian%20Beedi%20Industry.pdf (accessed 30 August 2020).

101 M Sarwer 'Burning both ends: Many young girls in Murshidabad are child labourers' *The Hindu* 7 July 2018.

12.5.3 Tobacco and protection of the environment

Given the current climate crisis, attention has turned to how the consumption and production of tobacco products negatively impact the environment. The WHO in a recent report highlights how 'from tobacco cultivation and curing to cigarette manufacturing, distribution, consumption and discarding, every stage in the global tobacco supply chain involves considerable resource inputs, and results in the production of wastes and emissions'.[102] The report uses the framework of the UN Sustainable Development Goals (SDGs) to advance the health of the environment. India renewed its commitment to the SDGs by releasing a report highlighting its baseline goals for the year 2030. Specific to tobacco, SDG 3.A mentions the implementation of article 18 of the FCTC, which talks about protecting the environment with regard to tobacco cultivation and manufacturing.

India is no exception, and being among the world's largest tobacco producer and consumer countries, tobacco exerts a huge impact on the environment. As discussed earlier, there are statutory bodies that promote tobacco cultivation and research to enhance tobacco yield in India. There is an urgent need to reconsider the tobacco-promoting mandate of certain public agencies and align policies across sectors in the interest of public health. There is a need to enhance focus on supply-side regulations that contain tobacco production. This also implies the need to make serious efforts towards creating safer alternative livelihoods for tobacco growers and workers in India. We currently lack a clear strategy and plan in this regard.

12.5.4 Tobacco business and human rights

One of the avenues to make the tobacco industry accountable is the UN Guiding Principles on Business and Human Rights, which require governments to protect the human rights of individuals from third-party abuse, including business enterprises, and set out expectations for business enterprises to respect human rights throughout their operations.[103] These foundational principles are backed by operational provisions that states may build upon to protect, respect and remedy human rights in relation to corporate interference. India is still in the process of formulating its National Action Plan on Business and Human Rights after

102 WHO 'Cigarette smoking: An assessment of tobacco's global environmental footprint across its entire supply chain, and policy strategies to reduce it' (2018) Abstract https://www.who.int/fctc/publications/WHO-FCTC-Enviroment-Cigarette-smoking.pdf?ua=1 (accessed 30 August 2020).

103 United Nations 'Guiding principles on business and human rights: Implementing the United Nations "Protect, respect and remedy" framework' (2011) https://www.ohchr.org/documents/publications/guidingprinciplesbusinesshr_en.pdf (accessed 30 August 2020).

having committed to do so in accordance with the principles.[104] The Draft Plan put out by the Ministry of Corporate Affairs for public comments did not refer to the tobacco or tobacco industry. However, the consultations with communities and civil society actors in this regard do point to many concerns with regard to the tobacco sector ranging from labour exploitation, occupational hazards to public investments in tobacco companies and widespread use of so-called corporate social responsibility by tobacco companies.[105;106]

12.6 Implementation of tobacco control laws

We discussed the development of tobacco control laws in India and how they relate to commitments that India has made to realising the right to health. We now look at how well the prevailing laws in post-FCTC India are implemented, especially at the national level.

12.6.1 Data from the Global Tobacco Surveillance System

We first look at the two important nationwide surveys conducted in India as part of the Global Tobacco Surveillance System: the Global Youth Tobacco Survey (GYTS) among school-going youth aged 13–15 years, and the Global Adult Tobacco Survey (GATS) among people aged 15 years and above. We look at the two rounds of both these surveys conducted post-FCTC providing comparative data on indicators suggesting the implementation of the four major provisions of the COTPA 2003; that is, prohibition of smoking in public places, prohibition on tobacco advertisements, prohibition on the sale of tobacco to minors and mandatory health warnings on tobacco packs.

As reflected in Table 12.2, there has been an improvement in all the proxy indicators of implementation of major provisions of COTPA among adults between 2010 and 2017. However, the data also suggest that none of these provisions has achieved a significant level of compliance. The data on similar indicators for youth show some improvement between 2006 and 2019, except for exposure of youth to cigarette advertisement that in fact increased between 2006 and 2009. Together, these data present a picture of incremental improvement in the implementation of tobacco control law over time.

104 Ministry of Corporate Affairs 'India's national action plan on business & human rights' (2020) http://www.mca.gov.in/Ministry/pdf/NationalPlanBusinessHumanRight_13022019.pdf (accessed 30 August 2020).

105 Praxis 'Status of corporate responsibility in India, 2019' (2019) https://www.traffickingmatters.com/wp-content/uploads/2019/10/Status_of_CR_Report_2019-2.pdf (accessed 30 August 2020).

106 Partners in Change 'Voices from the margins' (2019) http://www.picindia.org/wp-content/uploads/NAP-community-consultations_v1.pdf (accessed 30 August 2020).

Table 12.2 Proxy indicators on implementation of COTPA in post-FCTC India

	Adults (15 years and above)		
	GATS 1 (2009–2010)[107]	*GATS 2 (2016–2017)*[108]	
Exposure to second-hand smoke at any public place	29%	25.7%	
Exposure to tobacco advertising or promotion	34.7%	26.9%	
Sale of tobacco products to or by minors*	8.59%	5.27%	
Exposure to tobacco pack warnings	62.5%	69%	
	Youth (15–18 years)		
	GYTS (2006)[109]	GYTS (2009)[110]	GYTS (2019)[111]
Exposure to second-hand smoke in places outside their home	40.3%	36.6%	23.4%
Purchase of cigarettes from a store	51.9%	47%	39.7%
Exposure to pro-cigarette advertisements on billboards	71.6%	74.4%	**
Offered free cigarettes by a tobacco company representative	11.2%	8.1%	**

* The sample here contains respondents between 15–18 years of age
** Comparable data not available in the GYTS Factsheet 2019

107 Ministry of Health and Family Welfare, Government of India 'Global adult tobacco survey India 2009–2010' (2010).
108 WHO *GATS India Report 2016–17* (n 10).
109 'India (ages 13–15) global youth tobacco survey (GYTS) factsheet' (2006) https://nada.searo.who.int/index.php/catalog/40/download/281 (accessed 30 August 2020).
110 'India (ages 13–15) global youth tobacco survey (GYTS) factsheet' (2009) http://www.who.int/fctc/reporting/Annexoneindia.pdf?ua=1 (accessed 30 August 2020).
111 Government of India, International Institute for Population Sciences (n 14).

Case studies of specific jurisdictions within India explain several barriers to implementation which include lack of prioritisation, resources, monitoring and evaluation; the need for institutionalisation and horizontal coordination across departments for effective implementation of COTPA.[112;113] Some of the facilitators include an active and vibrant civil society presence and engagement in the policy process, advocacy, capacity building of the diverse set of actors that need to coordinate and work synergistically to achieve effective implementation.[114;115]

12.6.2 Reports from India to the FCTC Secretariat

The other important data source for understanding the implementation of tobacco control laws are the reports submitted by the Ministry of Health and Family Welfare (Government of India) to the FCTC Secretariat. We found five such reports so far for the years 2007, 2010, 2012, 2016 and 2018.

The 2007 report[116] indicates compliance to several of the obligations of the FCTC including the national coordinating mechanism provided by the National Tobacco Control Cell in 2001. Though the report does not articulate clear measures to protect policies from industry interference, it does highlight some of the implementation challenges: intermittent public awareness efforts, limited data and surveillance, need to upscale cessation services and public awareness, need to strengthen enforcement at the state level, several court cases challenging the tobacco control laws, and lack of resources for capacity building.

The 2010 report[117] highlights resources invested in terms of the National Tobacco Control Programme, Inter-ministerial Task Forces, a high-level national steering committee, and state- and district-level committees to look into the issue of direct and indirect advertisements. Some of the other major steps include the smoke-free rules of 2008 setting up a mechanism for monitoring and enforcing smoke-free laws as well as a national 24/7 toll-free tobacco control helpline number to receive any violations related to tobacco control laws. The report reveals a significant focus on raising public awareness through a logo, television, radio,

112 D Persai, R Panda & A Gupta 'Examining implementation of tobacco control policy at the district level: A case study analysis from a high burden state in India' (2016) *Advances in Preventive Medicine* Article ID 4018023.

113 PB Hebbar & others 'From policy to practice: Lessons from Karnataka about implementation of tobacco control laws' (2017) 42 *Indian Journal of Community Medicine* 77.

114 M Kashiwabara & others 'Local governments and civil society lead breakthrough for tobacco control: Lessons from Chandigarh and Chennai' (2011) 55 *Indian Journal of Public Health* 234.

115 J Kaur & PV Mohan 'Advocacy for tobacco control in India – a step forward' (2012) 126 *Public Health* 675.

116 'FCTC 2007 India report' https://untobaccocontrol.org/impldb/wp-content/uploads/reports/india_report.pdf (accessed 30 August 2020).

117 'FCTC 2010 India report' https://untobaccocontrol.org/impldb/wp-content/uploads/reports/India_5y_report_final.pdf (accessed 30 August 2020).

posters, stickers, street plays and the postal department, amongst others. Another area of focus was cessation services and their integration into other national government programmes, health facilities, and medical and dental curricula.

The 2012 report[118] highlights the Food Safety and Standards Act 2006, which paved the way for banning smokeless tobacco products in India. The report also mentions a draft code of conduct for public officials in line with article 5.3 of the FCTC to prevent tobacco industry interference. Taxes on tobacco were hiked, both in form of the excise duty at the national level as well as the VAT in 13 states in this reporting period. A focus on the enforcement of pictorial health warnings with notifications, guidelines and resources in 18 Indian languages was seen. The attention on raising public awareness continued by engaging other sectors such as transport, celebrities and generating earned media support. Some decentralised state-level local tools for tobacco control such as licensing tobacco shops were noticed in this report. The operational guidelines were developed and circulated to make schools tobacco-free. A multi-sector supply-side measure of supporting a shift to alternate crops for flue-cured Virginia tobacco growers was initiated, including research projects on the same. Another important legal tool used to support the implementation of a ban on smokeless tobacco products was the banning of the use of plastic sachets for packaging smokeless tobacco products by the Ministry of Environment and Forests in 2011. The data from the first round of the GATS were disseminated widely in this period, building the capacity of a diverse set of actors including policymakers, media and others. One of the barriers to the implementation mentioned was the large unorganised home-based bidi industry employing women from the lower socio-economic strata.

The 2016 report[119] highlighted findings from the economic burden of tobacco diseases study, which provided crucial data to support the implementation of tobacco control policies. The state governments had identified nodal officers for tobacco control. The mCessation services and a toll-free quit-line were also introduced in this period to support upscaling of cessation services. The draft code of conduct mentioned in the earlier report was still under discussion by the Inter-ministerial Taskforce. Although a steady increase in central excise and state-level VAT on cigarettes was being implemented, bidis were being left out of such measures. Efforts have been made at the district level to enhance compliance with tobacco control laws by integrating reporting of violations of tobacco control law into monthly crime review reports and meetings by police departments. Another major advancement was notification of new pictorial warnings that should cover 85 per cent of the tobacco package's surface area. The health ministry at the national level strived to enhance tobacco control by issuing circulars to education

118 'FCTC 2012 India report' https://untobaccocontrol.org/impldb/wp-content/uploads/reports/india_2012_report.pdf (accessed 30 August 2020).

119 'FCTC 2018 India report' https://untobaccocontrol.org/impldb/wp-content/uploads/India_2018_report.pdf (accessed 30 August 2020).

departments on avoiding sponsorships by the tobacco industry, to the ministry of information and broadcasting on the issue of surrogate advertising, and to the ministry of agriculture to examine the 'barn buy-out scheme' to phase out the flue-cured Virginia tobacco cultivation.

The 2018 report[120] mentioned the establishment of three tobacco testing laboratories and the setting up of a global knowledge hub on smokeless tobacco in India. With the national tax reforms in form of the GST, the bidis (which generally escaped the taxation gaze in the past) were incorporated with other tobacco products into the highest tax bracket of 28 per cent. The quit-line number was added to the warnings on tobacco packs. The report mentioned the ministry of agriculture and farmers' welfare implementing a crop diversification programme supporting tobacco farmers to diversify to other economically viable crops. Similarly, it mentioned the ministry of labour and employment implementing a skill development programme to shift bidi rollers to alternative vocations. In a timely intervention, the health ministry issued an advisory against electronic nicotine delivery systems.

12.6.3 Tobacco industry interference index

Since 2018, researchers and practitioners in India are making efforts at monitoring the implantation of article 5.3 of the FCTC through bringing out the Tobacco Industry Interference Index for India. This Index uses a standardised tool[121] and systematic gathering of data from the public domain on various aspects of tobacco industry interference. It highlights instances of industry interference in public health policy related to tobacco control in India. The overall score of the Index (out of a total score of 100) indicates the degree of tobacco industry interference: the lower the score, the lesser the interference. Post the FCTC, 14 states in India adopted a code of conduct for public officials preventing tobacco industry interference. More recently, the Ministry of Health and Family Welfare adopted such a code for officials of the ministry as well as of the institutions governed by the ministry. The score of 61/100 for the Index 2020 indicates reduction, albeit of a smaller proportion, in tobacco industry interference in India compared to Index 2019 (69/100) and Index 2018 (71/100).[122;123;124]

120 As above.

121 M Assunta & EU Dorotheo 'SEATCA tobacco industry interference index: A tool for measuring implementation of WHO framework convention on tobacco control article 5.3' (2016) 25 *Tobacco Control* 313.

122 Bhojani (n 63).

123 Chugh & others (n 81).

124 HRIDAY 'Tobacco industry interference index: India report on implementation of WHO FCTC article 5.3' (2019).

12.7 Litigation and the role of the judiciary in tobacco control

Tobacco as a commodity represents diverse interests and hence attracts a gamut of laws and regulations initiated through varied public agencies.[125] The legal framework for tobacco control in India has been substantially influenced by litigation. This is partly due to the important role played by the tobacco control community filing PIL in seeking better implementation and enforcement of the law in the public interest and partly due to a scourge of litigation by the tobacco industry challenging nearly all the tobacco control regulations.[126,127,128] In dealing with this litigation, courts in India have interpreted the law while at the time nudging governments for clarity and stricter implementation of the law. Against this backdrop, we shall discuss some important cases that have shaped tobacco control in the Indian context.

12.7.1 Smoke-free public places

In 1999, the Kerala High Court, as part of PIL, unanimously declared smoking in public places as unconstitutional as it violates article 21 of the Indian Constitution that guarantees the right to life and personal liberty.[129] While acknowledging its inability to frame an anti-smoking policy – as this is the role of the executive – the court operationalised the existing law by declaring smoking as a public nuisance and a contributor to air pollution, therefore making smoking in public places a punishable offence in Kerala. This landmark pronouncement by the Kerala High Court categorically noted the deleterious effect of smoking by acknowledging the widespread public health effects of smoking together with the need for a policy response. The court went on to highlight how India had signed a series of relevant (pre-FCTC) WHO resolutions that had not been adhered to in practice. A couple of years later, the Supreme Court of India comprehensively prohibited smoking in public places, and directed national and state governments to take effective steps to enact the ban.[130] Interestingly, these judicial pronouncements came before the FCTC and paved the way for (more) comprehensive anti-smoking provisions that were later embedded into India's national tobacco control law: COTPA 2003.

125 U Bhojani & W Soors 'Tobacco control in India: A case for health-in-all policy approach' (2015) 28 *National Medical Journal of India* 86.
126 U Bhojani 'Litigation for claiming health rights: Insights from tobacco control' *Health and Human Rights* (2014).
127 A Yadav & others 'Smokeless tobacco control: Litigation & judicial measures from Southeast Asia' *Indian Journal of Medical Research* (2018).
128 J Kaur, AV Rinkoo & R Singh 'Using public interest litigation for tobacco control: Insights from India' (2017) *Indian Journal of Public Health*.
129 *K Ramakrishnan v State of Kerala* AIR 1999 Ker 385.
130 *Murli S Deora v Union of India* AIR 2002 SC 40.

12.7.2 *Regulating smokeless tobacco and products alike*

In earlier attempts to regulate tobacco, India prioritised smoking tobacco, specifically cigarettes. However, in actuality, smokeless tobacco products, as well as bidi, remain dominant forms of tobacco consumption in India. Several localised forms of tobacco ranging from chewing tobacco to tobacco in paan, water, pastes and powder remain pervasive across Indian states.

Realising this paradoxical policy position, the governments in India sought to extend the application of existing laws to regulate these so far unregulated forms of tobacco. For example, the national government exercised power under the Drugs and Cosmetics Act 1940 to prohibit the manufacture (and sale) of tobacco dentifrices: toothpaste/powder mixed with tobacco.[131] These efforts were hamstrung by the tobacco industry, first before the Rajasthan High Court and later by the Supreme Court of India. Rejecting the industry's claim that their right to trade had been infringed by the impugned notification, the Rajasthan High Court held that policies promulgating the state's public health duty, under Part IV of the Constitution, could not be invalidated for violating fundamental rights of an individual. By maintaining this position of law, not only did the Court uphold the impugned notification, but it also directed the national government to appoint an expert committee to oversee the usage of other similar products such as pan masala and gutka, and further chalk out the possible public health effects.[132] Of course, the industry appealed before the Supreme Court of India, but the Court unequivocally upheld the ban in the public interest.[133]

Similarly, Courts played an important role in sustaining regulations issued by various state governments banning certain forms of smokeless tobacco products.[134] Indian states tactically operationalised provisions of food laws to curb the proliferation of chewing tobacco products that are relatively inexpensive and are products known to initiate youth to a lifetime of consumption of tobacco. Initially, some of the states used provisions of the Prevention of Food Adulteration Act, 1954 to taper the usage of adulterated tobacco products and certain chewing tobacco products, arguing that these are food products and hence ought not to contain harmful ingredients. While these regulations were challenged by the tobacco industry and were later struck down by the Supreme Court of India,[135] state governments pursued this line of regulations afresh under the new food law: the Food Safety and Standards Act, 2006 (FSSA). Regulation under the FSSA prohibited the usage of articles that are injurious to health, such as tobacco and nicotine. This time, nearly all the states and union territories used the provisions of this food law to ban one or more forms of chewing tobacco. Although the tobacco industry challenged the new wave of notifications, the courts'

131 Notification (No. X. 11014/3/91-DM-S & PFA).
132 *Kastoori Udyog v The Union of India* Civil Writ Petition 3354 of 1993.
133 *Laxmikant v The Union of India* 1997 (4) SCC 739 1997.
134 Dsouza & Bhojani (n 60).
135 *Godawat Pan Masala Products v Union of India* (2004) 7 SCC 68.

interpretation of what constitutes food under the new food law made it possible to sustain these efforts.

While there have been concerns about the suboptimal implementation of such prohibitions, these regulations marked a new shift in tobacco regulations. The COTPA (national tobacco control law) provides for limited restrictions on certain aspects of trade in tobacco products, while the food law was able to go beyond the confines of COTPA and allowed states to ban these chewing tobacco products.[136] While being strategic, these bans are vulnerable to legal challenges by the industry leaving courts to decide their fate. A systematic study of these judicial pronouncements illustrates how the effectiveness of such bans, when challenged in court, are contingent on whether the court reads the impugned tobacco product as 'food' (the very logic underpinning the bans). Finally, in *Ankur Gupta v India Asthma Care Society*,[137] the Supreme Court of India ordered states and union territories that had not yet issued notifications (enacting the bans on chewing tobacco products) to provide the Court with reasons for their inaction. Through this order, the Supreme Court sought to oversee the implementation by making states accountable for their non-compliance, hence strengthening the working of the bans.

12.7.3 Demanding stricter enforcement of laws

With the enactment of COTPA and the use of many other laws tangentially dealing with tobacco, India can be said to have a relatively robust legal infrastructure regulating tobacco. However, as we saw earlier, there remain challenges in achieving optimal compliance to these laws. Public-spirited citizens and organisations have frequented courts with regard to the implementation and enforcement of these laws, especially COTPA. In *Rahul Joshi v Union of India*,[138] a practising advocate concerned with the health burden of tobacco filed PIL for the implementation and enforcement of the COTPA amendment rules, 2014 (amongst a set of other policy considerations). These rules mandate that at least 85 per cent of tobacco pack areas be covered with pictorial health warnings, and these rules had been indefinitely deferred. After a comprehensive examination of the evidence proffered by the petitioner and in the larger interest of the public, the Rajasthan High Court directed that these rules come into force immediately. Again, in *Cancer Patient Association v State of Karnataka*,[139] PIL was filed for strict implementation of section 6(b) of COTPA, which prohibits the sale of tobacco products to minors and in close proximity to educational institutions. The petitioner furnished the court with evidence of non-compliance; in response,

136 Dsouza & Bhojani (n 60).
137 Petition(s) for Special Leave to Appeal Civil No(s). 16308/2007, Supreme Court of India (3 April 2013).
138 WP 8680/2015, High Court of Judicature at Rajasthan, Jaipur Bench, 2015.
139 WP 17958, High Court of Karnataka at Bangalore (2011).

the court responded with a slew of directives. In its final order, Karnataka High Court piloted a project where an officer of the education department along with the petitioner were to visit the school premises and oversee compliance with the law. The Court further instructed that the state government take required steps including dismantling unauthorised structures selling tobacco, in abrogation of the law.

Our intent was not to be exhaustive given the limitation of the space in this chapter but to use a few select cases in highlighting the role of litigation/courts in tobacco control. On the whole, we observe that the tobacco industry has used litigation widely as a means to challenge tobacco control regulations. There is also a good amount of litigation by public-spirited citizens and organisations asking for tobacco control regulations and their implementation in the public interest. The courts, in general, have been supportive of governments' efforts at regulating tobacco products in the interest of public health. Some of the cases, including ones outlined in this section, have established precedents that are promising in the use of a diverse set of laws and judicial recourse for tobacco control.

12.8 Conclusion

Tobacco is consumed in myriad ways with a range of smokeless and smoking products in India. The consumption varies a lot across Indian states and is based on gender, socio-economic position and location (urban/rural). Tobacco exacts a huge disease burden, causing about 1.3 million premature deaths annually. Tobacco consumption and attributable diseases cause a significant economic burden on households, health systems and India's economy as a whole.

India is also among the world's largest producers and exporters of tobacco. Hence, tobacco as a commodity evokes diverse and at times conflicting interests within governments. India has developed a strong tobacco control law over time. While the contemporary tobacco control law has evolved incrementally with its origins already in multiple sectors (e.g. environment, food safety and pharmaceuticals), there remains room to enhance policy coherence for tobacco control. The policies in the agriculture and commerce sectors tend to promote tobacco production and trade.

India was among the earlier countries to sign and ratify the FCTC in 2004. On several aspects of tobacco control, the Indian law is fully compliant with the FCTC requirements. In fact, India has several good practices to offer to the world in these areas. These include (1) large-sized – among the largest in the world – pictorial health warnings on tobacco control packs; (2) preventing youth access to tobacco through age restrictions in tobacco sales, a ban on sales around educational institutions and a ban on e-cigarettes and many forms of smokeless tobacco; and (3) reducing exposure to second-hand smoke through smoke-free public places. While India has also put in place other regulatory measures (e.g. a ban on tobacco advertisements), considering the FCTC requirements as well as framing tobacco control as a health rights issue, we identify certain areas where there is a need to do more.

The existing tobacco control policies seem to be yielding results in terms of reducing tobacco use prevalence. However, India lacks a nationwide policy in line with article 5.3 of the FCTC to protect these public health policies from the vested and commercial interests of the tobacco industry. While the health ministry has recently adopted a code of conduct for public officials in line with article 5.3, this code does not apply to other ministries/departments and many avenues of potential tobacco industry interference remain unchecked (e.g. public investments in tobacco firms, political funding by tobacco firms, so-called corporate social responsibilities by tobacco firms). In general, India could do more to make the tobacco industry accountable. There is a need to plan for and systematically pursue alignment of agricultural and commercial policies with that of public health goals of reducing tobacco use. The exploitation of certain categories of workers in the tobacco sector – their economic and labour rights – is well known. There is a need for urgent and serious attention to promote safer and viable non-tobacco livelihoods for tobacco growers and workers.

The other area that India ought to do more in is to raise taxes sufficiently on tobacco products to reduce its demand. At present, taxes remain a very small part of the retail costs of tobacco products. The majority of tobacco products have become more affordable over time, as taxes have not kept pace with rising purchase power. There are further areas where the existing regulations have gaps or ambiguity and hence need refinements. For example, while there is a ban on tobacco advertisements, there are some exceptions including at points of sale and on tobacco packs. Furthermore, tobacco promotion on the internet and on-demand streaming platforms and cross-border broadcasts are yet to be effectively regulated. While there is a ban on sale of tobacco to minors, measures that prohibit sale of single/loose sticks of cigarettes or tobacco sales through unlicensed vendors exist in limited jurisdictions. Finally, our focus in this chapter has been on policies and regulations. The compliance to many of these regulations remains suboptimal implying need for enhancing enforcement/implementation of the existing law.

Funding declaration

Upendra Bhojani, Riddhi Dsouza, Adhip Amin and Amiti Varma were supported through the DBT/Wellcome Trust India Alliance Fellowship awarded to Upendra Bhojani (IA/CPHI/17/1/503346). Pragati Hebbar was supported through the DBT/Wellcome Trust India Alliance fellowship (IA/CPHE/17/1/503338) awarded to her.

Bibliography

Ankur Gupta v India Asthma Care Society, Petition(s) for Special Leave to Appeal Civil No(s) 16308/2007, Supreme Court of India (3 April 2013)

Arora, M; Tewari, A; Nazar, G & Gupta, VK 'Ineffective pictorial health warnings on tobacco products: Lessons learnt from India' (2012) 56 *Indian Journal of Public Health* 61

Arora, M & Yadav, A 'Pictorial health warnings on tobacco products in India: Socio-political and legal developments' (2010) 23 *National Medical Journal of India* 357Assam Students and Juvenile Smoking Act, 1923

Bhojani, U 'Litigation for claiming health rights: Insights from tobacco control' (2014) *Health and Human Rights*

Bhojani, U & Soors, W 'Tobacco control in India: A case for Health-in-All Policy approach' (2015) 28 *National Medical Journal of India* 86

Bhojani, U; Venkataraman, V & Manganawar, B 'Public policies and the tobacco industry' (2011) 27 *Economic and Political Weekly*

Bombay Smoke Nuisances Act, 1912

Bombay Smoke Nuisances (Provision for Extension and Amendment) Act, 1961

The Cable Television Act, 1955

Cabrera, OA & Gostin, LO 'Human rights and the framework convention on tobacco control: Mutually reinforcing systems' (2011) 7 *International Journal of Law in Context* 285 Canadian Cancer Society 'Cigarette package health warnings international status report' (6th ed 2018) 4

Cancer Patients Aid Association v State of Karnataka WP 17958, High Court of Karnataka at Bangalore (2011)

CESCR General Comment 14: The Right to the Highest Attainable Standard of Health (Art 12) (2000) UN Doc E/C.12/2000/4 Dated 11 August 2000

Chugh, A; Bassi, S; Nazar, GP; Bhojani, U; Alexander, C; Lal, P; Gupta, PC & Arora, M 'Tobacco industry interference index: Implementation of the world health organization's framework convention on tobacco control article 5.3 in India' (2020) 32 *Asia Pacific Journal of Public Health* 172

Cigarette Act, 1975

Cigarette & Other Tobacco Products Act (Prohibition of Advertisement and Regulation of Trade and Commerce, Production, Supply and Distribution) Act, 2003

The Cinematograph Act, 1952

Directions Under Section 5 of the Environment (Protection) Act, 1986 Regarding Implementation of Plastic Waste

Drope, J; Schluger, N; Cahn, Z; Drope, J; Hamill, S; Islami, F; Liber, A; Nargis, N & Stoklosa M *The tobacco atlas* (American Cancer Society and Vital Strategies 2018)

The Drugs and Cosmetics Act, 1940

Dube, Y & Mohandoss, G 'A study on child labor in Indian bidi industry' National Commission for Protection of Child Rights (2013) http://www.nipccd-earchive.wcd.nic.in/sites/default/files/PDF/A%20study%20on%20Child%20Labour%20in%20Indian%20Beedi%20Industry.pdf (accessed 30 August 2020)

'FCTC 2007 India report' https://untobaccocontrol.org/impldb/wp-content/uploads/reports/india_report.pdf (accessed 30 August 2020)

'FCTC 2010 India report' https://untobaccocontrol.org/impldb/wp-content/uploads/reports/India_5y_report_final.pdf (accessed 30 August 2020)

'FCTC 2012 India report' https://untobaccocontrol.org/impldb/wp-content/uploads/reports/india_2012_report.pdf (accessed 30 August 2020)

'FCTC 2018 India report' https://untobaccocontrol.org/impldb/wp-content/uploads/India_2018_report.pdf (accessed 30 August 2020)

Food Safety and Standards Act, 2006

Food Safety and Standards (Prohibition and Restrictions on Sales) Regulations 2011

Gispen, MEC & Toebes, BC 'The human rights of children in tobacco control' (2019) 41 *Human Rights Quarterly* 340

Godawat Pan Masala Products I.P Ltd v Union of India (UOI), MANU/SC/0574/2004

Gupta, PC 'Mouth cancer in India: A new epidemic?' (1999) 97 *Journal of the Indian Medical Association* 373

Hebbar, PB; Bhojani, U; Kennedy, J & Rao, J 'From policy to practice: Lessons from Karnataka about implementation of tobacco control laws' (2017) 42 *Indian Journal of Community Medicine* 77

Himachal Pradesh Juvenile (Prevention of Smoking) Act, 1952

'India (ages 13–15) global youth tobacco survey (GYTS) factsheet' (2006) https://nada.searo.who.int/index.php/catalog/40/download/281(accessed 30 August 2020)

'India (ages 13–15) global youth tobacco survey (GYTS) factsheet' (2009) http://www.who.int/fctc/reporting/Annexoneindia.pdf?ua=1 (accessed 30 August 2020)

'India: First to adapt the Global Monitoring Framework on noncommunicable diseases (NCDs)' *WHO Features* 2015 https://www.who.int/features/2015/ncd-india/en/ (accessed 10 August 2020)

India Tiny Targets Report 'Tobacco advertisement, sales, product displays, and purchase incentives around primary and secondary schools' (2018) https://www.takeapart.org/wp-content/uploads/2019/02/India-Tiny-Targets-Report.pdf (accessed 30 August 2020)

Indian Council of Medical Research, Public Health Foundation of India & Institute for Health Matrics and Evaluation 'India: Health of the Nation's States – the India state-level disease burden initiative' New Delhi, India (2017)

Jha, JA & others 'A nationally representative case – control study of smoking and death in India' (2008) 358 *New England Journal of Medicine* 1137

John, RM 'Crowding out effect of tobacco expenditure and its implications on household resource allocation in India' (2008) 66 *Social Science & Medicine* 1363

John, RM; Rout, SK; Kumar, BR & Arora, M 'Economic burden of tobacco related diseases in India' (2014) New Delhi, India

Juvenile Justice (Care and Protection of Children) Act, 2015 (Act 2 of 2016)

K Ramakrishnan v State of Kerala MANU/KE/0551/1999

Kashiwabara, M; Arul, M; Goswami, H; Narain, JP & Armada, F 'Local governments and civil society lead breakthrough for tobacco control: Lessons from Chandigarh and Chennai' (2011) 55 *Indian Journal of Public Health* 234

Kastoori Udyog v Union of India, Civil Writ Petition 3354 of 1993

Kaur, J & Mohan, PV 'Advocacy for tobacco control in India – A step forward' (2012) 126 *Public Health* 675

Kaur, J; Rinkoo, AV & Singh, R 'Using public interest litigation for tobacco control: Insights from India' (2017) *Indian Journal of Public Health* (2017)

Kumar, G & Kumar, P 'Ban on Gutka in India: Symbolic victory or actual end-game for smokeless tobacco. Large-scale household survey in Delhi finds out!' (2018) 16 *Tobacco Induced Diseases* A36

Laxmikant v Union of India MANU/SC/1166/1997

Management Rules, 2016 by the manufacturers of Gutkha, Tobacco and Pan Masala http://www.indiaenvironmentportal.org.in/files/file/Direction%20PWMR%20Rules%202016.PDF (accessed 23 August 2020)

Mehrotra, R; Mehrotra, V & Jandoo, T 'Tobacco control legislation in India: Past and present' (2010) *Indian Journal of Cancer* 806

Ministry of Corporate Affairs 'India's national action plan on business & human rights' (2020) http://www.mca.gov.in/Ministry/pdf/NationalPlanBusinessHumanRight_13022019.pdf (accessed 30 August 2020)

Ministry of Health and Family Welfare, Government of India 'Global adult tobacco survey India 2009–2010' (2010)

Ministry of Health and Family Welfare, Government of India 'Guidelines for tobacco free educational institution (revised)' https://ntcp.nhp.gov.in/assets/document/TEFI-Guidelines.pdf (accessed 30 August 2020)

Ministry of Health and Family Welfare 'MOHFW GSR 182(E) 15 March 2008' https://www.tobaccocontrollaws.org/files/live/India/India%20-%20G.S.R.%20182%28E%29.pdf (accessed 30 August 2020) at 3–4

Ministry of Health and Family Welfare 'MOHFW GSR 331(E) 3 April 2018' https://www.tobaccocontrollaws.org/files/live/India/India%20-%20G.S.R.%20331%28E%29.pdf (accessed 30 August 2020) at 4

Ministry of Health and Family Welfare 'MOHFW GSR 345(E) 31 May 2005' https://www.tobaccocontrollaws.org/files/live/India/India%20-%20G.S.R.%20345%28E%29.pdf (accessed 30 August 2020) at 34–37

Ministry of Health and Family Welfare 'MOHFW GSR 417(E) 30 May 2008' https://www.tobaccocontrollaws.org/files/live/India/India%20-%20G.S.R.%20417%28E%29.pdf (accessed 30 August 2020) at 3–4

Ministry of Health and Family Welfare 'MOHFW GSR 561(E) 1 September 2004' https://www.tobaccocontrollaws.org/files/live/India/India%20-%20G.S.R.%20561%28E%29%20.pdf (accessed 30 August 2020) at 2

Ministry of Health and Family Welfare 'MOHFW GSR 739(E) 24 September 2015' https://www.tobaccocontrollaws.org/files/live/India/India%20-%20G.S.R.%20727%28E%29.pdf (accessed 30 August 2020) at 6

Ministry of Health and Family Welfare 'National tobacco control programme (NTCP)' https://nhm.gov.in/index1.php?lang=1&level=2&sublinkid=1052&lid=607 (accessed 30 August 2020)

Ministry of Health and Family Welfare 'Operational guidelines for national tobacco testing laboratories' (2019)

Murli S Deora v Union of India MANU/SC/0703/2001

National Health Systems Resource Centre 'National health accounts: Estimates for India 2013–14' (2016)

'Non-communicable diseases threaten health of India's population HSPH in the News (Boston)' (2012) https://www.hsph.harvard.edu/news/hsph-in-the-news/david-bloom-ncds-india/ (accessed 10 August 2020)

Notification (No X 11014/3/91-DM-S & PFA)

Orissa Prohibition of Smoking (In Show Houses) Act 1961

Parliamentary Standing Committee on Science & Technology, Environment & Forests 'Effects of tobacco curing on environment and health' Parliament of India, Rajya Sabha 285th Report (2016)

Partners in Change 'Voices from the margins' (2019) http://www.picindia.org/wp-content/uploads/NAP-community-consultations_v1.pdf (accessed 30 August 2020)

Persai, D; Panda, R & Gupta, A 'Examining implementation of tobacco control policy at the district level: A case study analysis from a high burden state in India' (2016) *Advances in Preventive Medicine* Article ID 4018023

Praxis 'Status of corporate responsibility in India, 2019' (2019) https://www.traffickingmatters.com/wp-content/uploads/2019/10/Status_of_CR_Report_2019-2.pdf (accessed 30 August 2020)

Prevention of Food Adulteration Act, 1954

Rahul Joshi v Union of India WP 8680/2015, High Court of Judicature at Rajasthan, Jaipur Bench, 2015

Rajasthan Prevention of Smoking Act, 1950

Rao, N; Bhojani, U; Shekar, P & Daddi, S 'Conflicts of interest in tobacco control in India: An exploratory study' (2016) 25 *Tobacco Control* 715

Ray, K 'Govt sets up three tobacco testing labs' *Deccan Herald* (New Delhi) 15 September 2019

Reddy, S & Gupta, PC 'Report on tobacco control in India' (2004)

Sarwer, M 'Burning both ends: Many young girls in Murshidabad are child labourers' *The Hindu* 7 July 2018

Sinha, DN; Palipudi, KM; Gupta, PC; Singhal, S; Ramasundarahettige, C; Jha, P; Indrayan, A; Asma, S & Vendhan, G 'Smokeless tobacco use: A meta-analysis of risk and attributable mortality estimates for India' (2014) 51 *Indian Journal of Cancer* 75

Strong, K; Mathers, C; Leeder, S & Beaglehole, R 'Preventing chronic diseases: How many lives can we save?' (2005) 366 *Lancet* 1578

Tobacco Board Act, 1975

Tobacco Board 'Main activities' https://tobaccoboard.com/bactivities.php (accessed 30 August 2020)

Tobacco Board 'Production regulation' https://tobaccoboard.com/propolicy.php (accessed 30 August 2020)

Tobacco Cess Act, 1975

Toebes, B; Gispen, ME; Been, JV & Sheikh, A 'A missing voice: The human rights of children to a tobacco-free environment' (2018) 27 *Tobacco Control* 3

UN Committee on the Rights of the Child (CRC), General Comment 4 (2003): Adolescent Health and Development in the Context of the Convention on the Rights of the Child (1 July 2003) UN Doc CRC/GC/2003/4 (2003)

UN General Assembly, Convention on the Rights of the Child, 20 November 1989, United Nations, Treaty Series, vol 1577, 3

UN General Assembly, International Covenant on Economic, Social and Cultural Rights, 16 December 1966, United Nations, Treaty Series, vol 993, 3

United Nations 'Guiding principles on business and human rights: Implementing the United Nations "protect, respect and remedy" framework' (2011) https://www.ohchr.org/documents/publications/guidingprinciplesbusinesshr_en.pdf (accessed 30 August 2020)

Uttar Pradesh Prohibition of Smoking (Cinema Houses) Act, 1952

WHO 'Cigarette smoking: An assessment of tobacco's global environmental footprint across its entire supply chain, and policy strategies to reduce it' (2018) https://www.who.int/fctc/publications/WHO-FCTC-Enviroment-Cigarette-smoking.pdf?ua=1 (accessed 30 August 2020)

WHO 'Fact sheet on tuberculosis and tobacco world health organization' (2009) https://www.who.int/tobacco/publications/health_effects/factsheet_tub_tob.pdf?ua=1 (accessed 10 August 2020)

WHO Framework Convention on Tobacco Control (2003) https://apps.who.int/iris/bitstream/handle/10665/42811/9241591013.pdf?sequence=1. (accessed 30 August 2020)

WHO 'NCD mortality and morbidity' https://www.who.int/gho/ncd/mortality_morbidity/en/ (accessed 30 August 2020)

WHO 'Noncommunicable Diseases (NCD) Country Profiles – India (2018) https://www.who.int/nmh/countries/2018/ind_en.pdf?ua (accessed 10 August 2020)

WHO 'Tobacco free initiative global adult tobacco survey (GATS) India report 2016–17' (2017)

Yadav, A; Singh, A; Khadka, BB; Amarasinghe, H; Yadav, N & Singh, R 'Smokeless tobacco control: Litigation & judicial measures from Southeast Asia' (2018) 148 *Indian Journal of Medical Research* 25

13 Beyond tobacco

Lessons on non-communicable diseases from the Inter-American Human Rights System

Isabel Barbosa and Margherita M Cinà

13.1 Introduction

Non-communicable diseases (NCDs), also known as chronic diseases, account for 71 per cent of deaths globally, with 85 per cent of premature deaths from NCDs occurring in low- and middle-income countries (LMICs).[1] Cardiovascular diseases, cancers, chronic respiratory diseases and diabetes are all examples of NCDs and together account for the largest proportion of NCD deaths around the world.[2] While the development of these NCDs may have complex aetiologies that include factors such as genetics, many can be largely attributable to four main modifiable risk factors: tobacco use, alcohol consumption, unhealthy diets and physical inactivity.[3]

In Africa, where communicable diseases, also known as infectious diseases, have historically been the largest health concern, the prevalence of NCDs is quickly on the rise, set to become the leading cause of disability and mortality in sub-Saharan Africa by 2030.[4] Across the Atlantic, the Americas are further along in the epidemiological shift from communicable diseases to NCDs as the primary health burden, with NCDs accounting for 81 per cent of all deaths in 2016.[5] Undoubtedly, the use and consumption of tobacco, alcohol and unhealthy foods and beverages, combined with increasing physical inactivity, have played a key role in this shift from communicable to non-communicable diseases.[6]

Although the modifiable risk factors of NCDs ensure their preventable nature, progress towards addressing these risk factors has been slow. For instance, despite

1 WHO 'Noncommunicable diseases' (1 June 2018) https://www.who.int/news-room/fact-sheets/detail/noncommunicable-diseases (accessed 20 September 2021).
2 As above.
3 As above.
4 JJ Bigna 'The rising burden of non-communicable disease in Sub Saharan Africa' (2019) 7 *The Lancet Global Health* e1295.
5 PAHO 'Evidence and intelligence for action in health department/health analysis, metrics and evidence unit. PLISA database. Core indicators 2019: Health trends in the Americas' (2019) 16.
6 WHO 'Global action plan for the prevention and control of noncommunicable diseases 2013–2020' (2013).

DOI: 10.4324/9781003264248-16

the global progress made in the tobacco control arena since the adoption of the Framework Convention on Tobacco Control (FCTC), LMICs will experience a doubling of tobacco-related deaths between 2002 and 2030.[7] Moreover, in Latin America, where approximately 600,000 people die every year due to diseases related to poor diet and obesity,[8] the per capita sale of ultra-processed food and drink increased by about 20 per cent from 2009 to 2019.[9] In Africa, where approximately 3,000,000 people die every year from NCDs,[10] the per capita sale of ultra-processed food and ultra-processed drinks increased from 58 per cent in 2002 to 71 per cent in 2016.[11] Where tobacco use and unhealthy diets directly impact the rising number of NCDs in both Latin America and Africa, our globalised economy encourages corporations that derive profits from these unhealthy products to establish their dominance within LMICs.

The adoption of the FCTC in 2003 was not only the World Health Organization's (WHO) first and only legally binding treaty created under article 19 of its Constitution, but it also signalled a powerful step towards global action to tackle one of the deadly NCD risk factors.[12] Following the FCTC, the global community has also increasingly acknowledged the urgency of addressing the NCD problem more generally, going beyond tobacco. From the United Nations political declarations on the prevention and control of NCDs, to the inclusion of the target to reduce by one-third premature mortality from NCDs in the 2030 Sustainable Development Goals, to the WHO 2013–2020 Global Action Plan for the Prevention and Control of NCDs, there is a global recognition that the rising number of NCDs must be tackled by addressing all four major modifiable risk factors.[13]

Nevertheless, these efforts have not risen to the level of a comprehensive treaty, as was the case with tobacco control. Meanwhile, it has become increasingly important to turn to other legal frameworks, one being international human rights law. Even as many of the tobacco-related developments relied on the

7 WHO Africa 'Tobacco control' https://www.afro.who.int/health-topics/tobacco-control (accessed 20 September 2021).

8 UN 'La Obesidad Se Triplica en América Latina por un mayor consumo de ultraprocesados y comida rápida' (12 November 2019) https://news.un.org/es/story/2019/11 /1465321 (accessed 20 September 2021).

9 PAHO 'Ultra-processed food and drink products in Latin America: Sale sources, nutrient profiles and policy implications' (2019) 9.

10 WHO *Summary tables of mortality estimates by cause, age and sex, globally and by region* (2000–2016).

11 S Vandevijvere & others 'Global trends in ultraprocessed food and drink product sales and their association with adult body mass index trajectories' (2019) 20 *Obesity Reviews* 10.

12 See, in general, WHO 'Framework Convention on Tobacco Control' (2003).

13 See, in general, UN General Assembly, Political Declaration of the Third High-Level Meeting of the General Assembly on the Prevention and Control of Non-Communicable Diseases (10 October 2018) UN Doc A/RES/73/2 (2018); UN General Assembly 'Transforming our World: The 2030 Agenda for Sustainable Development' (25 September 2015) UN Doc A/RES/70/1 (2015) 16; WHO 'Global Action Plan for the Prevention and Control of NCDs 2013–2020' (2013).

FCTC to spur global action, the human rights framework more generally has also proven to be a useful tool to address tobacco use as an NCD risk factor – and has potential in relation to other NCD risk factors as well. For instance, the Inter-American Human Rights System (IAHRS), which has already touched upon tobacco-related rights, albeit in a limited capacity, has started to pave the way for an increased understanding of how regional human rights bodies can be used to reduce the overall burden of NCDs.

This chapter will explore the potential of human rights frameworks in addressing NCD risk factors, looking beyond the achievements and promises of the FCTC. In particular, it will focus on the IAHRS as an example of how regional human rights systems can create opportunities to examine NCD risk factors outside of their topic-specific silos. To do so, Section 2 begins by examining how NCDs are understood both internationally and regionally as a human rights issue, including how human rights played a role in the FCTC. Section 3 outlines the governance system of the IAHRS, and Section 4 examines the NCD-relevant developments within the Americas. Section 5 discusses ways forward for both the IAHRS and the African Human Rights System (AHRS) seeking to further develop NCDs and human rights within their regions.

13.2 NCDs and the right to health

There are established links between human rights and NCDs – and consequently between human rights and NCD risk factors. Beyond the fact that the failure to adequately prevent and control NCDs endangers the right to the highest attainable standard of physical and mental health, it also comprises significant social and economic costs that threaten to lower the living standards of millions, impoverishing families, jeopardising universal health coverage, and increasing health disparities within and between countries.[14] In other words, NCDs directly impact health and health-related rights.

This human rights approach to NCDs is perhaps most famous in the form of tobacco control. Although not a human rights treaty, the FCTC created a critical foundation for the link between human rights and the regulation of this particular risk factor by specifically referring to the right to health in the International Covenant on Economic, Social and Cultural Rights (ICESCR), the Constitution of the WHO, and the Convention on the Rights of the Child.[15] In addition to these concrete references to human rights, the FCTC created standards against which state action can be measured, thereby informing the content of the right to health.[16]

14 PAHO 'Comprender la dimensión económica de las ENT y herramientas para abordarlas de manera efectiva' https://www.paho.org/hq/index.php?option=com_content&view=article&id=15536:understanding-the-economic-dimension-of-ncds-and-tools-to-effectively-address-them&Itemid=72568&lang=es (accessed 19 September 2020).

15 See, in general, the FCTC.

16 See O Cabrera & L Gostin 'Human rights and the framework convention on tobacco control: Mutually reinforcing systems' (2011) 7 *International Journal of Law in Context* 285 at 292.

For these and other reasons, as argued by Cabrera and Gostin, human rights and tobacco control have been understood as mutually reinforcing legal frameworks.[17] Where human rights have an important link to this one NCD risk factor, it is critical to understand how other risk factors (alcohol consumption, unhealthy diets and physical inactivity) also have serious consequences for the realisation of a wide range of health and health-related human rights; and most importantly, for the purpose of this chapter, how human rights frameworks can be further explored for addressing NCD risk factors. In this sense, the FCTC has paved the way for an understanding of how existing international and regional human rights law can play a critical role in tackling the growing rates of NCDs.

Under international human rights law, states are expected to carry out the necessary measures to reduce all major risk factors for NCDs.[18] In particular, the right to health, protected under article 12 of the ICESCR, is an inclusive right that extends not only to timely and appropriate medical care but also to the underlying determinants of health, including adequate food – a right itself, enshrined in article 11 of the ICESCR – and health-related education and information, among others.[19] Importantly, given that the right to health includes 'the prevention, treatment and control of epidemic, endemic, occupational and other diseases', the prevention of NCDs is well within the human rights obligations under the ICESCR.[20]

Further proof of this link between NCD risk factors and human rights is found in multiple references within the Universal System of Human Rights. For example, the Committee on Economic, Social and Cultural Rights (CESCR), the main interpreter of the ICESCR, addressed health and tobacco use in Argentina in 2018 and health and NCDs in Mauritius in 2019.[21] Furthermore, Anand Grover and Dainius Pūras, both former Special Rapporteurs on the right of everyone to the enjoyment of the highest attainable standard of physical and mental health, have discussed NCDs in official statements. The first issued a report on unhealthy foods, NCDs, and the right to health.[22] The second issued a recent statement

17 As above.

18 WHO 'Global Action Plan' (n 6).

19 UN Committee on Economic, Social and Cultural Rights (CESCR), General Comment 14: The Right to the Highest Attainable Standard of Health (2000) UN Doc E/C.12/2000/4 Dated 11 August 2000 para 11.

20 UN General Assembly, International Covenant on Economic, Social and Cultural Rights, 16 December 1966, United Nations, Treaty Series, vol 993, 3 art 12(2)(c) https://www.ohchr.org/en/professionalinterest/pages/cescr.aspx (accessed 19 September 2020).

21 Concluding Observations on the fourth periodic report of Argentina, Committee on Economic, Social and Cultural Rights (1 November 2018) UN Doc E/C.12/ARG/CO/4 (2018) paras 51–52; Concluding Observations on the Fifth Periodic Report of Mauritius, Committee on Economic, Social and Cultural Rights (5 April 2019) UN Doc E/C.12/MUS/CO/5 (2019) paras 51–52.

22 UN General Assembly 'Report of the Special Rapporteur on the Right of Everyone to the Enjoyment of the Highest Attainable Standard of Physical and Mental Health: UN General Assembly, Anand Grover' (1 April 2016) UN Doc A/HRC/26/31.

about the adoption of front-of-package warning labelling to tackle NCDs, endorsed by both the Special Rapporteur on the right to food and the Working Group on the issue of human rights and transnational corporations and other business enterprises.[23] In the same line, Hilal Elver, the Special Rapporteur on the right to food, issued a report about nutrition that touched upon unhealthy eating environments and the growing threat of NCDs, thereby building the connection between the rights to health and adequate food.[24]

The human rights framework at the global level engages three critical obligations on states in relation to combating the rising burden of NCDs: the obligations to *respect, protect* and *fulfil.*[25] First, the obligation to *respect* requires states to refrain from interfering either directly or indirectly with the enjoyment of human rights. Therefore, states cannot engage in behaviours that may contribute to preventable morbidity and mortality.[26] Second, under the obligation to *protect*, states must take legislative and other measures to prevent non-state actors, including corporations, from interfering with the enjoyment of human rights, one being the right to health.[27] Finally, states must, under the obligation to *fulfil*, adopt legislation and national health policies to advance the full realisation of human rights. In the context of the right to health, this includes, but is not limited to, the need to provide information that supports healthy decisions.[28]

These three layers of obligations provide a legal basis upon which to monitor whether or not states are taking the necessary actions to address the rising prevalence of NCDs. In other words, human rights provide a framework for holding states accountable, which is especially relevant in a field where the industry often pushes for self-regulation and public-private partnerships, despite the lack of evidence of their effectiveness or safety.[29] By means of the obligations to take necessary steps to respect, protect and fulfil different aspects of the right to health and health-related rights in connection with NCDs, the human rights framework ensures that states move towards health-enabling environments.

Regionally, in Africa, the right to health is protected under the African Charter on Human and Peoples' Rights (Banjul Charter); in the Americas, it has been

23 UN Human Rights Office of the High Commissioner 'Statement by the UN Special Rapporteur on the Right to Health on Adoption of Front-of-Package Warning Labelling to Tackle NCDs' (27 July 2020) https://www.ohchr.org/EN/NewsEvents/Pages/DisplayNews.aspx?NewsID=26130&LangID=E#_ednref16 (accessed 20 September 2020).

24 UN General Assembly 'Report of the Special Rapporteur on the Right to Food' (3 August 2016) UN Doc A/71/282.

25 General Comment 14 (n 19) para 33.

26 General Comment 14 (n 19) para 34; UNGA Report of the Special Rapporteur (n 22) para 14; Statement by the UN Special Rapporteur (n 23).

27 General Comment 14 (n 19) para 35; Report of the Special Rapporteur (n 22) para 15; Statement by the UN Special Rapporteur (n 23).

28 General Comment 14 (n 19) para 34; Report of the Special Rapporteur (n 22) para 16; Statement by the UN Special Rapporteur (n 23).

29 See R Moodie & others 'Profits and pandemics: Prevention of harmful effects of tobacco, alcohol, and ultra-processed food and drink industries' (2013) 381 *The Lancet* 670.

developed through an interpretation of the American Convention on Human Rights (ACHR or American Convention) and found in the Additional Protocol to the American Convention on Human Rights in the area of Economic, Social, and Cultural Rights (Protocol of San Salvador), as explored in more detail throughout this chapter. The development of a rights-based approach to NCDs at the global and regional levels are not disconnected, given that there is often a dialogue among the institutions that make up different human rights systems (as exemplified by the Inter-American Court's reference to General Comment 14, issued by the CESCR, mentioned in the following section). In this sense, given that this chapter provides a deep dive into the IAHRS, the aforementioned statements within the Universal System of Human Rights are merely referred to as examples that provide useful context on the normative development around a rights-based approach to NCDs.

As the African continent continues to see a worrisome rise in NCDs, and with an understanding that this public health threat is deeply connected to the realisation of human rights in the region, it is critical to go beyond the FCTC and understand how the AHRS, the youngest of regional human rights systems,[30] may provide an avenue for addressing this growing burden in the region. In this sense, it is useful to draw on experiences developed within the IAHRS that are directly or indirectly relevant for NCD risk factors. Where the FCTC provides an avenue to tackle one particular NCD risk factor, examining the IAHRS is a powerful exercise to strengthen the interconnections between NCD risk factors and human rights in both regions – the Americas and Africa – particularly in the absence of treaties for all the major NCD risk factors.

13.3 The Inter-American Human Rights System: governance

The IAHRS is the regional human rights system responsible for monitoring, promoting and protecting human rights in member countries of the Organization of American States (OAS).[31] It has historically played a fundamental role in shaping the human rights discourse in the region, including defining what constitutes human rights violations and how to address them from a human rights perspective.[32]

Similar in structure to the AHRS, the IAHRS is composed of two principles, autonomous entities serving complementary functions to protect and promote human rights within the OAS: (1) the Inter-American Commission on Human Rights (Inter-American Commission), with a general mandate to promote and

30 See International Justice Resource Center 'African human rights system' https://ijrcenter.org/regional/african/ (accessed 20 September 2021).

31 See Organisation of American States 'IACHR' https://www.oas.org/en/iachr/mandate/what.asp (accessed 20 September 2020).

32 See O Cabrera & A Constantin 'Tobacco control in the inter-American human rights system' in ME Gispen & B Toebes (eds) *Human rights and tobacco control* (2020) 45.

protect human rights, expressed in the individual petitions and case system and through country and thematic monitoring within all member states; and (2) the Inter-American Court of Human Rights (Inter-American Court), with a narrower mandate to decide contentious cases and respond to advisory opinion requests.[33]

The Inter-American Commission and the Inter-American Court engage in a number of functions to protect and promote human rights within the OAS, many of which are in parallel with those of the African Commission on Human and Peoples' Rights (African Commission) and the African Court on Human and Peoples' Rights (African Court). Notably, both the Inter-American Commission and the Inter-American Court analyse individual complaints regarding alleged violations of the American Declaration of the Rights and Duties of Man, the American Convention on Human Rights, and other regional human rights treaties.[34] Moreover, both entities may also issue precautionary and provisional measures, respectively, in order to prevent irreparable harm in serious and urgent situations.[35]

In both regional human rights systems, individual petitions can be analysed by the commission and the court.[36] In the case of the IAHRS, the Inter-American Commission investigates human rights violations and then issues recommendations to the state in question to restore the enjoyment of rights wherever possible, to make reparations for the harm caused to the victims, and to prevent the repetition of similar events.[37] In the event that the recommendations are not followed by the state, the Inter-American Commission can submit the case to the Inter-American Court.[38] In the AHRS, the African Court similarly acts to complement and reinforce the work done by the African Commission to protect human rights, both by receiving its own petitions and those that have been transferred from the African Commission.[39]

Besides receiving and processing individual complaints and utilising the precautionary measures mechanism, the Inter-American Commission engages in a

33 See Organisation of American States 'Charter of the organisation of American states' (1993) ch XV art 106; Organisation of American States 'American Convention on Human Rights' (1969) sec 2; International Justice Resource Center 'Inter-American human rights system' https://ijrcenter.org/regional/inter-american-system/ (accessed 20 September 2021).

34 See arts 33, 44, 61 American Convention on Human Rights (1969).

35 'Charter of the Organisation of American States' (n 33) art 106.

36 Rules of Procedure of the African Commission on Human and Peoples' Rights of 2020 (Rules of the Commission) Rule 118 https://www.achpr.org/legalinstruments/detail?id=72 (accessed 20 September 2021); 'American Convention on Human Rights' (n 33) sec 2 art 41.

37 Organisation of American States 'Mandato y Funciones de la CIDH' http://www.oas.org/es/cidh/mandato/funciones.asp (accessed 20 September 2021).

38 See D Shelton 'The rules and the reality of petition procedures in the Inter-American Human Rights System' (2015) 5 *Notre Dame Journal of International & Comparative Law* 1.

39 Organisation of African Unity (OAU), Protocol to the African Charter on Human and Peoples' Rights on the Establishment of an African Court on Human and Peoples' Rights, 10 June 1998, arts 2 and 6(3).

wide array of human rights monitoring and promotion activities, undertaking country visits to investigate specific situations, monitoring the general human rights situation in the member states, including issuing country-specific and thematic reports, and holding thematic hearings on specific areas of concern.[40] Part of these functions are carried out by its rapporteurships, which include a Special Rapporteurship on Economic, Social, Cultural, and Environmental Rights (ESCER) that supports the Commission in fulfilling its mandate to promote and protect economic, social and cultural rights in the Americas.[41] Similarly, in addition to acting as a quasi-judicial body to promote, protect, and interpret the rights found within the Banjul Charter, the African Commission has the ability to appoint special rapporteurs to address specific thematic areas of work.[42]

In turn, the Inter-American Court also has powers beyond adjudicating individual complaints and issuing provisional measures. The Inter-American Court is empowered to issue advisory opinions regarding the interpretation of rights within Inter-American instruments, at the request of an OAS agency or a member state.[43] This advisory opinion competence is shared with the African Court, which may receive requests from the African Commission, the African Union member states, African Union organs, or any recognised organisation of the African Union to interpret relevant human rights instruments.[44]

While much of the governing structures of both systems share similarities, they each protect the right to health in different ways. Where the AHRS explicitly protects the right to health under the Banjul Charter,[45] there is no explicit right to health found within the American Convention on Human Rights, though within the IAHRS its content and scope have been clarified based on additional human rights instruments and by means of interpretation. For instance, though the right to health is enshrined within the Protocol of San Salvador,[46] its direct justiciability is excluded by article 19 of this instrument. Nevertheless, the Inter-American Commission and Court have been able to interpret the right to health in relation to other rights (e.g. the rights to life, personal integrity, and access to information) and have also recently derived a stand-alone right to health from article 26 of the of the American Convention, which protects 'rights implicit in

40 'Inter-American Human Rights System' (n 33).

41 Organisation of American States 'REDESCA: Mandato y Funciones' https://www.oas.org/es/cidh/desca/mandato/mandato.asp (accessed 20 September 2021).

42 See Organisation of African Unity (OAU), African Charter on Human and Peoples' Rights (Banjul Charter), 27 June 1981, CAB/LEG/67/3 rev 5, 21 ILM 58 (1982) art 45; Rules of Procedure of the African Commission on Human and Peoples' Rights of 2020 (Rules of the Commission) Rule 25 https://www.achpr.org/legalinstruments/detail?id=72 (accessed 20 September 2021).

43 Art 64 American Convention on Human Rights.

44 Protocol to the African Charter (n 39) art 4.

45 Banjul Charter (n 42) art 16.

46 See art 10 Additional Protocol to the American Convention on Human Rights in the Area of Economic, Social and Cultural Rights (Protocol of San Salvador) (adopted 1988, entered into force 1999).

the economic, social, educational, scientific, and cultural standards set forth in the Charter of the Organization of American States as amended by the Protocol of Buenos Aires'.[47] These interpretations of the right to health are explored in more detail in the following section.

13.4 The Inter-American Human Rights System: NCD-relevant developments

Beyond the avenues created by the FCTC to tackle tobacco use, the IAHRS, in recent years, has proven to be another useful venue to address NCD risk factors – or relevant related issues – to varying degrees. Two avenues have been particularly relevant: its monitoring mechanisms, on the one hand, and the development of relevant jurisprudence, on the other hand. Using its monitoring mechanisms, the Inter-American Commission has explicitly addressed tobacco use, alcohol consumption and diet-related risk factors, and has explored the impact of corporations on the enjoyment of human rights, including by expressing concern about the corporate capture of policymaking. Moreover, despite the fact that no case specific to NCD risk factors has yet been processed and decided by the Inter-American Commission and Court, there is a solid jurisprudence around issues that are central to this legal debate. In this respect, though there are plenty of legal obligations worthy of notice,[48] this chapter will focus on those stemming from the rights to health and adequate food – in relation to the right to information – and the cross-cutting obligation of due diligence.

13.4.1 Monitoring mechanisms

For the first time, in April 2016, the Inter-American Commission specifically received information on a risk factor to NCDs and acknowledged that this was a human rights issue relevant to its mandate. Upon request of the O'Neill Institute for National Global Health Law at Georgetown Law School (O'Neill Institute), in collaboration with the Fundación InterAmerican del Corazón Argentina (FIC) and Action on Smoking and Health (ASH), it held a thematic hearing on the 'Right to Health and Tobacco Addiction in the Americas', which explored the intersection between tobacco control and human rights.[49] The Inter-American Commission received information on the public health consequences of tobacco use,[50] and the participating organisations argued that the FCTC created specific measures that states must implement in order to uphold human rights.[51]

47 See Banjul Charter (n 42) art 26.
48 See Cabrera & Constantin (n 32) 45.
49 As above.
50 CIDH 'Informe sobre el 157 Período de Sesiones de la CIDH' (April 2016) https://www.oas.org/es/cidh/prensa/docs/Informe-157.pdf (accessed 20 September 2021).
51 As above.

In particular, the aforementioned organisations made considerations on (1) the lethality, illness and disability caused by tobacco products; (2) the disproportionate impact on groups of people that have historically faced discrimination; (3) the tobacco industry's unethical and/or illegal efforts to advertise the aforementioned groups, such as children and adolescents, women and LGBTI persons, while simultaneously thwarting the government's efforts to regulate tobacco and promote public health; and (4) the evidence in support of policies to slow down the epidemic of tobacco addiction and uphold human rights. Finally, the organisations called for the implementation of tobacco control measures, as well as transparency in governments' dealings with the tobacco industry. The Inter-American Commission acknowledged that this was a new topic to the IAHRS, stressing the 'opportunity to learn together' about the intersection of tobacco and human rights.[52]

More recently, in November 2019, the Inter-American Commission released a report titled 'Business and Human Rights: Inter-American Standards', authored by the Special Rapporteur on Economic, Social, Cultural, and Environmental Rights (Special Rapporteur).[53] This report touched on NCDs, going beyond the scope of the 2016 thematic hearing, which focused solely on tobacco, to also include other risk factors to NCDs, such as alcohol and unhealthy food and beverages. Particularly, this report discussed corporate capture in policymaking, using the food and beverage industry as an example of the undermining of the government's ability to regulate and supervise commercial activities. In this respect, the Inter-American Commission stressed the importance of transparency in the relationship between the public and private sectors for upholding human rights.[54]

Furthermore, the Special Rapporteur expressed concern about children and adolescents, focusing on the rates of overweight and obesity and on their use of tobacco and alcohol. Notably, she suggested that data indicates a high consumption of products that put children and adolescents' right to health at risk. The Special Rapporteur indicated that both states and corporations are at fault for this situation: states for failing to comply with international obligations in addressing the problem, and corporations for undertaking actions that hinder public policies, put pressure on decision makers, and financially support biased studies to back their own interests.[55] Thus, the Inter-American Commission called upon states to abide by the legal frameworks in place and adopt measures to effectively

52 Inter-American Commission on Human Rights 'Report on the 157th session of the IACHR' (13 June 2016) https://www.oas.org/en/iachr/media_center/PReleases/2016/049A.asp (accessed 20 September 2020).

53 See Inter-American Commission on Human Rights 'Empresas y Derechos Humanos: Estándares Interamericanos' (1 November 2019) OEA/Ser.L/V/II. CIDH/REDESCA/INF.1/19.

54 'Empresas y Derechos Humanos: Estándares Interamericanos' (n 53) paras 265–266.

55 As above para 360.

prevent, address, and sanction commercial activities that negatively affect children's and adolescents' rights.[56]

Shortly after, in December 2019, the Inter-American Commission released another relevant report, titled 'Corruption and Human Rights: Inter-American Standards'.[57] Despite not explicitly discussing NCD risk factors, this report addressed corporate capture from the perspective of corruption. Discussing the impact of corruption on the rule of law, the Inter-American Commission stated that corporate access to decision makers diverts public policies from the common good to private interests, ultimately posing a threat to democracy itself.[58] In this sense, the Inter-American Commission highlighted that corruption may take the form of political and technical pressure over decision makers, ultimately undermining regulations, favouring commercial activities, or defining the relationship with land, endangering, for example, access to adequate food and water.[59]

These developments signal not only the growing importance of discussing NCD risk factors from a human rights perspective but also the opportunities present within regional human rights systems for expanding this understanding, going beyond an NCD risk factor–specific treaty such as the FCTC. While the IAHRS first considered this issue through a thematic hearing specifically in relation to tobacco, the Inter-American Commission has since confirmed that it may consider both tobacco use and NCD risk factors more generally as human rights issues well within its mandate. Moreover, NCD risk factors first came to the attention of the Inter-American Commission though a thematic hearing requested by academia and civil society organisations, only to be later picked up (and broadened) in two unrelated thematic reports. In doing so, the Inter-American Commission relied on sources such as the Lancet Commission and the Pan American Health Organisation (PAHO), indicating that the IAHRS is mindful of academia, on the one hand, and other relevant institutions in the region, on the other hand.

13.4.2 Litigation

Despite the progress made within the IAHRS on NCD risk factors, it has so far consisted of monitoring carried out by the Inter-American Commission through a thematic hearing and thematic reports. As of 2021, no case specifically related to NCD risk factors has been litigated within the IAHRS. Nonetheless, the IAHRS has developed a solid jurisprudence on issues that are unquestionably relevant to this legal debate. This section will explore two of these issues: the development of the rights to health and adequate food, in relation to the right to information, and the cross-cutting obligation of due diligence.

56 As above para 361.
57 See, in general, Inter-American Commission on Human Rights 'Corrupción y Derechos humanos: Estándares Interamericanos' (6 December 2019) OEA/Ser.L/V/II. Doc 236.
58 'Corrupción y Derechos humanos: Estándares Interamericanos' (n 57) para 133.
59 As above para 173.

13.4.2.1 *The right to health*

Over the years, the Inter-American Commission and the Inter-American Court have processed and decided a number of cases that involved social, economic and cultural rights, including the right to health.

Prior to 2017, economic, social and cultural rights were generally adjudicated in connection with civil and political rights rather than as rights of their own.[60] In consequence, even if a given case revolved around the right to health, the decisions have ultimately been analysed and resolved under the rights to life and/ or personal integrity. For example, *Ximenes Lopes v Brazil*[61] (a case about the death of a person who had been committed to a psychiatric ward), *Suárez Peralta v Ecuador*[62] (a case about medical malpractice), and *Gonzales Lluy et al. v Ecuador*[63] (a case about HIV contagion through blood transfusion) were all framed as violations of the rights to life and/or personal integrity, despite the fact that the Inter-American Court heavily relied on the right to health, including its contents established within General Comment 14 in the reasoning.

In 2017, the Inter-American Court issued a ruling that signalled a bold shift in its jurisprudence towards a direct adjudication of economic, social and cultural rights that was soon applied to the right to health and, more recently, to the right to adequate food. In *Lagos del Campo v Peru*, the state was held responsible for the violation of article 26 of the American Convention on Human Rights, indicating that economic, social and cultural rights were henceforth subject to direct adjudication, no longer necessarily tied to civil and political rights.[64] Following this leading case, the Court directly analysed the right to health in cases such as *Poblete Vilches v Chile*,[65] *Cuscul Pivaral v Peru*[66] and *Hernández v Argentina*,[67] cases about the lack of appropriate medical care received by an elderly person, by a group of persons living with HIV, and by a person deprived of liberty, respectively.

Both phases of the development of the right to health (indirect and direct adjudication) should be understood as complementary, given that an independent

60 See S Serrano Guzmán 'Comentarios sobre el giro jurisprudencial de la Corte Interamericana en materia de justiciabilidad de los derechos económicos, sociales, culturales y ambientales a la luz de seis sentencias emitidas entre 2017 y 2019' in M Morales Antoniazzi & others (coord) *Interamericanización de los DESCA: El Caso Cuscul Pivaral de la Corte IDH* (2020).

61 (Merits, Reparations and Costs) IACHR (4 July 2006) Ser C/149.

62 (Preliminary Objections, Merits, Reparations and Costs) IACHR (21 May 2013) Ser C/261.

63 (Preliminary Objections, Merits, Reparations and Costs) IACHR (1 September 2015) Ser C/298.

64 Serrano Guzmán (n 60).

65 (Merits, Reparations and Costs) IACHR (8 March 2018) Ser C/349.

66 (Preliminary Objection, Merits, Reparations and Costs) IACHR (23 August 2018) Ser C/359.

67 (Preliminary Objection, Merits, Reparations and Costs) IACHR (22 November 2019) Ser C/395.

analysis of social, economic, and cultural rights under article 26 of the American Convention does not exclude the existence of correlated violations of civil and political rights related to health rights.[68] Ultimately, the most recent decisions build on precedents that have contributed to the development of the right to health in the region. In this sense, judgments of both phases bring important topics to the table when it comes to the possibility of tackling NCDs in the future.

First, it is important to discuss how the Inter-American Court has elucidated the content of the right to health within its jurisprudence. Echoing the ICESCR and expanding on General Comment 14, the right to health refers to the enjoyment of the highest attainable standard of physical, mental and social wellbeing, 'derived from a lifestyle that allows the individual to achieve an overall balance'.[69] It encompasses healthcare in accordance with the principles of availability, accessibility, acceptability and quality,[70] but also the regulation of public and private services[71] in relation to both prevention and care.[72] Moreover, the Inter-American Court has discussed the underlying determinants of health, referring to, for example, the importance of a healthy diet for individuals with HIV.[73] If ever the Inter-American Court were to decide a case specifically about risk factors to NCDs, it would certainly build on this groundwork.

Second, it is noteworthy that the Inter-American Court often highlights the connection between the right to health and other human rights; perhaps a legacy from the indirect adjudication of economic, social and cultural rights through their connection to civil and political rights. However, Serrano Guzmán points out that this strategy not only allowed for indirect adjudication at a time when this was particularly important but also shaped legal interpretation by highlighting the 'multi-offensive' nature of certain conducts – meaning that either a given conduct violates several rights at once or it is made of elements that violate different rights.[74] This reasoning continues to be relevant even as the Inter-American Court embraces the direct adjudication of economic, social and cultural rights.[75]

In the context of NCD risk factors, the interdependence of human rights is particularly relevant with regard to the connection between the right to health and the right to information, which has also been developed within the IAHRS. In *Poblete Vilches v Chile*,[76] the Inter-American Court described informed consent as an essential part of accessibility in the right to health.[77] Later, in

68 Serrano Guzmán (n 60) 107.
69 *Cuscul Pivaral v Guatemala* (Preliminary Objection, Merits, Reparations and Costs) IACHR (23 August 2018) Ser C/359 para 105.
70 *Cuscul Pivaral v Guatemala* (n 69) para 107.
71 As above para 106.
72 As above para 108.
73 As above para 112.
74 Serrano Guzmán (n 60) 106.
75 As above.
76 (Reparations and Costs) IACHR (8 March 2018) Ser C/349.
77 *Poblete Vilches v Chile* (n 76) para 160.

Cuscul Pivaral v Guatemala, the Inter-American Court recalled that information accessibility includes 'the right to seek, receive and impart information and ideas concerning health issues'.[78] Thus, the Court has elaborated on how access to information plays an instrumental role in the realisation of the right to health. This development of the right to health will be very relevant to an eventual case regarding NCD risk factors, since ensuring that consumers have access to information about risk factors to NCDs is one of the priorities in this area.[79]

In *Poblete Vilches v Chile*, the Inter-American Court also analysed the right to health in relation to non-discrimination. It emphasised the immediate nature of the obligation of non-discrimination tied to economic, social and cultural rights, including the right to health. In particular, the Court stated that such obligation consisted in adopting effective measures to guarantee access, without discrimination, to the benefits recognised for each right, adding that these measures 'must be adequate, deliberate, and specific in order to achieve the full realization of such rights'.[80] Considering the disproportionate burden of NCDs on vulnerable groups, these observations on non-discrimination are relevant for potential litigation around this issue.

The recent developments towards a more direct adjudication of the right to health signal the inevitable expansion of the study of the right to health within the IAHRS. In the coming years, the Inter-American Court is likely to continue to develop an independent analysis of the right to health under article 26 of the American Convention, exploring the correlated obligations that fall upon the state, and addressing corresponding health-related matters. Considering that NCDs are one of the major challenges of the 21st century,[81] sooner or later they will reach the Inter-American Court, and this will be an unparalleled opportunity to use the current landscape of the IAHRS to frame the risk factors to NCDs from a human rights perspective.

13.4.2.2 The right to adequate food

The direct adjudication of social, economic and cultural rights also allowed for the unprecedented analysis of other rights within the IAHRS, including health-related rights such as the right to adequate food.

Before the precedent in *Lagos del Campo v Peru*,[82] the Inter-American Court had previously touched upon the issue of food in the time of indirect adjudication. In *Yakye Axa v Paraguay*, about an indigenous community's land rights, it stated that access to food and clean water impacted the right to a dignified

78 General Comment 14 (n 19) para 12; *Cuscul Pivaral v Guatemala* (Preliminary Objection, Merits, Reparations and Costs) IACHR (23 August 2018) Ser C/359 para 106.

79 See 'Statement by the UN Special Rapporteur' (n 23).

80 (Reparations and Costs) IACHR (8 March 2018) Ser C/349 para 104.

81 WHO 'Global status report on non-communicable diseases' (2014).

82 (Preliminary Objections, Merits, Reparations and Costs) IACHR (31 August 2017) Series C/340.

existence.[83] However, after urging the state to guarantee the right of the elderly to adequate food, the Inter-American Court proceeded to declare a violation to the right to life.[84]

Similar to the development of the right to health, the jurisprudential turn within the IAHRS has since opened new possibilities for the direct adjudication of the right to adequate food. For example, in ***Indigenous Communities of the Lhaka Honhat Association (Our Land) v Argentina***, another land rights case, the Inter-American Court started developing the content of the right to adequate food, tying the understanding of food to nutrition that is adequate to ensure health, even specifically stating that the right to food should not be narrowly interpreted as a minimum package of calories.[85] Clarifying further, the Court established that 'it is not just any type of food that satisfies the right; rather there are a number of factors that must be taken into account when determining whether particular food is "appropriate"'.[86] The Inter-American Court also established that consumer acceptability within the context of the right to food 'implies the need to also take into account, as far as possible, perceived non-nutrient-based values attached to . . . food consumption',[87] quoting the CESCR.

This development on the right to food is an important precedent for diet-related risk factors to NCDs, since it puts forth the notion that nutrition should be adequate to ensure health. In the coming years, the Inter-American Court will likely have the opportunity to further develop the right to adequate food, as well as the correlated obligations that fall upon the states.

13.4.2.3 State duty of due diligence

Throughout its jurisprudence, the Inter-American Court has extensively developed the concept of due diligence as a duty that falls upon the state. This duty provides useful insights into states' obligations in relation to health and health-related rights.

In the Inter-American Court, *Velásquez Rodríguez v Honduras* is the landmark case in which the Inter-American Court established that

> in principle, any violation of rights recognised by the Convention carried out by an act of public authority or by persons who use their position of authority is imputable to the State. However, this does not define all the circumstances in which a State is obligated to prevent, investigate and punish human rights violations, nor all the cases in which the State might be found responsible for

83 (Merits, Reparations and Costs) IACHR (17 June 2005) Ser C/125 para 167.

84 *Yakye Axa v Paraguay* (n 83) paras 175–176.

85 (Merits, Reparations and Costs) IACHR (6 February 2020) Ser C/400 para 216.

86 *Our Land v Argentina* (n 85) para 220.

87 Committee on Economic, Social and Cultural Rights, General Comment 12: The Right to Adequate Food (art 11) (1999) UN Doc UN Doc. E/C.12/1999/5 (12 May 1999) paras 7 and 11; *Our Land v Argentina* (n 85) para 220.

> an infringement of those rights. An illegal act which violates human rights and which is initially not directly imputable to a State (for example, because it is the act of a private person or because the person responsible has not been identified) can lead to international responsibility of the State, not because of the act itself, but because of the lack of due diligence to prevent the violation or to respond to it as required by the Convention.[88]

In the years that followed, the Inter-American Court had the opportunity to apply the concept of due diligence in relation to a range of rights enshrined in the American Convention, setting different standards of due diligence depending on the circumstances of each human rights violation. Connecting with the broader international human rights framework, the concept of due diligence is particularly relevant to the obligation to protect, referred to above, which requires states to ensure that third parties do not interfere with the enjoyment of a particular right.

In *González (Cotton Field) v Mexico*, when discussing the notion of prevention within the IAHRS, the Inter-American Court clarified that the state cannot be held responsible for every human rights violation committed by private actors within its jurisdiction, thus establishing a set of criteria for obligations of due diligence that are primarily centred around the notion of risk: (1) there must be a situation of real and immediate risk; (2) this situation must threaten a specific individual or group; (3) the state must know or should have known of the existence of the risk; and (4) the state could have reasonably prevented or avoided the materialisation of the risk.[89] In particular, a situation of generalised risk helps define the predictability and avoidability of a particular risk;[90] therefore, the context may enhance the obligation of due diligence. In all cases, 'the specific circumstances of the case and the discharge of such obligation to guarantee must be taken into account'.[91]

However, the concept of due diligence is even broader. In the context of the right to health – both in relation to other rights, such as the rights to life and/or personal integrity, and as an independent analysis – the Inter-American Court has repeatedly stated that states have the obligation to regulate and supervise private actors. In the aforementioned *Ximenes Lopes v Brazil*, the Inter-American Court established that

> states must regulate and supervise all activities related to healthcare given to the individuals under the jurisdiction thereof, as a special duty to protect life

88 *Velásquez Rodríguez v Honduras* Merits (29 July 1988) Ser C/4 para 172.

89 See Cabrera & Constantin (n 32) 45.

90 V Abramovich 'Responsabilidad estatal por violencia de género: comentario s sobre el caso "Campo Algodonero" en la Corte Interamericana de Derechos Humanos' (2010) 6 *Anuario de Derechos Humanos* 167 at 179.

91 (Preliminary Objection, Merits, Reparations and Costs) IACHR (16 November 2009) Ser C/205 para 280.

> and personal integrity, regardless of the public or private nature of the entity giving such healthcare.[92]

Furthermore, the Inter-American Court indicated that

> the failure to regulate and supervise such activities gives rise to international liability. . . . [U]nder the American Convention international liability comprises the acts performed by private entities acting in a State capacity, as well as the acts committed by third parties when the State fails to fulfil its duty to regulate and supervise them. Therefore, the duty of the States to regulate these acts is not limited to public hospitals but includes any and all healthcare institutions.[93]

Other health-related cases followed the same reasoning, both in the time of indirect and direct adjudication.[94] Notably, in *Gonzales Lluy et al. v Ecuador*, the case about HIV contagion through a blood bank, the Inter-American Court emphasised the severity of the illness involved and the risks that the victim may face at different stages of her life.[95]

In fact, the Inter-American Court has already applied the duty to regulate and supervise risky activities in contexts other than healthcare; particularly, in a case in Brazil about the employees of the fireworks factory at Santo Antônio de Jesus and their family members.[96] Similarly, in a case about indigenous peoples engaged in diving activities on behalf of the fishing industry, the Inter-American Court again stated the duty to regulate and supervise risky activities carried out by corporations.[97] In this sense, it is worth considering the argument of not limiting such duties to healthcare providers but extending them to other actors whose activities may affect the rights at stake.

92 (Reparations and Costs) IACHR (4 July 2006) Ser C/149 para 89.

93 *Ximenes Lopes v Brazil* (n 92) para 90.

94 See *Suárez Peralta v Ecuador* (Preliminary Objections, Merits, Reparations and Costs) IACHR (21 May 2013) Ser C/261 paras 130–132; *Gonzales Lluy v Ecuador* (Preliminary Objections, Merits, Reparations and Costs) (1 September 2015) Ser C/298 para 190. *Cuscul Pivaral v Guatemala* (Preliminary Objection, Merits, Reparations and Costs) IACHR (23 August 2018) Ser C/359 para 115 and operative para 14. *Poblete Vilches v Chile* (Merits, Reparations and Costs) IACHR (8 March 2018) Ser C/349 para 152. *Hernández v Argentina* (Preliminary Objection, Merits, Reparations and Costs) (22 November 2019) Ser C/395 para 77.

95 *Gonzales Lluy v Ecuador* (Preliminary Objections, Merits, Reparations and Costs) IACHR (1 September 2015) Ser C/298 para 190.

96 *Case of the Workers of the Fireworks in Santo Antônio de Jesus and Their Families v Brazil* (Preliminary Objections, Merits, Reparations and Costs) IACHR (15 July 2020) Ser C/407 para 118.

97 *Buzos Miskitos (Lemoth Morris et al) v Honduras* IACHR (31 August 2021) Ser C/432 para 55.

The same is true for the right to adequate food. In the aforementioned *Indigenous Communities of the Lhaka Honhat Association (Our Land) v Argentina*, the Inter-American Court stated that the state has the obligation to ensure that enterprises or individuals do not deprive other individuals of their access to adequate food. By failing to regulate activities of individuals or groups so as to prevent them from violating the right to food of others, the state itself incurred a human rights violation.[98]

The concept of due diligence is particularly important when addressing NCD risk factors from a human rights perspective, given the influence that unhealthy products industries have on the rising burden of NCDs. Through lobbying, litigating, and funding biased research on the one hand, and aggressively marketing and advertising of their products on the other hand, these industries have been successful in creating unhealthy environments and in influencing consumer choices.[99] Ultimately, actions that have interfered with government decision-making seeking to protect public health have directly impacted states' ability to uphold health and health-related human rights. Due diligence can and should be used as a tool within regional human rights systems to fight the epidemic of NCDs.

13.5 Conclusion: the way forward

NCDs are a grave problem in Africa and around the globe, as they negatively impact the realisation of a broad range of human rights. While the right to health is particularly impacted, the interdependence of human rights triggers a domino effect that necessarily affects other rights.

In this context, in addition to relying on existing international law such as the FCTC, it is important to consider how human rights mechanisms, such as the IAHRS and the AHRS, can be activated as a powerful tool to address all major NCD risk factors, particularly calling upon states to uphold their human rights obligations in this regard. The developments by the Inter-American Commission and Court explored throughout this chapter indicate that, in the absence of treaties that specifically tackle NCD risk factors beyond tobacco use, all NCD risk factors can and should be addressed within regional human rights systems. While the IAHRS has yet to develop a robust set of human rights standards specific to NCD risk factors, there are promising trends which might be relevant for other human right systems seeking to achieve similar goals.

98 *Our Land v Argentina* (n 85) para 221.

99 See V Tangcharoensathien & others 'Addressing NCDs: Challenges from industry market promotion and interferences' (2019) 8 *International Journal of Health Policy and Management* 256; The Lancet 'Stop industry interference, save lives' (2019) 7 *Global Health* 256.

The first and perhaps most important lesson moving forward is the necessity of framing NCD risk factors as a human rights issue. Frequently, regulating NCD risk factors and upholding human rights are seen as competing (as opposed to mutually reinforcing) legal interests. However, the developments within international human rights law indicate that regulating NCD risk factors should be understood as a means to realise human rights. The legal debate is already advancing in this direction, including within the IAHRS. In the coming years, the AHRS should also advance this debate, using some of the developments that have transpired in the IAHRS, explored throughout this chapter, as useful input in pursuing this goal.

Second, as the AHRS seeks to address NCD risk factors broadly, it must consider the interdependence of human rights within the NCD context as playing a key role in the development of normative and jurisprudential instruments. However, the rights to health and adequate food, including how they relate to the right to information, are particularly important in the development of a cohesive human rights discourse across the globe. Likewise, it will be important for the AHRS to consider the argument of non-discrimination in light of the disproportionate burden of NCDs on vulnerable groups.

Third, due diligence is a critical concept that could be further developed by regional human rights systems like the AHRS within this field, given corporations' involvement in the (predictable and avoidable) NCD health crisis, by both hindering regulations often considered rights compliant and engaging in a wide array of unethical and/or illegal conduct in the sale of unhealthy commodities, such as tobacco, alcohol and unhealthy foods and beverages.

Finally, while it is only natural that tobacco control – grounded on the development of the FCTC – has spearheaded the discussion on NCDs and human rights, the time has come for a comprehensive approach to NCD risk factors. In order to break down silos, thereby enhancing the efforts on all fronts against NCDs, it is necessary for regional human rights systems like the AHRS, to build on the existing human rights frameworks in order to further explore the intersection between human rights and NCDs. Treaties such as the FCTC are undoubtedly useful for the analysis at the regional level but, in the absence of a broader treaty that encompasses other NCD risk factors beyond tobacco, the AHRS should not be deterred from using its existing avenues for advancing the legal debate in this area. There are human rights instruments already in place that will, if used strategically, allow for a more comprehensive approach.

Acknowledgements

The authors are grateful for the insightful and valuable guidance provided by Oscar A Cabrera and Silvia Serrano Guzmán, as well as the research support provided by William Shefelman.

Bibliography

Abramovich, V 'Responsabilidad estatal por violencia de género: comentario s sobre el caso "Campo Algodonero" en la Corte Interamericana de Derechos Humanos' (2010) 6 *Anuario de Derechos Humanos* 167

Additional Protocol to the American Convention on Human Rights in the Area of Economic, Social and Cultural Rights (Protocol of San Salvador) (Adopted 1988, Entered into Force 1999)

American Convention on Human Rights (1969)

Bigna, JJ 'The rising burden of non-communicable disease in Sub Saharan Africa' (2019) *The Lancet Global Health* E1925

Buzos Miskitos (Lemoth Morris et al) v Honduras IACHR (31 August 2021) Ser C/432

Cabrera, O & Constantin, A 'Tobacco control in the Inter-American Human Rights System' in Gispen, ME & Toebes, B (eds) *Human rights and tobacco control* (Edward Elgar 2020)

Cabrera, O & Gostin, L 'Human rights and the framework convention on tobacco control: Mutually reinforcing systems' (2011) 7 *International Journal of Law in Context* 285

CIDH 'Informe sobre el 157 Período de Sessiones de la CIDH' (April 2016) https://www.oas.org/es/cidh/prensa/docs/Informe-157.pdf (accessed 20 September 2021)

Committee on Economic, Social and Cultural Rights, General Comment 12: The right to adequate food (1999) UN Doc E/C.12/1999/5 dated 12 May 1999

Committee on Economic, Social and Cultural Rights (CESCR) General Comment 14: The Right to the Highest Attainable Standard of Health (11 August 2000) UN Doc E/C.12/2000/4 (2000)

Concluding Observations on the Fifth Periodic Report of Mauritius, Committee on Economic, Social and Cultural Rights (5 April 2019) UN Doc. E/C.12/MUS/CO/5 (2019)

Concluding Observations on the fourth periodic report of Argentina, Committee on Economic, Social and Cultural Rights (1 November 2018) UN Doc E/C.12/ARG/CO/4 (2018)

Cuscul Pivaral v Peru (Preliminary Objection, Merits, Reparations and Costs) IACHR (23 August 2018) Ser C/359

González et al. (Cotton Field) v Mexico (Preliminary Objection, Merits, Reparations and Costs) IACHR (16 November 2009) Ser C/205

Gonzales Lluy et al. v Ecuador (Preliminary Objections, Merits, Reparations and Costs) IACHR (1 September 2015) Ser C/298

Hernández v Argentina (Preliminary Objection, Merits, Reparations and Costs) IACHR (22 November 2019) Ser C/395

Inter-American Commission on Human Rights 'Corrupción y Derechos humanos: Estándares Interamericanos' (6 December 2019) OEA/Ser.L/V/II. Doc 236

Inter-American Commission on Human Rights 'Empresas y Derechos Humanos: Estándares Interamericanos' (1 November 2019) OEA/Ser.L/V/II. CIDH/REDESCA/INF.1/19

Inter-American Commission on Human Rights 'Report on the 157th session of the IACHR' (13 June 2016) https://www.oas.org/en/iachr/media_center/PReleases/2016/049A.asp (accessed 20 September 2021)

Inter-American Commission on Human Rights 'IACHR takes case involving Brazil to the inter-American court of human rights' (4 October 2018) https://www.oas.org/en/iachr/media_center/PReleases/2018/218.asp (accessed 21 September 2021)

Inter-American Commission on Human Rights 'Informe No. 25/18 Caso 12.428 Admisibilidad y fondo Empleados de la fábrica de fuegos en Santo Antonio de Jesus y su familiares' (2 March 2018) OEA/Ser.L/V/II.167 Doc. 29

International Covenant on Economic, Social and Cultural Rights, UN General Assembly (16 December 1966) https://www.ohchr.org/en/professionalinterest/pages/cescr.aspx (accessed 21 September 2020)

International Justice Resource Center 'African human rights system' https://ijrcenter.org/regional/african/ (accessed 20 September 2021)

International Justice Resource Center 'Inter-American human rights system' https://ijrcenter.org/regional/inter-american-system/ (accessed 20 September 2021)

Lagos del Campo v Peru (Preliminary Objections, Merits, Reparations and Costs) IACHR (31 August 2017) Series C/340

Moodie, R; Stuckler, D; Monteiro, C; Sheron, N; Neal, B; Thamarangsi, T; Lincoln, P; Casswell, S & Lancet NCD Action Group 'Profits and pandemics: Prevention of harmful effects of tobacco, alcohol, and ultra-processed food and drink industries' (2013) 381 *The Lancet* 670

Organisation of African Unity (OAU), African Charter on Human and Peoples' Rights (Banjul Charter), 27 June 1981, CAB/LEG/67/3 rev 5, 21 ILM 58 (1982)

Organisation of African Unity (OAU), Protocol to the African Charter on Human and Peoples' Rights on the Establishment of an African Court on Human and Peoples' Rights, 10 June 1998

Organisation of American States 'American Convention on Human Rights' (1969)

Organisation of American States 'Charter of the Organisation of American States' (1993)

Organisation of American States 'IACHR' https://www.oas.org/en/iachr/mandate/what.asp (accessed 20 September 2021)

Organisation of American States 'Mandato y Funciones de la CIDH' http://www.oas.org/es/cidh/mandato/funciones.asp (accessed 20 September 2021)

Organisation of American States 'REDESCA: Mandato y Funciones' https://www.oas.org/es/cidh/desca/mandato/mandato.asp (accessed 20 September 2021)

PAHO 'Comprender la dimensión económica de las ENT y herramientas para abordarlas de manera efectiva' https://www.paho.org/hq/index.php?option=com_content&view=article&id=15536:understanding-the-economic-dimension-of-ncds-and-tools-to-effectively-address-them&Itemid=72568&lang=es (accessed 20 September 2021)

PAHO 'Evidence and intelligence for action in health department/health analysis, metrics and evidence unit. PLISA database. Core indicators 2019: Health trends in the Americas' (2019)

PAHO 'Ultra-processed food and drink products in Latin America: Sale sources, nutrient profiles and policy implications' (2019)

Poblete Vilches v Chile (Merits, Reparations and Costs) IACHR (8 March 2018) Ser C/349

Report of the Special Rapporteur on the Right of Everyone to the Enjoyment of the Highest Attainable Standard of Physical and Mental Health, Anand Grover, UN General Assembly (1 April 2016) UN Doc A/HRC/26/31

Rules of Procedure of the African Commission on Human and Peoples' Rights of 2020 (Rules of the Commission) (https://www.achpr.org/legalinstruments/detail?id=72 (accessed 20 September 2021)

Serrano Guzmán, S 'Comentarios sobre el giro jurisprudencial de la Corte Interamericana en materia de justiciabilidad de los derechos económicos, sociales, culturales y ambientales a la luz de seis sentencias emitidas entre 2017 y 2019' in Morales Antoniazzi, M; Ronconi, L & Clérico, L (coord) *Interamericanización de los DESCA: El Caso Cuscul Pivaral de la Corte IDH* (2020)

Shelton, D 'The rules and the reality of petition procedures in the Inter-American Human Rights System' (2015) 5 *Notre Dame Journal of International & Comparative Law* 1

Statement by the UN Special Rapporteur on the Right to Health on Adoption of Front-of-Package Warning Labelling to Tackle NCDs, UN Human Rights Office of the High Commissioner https://www.ohchr.org/EN/NewsEvents/Pages/DisplayNews.aspx?NewsID=26130&LangID=E#_ednref16 (accessed 20 September 2021)

'Stop industry interference, save lives' (2019) 7 *The Lancet Global Health* e1584

Suárez Peralta v Ecuador (Preliminary objections, merits, reparations and costs) IACHR (21 May 2013) Ser C/261

Tangcharoensathien, V; Chandrasiri, O; Kunpeuk, W; Markchang, K & Pangkariya, N 'Addressing NCDs: Challenges from industry market promotion and interferences' (2019) 8 *International Journal of Health Policy and Management* 256

UN General Assembly 'Political Declaration of the Third High-Level Meeting of the General Assembly on the Prevention and Control of Non-Communicable Diseases' (10 October 2018) UN Doc A/RES/73/2 (2018)

UN General Assembly 'Transforming our World: The 2030 Agenda for Sustainable Development' (25 September 2015) UN Doc A/RES/70/1

UN 'La Obesidad Se Triplica en América Latina por un mayor consumo de ultraprocesados y comida rápida' (12 November 2019) https://news.un.org/es/story/2019/11 /1465321 (accessed 20 September 2021)

UN 'Statement by the UN Rapporteur on the right to health on the adoption of front-of-package warning labelling to tackle NCDs' (20 September 2021)

Vandevijvere, S; Jaacks, LM; Monteiro, CA; Moubarac, JC; Girling-Butcher, M; Lee, AC; Pan, A; Bentham, J & Swinburn, B 'Global trends in ultraprocessed food and drink product sales and their association with adult body mass index trajectories' (2019) 20 *Obesity Reviews* 10

Velásquez Rodríguez v Honduras (Merits) (29 July 1988) Ser C/4

WHO 'Global action plan for the prevention and control of noncommunicable diseases 2013–2020' (2013)

WHO 'Global status report on non-communicable diseases' (2014)

WHO 'Noncommunicable diseases' (1 June 2018) https://www.who.int/news-room/fact-sheets/detail/noncommunicable-diseases (accessed 20 September 2021)

WHO *Summary tables of mortality estimates by cause, age and sex, globally and by region, 2000–2016* (accessed 20 September 2021)

WHO 'World Health Organization framework convention on tobacco control' (2003)

WHO Africa 'Tobacco control' https://www.afro.who.int/health-topics/tobacco-control (accessed 20 September 2021)

Workers of the Fireworks Factory in Santo Antônio de Jesus and their Families v Brazil (Preliminary objections, merits, reparations and costs) IACHR (15 July 2020) Ser C/407

Ximenes Lopes v Brazil (Merits, Reparations and Costs) IACHR (4 July 2006) Ser C/149

Yakye Axa v Paraguay (Merits, Reparations and Costs) IACHR (17 June 2005) Ser C/125

Index